EIGHTH EDITION

MANAGEMENT MISTAKES AND SUCCESSES

Robert F. Hartley
Cleveland State University

JOHN WILEY & SONS, INC.

Associate Publisher/Acquisitions Editor	*Judith Joseph*
Marketing Manager	*David Woodbury*
Editorial Assistant	*Jessica Bartelt*
Associate Production Manager	*Kelly Tavares*
Production Editor	*Sarah Wolfman-Robichaud*
Managing Editor	*Kevin Dodds*
Illustration Editor	*Wendy Stokes Hodge*

This book was set in 10/12 New Caledonia by Leyh Publishing LLC, and printed and bound by Courier Westford. The cover was printed by Lehigh Press.

This book is printed on acid-free paper. ∞

ISBN 0-471-66202-X

Printed in the United States of America

10 9 8 7 6 5 4

PREFACE

The American philosopher George Santayana noted, "Those who cannot remember the past are doomed to repeat it." We offer in these books learning insights from the past that can benefit those who come after.

Welcome to this eighth edition of *Management Mistakes*. It has now been around for more than twenty years. Who would have thought that interest in mistakes would have been so enduring.

I doubt that anybody has used all the editions. If anyone has, going back to 1983, I would really like to hear from you. I know that many of you are past users though, and hope you will find this eighth edition with its new and updated cases a worthy successor to earlier editions.

After so many years of treating mistakes, and more recently some successes as well, it might seem a monumental challenge to keep these new editions fresh and interesting and still provide good learning experiences. But the task of doing so, and the joy of the challenge, has made this an intriguing labor through the decades. It is always difficult to abandon interesting cases that have stimulated student discussions and provided good learning experiences, but newer case possibilities are ever competing for inclusion. Examples of good and bad handling of problems and opportunities are always emerging.

For new users, I hope the book will meet your full expectations and be an effective instructional tool. Although case books abound, you and your students may find this somewhat unique and very readable, a book that can help transform dry and rather remote concepts into practical reality, and lead to lively class discussions, and even debates amid the arena of decision making.

NEW TO THIS EDITION

In contrast to the early editions, which examined only notable mistakes, and based on your favorable comments about recent editions, I have again included some well-known successes. While mistakes provide valuable learning insights, we can also learn from successes, and we can learn by comparing the unsuccessful with the successful.

We have continued two sections that were added last time: (1) Crisis Management, now expanded a bit to include Change Management; and (2) Risks in Merger Mania, the contagion sweeping the business environment to the detriment of employees, communities, and sometimes even the executives involved and their shareholders.

Although the Entrepreneurial Adventures section was continued, I did drop the separate sections for great comebacks and ethical misconduct, but have placed appropriate cases with other sections. (For those of you with more interest in ethical problems, I have a new book, *Business Ethics: Mistakes and Successes,* due from Wiley in late 2004.) I have tried to keep the cases as current as possible with updates where appropriate. Some of these updates were inserted just before the book went into the production process.

A number of you have asked that I identify which cases would be appropriate for the traditional coverage of topics as organized in most management texts. With many cases, it is not possible to truly compartmentalize the mistake or success strictly according to one topic. The patterns of success or failure tend to be more pervasive. Still, I think you will find the following classification of cases by subject matter to be helpful. I thank those of you who made this and other suggestions.

Table 1: Classification of Cases by Major Management Topics

Topics	Most Relevant Cases
Change and Crisis Management	Scott Paper, Sunbeam, Perrier, MetLife, Maytag, United Way, Boeing/Airbus, Firestone/Ford, Philip Morris, Johnson & Johnson (J&J)
Mergers	DaimlerChrysler, Snapple, Newell Rubbermaid, Maytag, Boeing/Airbus, Hewlett-Packard
Great Comebacks	Continental Air, Harley Davidson
Planning	Euro Disney, Coca-Cola/Pepsi, Vanguard, Boston Beer, Office Max, Philip Morris, Dell, McDonald's, Hewlett-Packard
Executing	Boeing/Airbus, Continental, Harley Davidson, Boston Beer, Maytag, J&J, Perrier, MetLife, Firestone/Ford, United Way, Office Max, Dell, Newell Rubbermaid
Controlling	United Way, MetLife, McDonald's, Maytag, Boeing/Airbus, Firestone/Ford, Dell
Global Applications	Euro Disney, McDonald's, Boeing/Airbus, Harley Davidson, DaimlerChrysler, Perrier, Maytag, Dell, Coca-Cola/Pepsi
Entrepreneurial	Boston Beer, Office Max, Dell, Gateway
Ethical	United Way, MetLife, J&J, DaimlerChrysler, Firestone/Ford, Scott Paper and Al Dunlap
Customer relations	Newell Rubbermaid, Vanguard, Maytag, Harley Davidson, Firestone/Ford, MetLife, United Way

TARGETED COURSES

As a supplemental text, this book can be used in a variety of courses, both undergraduate and graduate, ranging from principles of management to strategic management. It can be used in courses in business ethics and organizational theory. It certainly can be used in training programs and even for those nonprofessionals who look for a good read about well-known firms and personalities.

TEACHING AIDS

As in the previous editions, this edition contains a number of teaching aids within and at the end of each chapter. Some of these will be common to several cases, and illustrate that certain successful and unsuccessful practices tend to cross company lines.

Information Boxes and Issue Boxes are included within each chapter to highlight relevant concepts and issues, or related information. Learning insights help students see how certain practices—both errors and successes—cross company lines and are prone to be either traps for the unwary or success modes. Discussion Questions and Hands-On Exercises encourage and stimulate student involvement. A recent pedagogical feature is the Team Debate Exercise, in which formal issues and options can be debated for each case. New in certain cases is the "Be a Devil's Advocate" exercise, in which students can argue against a proposed course of action to test its merits. Invitation to Research suggestions allow students to take the case a step further, to investigate what has happened since the case was written. In the final chapter, the various learning insights are summarized and classified into general conclusions.

An Instructor's Manual written by the author accompanies the text to provide suggestions and considerations for the pedagogical material within and at the ends of chapters.

ACKNOWLEDGMENTS

It seems fitting to acknowledge all those who have provided encouragement, information, advice, and constructive criticism through the years since the first editions of these Mistakes books. I hope you all are well and successful, and I truly appreciate your contributions. I apologize if I have missed anybody, and would be grateful to know such so I can rectify this in future editions. I welcome updates of present affiliations.

Beverlee Anderson, University of Cincinnati; Y.H. Furuhashi, Notre Dame; W. Jack Duncan, University of Alabama—Birmingham; Mike Farley, Del Mar College; Joseph W. Leonard, Miami University (Ohio); Abbas Nadim, University of New Haven; William O'Donnell, University of Phoenix; Howard Smith, University of New Mexico; James Wolter, University of Michigan—Flint; Vernon R. Stauble, California State Polytechnic University; Donna Giertz, Parkland College; Don Hantula, St. Joseph's University; Milton Alexander, Auburn University; James F. Cashman, University of Alabama; Douglas Wozniak, Ferris State University; Greg Bach, Bismarck State College; Glenna Dod, Wesleyan College; Anthony McGann, University of Wyoming; Robert D. Nale, Coastal Carolina University; Robert H. Votaw, Amber University; Don Fagan, Daniel

Webster University; Andrew J. Deile, Mercer University; Samuel Hazen, Tarleton State University; Michael B. McCormick, Jacksonville State University.

Also: Barnett Helzberg, Jr. of the Shirley and Barnett Helzberg Foundation. My present and former colleagues from Cleveland State: Dean Ephraim Smith, Ram Rao, Sanford Jacobs, Andrew Gross, and Benoy Joseph. From Wiley: Tim Kent, Ellen Ford, Brent Gordon, Jeff Marshall, Judy Joseph, and Jessica Bartelt.

Robert F. Hartley
Professor Emeritus
Cleveland State University
Cleveland, Ohio
RFHartley@aol.com

CONTENTS

CHAPTER ONE

Introduction

*I*n this eighth edition of *Management Mistakes and Successes*, we have added five new cases. Five other cases have been dropped to make room for the new entries, with the rest revamped and updated, and in some instances reclassified. Many of these cases are as recent as today's headlines; some have still not come to complete resolution.

In accordance with your expressed preferences, we have kept the format of the last several editions by examining not only notable mistakes but also some notable successes. We continue to seek what can be learned—insights that are transferable to other firms, other times, and other situations. What key factors brought monumental mistakes for some firms and resounding successes for others? Through such evaluations and studies of contrasts, we may learn to improve the "batting average" in the intriguing, ever-challenging art of management decision making.

We will encounter examples of the phenomenon of organizational life cycles, with an organization growing and prospering, then failing (just as humans do), but occasionally resurging. Success rarely lasts forever, but even the most serious mistakes can be (but are not always) overcome.

As in previous editions, a variety of firms, industries, mistakes, and successes are presented. You will be familiar with most of the organizations, although probably not with the details of their situations.

We are always on the lookout for particular cases that bring out certain points or caveats and that give a balanced view of the spectrum of management problems. We have sought to present examples that provide somewhat different learning experiences, where at least some aspect of the mistake or success is unique. Still, we see similar mistakes occurring time and again. The prevalence of some of these mistakes makes us wonder how much decision making has really improved over the decades.

Let us then consider what learning insights we can gain, with the benefit of hindsight, from examining these examples of successful and unsuccessful management practices.

LEARNING INSIGHTS

Analyzing Mistakes

In looking at sick companies, or even healthy ones that have experienced difficulties with certain parts of their operations, we are tempted to be unduly critical. It is easy to criticize with the benefit of hindsight. Mistakes are inevitable, given the present state of decision making and the dynamic environment facing organizations.

Mistakes can be categorized as errors of omission and of commission. Mistakes of omission are those in which no action was taken and the status quo was contentedly embraced amid a changing environment. Such errors, which often typify conservative or stodgy management, are not as obvious as the other category of mistakes. They seldom involve tumultuous upheaval; rather, the company's fortunes and competitive position slowly fade, until management at last realizes that mistakes having monumental impact have been allowed to happen. The firm's fortunes often never regain their former luster. But sometimes they do, and we have described the cases of Continental Airlines and Harley Davidson that fought back successfully from adversity.

Mistakes of commission are more spectacular. They involve bad decisions, wrong actions taken, misspent or misdirected expansion, and the like. Although the costs of the erosion of competitive position coming from errors of omission are difficult to calculate precisely, the costs of errors of commission are often fully evident. We have devoted Part II to a particularly costly type of errors of commission, those involving unwise mergers and acquisitions. But errors of commission are seen in many other cases throughout the book. Looking at a few such examples, the costs associated with the misdirected efforts of MetLife in fines and restitution totaled nearly $100 million. With Euro Disney, in 1993 alone the loss was $960 million; it improved in 1994 with only a $366 million loss. With Maytag's overseas Hoover division, the costs of an incredibly bungled sales promotion brought it a loss of $315 million (10.4 percent of revenues) in 1992, with losses continuing to mount after that.

Although they may make mistakes, organizations with alert and aggressive management show certain actions or reactions when reviewing their own problem situations:

1. Looming problems or present mistakes are quickly recognized.
2. The causes of the problem(s) are carefully determined.
3. Alternative corrective actions are evaluated in view of the company's resources and constraints.
4. Corrective action is prompt. Sometimes this requires a ruthless axing of the product, the division, or whatever is at fault.
5. Mistakes provide learning experiences. The same mistakes are not repeated, and future operations are consequently strengthened.

When a company is slow to recognize emerging problems, we think that management is lethargic and incompetent or that controls have not been established to provide prompt feedback at strategic control points. For example, a declining competitive position in one or a few geographical areas should be a red flag to management that something is amiss. To wait months before investigating or taking action may mean a permanent loss of business. Admittedly, signals sometimes get mixed, and complete information may be lacking, but procrastination cannot be easily defended.

Just as problems should be quickly recognized, the causes of these problems— the "why" of the unexpected results—must be determined as quickly as possible. It is premature, and rash, to take action before knowing where the problems really lie. To go back to the previous example, the loss of competitive position in one or a few areas may reflect circumstances beyond the firm's immediate control, such as an aggressive new competitor who is drastically cutting prices to "buy sales." In this situation, all competing firms will likely lose market share, and little can be done except to stay as competitive as possible with prices and servicing. However, closer investigation may reveal that the erosion of business was due to unreliable deliveries, poor quality control, uncompetitive prices, or incompetent sales staff.

With the cause(s) of the problem defined, various alternatives for dealing with it should be identified and evaluated. This may require further research, such as obtaining feedback from customers or from field personnel. Finally the decision to correct the situation should be made as objectively and prudently as possible. If drastic action is needed, there usually is little rationale for delaying. Serious problems do not go away by themselves: They tend to fester and become worse.

Finally, some learning experience should result from the misadventure. The president of one successful firm told me:

> I try to give my subordinates as much decision-making experience as possible. Perhaps I err on the side of delegating too much. In any case, I expect some mistakes to be made, some decisions that were not for the best. I don't come down too hard usually. This is part of the learning experience. But God help them if they make the same mistake again. There has been no learning experience, and I question their competence for higher executive positions.

Analyzing Successes

Successes deserve as much analysis as mistakes, although admittedly the urgency is less than with an emerging problem that requires remedial action lest it spread.

Any analysis of success should seek answers to at least the following questions:

Why were such actions successful?

- Was it because of the nature of the environment, and if so, how?
- Was it because of particular research and planning efforts, and if so, how?
- Was it because of particular engineering and/or production achievements, and if so, can these be adapted to other aspects of our operations?
- Was it because of any particular element of the strategy—such as service, promotional activities, or distribution methods—and if so, how?
- Was it because of the specific elements of the strategy meshing well together, and if so, how was this achieved?

Was the situation unique and unlikely to be encountered again?

- If not unique to the situation, how can we use these successful techniques in the future or in other operations at the present time?

ORGANIZATION OF BOOK

In this eighth edition we have expanded two sections.

Managing Change and Crises is a topic that has received considerable attention of late, and Part I looks at how five firms handled such extreme situations. Three fumbled big time, one is in the process of adjusting to a toned-down growth scenario, and one became the classic masterpiece in handling a crisis of the worst kind: loss of life.

The last decade has seen a rash of firms salivating to merge or make acquisitions, and many of these turned out to be disasters. We have devoted Part II to three cases on the Perils of Merger Mania, plus one as a model for effective assimilation.

We have continued an addition that many of you approved of: Entrepreneurial Adventures. Polls of students show that interest in entrepreneurship has never been greater, and Entrepreneurial Adventures gives us two intriguing cases with their challenges and triumphs. Another case, Dell Computer, could well have been placed in this section, but we opted to place it instead in the Executing section because of Dell's remarkable rise to dominate the PC market.

Otherwise, we have categorized cases under traditional management functions of Planning and Controlling, and have combined the organization and leadership functions under Executing. Social responsibility and ethical concerns can hardly be ignored in the close scrutiny of business practices today, but rather than devoting a specific section to this we have interspersed several such cases in other sections. Similarly, instead of a separate section on "great comebacks," we have placed two such salient cases in the Executing section.

Managing Change and Crises

Product safety lapses that result in injuries and even loss of life of users are among the worst ethical and social responsibility abuses. Even more reprehensible is when such risks are allowed to continue for years, with no responsibility admitted. Ford Explorers equipped with Firestone tires were implicated in more than 200 deaths from tire failures and vehicle rollovers. After revelations about the accidents surfaced in the media, Ford and Firestone each blamed the other for the deaths. Eventually, a host of lawsuits led to massive recalls and billions in damages.

McDonald's in the last decade seemed to have entered the maturity stage of its life cycle, and had difficulty lowering its expectations from its tradition of often frenetic expansion. Under new management it has embraced a policy of moderation, and, surprisingly, the price of its shares have gone up.

Perrier, the bottled-water firm, encountered adversity when traces of benzene were found in some of its product. Responsibly, it ordered a sweeping recall of all bottles in North America and a few days later in the rest of the world, while the company sought to correct the problem. For five months Perrier was off the market, thereby giving competitors an unparalleled windfall and savaging its market share.

Added to this was public recognition that the claims regarding purity of its product were false.

Albert Dunlap had gained a well-deserved reputation of being the premier hatchet man, the one who would come into a sick organization and fire enough people to make it temporarily profitable—they called him "Chainsaw Al." Somehow, with Sunbeam this seemingly proven downsizing strategy did not work. Dunlap himself was fired by the board of directors.

Johnson & Johnson exemplified crisis management under the most severe circumstances: loss of life directly connected with its flagship product, Tylenol. Johnson & Johnson became a role model on how to "keep the faith" with its customers, putting their best interests ahead of the firm's and in the process enhancing a public image as a responsive and caring firm.

Perils of Merger Mania

Snapple, a marketer of noncarbonated fruit-flavored and iced tea drinks, was acquired by Quaker Oats in late 1994 for $1.7 billion. As sales declined and losses mounted, it soon became apparent to all but the CEO of Quaker that far too much had been paid for this acquisition. No strategy changes were able to turn Snapple around. In 1997, Snapple was sold for $300 million, a loss of $1.4 billion in only three years.

The merger of Chrysler with the huge German firm Daimler, maker of Mercedes, was supposed to be a merger of equals. But Chrysler management quickly found this was not so, as top Chrysler executives were soon replaced by executives from Stuttgart, Germany. Problems of assimilation and coordination plagued the merger for years. Adding to the problems, the industry and the economy soured.

Newell, a consumer-products firm, had successfully geared its operations to meeting the demands of giant retailers, particularly Wal-Mart. Rubbermaid had in recent years been unable to meet those stringent requirements. In 1999, Newell acquired Rubbermaid, confident of turning its operation around, only to find that Rubbermaid's problems were not easily corrected and had a negative impact on the fortunes of Newell as well.

In July 1999, Hewlett-Packard, the world's second biggest computer maker, chose Carly Fiorina to be its CEO. Thus she became the first outsider to take the reins in HP's sixty-year history. Three years later she engineered the biggest merger in the high-tech industry, with Compaq Computer. Only a year later, HP was able to boast that this merger had become a model of effectively assimilating two giant organizations.

Planning

In April 1992, just outside Paris, Disney opened its first European theme park. It had high expectations and supreme self-confidence (critics called it arrogance). The earlier Disney parks in California, Florida, and more recently Japan, were spectacular successes. But the rosy expectations soon became a delusion as a variety of planning miscues finally showed Disney that Europeans, and particularly the French, were not carbon copies of visitors elsewhere.

Pepsi and Coca-Cola for decades competed both domestically and internationally. Usually Coca-Cola won out, but it could never let its guard down, and it recently did so in Europe.

The tobacco industry, and Philip Morris in particular, had long contested the assertions of health experts that tobacco was life threatening. Only in the last few years, facing multibillion-dollar legal settlements and smoking bans sweeping the world, has Philip Morris begun to change its strategy.

Vanguard is fighting Fidelity to become the largest mutual fund company. Vanguard's strategy has been to walk a road less traveled, downplay marketing and shunning the heavy advertising and overhead of its competitors. It provided investors with better returns through far lower expense ratios, relying on word-of-mouth and unpaid publicity to gain new customers while old customers continued to pour money into the best values in the mutual fund industry.

Executing

Boeing had an interesting dilemma: too much business. It was unable to cope with a deluge of orders in the mid- and late 1990s. Months, and then years, went by as it tried to make its production more efficient. In the meantime, a foreign competitor, Airbus, emerged to oust Boeing in 2003 as number one in the commercial passenger plane market.

In the early 1960s, Harley Davidson dominated a static motorcycle industry. Suddenly, Honda burst on the scene and Harley's market share dropped from 70 percent to 5 percent in only a few years. It took Harley nearly three decades to revive, but now it has created a mystique for heavy motorcycles and gained a new type of user.

The comeback of Continental Airlines from extreme adversity and devastated employee morale to become one of the best airlines in the country is an achievement of no small moment. New CEO Gordon Bethune brought human-relations skills to one of the most rapid turnarounds ever, after a decade of raucous adversarial relations.

What made the competition between Dell Computer, Gateway, and Hewlett-Packard all the more fascinating was that it took place in an economic downturn particularly hard on technology firms. But Dell prospered despite this adversity.

Controlling

United Way of America is a not-for-profit organization. The man who led it to become the nation's largest charity perceived himself as virtually beyond authority. Exorbitant spending, favoritism, conflicts of interest—these went uncontrolled and uncriticized until investigative reporters from the *Washington Post* publicized the scandalous conduct. Amid the hue and cry, contributions nationwide drastically declined.

The problems of Maytag's Hoover subsidiary in Great Britain almost defy belief. The subsidiary, acquired in the late 1980s, was allowed to operate under very loose reins from corporate Maytag. In 1992 it planned a promotional campaign so generous that it was overwhelmed with takers; it was unable either to supply the products or to grant the prizes. Maytag was left to foot the bills while trying to appease irate customers and stockholders, to the tune of over $300 million.

The insurance firm MetLife, whether through loose controls or tacit approval, permitted an agent to use deceptive selling tactics on a grand scale, and enrich himself in the process. Investigations of several state attorneys general forced the company to cough up almost $2 billion in fines and restitutions.

Entrepreneurial Adventures

Boston Beer burst on the microbrewery scene with Samuel Adams beers, higher priced even than most imports. Notwithstanding this—or maybe because of it— Boston Beer became the largest microbrewer. It showed that a small entrepreneur can compete successfully against the giants in the industry, and do this on a national scale.

OfficeMax, an office-supply category-killer chain, grew to $2.5 billion in sales in only a few years. The dedication and creative efforts of its founder serve as a model for any would-be entrepreneur who aspires to make it big. Yet, it was number three in its industry with the heady years of profitable growth seemingly over. In October 2003, Michael Feuer, the founder, agreed for his firm to be acquired by Boise Cascade, a giant lumber firm.

GENERAL WRAP-UP

When possible, we have depicted the major personalities involved in these cases. Imagine yourself in their positions, confronting the problems and facing choices at their points of crisis or just-recognized opportunities. What would you have done differently, and why? We invite you to participate in the discussion questions, the hands-on exercises, and, yes, the debates appearing at the ends of chapters. There are also discussion questions for the various boxes within chapters. We urge you to consider the pros and cons of alternative actions.

In so doing you may feel the excitement and challenge of decision making under conditions of uncertainty. Perhaps you may even become a better future executive and decision maker.

QUESTIONS

1. Do you agree that it is impossible for a firm to avoid mistakes? Why or why not?

2. How can a firm speed up its awareness of emerging problems so that it can take corrective action? Be as specific as you can.

3. Large firms tend to err on the side of conservatism and are slower to take corrective action than smaller ones. Why do you suppose this is?

4. Which do you think is likely to be more costly to a firm, errors of omission or errors of commission? Why?

5. So often we see the successful firm eventually losing its pattern of success. Why is success not more enduring?

PART ONE

MANAGING CHANGE
AND CRISES

CHAPTER TWO

McDonald's Struggles with Maturity

*F*ew business firms anywhere in the world have been able to match the sustained growth of McDonald's. Initially, it grew with one simple product, a hamburger, and while it has broadened its product mix today, it still remains uniquely undiversified.

The foundation for McDonald's success had always been the most rigid standards and controls to be found anywhere. The company insisted these be adhered to by all outlets, company-owned as well as franchised, and therein was an enduring management strategy. For decades, no competitor could match the standards of quality, service, and cleanliness that made McDonald's unique, and it seemed the growth mode would last forever.

In recent years, however, McDonald's appeared to have entered the maturity stage of its life cycle, and was not handling well this new environment. Its standards and controls had slipped, while competitors countered its former advantage. And, after decades of seemingly unlimited demand for hamburgers, suddenly the market both here and abroad appeared saturated. But before we delve into this, let's see how McDonald's got started and the glorious decades that followed.

RAY KROC'S DREAM

Ray Kroc faced a serious dilemma. He was fifty-seven-years old and all his life had dreamed of becoming rich, and worked hard at it, but real success eluded him. He had played piano with dance bands, then turned to selling paper cups for a firm called Lily-Tulip. He also moonlighted at a Chicago radio station, accompanying singers and arranging the music programs. Then he thought he might make his fortune by selling land in a Florida land boom. But this did not work out, and he returned to Chicago a year later almost broke. Lily-Tulip gave him back his old job and he stayed there for more than ten years.

In 1937, he became intrigued with a new gadget, a simple electrical appliance that could mix six milkshakes at the same time, and he quit Lily-Tulip again and made a deal with the inventor. He soon became the world's exclusive agent for the Prince

Castle Multi-Mixer and for the next twenty years traveled all over the country peddling it. Though he didn't yet know it, at long last he was on the threshold of his dream.

In 1954, Kroc received an order for eight of the Multi-Mixers from a small hamburger stand in San Bernardino, California. He wondered what wild kind of business sold so many milkshakes. So he decided to go out and see for himself this operation of Maurice and Richard McDonald that needed to make forty-eight milkshakes at the same time.

When Ray Kroc arrived, he was amazed. It was a self-service hamburger stand, and he saw crowds of people waiting in line under golden arches. He was even more impressed with the speed of service and the cleanliness. Kroc badly wanted in on this business, and hounded the McDonald brothers until they allowed him to start selling franchises. By 1960 he had sold some 200 franchises.

Kroc bought out the McDonald brothers, though he kept their name, and they took their money and quietly retired to their hometown of Bedford, New Hampshire. Now in control, Kroc took only seventeen years to reach the billion-dollar milestone. It gave him great satisfaction to think that IBM needed forty-six years to do this. Kroc would boast in his autobiography that the company was responsible for making more than 1,000 millionaires, the franchise holders.[1]

When Kroc retired in 1968, the company had more than 1,200 restaurants, and sales were $400 million. He had laid the foundation for great growth, and by 1972 the number of outlets had climbed to 2,272 and sales were accelerating beyond $1 billion.

THE MCDONALD'S GROWTH MACHINE

In its 1995 Annual Report, McDonald's management was justifiably proud. Sales and profits had continued the long trend upward, and even seemed to be accelerating. See Table 2.1 for sales and profits through 1998. Far from reaching a saturation point, the firm was opening more restaurants than ever, some 2,400 around the world in 1995, up from 1,800 the year before. "We plan to add between 2,500 and 3,200 restaurants in both 1996 and 1997, with about two thirds outside of the U.S. In other words, we opened more than six restaurants per day in 1995; over the next two years, we plan to open eight a day."[2] And, "Our growth opportunities remain significant: on any given day, 99 percent of the world's population does not eat at McDonald's ... yet."[3]

Company management extolled the power of the McDonald's brand overseas, and how on opening days lines were sometimes "miles" long. "Often our challenge is to keep up with demand. In China, for example, there are only sixty-two McDonald's to serve a population of 1.2 billion."[4] By the end of 1995, the company had 7,012 outlets in 89 countries of the world, with Japan alone having 1,482. Table 2.2 shows the top ten countries in 1999 in number of McDonald's units.

[1] Ray Kroc and Robert Anderson, *Grinding It Out: The Making of McDonald's* (New York: Berkley Publishing, 1977), p. 200.

[2] *McDonald's 1995 Annual Report*, p. 8.

[3] *Ibid.*, p. 7.

[4] *Ibid.*

TABLE 2.1 Growth in McDonald's Sales and Profits, 1985–1998

	Sales (millions)	Percent Gain	Income (millions)	Percent Gain
1985	$11,011	—	$433	
1986	12,432	12.9%	480	12.2%
1987	14,330	15.3	549	14.4
1988	16,064	12.1	646	17.7
1989	17,333	7.9	727	12.5
1990	18,759	8.2	802	10.3
1991	19,928	6.2	860	7.2
1992	21,885	9.8	959	11.5
1993	23,587	7.8	1,083	12.9
1994	25,987	10.2	1,224	13.0
1995	29,914	15.1	1,427	16.6
1996	31,812	6.3	1,573	10.2
1997	33,638	5.7	1,642	4.3
1998	35,979	6.9	1,550	–5.6

Source: 1998 Annual Report.

Commentary: Of particular interest is how the new expansion policies brought a burst of revenues and profits in the mid-1990s. But after 1995, growth in sales and earnings slowed. Note in particular the first decline in profit gain in 1998, a harbinger of things to come.

TABLE 2.2 Top Ten Foreign Markets in Number of Units at the Beginning of 1999

Japan	2,852 McDonald's restaurants
Canada	1,085
Germany	931
England	810
France	708
Brazil	672
Australia	666
Taiwan	292
China	220
Italy	201

Source: 1998 Annual Report.

Commentary: Is the popularity in Japan a surprise?

Sometimes in marketing its products in different cultures, adjustments had to be made. Nowhere was this more necessary than in Yugoslavia during the NATO bombings in the Kosovo confrontation. The following Information Box describes the changes McDonald's made there for these turbulent times.

Growth Prospects in the United States

In 1995, with 11,368 of its restaurants in the United States, wasn't McDonald's reaching saturation in its domestic market? Top management vehemently disputed this conclusion. Rather, it offered a startling statistical phenomenon to support accelerating

---

INFORMATION BOX

MCDONALD'S SUCCESSFUL ADVENTURES IN SERBIA, 1999

The NATO air war against Yugoslavia lasted seventy-eight days. At first the fifteen McDonald's restaurants in Yugoslavia were closed due to angry mobs bent on vandalizing. Fanned by media attacks on "NATO criminals and aggressors," mobs of youths smashed windows and painted insults. But the restaurants soon reopened, downplaying their U.S. citizenship and presenting McDonald's as a Yugoslav company.

The restaurants promoted the McCountry, a domestic pork burger with paprika garnish. (Pork is considered the most Serbian of meats.) To cater to Serbian identity and pride, they brought out posters and lapel buttons showing the golden arches topped with a traditional Serbian cap called the sajkaca. Dragoljub Jakic, the forty-seven-year-old managing director of McDonald's in Yugoslavia, noted that the cap "is a strong, unique Serbian symbol. By adding this symbol of our cultural heritage, we hoped to denote our pride in being a local company."[5] They also handed out free cheeseburgers at anti-NATO rallies. One restaurant's basement in Belgrade even became a bomb shelter.

The result? In spite of falling wages, rising prices, and lingering anger at the United States, the McDonald's restaurants were thronged with Serbs.

Still, McDonald's globally is a prominent symbol of American culture and attracts outbursts of anti-American sentiment. For example, in August 1999, a McDonald's in Belgium was burned down by suspected animal-rights activists. And India has seen militant critics: "… they [McDonald's] are the chief killers of cows in the world. We don't need cow killers in India."[6]

Do you think McDonald's in Serbia went too far in downplaying—some would say even denying—its American roots? Did it have any other reasonable option if it were to keep operating?

Should militant activists become more violent about McDonald's "conducting a global conspiracy against cows." Do you think McDonald's should abandon the India markets? Why or why not?

---

[5] Robert Block, "How Big Mac Kept From Becoming a Serb Archenemy," *Wall Street Journal*, September 3, 1999, p. B3.

[6] "Delhi Delights in McMutton Burgers," *Cleveland Plain Dealer*, November 6, 1999, p. 3D.

expansion. Called "Greenberg's Law," after newly appointed McDonald's U.S. chairman Jack Greenberg, it maintained that the more stores McDonald's put in a city the more per-capita transactions will result. Thus, with two stores in a city there might be sixteen transactions per capita per year. Add two or four more stores and the transactions will not only double, or quadruple, but may even do better than that. The hypothesized explanation for this amazing phenomenon seemingly rested on two factors: convenience and market share. With more outlets, McDonald's increased its convenience to consumers, and added to its market share at the expense of competitors. Hence, the justification for the expansion binge.

In the quest for this domestic expansion, the company over the last five years had been able to reduce the cost of building a new U.S. traditional restaurant by 26 percent through standardizing building materials and equipment and global sourcing, as well as improving construction methods and building designs. It had also found abundant market opportunities in satellite restaurants. These were smaller, had lower sales volume, and served simplified menus. This format proved cost efficient in such nontraditional places as zoos, hospitals, airports, museums, and military bases as well as in retail stores such as Wal-Mart, The Home Depot, and other major stores. For example, such satellite restaurants were in some 800 Wal-Mart stores by the end of 1995, with more planned. In October 1996, a McDonald's Express opened in an office building in Lansing, Michigan, perhaps a harbinger of more such sites to come.

In its eager search for more outlets, McDonald's did something it had never done before. It took over stores from weak competitors. In late summer 1996, it bought 184 company-owned Roy Rogers outlets. "Here was an opportunity that was maybe once in a lifetime," Greenberg stated.[7] Earlier the same year, it acquired Burghy's, an eighty-store fast-food chain in Italy. And in New Zealand, it added seventeen restaurants from the Georgie Pie chain.

The new stores being opened were seldom like the old ones. The popular drive-thru windows generated 55 percent of U.S. sales, and in the process fewer seats were needed inside. This left more space available for gas stations or for indoor playgrounds—"Ronald's Playplaces"—to attract families. McDonald's made joint ventures with Chevron and Amoco to codevelop properties. It also signed an exclusive marketing deal with Disney for promoting each other's brands.

McDonald's had always been a big spender for advertising, and this had been effective. Even back in the 1970s, a survey of school children found that 96 percent could identify Ronald McDonald, ranking him second only to Santa Claus.[8] In 1995, advertising and promotional expenditures totaled $1.8 billion, or 6 percent of sales.[9]

Factors in the Invincibility of McDonald's

Through the third quarter of 1996, McDonald's could proudly claim 126 consecutive quarters of record earnings. Since its earliest days, the ingredients of success were simple, but few competitors were able to effectively emulate them. The basic aspects were:

[7] Gary Samuels, "Golden Arches Galore," *Forbes*, November 4, 1996, p. 48.

[8] "The Burger That Conquered the Country," *Time*, September 17, 1973, pp. 84–92.

[9] *McDonald's 1995 Annual Report*, p. 9.

- A brief menu, but having consistent quality over thousands of outlets
- Strictly enforced and rigorous operational standards controlling service, cleanliness, and all other aspects of the operation
- Friendly employees, despite a high turnover of personnel because of the monotony of automated food handling
- Heavy mass media advertising directed mostly at families and children
- Identification of a fertile target market—the family—and directing the strategy to satisfying it with product, price, promotional efforts, and site locations (in the early years, at least, this meant locating in suburbs with their high density of families)

However, by the end of 1996, international operations were the real vehicle of growth, providing 47 percent of the company's $30 billion sales and 54 percent of profits. Of no small concern, the domestic operation had not blossomed accordingly.

PROBLEMS AS MATURITY APPROACHED: STORM CLOUDS FOR THE DOMESTIC OPERATION

Souring Franchisee Relations

In the market-share game, in which McDonald's dominated all its competitors, corporate management concluded that the firm with the most outlets in a given community wins. But as McDonald's unprecedented expansion continued, many franchisees were skeptical of headquarters' claim that no one loses when the company opens more outlets in a community because market share rises proportionately. The franchise holders had to wonder how much their sales would diminish when another McDonald's opened down the street.

The 7,000-member American Franchisee Association, an organization formed to look after franchisees' rights, claimed that McDonald's operators were joining in record numbers.[10] Other franchisees formed a clandestine group called the Consortium, representing dissidents who felt present management was unresponsive to their concerns. They remembered a kinder and gentler company. See the following Information Box for contrasting franchisee views on the high-growth market share policy.

Another concern of franchisees was a new set of business practices developed by corporate headquarters, known as Franchising 2000. The company claimed it instituted this as a way to improve standards for quality, service, cleanliness, and value by giving franchisees better "tools." But some saw this as a blatant attempt to gain more power over the franchised operations. One provision revived a controversial A, B, C, and F grading system, with only franchisees who received A's and B's eligible for more restaurants. Furthermore, McDonald's began using Franchising 2000 to enforce a single pricing strategy throughout the chain, so that a Big Mac, for example, would

---

[10] Richard Gibson, "Some Franchisees Say Moves by McDonald's Hurt their Operations," *Wall Street Journal*, April 17, 1996, pp. A1, A8.

INFORMATION BOX

THE CONTENTMENT OF TWO MCDONALD'S FRANCHISES

In 1980, Wayne and Mary Jane Kilburn took over the only McDonald's in Ridgecrest, California, a town of 26,000. The Kilburns prospered in the years to come. Then McDonald's instituted its "market-share plan" for Ridgecrest. Late in 1995, it put a company-owned restaurant inside the local Wal-Mart. A few months later it built another outlet inside the China Lake Naval Weapons Center. A third company-owned store went up just outside the naval base. "Basically, they killed me," *Forbes* reported Wayne Kilburn saying. And he claimed his volume dropped 30 percent.[11]

In its *1995 Annual Report*, corporate headquarters offered another view concerning franchisee contentment. Tom Wolf was a McDonald's franchisee with fifteen restaurants in the Huntington, West Virginia, and Ashland, Kentucky, markets. He opened his first McDonald's in 1974, had eight by the end of 1993, and opened seven more in the last two years, including two McDonald's in Wal-Mart stores and another in an alliance with an oil company; in addition he added indoor Playplaces to two existing restaurants.

Has all this investment in growth made a difference? The Annual Report quotes Tom: "I wouldn't change a thing. Sales are up. I'm serving more customers, my market share is up and I'm confident about the future. Customers say that the Playplaces and Wal-Mart units are 'a great idea.' The business is out there. We've got to take these opportunities now, or leave them for someone else to take."[12]

"The high growth, market share policy should not bother any franchisee. It simply creates opportunities to invest in more restaurants." Evaluate this statement.

cost the same everywhere. The corporation maintained that such uniformity was necessary for the discounting needed to build market share. Those not complying risked losing their franchise.

Franchise relations should not be a matter of small concern to McDonald's. Table 2.3 shows the ratio of franchised restaurants to total restaurants up to 1998. As can be seen, franchises constituted by far the largest proportion of restaurants.

Menu Problems

Since 1993, domestic per-store sales slumped from a positive 4 percent annual rate to a negative 2 percent by the third quarter of 1996, this being the fifth quarter in a row of declining sales. In part this decline was thought to be attributable to older customers drifting away: "Huge numbers of baby-boomers ... want less of the cheap, fattening foods at places like McDonald's. As soon as their kids are old enough, they go elsewhere."[13]

[11] Samuels, p. 48.

[12] *McDonald's 1995 Annual Report*, p. 32.

[13] Shelly Branch, "McDonald's Strikes Out With Grownups," *Fortune*, November 11, 1996, p. 158.

TABLE 2.3 Percent of Franchised to Total Traditional McDonald's Restaurants, Selected Years, 1985–1998

	1985	1992	1995	1998
Total	8,901	13,093	16,809	24,800
Operated by franchisees	6,150	9,237	11,240	15,281
Percent of franchised to total	69.1%	70.5%	66.9%	61.6%

Source: Calculated from *1998 Annual Report.*

Commentary: While by 1998, the ratio of franchised to total restaurants had dropped, still more than 60 percent are operated by franchisees. Perhaps this suggests that franchisee concerns ought to receive full consideration by corporate headquarters.

In an attempt to garner more business from this customer segment, McDonald's with a $200 million promotional blitz launched its first "grownup taste" sandwich, the Arch Deluxe line of beef, fish, and chicken burgers. It forecast that this would become a $1 billion brand in only its first year. But before long, some were calling this a McFlop. In September 1996, Edward Rensi, head of U.S. operations, tried to minimize the stake in the new sandwich, and sent a memo to 2,700 concerned franchisees, "the Arch Deluxe was never intended to be a silver bullet."[14] On October 8, Rensi was replaced by Jack Greenberg.

McDonald's domestic troubles were not entirely new. As far back as the late 1980s, competitors, including Pizza Hut and Taco Bell, were nibbling at McDonald's market share, and Burger King was more than holding its own. Even the great traditional strength of McDonald's of unsurpassed controlled standards over food, service, and cleanliness seemed to be waning: A 1995 Restaurants and Institutions Choice in Chains survey of 2,849 adults gave McDonald's low marks on food quality, value, service, and cleanliness. Top honors instead went to Wendy's.[15]

In 1991, McDonald's reluctantly tried discounting, with "Extra Value Meals," largely to keep up with Taco Bell's value pricing. But by 1995, price promotions were no longer attracting customers, and per-store sales began slumping.

The new, adult-oriented Deluxe line was not only aimed at older adults, but with its prices 20 percent more than regular items, the hope was to parry the discounting.

The company had had previous problems in expanding its menu. The McDLT was notably unsuccessful despite heavy promotion. More recently, the low-fat McLean, an effort to attract weight-conscious adults, was a complete disaster. In fact this beef and seaweed concoction sold so badly that some operators kept only a few frozen patties on hand, while others, as revealed in an embarrassing TV exposé, sold fully fatted burgers in McLean boxes to the few customers asking for them.

Some years before, the company had tried but failed to develop an acceptable pizza product. It also was unable to create a dinner menu that would attract evening-hour traffic. Two other experiments were also abandoned: a 1950s-style cafe and a family-type concept called Hearth Express that served chicken, ham, and meatloaf.

[14] *Ibid.*
[15] *Ibid.*

THE SITUATION IN THE NEW MILLENNIUM

Jack Greenberg was promoted to CEO in August 1998, and then to chairman of the board in May 1999. There was hope that he would lessen the alienation felt by many franchisees. He bought Donatos Pizza, a Midwestern chain of 143 restaurants, proclaiming: "We would like to make this a growth opportunity for our franchisees."[16] In imitation of its competitors, particularly Wendy's, the company installed a new cooking system to deliver sandwiches to order, "Made for You," which meant fresher with less waste compared with the old system of holding bins.

Despite Greenberg's leadership, McDonald's domestic operations continued to falter. By 2001, it was averaging only 1 percent same-store sales growth, far behind the 4 percent average of Burger King and Wendy's. After forty-four years as one of America's premier growth companies, market saturation seemed imminent. The main reason was thought to be a stale menu, but this was hardly a new insight.

Of perhaps just as much concern was the deterioration of the stringent controls that for decades had made McDonald's the paragon among all firms. A 2001 University of Michigan study on customer satisfaction showed that conditions had worsened from the 1995 survey that had given it low marks on food, service, and cleanliness. Estimates were that unhappy customers could mean an average of $60,000 in lost sales per year per store.

Undoubtedly such problems reflected the difficulty many businesses were having in hiring good help in the low unemployment of the late 1990s and beginning the new millennium. But other fast-food chains were doing better in this regard than McDonald's. Perhaps another factor contributed to the quality control problems. In recognition of franchisee complaints, Greenberg threw out the Franchise 2000 rulebook with its eighty pages of onerous regulations, and gave franchisees more say in their local menus.

The frenetic growth in outlets of the mid-1990s was over, as many angry franchisees saw their sales decline as much as 30 percent due to cannibalization. In 1999, only 150 new outlets were added, down sharply from the 1,100 of a few years before.

Increasingly, Greenberg turned his attention to food diversifications. He planned to grow the 143-store Donatos Pizza regional chain to a national one of 1,000 stores. He bought into Chipotle Mexican Grill, a popular Denver-based chain of Mexican restaurants. The purchase of Aroma, a coffee-and-sandwich bar in London, England, showed perhaps the most promise. In the UK, the cold-sandwich market was almost double the size of the burger market and growing twice as fast. It appealed to mostly single, health-conscious females with practically no overlap with the burger crowd—therefore, no cannibalization. Some 150 stores were planned by 2002.

In another major acquisition, the faltering Boston Market chain was acquired on May 26, 2000. Almost 100 underperforming Boston Market restaurants were closed, with others converted to McDonald's, Chipotle Mexican Grill, and Donatos Pizza. This still left more than 750 Boston restaurants that could be a challenge in achieving profitability.

---

[16] James P. Miller and Richard Gibson, "Did Somebody Say Pizza?" *Wall Street Journal*, May 1, 1999, p. A4.

In a major menu thrust beyond burgers, more new products were coming out of McDonald's test kitchens than ever before, many of these appealing regionally rather than nationally: for example, the McBrat, a $1.99 sandwich with sauerkraut and onion on the bratwurst, a big hit in Minnesota and Wisconsin; a McLobster Roll in New England; Homestyle Burger with hot mustard in Texas; the Brutus Buckeye Burger for Ohioans; and even bagel breakfast sandwiches, already doing well in 6,000 stores.[17]

Still, U.S. sales grew just 3 percent in 2000, while fourth-quarter net earnings declined 7 percent. McDonald's responded with a "New Tastes Menu," a collection of forty-four items to be rotated four at a time. An analyst noted, however, that these were mostly "tired old products with such startling innovations like a strip of bacon or a dollop of ranch dressing."[18]

The Situation in the Rest of the World

In Europe, mad cow hysteria and currency woes were playing havoc, and McDonald's stock was at a two-year low. But non-U.S. restaurants continued to offer the best opportunities, and by the end of 2000 foreign restaurants outnumbered U.S. outlets, 15,900 to 12,408 in the United States. International business contributed 52 percent of total operating income by 2000.[19] The success of the international operations partly reflected McDonald's adaptations in foreign environments. (We saw an example of this earlier in the Serbian Information Box.)

Japan especially was a lucrative foreign market, and by 2001 the almost 3,600 McDonald's restaurants there had changed the eating habits of the nation, making fast food a part of everyday life. McDonald's—"Maku" in Japanese shorthand—controlled about 65 percent of the fast-food burger market, serving 1.3 billion customers a year. The mad cow disease scare that had so severely affected demand in Europe was at first largely averted in Japan, which used beef from Australia, where there had been no disease. Later, the stigma also began to affect Japanese demand.

LATER DEVELOPMENTS

CEO Jack Greenberg, at sixty, stepped down at the end of 2002, well ahead of his planned 2005 retirement. His had been a frustrating four-year effort to reinvent the firm and start it on a new growth pattern.

Greenberg's reinvention efforts included starting a fierce price war by selling two of McDonald's biggest sandwiches for $1 each, introducing some forty menu items, and spending $151 million to overhaul the company's U.S. kitchens in order to make food hotter and fresher, as well as acquiring other restaurant chains. In November 2002, customers were even given the option of paying with credit cards and earning frequent flyer miles.

Except for the acquisitions, customer response to all these efforts was poor. The price war mostly resulted in all burger chains facing lower profits with little increase in

---

[17] Bruce Upbin, "Beyond Burgers," *Forbes*, November 1, 1999, pp. 218–223.

[18] Brandon Copple, "Same Old, Same Old," *Forbes*, February 19, 2001, p. 60.

[19] Company public information.

sales. The new "Made for You" kitchens sacrificed speed and service. And Greenberg could never bring customer service up to historic levels, despite sending mystery shoppers to evaluate service. The mad cow scare of 2000 in Europe dragged down profits as well, but profitability was not regained with the end of mad cow concerns.[20]

James R. Cantalupo succeeded Greenberg as CEO in January 2003. He had briefly retired as CEO of McDonald's International, and now was brought in to return the company to its core business. Profits had fallen in seven of the last eight quarters, and the stock price had sunk to a seven-year low. The bottom came in January 2003, when the company announced its first quarterly loss since going public in 1965, almost forty years before.

Cantalupo promised to slice capital expenditures (new stores), hold back on global expansion, shoot for lower growth targets, and raise the dividend. The lower growth expectations was a long overdue admission that McDonald's was now in the maturity stage of its life cycle.

The insistence of former top management on pushing for double-digit growth had tormented franchisees who shuddered at the cannibalization new outlets brought them, and also tormented investors who saw costly expansion efforts playing havoc with profitability.

The foreign markets that had long sustained the growth mode were also faltering. Germany was the largest European market, but McDonald's growth there stagnated as competition grew from Burger King, which expanded from 268 stores in 2000 to 390 in 2002, and from local retailers such as gas-station food marts and traditional mom-and-pop bakeries. In the UK, McDonald's problems with service and cleanliness, as well as changes in consumer tastes, now throttled its expansion efforts. In Japan, long the crown jewel in McDonald's foreign operations, the chain's 3,800 stores there faced a saturated market, with its core customers—families with children—shrinking with a declining birthrate, while local competitors became stronger. Same-store sales in Japan fell 12.1 percent in 2002 and were expected to fall an additional 3.5 percent in 2003.

Domestically, even the restaurant chains that Greenberg acquired in his modest diversification efforts were not producing the expected profits. Boston Market and its other partner brands as a group lost $67 million on sales of $1.07 billion in 2002. Some of these could face divestiture by a top management less growth-minded. Still, a company willing to work hard on its core business and forsake reckless growth could provide reasonable satisfaction to customers, franchisees, and investors.[21]

The attractiveness of Cantalupo's new low-growth policy of was fully evident in the summer and fall of 2003 when the dividend was raised 70 percent and the stock

[20] Shirley Leung and Ron Lieber, "The New Menu Option at McDonald's: Plastic," *Wall Street Journal*, November 26, 2002, pp. D1–2; Shirley Leung, "McDonald's Chief Plans to Leave," *Wall Street Journal*, December 6, 2002, pp. A3, A6.

[21] Compiled from Nick Pachetti, "Back to the Kitchen," *Money*, July 2003, pp. 44–45; Martin Fackler, "Will Ratatouille Bring Japanese to McDonald's?" *Wall Street Journal*, August 14, 2003, pp. B1, B5; Erin White and Shirley Leung, "McDonald's German Sales Stall," *Wall Street Journal*, September 23, 2003, p. B4; and Julie Dunn, "Is McDonald's Losing Its Taste for Non-Burger Chains?" *New York Times* as published in *Cleveland Plain Dealer*, May 5, 2003, p. E4.

price rose from $18 to over $24 by early October. Was this a validation of a new philosophy: eschewing growth in the quest for more stability and profitability?

ANALYSIS

After decades of uninterrupted growth in sales, profits, and number of stores opened, McDonald's faced diminished prospects both domestically and foreign by the latter 1990s. Though no one wanted to admit it then, the evidence was rather compelling that the company life cycle was reaching maturity without major policy changes. Pouring more efforts into additional outlets seemed ill-advised, although it took a top management change to recognize and come to grips with this. But the siren call of growth is difficult to subdue.

McDonald's relations with its franchisees, formerly the best in the industry, had deteriorated as corporate management pursued policies more dictatorial and selfish than ever before, policies that signaled the end of the kinder and gentler stance franchisees remembered. In particular, the new expansion policy aimed at increased market share regardless of its effect on established franchisees, and portended worsening relations and the start of an adversarial instead of supportive climate.

The cost/benefit consequences of an aggressive expansion policy were rationalized as in the company's best interest, especially as recent store construction became more cost efficient. If total market share could be substantially increased, despite same-store sales declining, the accounting analyses supported more stores. But how much should the franchisee be considered in this aggressive strategy of McDonald's outlets competing not so much with Wendy's, Burger King, and Taco Bell as with other McDonald's outlets? And, couldn't profitability be improved by more carefully selecting fewer new store sites, and at the same time identifying marginal stores that perhaps should be closed?

A major domestic challenge for the growth-oriented McDonald's was the menu: how to appeal to adults and expand market potential. This offered another growth alternative, even more so if the dinner market could be tapped. But the last successful menu expansion had been the breakfast menu, and that was decades ago.

What menu changes should be made? Installing a salad bar—would this be the menu breakthrough needed? With a history of past failures, expectations could hardly be robust. Yet McDonald's, as any chain organization whether fast food or otherwise, can test different prices and strategies or different menus and different atmospheres in just a few outlets, and only if results are favorable expand further. A few stores then can provide a powerful research tool.

A major trouble spot was McDonald's seeming inability to enforce tighter controls over product quality and service. The rigid standards and controls imposed in the days of Ray Kroc that made McDonald's unique had somehow eroded. Admittedly, as more and more outlets were added, enforcing tight controls became more difficult. Yet competitors meantime were doing a better job of matching, and surpassing, McDonald's former high standards.

To summarize, is McDonald's likely to continue its great growth in sales and profits? Probably not, either domestically or foreign. The burger that sustained its growth for almost four decades had now become more mundane, with a host of competitors offering similar products while customers were becoming calloused.

McDonald's faces a situation that seemingly cries for diversification. Perhaps an inspired menu change. Maybe a new format to tap other customer segments. Or should it be content to stick to reenergizing its basic core position?

WHAT CAN BE LEARNED?

It is possible to have strong and enduring growth without diversification. For more than four decades, since 1955, McDonald's had grown continuously and substantially. In all this time, the product was essentially the hamburger in its various trappings and accompaniments. Almost all other firms in their quest for growth have diversified, sometimes wisely and synergistically, at other times imprudently and even recklessly.

For such an undeviating focus, the product should have universal appeal, be frequently consumed, and have almost unlimited potential. Along with beer, soft drinks, and tobacco, the hamburger probably meets these criteria better than practically any other product. And soft drinks, of course, are a natural accompaniment of the hamburger.

Eventually even the hamburger began to fall short in providing continued strong growth as the international market reached saturation and the domestic market oversaturation. McDonald's may be forced to seek judicious diversifications or lose the growth mode. There is risk: Firms in pursuit of growth often jump into acquisitions far too hastily and are faced with massive debt and overhead.

Beware the reckless drive for market share. A firm can usually "buy" market share, if it is willing to sacrifice profits to do so. It can step up advertising and sales promotions. It can reduce prices, assuming that lower prices would bring more demand. It can increase sales staff and motivate them to be more aggressive. Sales and competitive position then will usually rise. But costs may increase disproportionately. In other words, the benefits to be gained may not be worth the costs.

As we saw, McDonald's aggressively increased market share in the mid-1990s by opening thousands of new domestic units. As long as developmental costs could be kept sufficiently low for these new units to be profitable and not cannibalize business away from other McDonald's restaurants, then the strategy was defensible. Still, the costs of damaged franchisee relations resulting in lowered morale, reduced cooperation, and festering resentments could be real indeed. Interestingly, this market share growth strategy was toned down by early 2000.

Maintaining the highest standards requires constant monitoring. McDonald's heritage and its competitive advantage had long been associated with the highest standards and controls for cleanliness, fast service, dependable quality of food, and friendly and well-groomed employees. The following Information Box discusses strategy countering by competitors and the great difficulty in matching nonprice strengths.

INFORMATION BOX

MATCHING A COMPETITOR'S STRATEGY

Some strategies are easily countered or duplicated by competitors. Price cutting is the most easily countered. A price cut can often be matched within minutes. Similarly, a different package or a warranty is easily imitated by competitors.

But some strategies are not so easily duplicated. Most of these involve service, a strong and positive company image, or both. A reputation for quality and dependability is not easily countered, at least in the short run. A good company or brand image is hard to match because it usually results from years of good service and satisfied customers. The great controls of McDonald's with its high standards would seem to be easily imitated, but they proved not to be, as no other firm fully matched them until recent years.

The strategies and operations most difficult to imitate often are not the wildly innovative ones, nor the ones that are complex and well researched. Rather they seem to be the simple ones: doing a better job in servicing and satisfying customers and in performing even mundane operations cheerfully and efficiently.

What explanation can you give for competitors' inability for so long to match the standards of McDonald's?

Alas, in the last few years McDonald's has apparently let its control of operational standards slip. We have seen that surveys of customer satisfaction in 1995 and 2001 gave McDonald's low marks on food quality, value, service, and cleanliness, with its competitors showing up considerably better. Why this lapse? Without doubt, maintaining high standards among thousands of units, company-owned as well as franchised, requires constant monitoring and exhortation. But this was successfully done for over four decades. How was this lapse allowed to happen? We can only speculate that such standards became taken for granted, not emphasized as much. Then it became difficult to resurrect them.

Controls can be too stringent. In a belated attempt to improve standards and tighten corporate control, McDonald's instituted the controversial Franchising 2000. Among other things this called for grading franchisees, with those receiving the lower grades being penalized. McDonald's also wanted to take away any pricing flexibility for its franchisees: All restaurants now had to charge the same prices, or risk losing their franchise. Not surprising, some franchisees were concerned about this new "get tough" management.

Can controls be too stringent? As with most things, extremes are seldom desirable. All firms need tight controls over far-flung outlets to keep corporate management alert to emerging problems and opportunities and maintain a desired image and standard of performance. In a franchise operation this is all the more necessary since the company is dealing with independent entrepreneurs rather than hired managers. However, controls can be so rigid that no room is left for special circumstances and opportunities. If the enforcement is too punitive, the climate becomes more that of a police state than a teamwork relationship with both parties cooperating to their mutual advantages.

This brings us to the next insight for discussion.

There is a place for a kinder, gentler firm in today's hotly competitive environment. Many longtime McDonald's franchisees remembered with sadness a kinder, gentler company, an atmosphere nurtured by founder Ray Kroc. To be sure, Kroc insisted that customers be assured of a clean, family atmosphere with quick and cheerful service. To Kroc, this meant strict standards, not only in food preparation but also in care and maintenance of facilities, including toilets. Company auditors closely checked that the standards were adhered to, under Kroc's belief that a weakness in one restaurant could have a detrimental effect on other units in the system. Still, the atmosphere was helpful—the inspectors were "consultants"—rather than adversarial. Kroc was proud that he was responsible for making more than 1,000 millionaires, the franchise holders.

Many franchisees traced the deterioration of franchiser-franchisee relations to the 1992 death of Gerald Newman, McDonald's chief accounting officer. He spent much time interacting with franchisees, sometimes encouraging them—he had a reputation for a sympathetic ear—sometimes even giving them a financial break.[22]

So, is it possible and desirable to be a kind and gentle company? With franchisees? Employees? Suppliers? Customers? Of course it is. Organizations, and the people who run them, often forget this in the arrogance of power. They excuse a "get tough" mindset on the exigencies of competition and the need to be faithful to their stockholders.

Kind and gentle—is this an anachronism, a throwback to a quieter time, a nostalgia long past its usefulness? Let us hope not.

CONSIDER

Can you add other learning insights?

QUESTIONS

1. How do you account for the reluctance of competitors to imitate the successful efforts of another firm in their industry? Under what circumstances is imitation likely to be embraced?

2. To date McDonald's has shunned diversification into unrelated food retailing operations as well as nonfood options. Discuss the desirability of such diversification efforts.

3. "Eventually—and this may come sooner than most think—there will no longer be any choice locations anywhere in the world for new hamburger outlets. As a McDonald's stockholder, I'm getting worried." Discuss.

4. Does the size of McDonald's give it a powerful advantage over its competitors? Why or why not?

[22] Gibson, p. A8.

5. What do you think is McDonald's near-term and long-term potential? What makes you think this?

6. Is it likely that McDonald's has really found a saturated market for its hamburgers?

7. Discuss the importance of market share in the fast-food industry.

8. Discuss the desirability of McDonald's efforts to insist on the same price in all domestic restaurants.

9. Do you think McDonald's "adaptability" in such countries as Yugoslavia went too far in repudiating U.S. values? Why or why not?

HANDS-ON EXERCISES

1. You have been given the assignment by Edward Rensi in 1993 to instill a recommitment to improved customer service in all domestic operations. Discuss in as much detail as you can how you would go about fostering this among the 10,000 domestic outlets.

2. As a McDonald's senior executive, what long-term expansion mode would you recommend for your company?

3. As a Burger King senior executive, what long-term expansion mode would you recommend for your company to combat a McDonald's that has maybe grown a bit vulnerable?

TEAM DEBATE EXERCISE

1. Debate this issue: McDonald's is reaching the limits of its ability to grow without drastic change. (Note: the side that espouses drastic change should give some attention to the most likely directions for such, and be prepared to defend these expansion possibilities.)

2. Debate the issue of a "get-tough" attitude of corporate management toward franchisees even if it riles some, versus involving them more in future directions of the company. In particular, be prepared to address the challenge of bringing customer satisfaction up to traditional standards.

3. Debate this contention: Market share is overemphasized in this industry. (Both sides in their debate may want to consider whether this assertion may or may not apply to other industries.)

INVITATION TO RESEARCH

How have Cantalupo's slower growth policies fared? Has profitability been well restored? How about the company stock market valuation? Has McDonald's made any major acquisitions recently?

CHAPTER THREE

Ill-Handling the Firestone/Ford Explorer Tire Disaster

*P*roduct defects that lead to customer injuries and deaths through manufacturer carelessness constitute the most serious crises that any firm should face. In addition to destroying brand reputation, ethical and social responsibility abuses are involved with legal and regulatory consequences. Managing such a crisis becomes far worse, however, when the manufacturer knew about the problems and concealed them, or denied them.

This case is unique in that two manufacturers were culpable, but each blamed the other. As a result, Firestone and Ford were savaged by the press, public opinion, the government, and a host of salivating lawyers. Massive tire recalls destroyed the bottom line and even endangered the viability of Bridgestone/Firestone, while sales of the Ford Explorer, the world's best-selling sport-utility vehicle, plummeted 22 percent in April 2001 from the year before, while domestic sales of SUVs overall climbed 9 percent.

A HORROR SCENARIO

Firestone tires mounted on Ford Explorers were linked to more than 200 deaths from rollovers in the United States, as well as more than 60 in Venezuela and a reported 14 in Saudi Arabia and neighboring countries. A widely publicized lawsuit took place in Texas in the summer of 2001. It had been expected that the jury would determine who was more to blame for the deaths and injuries from Explorers outfitted with Firestone tires.

Ford settled its portion of the suit for $6 million one month before the trial began. While Firestone now became the sole defendant, jurors were asked to also assess Ford's responsibility for the accident.

The lawsuit was brought by the family of Marisa Rodriguez, a mother of three who was left brain-damaged and paralyzed after the steel belt and tread of a Firestone tire tore apart during a trip to Mexico in March 2000. As a result, the Explorer rolled over three times, crushing the roof above Mrs. Rodriguez in the rear seat, and also injuring her husband, Joel, who was asleep in the front passenger seat. The live pictures of Mrs. Rodriguez in a wheelchair received maximum coverage by network TV.

After the federal court jury in the Texas border town of McAllen had been deadlocked for four days, a settlement was reached with Bridgestone/Firestone for $7.85 million. (The plaintiffs originally had asked for $1 billion.)

The out-of-court settlements with both Ford and Firestone did not resolve the issue of who was more to blame for this and the hundreds of other injuries and deaths. But a lawyer for the Rodriguez family predicted that sooner or later a verdict would emerge: "There's going to be trials and there's going to be verdicts. We've got Marisa Rodriguezes all over the country."[1]

ANATOMY OF THE PROBLEM

The Ford/Firestone Relationship

Ford and Firestone have had a long, intimate history. In 1895, Harvey Firestone sold tires to Henry Ford for his first automobile. In 1906, the Firestone Tire & Rubber Company won its first contract for Ford Motor Company's mass-produced vehicles, a commitment that continued through the decades.

Henry Ford and Harvey Firestone became business confederates and best friends who went on annual summer camping trips, riding around in Model T's along with Thomas Edison and naturalist John Burroughs. Further cementing the relationship, in 1947 Firestone's granddaughter, Martha, married Ford's grandson, William Clay Ford, in a dazzling ceremony in Akron, Ohio, that attracted a Who's Who of dignitaries and celebrities. Their son, William Clay Ford, Jr., was to become Ford's chairman.

In 1988, Tokyo-based Bridgestone Corporation bought Firestone, twenty years after the Japanese company sold its first tires in the United States under the Bridgestone name. In 1990, Ford introduced the Explorer sport-utility vehicle to replace the Bronco II in the 1991 model year. It became the nation's top-selling SUV, and the Explorer generated huge profits for more than a decade. Bridgestone/ Firestone was the sole supplier of the Explorer's tires.

The Relationship Worsens

The first intimation of trouble came in 1999 when Ford began replacing tires of Explorers in Saudi Arabia and nearby countries after fourteen fatalities. The tire failures were blamed on hot weather and underinflated tires. At the time, overseas fatalities did not have to be reported to U.S. regulators, so the accidents received scant attention in the U.S. media.

---

[1] "Firestone Agrees to Pay $7.5 Million in Tire Suit," *Cleveland Plain Dealer*, August 25, 2001, pp. A1, A13; Milo Geyelin and Timothy Aeppel, "For Firestone, Tire Trial Is Mixed Victory," *Wall Street Journal*, August 27, 2001, pp. A3, A4.

The media caught the scent in early 2000 when television reports in Houston revealed instances of tread separation on Firestone's ATX tires, and the National Highway Traffic Safety Administration (NHTSA) started an investigation. By May, four U.S. fatalities had been reported, and NHTSA expanded the investigation to 47 million ATX, ATXII, and Wilderness tires.

In August 2000, as deaths began mounting leading to increasing pressure from consumers and multiple lawsuits, Firestone voluntarily recalled 14.4 million 15-inch radial tires because of tread separation. The Firestone plant in Decatur, Illinois, was implicated in most of these accidents. Ford and Firestone agreed to replace the tires, but estimated that 6.5 million were still on the road. Consumer groups sought a still wider recall, charging that Explorers with other Firestone tire models were also prone to separation leading to rollovers.

In December 2000, Firestone issued a report blaming Ford for the problems, claiming that the Explorer's design caused rollovers with any tread separations. On April 20, 2001, Ford gave NHTSA a report blaming Firestone for flawed manufacturing.

In May 2001, Ford announced that it was replacing all remaining 13 million Firestone Wilderness AT tires on its vehicles, saying that the move was necessary because it didn't have confidence in the tires' safety. "We feel it's our responsibility to act immediately," Ford CEO Jacques Nasser said. Ford said the move would cost the automaker $2.1 billion, although it hoped to get this back from Firestone.

Firestone Chairman and CEO John Lampe defended his tires, saying, "no one cares more about the safety of the people who travel on our tires than we do. When we have a problem, we admit it and we fix it."[2]

The Last Days

It is lamentable when a long-lasting close relationship is severed. But on May 21, 2001, Lampe abruptly ended the ninety-five-year Ford/Firestone association, accusing Ford of refusing to acknowledge safety problems with its vehicles and thus putting all the blame on Firestone.

The crisis had been brewing for months. Many Firestone executives did not trust Ford and even exchanging documents was done with rancor, with major disagreements in interpreting the data. Firestone argued that tread-separation claims occurred ten times more frequently on Ford Explorers than on Ranger pickups with the same tires, thus supporting their contention that the Explorer was mostly at fault. Ford rejected Firestone's charges about the Explorer, saying that for ten years the model "has ranked at or near the top in terms of safety among the 12 SUVs in its class." It stated that 2.9 million Goodyear tires mounted on more than 500,000 Explorers had "performed with industry-leading safety."[3]

The critical time came in a May 21 meeting of Lampe and a contingent of Ford officials with both sides maintaining that the other was to blame. Discussions broke

---

[2] Ed Garsten, Associated Press, as reported in "Ford Tire Tab $2.1 Billion," *Cleveland Plain Dealer*, May 23, 2001, pp. 1C, 4C.

[3] Timothy Aeppel, Joseph B. White, and Stephen Power, "Firestone Quits as Tire Supplier to Ford," *Wall Street Journal*, May 22, 2001, pp. A3, A12.

down on how the two companies could work together to examine the Explorer's role in the accidents. At that point, Lampe sent a letter to Ford's Nasser ending their relationship. Both sides then were left with the task of defending themselves before Congress and the court of public opinion, and ultimately a siege of lawsuits. See the accompanying Information Box, "How Emotion Influences Company Reputation," for a discussion of how emotion drives consumers in their perception, good and bad, of companies.

Advantage to Competitors

Major competitors Goodyear and Michelin and smaller competitors and private-label tire makers predictably raised tire prices 3 to 5 percent. Goodyear now tried to increase production robustly to replace the millions of Firestone tires recalled or soon to be, but it was trying to avoid overtime pay to bolster profits. In a written statement, Goodyear said, "We are working very closely with Ford to jointly develop an aggressive plan to address consumers' needs as quickly as possible."[4]

INFORMATION BOX

HOW EMOTION INFLUENCES COMPANY REPUTATION

The second annual corporate-reputation survey conducted by the Harris market-research firm and the Reputation Institute involving 26,011 respondents found that Emotional Appeal—trust, admiration and respect, and generally good feelings toward—was the driving force in how people rated companies. The survey found that advertising did not necessarily change opinions. For example, despite a $100 million advertising campaign about what a good citizen Philip Morris Company was in feeding the hungry and helping victims of domestic violence, the company still received low marks on trust, respect, and admiration. But the most recent poll showed that Philip Morris no longer had the worst reputation in America. This distinction went to Bridgestone/Firestone, with Ford receiving the lowest reputation rating among auto companies.

Once lost, a company's reputation or public image is usually difficult to regain. For example, ExxonMobil's reputation for environmental responsibility was still given low grades more than a decade after the destructive Alaskan oil spill involving the oil tanker Exxon Valdez.

Do you think Firestone can ever fix its reputation after the massive recall and publicity involving the failures of its tires? If so, how?

Source: Ronald Alsop, "Survey: Emotion Drives Public Perception of Companies," *Wall Street Journal*, February 11, 2001, p. 5H.

---

[4] Thomas W. Gerdel, "Goodyear, Michelin Raising Consumer Tire Prices," *Cleveland Plain Dealer*, May 23, 2001, pp. 1C, 4C.

The slowdown in auto sales in the slowing economy that began in 2000 had led Goodyear to production cutbacks, including cutting 7,200 workers worldwide as it posted an 83 percent decline in profits in 2000. Now it faced a challenge in gearing up to handle the windfall of the ending of the Ford/Firestone relationship.

WHERE LIES THE BLAME?

In years to come, courts and lawyers will sort out the culpability controversy. The final outcome is unpredictable, but the finger of blame points to a number of sources, though the weighting of the blame is uncertain. While major responsibility should be shared by Ford and Firestone, the NHTSA and the motoring public were hardly blameless.

Ford

Whether the design of Ford's Explorer made it more prone to roll over than other SUVs will be decided in the courtroom arena. One thing seems clear: Ford recommended a low inflation level for its tires, and this would subject them to more flex in the sidewall and greater heat buildup. For example, Ford's recommended tire pressure was 26 pounds and this would bring the car's center of gravity lower to the ground, which would seem good, but only at first look. Ford was alone among SUV makers in equipping the Explorer with "c" tires rather than the more heat-resistant "b" tires that were the near-universal standard on most sport utility vehicles. To make the "c" grade, tires had to withstand only two hours at 50 mph when properly inflated and loaded, plus another 90 minutes at speeds up to 85 mph. This standard dated back to 1968 when sustained highway speeds were much lower than today. Now, people drive hour after hour at speeds well above 70 mph. With high-speed driving in hot weather, such a high-profile vehicle would be more prone to roll over with any tire trouble, especially with inexperienced drivers.

The c-rated Firestones were used on millions of Ford pickup trucks without problems. However, in contrast with SUVs, most pickup trucks are not taken on long-haul, high-speed road trips filled with family and luggage.

Ford CEO Jacques Nasser justified replacing 13 million tires by claiming the Firestones were failing at a rate higher than Goodyears mounted on two million Explorers in the mid-1990s. But the Goodyears carried the "b" rating. The dangerous effect of heat buildup was shown by most Explorers' accidents taking place in hot Southern states and other hot-climate countries with high speed limits.

Ford engineers should have been aware of these dangers, if not immediately, certainly after a few years, and adapted the Explorer to customers who drive fast, pay little attention to tire maintenance, and are prone to panic with a blowout and flip the car. Unfortunately, the American legal environment, the tort system, makes the manufacturer vulnerable to lawsuits and massive damage claims should it acknowledge in retrospect that it had made a bad mistake in its tire selection and pressure recommendation. So the temptation was to blame the tiremaker, and spend millions to create it as a media monster.

Bridgestone/Firestone

Firestone tires were far from blameless. Early on, investigations of deadly vehicle accidents linked the causes to tire failure, notably due to shoddy manufacturing practices at the Firestone Decatur, Illinois, plant; the 6.5 million tire recall by Firestone was of the 15-inch radial ATX and ATX11 tires and Wilderness AT tires made in this plant. In June 27, 2001, the company announced the plant would be closed. But Firestone's poorly controlled manufacturing process proved not to be limited to this single operation. See the accompanying Information Box about the whistleblower who exposed another plant's careless disregard of safe tire production.

Still, there were contrary indications that the fault was not all Bridgestone/Firestone's, that Ford shared the blame. General Motors had detected no problems with Firestones it used as standard equipment in fourteen of its models. In fact, in July 2001 GM named Firestone as its supplier of the year for the sixth consecutive time.

INFORMATION BOX

A WHISTLEBLOWER "HERO"

Alan Hogan was honored in June 2001 by the Civil Justice Foundation for exposing how employees at a Bridgestone/Firestone plant in North Carolina routinely made defective tires. This consumer advocacy group, founded by the Association of Trial Lawyers of America, bestowed similar "community champion" awards on tobacco whistleblower Jeffrey Wigand, and on Erin Brockovich, who exposed hazardous-waste dangers and was the subject of a popular movie.

With his insider's knowledge of shoddy tire-building practices, Hogan was widely credited with bringing about the first recall. He testified at a wrongful-death lawsuit in 1999 that he witnessed the crafting of countless bad tires built with dried-out rubber and wood bits, cigarette butts, screws, and other foreign materials mixed in. Hogan, who had quit the company and opened an auto-body shop in his home town, became a pariah among many people for his revelations about the major employer of the community, and company attorneys looked into his work and family life for anything they could use to discredit him. They tried to portray him as a disgruntled former employee. An anonymous fax accused him of spreading "vicious, malicious allegations" about the company. Employees were warned not to do business with car dealerships that dealt with his body shop.

But he persevered, and eventually won recognition and accolades. "I'm surprised it took this long," he said. "Maybe now people will see this is the way it's been since 1994, 1995, when they started covering this up." His whistle-blowing credentials were now in high demand as an expert witness in other lawsuits.

Do you see any reasons why Hogan may not have been completely objective in his whistle-blowing efforts?

Source: Dan Chapman, Cox News, as reported in "Firestone Ex-Worker Called Hero in Recall," *Cleveland Plain Dealer*, May 29, 2001, p. 1C.

Honda of America was also loyal to Firestones, which it used on its best-selling Civics and Odysseys.[5]

On September 14, 2001, months after all Firestones had been recalled from Ford Explorers, an apparently skilled driver, a deputy bailiff driving home from court, was killed when he lost control of his Explorer and it flipped over a guardrail, slid down an embankment, and rolled over several times.[6]

Government

Public Citizen and other consumer groups were critical of the government, maintaining that it was too slow in completing its initial Firestone investigation and had delayed its investigation of the Explorer. A Public Citizen study saw the use of the specific Firestone tires as coming from cost- and weight-saving miscalculations and gambles by Ford, "making what was already a bad problem into a lethal one." Not just the companies were at fault, but federal regulators were lax in not toughening standards on SUVs to prevent roofs from collapsing in rollover crashes. "The human damage caused is barbaric and unnecessary," the study concluded.[7]

The Driver

There is no doubt that drivers contributed to accidents by neglecting tire pressure so that it was often below even the low recommendations of Ford, by heavily loading vehicles, and by driving too fast over long periods so that tires could heat up to dangerous levels. Added to this, a lack of driving expertise to handle emergency blowouts was often the fatal blow. Yet could a carmaker, tiremaker, or government really expect the average consumer to act with strict prudence? Precautions, be they car standards or tire standards, needed to be imposed with worst scenarios in mind as to consumer behavior.

CONSEQUENCES

Each company maneuvered primarily to cast blame on the other. Ford announced in May 2001 it would triple the size of the Firestone recall, a $2.8 billion prospect, a cost Ford wanted to shift to the tiremaker. Firestone, at that point, severed its long relationship with Ford by refusing to supply the company with more tires. Firestone CEO Lampe maintained Ford was trying to divert scrutiny of the rollover-prone Explorer by casting doubt on the safety of Firestone tires.

Both parties suffered in this name-calling and buck-passing. By fall 2001, sales of Explorers were off sharply, as consumers wondered whether the hundreds of

[5] Ed Garsten, Associated Press, as reported in "Ford Tire Tab, $2.1 Billion," *Cleveland Plain Dealer*, May 23, 2001, pp, 1C and 4C; and Alison Grant, "Bridgestone/Firestone Faces Struggle to Survive," *Cleveland Plain Dealer*, August 5, 2001, pp. H1, H5.

[6] "SUV Flips, Killing Deputy Bailiff, 24," *Cleveland Plain Dealer*, September 15, 2001, p. B5.

[7] Alison Grant, "Government, Goodyear Still Navigating a Bumpy Road," *Cleveland Plain Dealer*, August 5, 2001, p. H5.

Explorer crashes were due to the SUV's design, or Firestone tires, or both. Ford lost market share to Toyota and other foreign rivals in the SUV market. In July 2001, it reported its first loss from operations since 1992. It also faced 200 product-liability lawsuits that involved Explorer rollovers. Still, Ford was big enough to absorb problems with one of its models.

Smaller Bridgestone/Firestone faced a more serious situation. In 2000, its earnings dropped 80 percent, reflecting the costs of recalling millions of tires as well as a special charge to cover legal expenses. The Firestone unit, which accounted for 40 percent of the parent company's revenue, posted a net loss of $510 million after it took a $750 million charge for legal expenses. Sales were forecast to plunge 20 percent in 2001, and costs of lawsuits could eventually reach billions of dollars, to the point where some analysts doubted Firestone as a brand could survive.[8]

Options Firestone Faced

This esteemed brand, launched more than a century ago, had been the exclusive tire supplier to the Indy 500. Now its future was in doubt, despite decades of brand loyalty. The brand faced three options:

Option #1: De-emphasize Firestone, and push business to the Bridgestone label. This would likely result in some loss of market segmentation and the flexibility of having distinct low-end, mid-level, and premium tires. Some thought, however, that such a half-hearted approach would simply prolong the agony of hanging on to a besmirched brand.

Option #2: Obliterate the Firestone name, it being irretrievable. "Firestone should just give up," said one public relations analyst. "They've damaged themselves so severely." A University of Michigan Business School professor called the brand dead: "Can you imagine any jury claiming that somebody who's suspected of building bad tires is innocent?"[9]

Option #3: Try to salvage the brand. Some questioned the wisdom of abandoning the century-old Firestone name, with its rich tradition and millions of cumulative advertising dollars. They thought that with money, time, and creative advertising, Bridgestone/Firestone should be able to restore its image. But to do so, Roger Blackwell of Ohio State University thought the company needed to make an admission of regret: "The lawyers will tell them not to admit blame. ... But they need to do what Johnson & Johnson did when someone was killed by their product [cyanide-tainted Tylenol]. A credible spokesman got on TV and had tears in his eyes when he spoke." (See Chapter 6 for this Johnson & Johnson classic case.) An independent tire dealer who lost $100,000 in sales in 2000 but was confident of a rebound supported this option: "The American public is quick to forget," he said.[10]

---

[8] Akiko Kashiwagi, "Recalls Cost Bridgestone Dearly; Firestone's Parent's Profit Drops 80%," *Washington Post*, Feb. 23, 2001, p. E3.

[9] Grant, "Bridgestone/Firestone Faces Struggle to Survive," p. H5.

[10] *Ibid.*

POSTMORTEM

For years, buyers of Ford Explorers equipped with Firestone tires faced far higher risks of deaths and injuries, both in the United States and abroad, than they would have from other models. The *New York Times* reported that the tire defects, and their contribution to accidents, were known in 1996.[11] Not until August 1999 did Ford begin replacing tires on Explorers in Saudi Arabia, calling the step a "customer notification enhancement program." Fourteen fatalities had already been reported. Not until March 2000, after television reports of problems, did federal regulators and the two manufacturers take all this seriously.

Ford, in its concern with the bottom line, stubbornly refused to admit that anything was wrong with its SUV, while Firestone couldn't seem to clean up its act in the Decatur, Illinois, plant, and even some other plants, where carelessness and lack of customer concern prevailed. Minor ethical abuses became major when lives were lost, but the foot-dragging continued until lawyers came on the scene. Then these two tried to cover their mistakes with finger pointing, while a vulnerable public continued to be in jeopardy. Throughout this whole time, saving lives did not apparently have a very high priority. Eventually the consequences came back to haunt the companies, with hundreds of lawsuits, millions of tire recalls, and public images denigrated.

How could this have been permitted to happen? After all, top management were not deliberately vicious men. They were well intentioned, albeit badly misguided. Perhaps their worst sin was to at first ignore, and then refuse to admit and to try to cover up increasingly apparent serious risk factors.

Part of the problem was the stubborn mindset of top executives that nothing was wrong: A few accidents reflected driver carelessness, not a defective product. Neither would assume the worst scenario: that this was a dangerous product used on a dangerous product that was killing people, and neither Ford nor Firestone could escape blame.

Forty years ago a somewhat similar situation occurred with the GM Corvair, a rear-engine car that exhibited instability under extreme cornering conditions causing it to flip over. Ralph Nader gained his reputation as a consumer advocate in his condemnation of this "unsafe" car with a best-selling book, *Unsafe At Any Speed.* But GM executives refused to admit there was any problem, until eventually the evidence was overwhelming and lawsuits flourished, and the federal government stepped in with the National Traffic and Motor Vehicle Safety Act of 1966, which among other things required manufacturers to notify customers of any defects or flaws later discovered in their vehicles.

GM executives, like those of Ford and Firestone forty years later, were honorable men. Yet, something seems to happen to the conscience and the moral sensitivity of top executives. They commission actions in their corporate personas that they would hardly dream of doing in their private lives. John DeLorean, former GM executive, was one of the first to note this dichotomy:

> "These were not immoral men who were bringing out this car [the Corvair]. These were warm, breathing men with families and children who as private individuals

---

[11] Keith Bradsher, "SUV Tire Defects Were Known in '96 but Not Reported; 190 Died in Next 4 Years," *New York Times*, June 24, 2001, p. 1N.

would never have approved [this project] for a minute if they were told, 'You are going to kill and injure people with this car.' But these same men, in a business atmosphere, where everything is reduced to terms of costs, corporate goals, and production deadlines, were able to approve a product most of them wouldn't have considered approving as individuals."[12]

We have to raise the question: Why this lockstep obsession with sales and profits at all costs? See the accompanying Information Box, "The 'Groupthink' Influence on Unethical Behavior," for a discussion of this issue.

UPDATE

On October 30, 2001, Ford Motor Company announced that Jacques Nasser would be replaced as CEO by William Clay Ford, Jr., age forty-four—the first Ford family member to be in charge since 1979. Ford is the son of William Clay Ford Sr., who is the grandson of founder Henry Ford and brother of Henry Ford II. Nasser had been under pressure for months for Ford's loss of market share and tumbling profitability and the adverse publicity of the Explorer.

In December 2001, the newly designed 2002 Ford Explorer received a top score in a crash test from the Insurance Institute for Highway Safety. Changes in the 2002 Explorer to improve passenger protection were part of the automaker's "commitment to continuous improvements," a Ford spokesperson said.[13]

Firestone also bounced back, despite dire predictions of the brand's demise as U.S. operations suffered a $1.7 billion loss in 2001 on top of a $510 million loss in 2000. Some called this "the most unlikely brand resurrection in marketing history." Much of the credit for the survival was credited to Firestone CEO John Lampe, who crisscrossed the country giving pep talks to hundreds of Firestone's 10,000 dealers. These dealers became fiercely loyal at a time when 75 percent of tire buyers were influenced by dealers' recommendations, according to industry estimates. Several splashy new tires were brought out, including the Firehawk Indy 500, which became a hit with racing fans. "We are selling as many Firestone tires as we've ever sold," one large dealer noted.

With communication improving between the two companies, Lampe could see signs that the rift with Ford was ending, and William Clay Ford even mentioned his great-grandfather Harvey Firestone in a Ford commercial. "It was a very honest thing to do. He didn't have to do that," Lampe observed.[14]

[12] J. Patrick Wright, *On a Clear Day You Can See General Motors* (Grosse Point, Mich.: Wright Enterprises, 1979), pp. 5–6.

[13] Christopher Jensen, *Cleveland Plain Dealer*, December 12, 2001, pp. C1, C4.

[14] Todd Zaun, "Defying Expectations, Bridgestone Embarks on a Turnaround," *Wall Street Journal*, March 12, 2002, p. A21; Jonathan Fahey, "Flats Fixed," *Forbes*, May 27, 2002, pp. 40–41.

INFORMATION BOX

THE "GROUPTHINK" INFLUENCE ON
UNETHICAL BEHAVIOR

The callousness about "killer" cars would, as John DeLorean theorized, probably never have prevailed if an individual was making the decision outside the corporate environment. But bring in groupthink, which is decision-by-committee, and add to this a high degree of organizational loyalty (versus loyalty to the public interest), and such callousness can manifest itself. Why can the moral standards of groupthink be so much lower than individual moral standards?

Perhaps the answer lies in the "pack mentality" that characterizes certain committees or groups highly committed to organizational goals. All else then becomes subordinated to the single-minded perspective of achieving these goals. Within any committee, individual responsibility for decision is diluted since this is a committee decision. Furthermore, without the contrary arguments of a strong "devil's advocate" (i.e., one who argues the opposing viewpoint, sometimes simply to be sure that all sides of an issue are considered), a follow-the-leader syndrome can take place, with no one willing to oppose the majority views.

But there is more to it than that. Chester Barnard, a business executive, scholar, and philosopher, noted the paradox: People have a number of private moral codes that affect behavior in different situations, and these codes are not always compatible. Codes for private life, regarding family and religion, may be far different from codes for business life. Throughout the history of business, it has not been unusual to find that the scrupulous and God-fearing churchgoer is far different when he or she conducts business during the week: A far lower ethical standard prevails during the week than on the Sabbath. Nor has it been unusual to find that a person can be a paragon of love, understanding, and empathy with his or her family but be totally lacking in such qualities with employees or customers.[15] We might add that even tyrants guilty of the most extreme atrocities, such as Hitler and Saddam Hussein, have been known to exude great tenderness and consideration for their intimates.

What does it take for a person to resist and not accept the majority viewpoint? What do you think would be the characteristics of such a person? Do you see yourself as such an individual?

WHAT CAN BE LEARNED?

A firm today must zealously guard against product liability suits. Any responsible executive needs to recognize that product liability suits, in today's litigious environment, can even bankrupt a firm. The business arena has become more risky, more fraught with peril for the unwary or the naively unconcerned. Consequently,

---

[15] Chester I. Barnard, *The Functions of the Executive* (Cambridge, Mass.: Harvard University Press, 1938), p. 263.

any firm needs careful and objective testing of any product that can affect customer health and safety. Sometimes such testing may require that production be delayed, even if competition gains some advantage from this delay. The risks of putting an unsafe product on the market outweigh competitive concerns.

Suspicions and complaints about product safety must be thoroughly investigated. We should learn from this case that immediate and thorough investigation of any suspicions or complaints must be undertaken, regardless of the confidence management may have in the product or of the glowing recommendations of persons whose objectivity could be suspect. To procrastinate or ignore complaints poses what should be unacceptable risks.

Sometimes the root of the problem is not obvious, or is more complex than first thought. In this Ford/Firestone case, objective research should have focused on both the Explorer and the Firestone tires, and how the situation could be remedied to minimize rollovers and save lives.

The health and safety of customers is entirely compatible with the well-being of the firm. It is a lose/lose situation if this is ignored: The customer is jeopardized, but eventually the firm is, too, as lawsuits grow and damages increase. Why, then, the corporate mindset of "us versus them"? There should be no conflicting goals. Both win when customer welfare is maximized.

In the worst scenario, go for a conciliatory salvage strategy. Ford and Firestone faced a crossroads by late 1999 and early 2000. Reports of fatalities linked to Ford Explorers and Firestone tires were trickling in, the first occurring in the hot climate of Saudi Arabia, and these were in a matter of months to become a flood. How should a company react?

A salvage strategy can be attempted by toughing it out, trying to combat the bad press, denying culpability, blaming someone else, and resorting to the strongest possible legal defense. This essentially is what Ford opted to do, as it blamed Firestone for everything and spent millions advertising to promote this contention.

Firestone was more vulnerable since its shredded tires could hardly be denied, and it was forced to recall millions of tires, although it stoutly maintained that the cause of the shredding was underinflation and the wrong quality of tire, as well as the Explorer itself. At stake were company reputations, economic positions, and even viability for Firestone, and, most importantly, also the lives of hundreds of users.

Conciliation usually is the better salvage strategy. This involves recognition and full admission of the problem and removal of the risk, even if this entails a full-market withdrawal until the source of the problem can be identified and correction made. Expensive, yes, but far less risky for the viability of the company and certainly for the health of those customers involved.

Neither strategy is without substantial costs. But the first course of action puts major cost consequences in the future, where they may turn out to be vastly greater as legal expenses and damage awards skyrocket. The second course of action poses an immediate impact on profitability, and will not avoid legal expenses, but may save the company and its reputation and return it to profitability in the near future.

Where blame is most likely shared, the solution of the problem lies not in confrontation but in cooperation. This is the most grievous component of the violations of the public trust by Ford and Firestone: denial and confrontation, rather than cooperation to solve the problem of product safety.

CONSIDER

Can you think of additional learning insights?

QUESTIONS

1. Can a firm guarantee complete product safety? Discuss.

2. Based on the information presented, which company do you think is more to blame for the deaths and injuries? What led you to your conclusion?

3. "If an Explorer driver never checks the tire pressure and drives well above the speed limit, he has no one to blame but himself in an accident—not the vehicle and not the tires." Discuss.

4. Do you think the government should be blamed in the Explorer deaths and injuries? Why or why not?

5. Would you give credence to the "community champion" awards bestowed by a consumer advocacy group founded by the Association of Trial Lawyers, and given to Alan Hogan in June 2001 for exposing careless tire production? Why or why not?

6. "Admittedly the groupthink mindset may be responsible for a few unethical and bad decisions, but this mindset is more likely to consider the consequences to the company of delivering unsafe products and to support aggressive corrective action." Evaluate this argument.

7. Have you had any experience with a Ford Explorer? If so, what is your perception of its performance and safety?

8. Have you had any experience with Firestone tires? What is your perception of their performance and safety?

HANDS-ON EXERCISES

1. Place yourself in the position of John Lampe, CEO of Firestone, as the crisis worsens and accusations mount. Discuss how you would try to change the climate with Jacques Nasser of Ford from confrontational to cooperative. Be as specific as you can. Do you think you would be successful?

2. Firestone is on its knees after massive tire recalls and monstrous damage suits. You are a consultant brought in to help the firm recover. Be as specific as you can in recommendations, and in the priority of things to do. Make any assumptions you need to, but keep them reasonable. Defend

your recommendations. (Do not be swayed by what actually happened. Maybe things could have been done better.)

3. You are a trusted aide of Nasser. Support his confrontational stance with Firestone before the Ford board of directors.

4. Be a devil's advocate. In a staff meeting the topic comes up that your SUVs have been involved in a number of deaths. The group passes this off as due to reckless drivers. Argue persuasively a contrary position.

TEAM DEBATE EXERCISE

Debate the issue of dropping or keeping the Firestone name. Defend your position and attack the other side.

INVITATION TO RESEARCH

Can you find statistics as to how competing tire companies, particularly Goodyear and Michelin, fared during and after the Firestone recall? Are Ford and Firestone friends again? Is the Ford Explorer still the top SUV?

CHAPTER FOUR

Perrier—Overresponding to a Crisis

On a Friday in early February 1990, the first news reached Perrier executive suites that traces of benzene had been found in its bottled water. Ronald Davis, president of the Perrier Group of America, ordered a sweeping recall of all bottles in North America. Just a few days later, Source Perrier S.A., the French parent, expanded the recall to the rest of the world, while the company sought to identify the source of the problem and correct it.

Although at first view such a reaction to an unexpected crisis seems zealous and the ultimate in customer concern and social responsibility, a deeper study reveals mistakes of major proportions.

BEFORE

In late 1989, Ronald Davis, forty-three-year-old president of Perrier's U.S. operations, had reason to be pleased. During his ten-year tenure, Perrier's U.S. sales had risen from $40 million to more than $800 million at retail, which was a significant 25 percent of the company's worldwide sales. He was also proud of his firm being depicted in a May 1989 issue of *Fortune* as one of six companies that compete best. *Fortune* captioned: "These are companies you don't want to come up against in your worst nightmare. In the businesses they're in, they amass crushing market share."[1]

A company report in 1987 described the French source, a spring in Vergeze, as follows:

> One of Perrier's identifying qualities is its low mineral (particularly sodium) content. This is because the water spends only a short time filtering through minerals. While flowing underground, the water meets gas flowing vertically through porous volcanic rocks. This is how Perrier gets its fizz ... the company assured us that production has never been limited by the source output. The company sells approximately one billion bottles of which 600 million are exported.[2]

[1] Bill Saporito, "Companies That Compete Best," *Fortune* (May 22, 1989), pp. 36ff.

[2] B. Facon, *Source Perrier—Company Report* (November 13, 1987), p. 4.

Davis recognized that he was in two businesses, albeit both involved bottled water: (1) sparkling water, in the famous green bottle, which he had been successful in positioning as an adult soft drink with a French mystique, an alternative to soft drinks or alcohol; and (2) still water, a tap-water replacement, with the product delivered to homes and offices and dispensed through watercoolers. This latter business he saw as more resembling package delivery such as UPS and Federal Express, and less akin to pushing soft drinks. Accordingly, he emphasized quality of professional service for his route drivers. While best known for the green-bottled Perrier, a mainstay of most restaurants and bars, the company owned nine other brands of bottled water, including Poland Spring, Great Bear, Calistoga, and Ozarka.

At a price of 300 to 1,200 times that of tap water, bottled water was the fastest growing segment of the U.S. beverage industry (see Table 4.1). Perrier controlled 24 percent of the total U.S. bottled-water business. Of the imported-bottled-water sector, the green bottle dominated with almost 50 percent of the market, although this market share had fallen when more competitors attempted to push into the rapidly growing market. In the 1980s, more than twenty firms had taken a run at the green bottle, but without notable success; these included such behemoths as Coca-Cola, PepsiCo, and Anheuser-Busch. Now Davis was more concerned with expanding the category, and was trying to shift the brand's image from chic to healthy, so as to make the brand more acceptable to the "masses."

THE CRISIS

The North American Recall

Davis, as he prepared his five-year plan in early 1990, wrote that competing in the 1990s would require not strategic planning, but "flexibility planning."[3] In retrospect, he seemed to be prophetic.

TABLE 4.1   Average Annual Growth of Beverage Sales, 1985–1989

Beverage Type	Percent of Growth
Bottled water	+ 11.1
Soft drinks	+ 3.2
Milk	+ 1.5
Tea	+ 1.2
Beer	+ 0.4
Coffee	− 0.4
Wine	− 2.0
Distilled spirits	− 2.6

Source: Beverage Marketing Corporation, as reported in *Fortune* (April 23, 1990), p. 277.

[3] Patricia Sellers, "Perrier Plots Its Comeback," *Fortune* (April 23, 1990), p. 277.

As he was fine-tuning his plan, the first news trickled in that a lab in North Carolina had discovered traces of benzene, a carcinogen, in some of the bottles. That same day, February 9, he ordered Perrier removed from distribution in North America.

Source Perrier officials were soon to inform reporters that the company believed the contamination occurred because an employee had mistakenly used cleaning fluid containing benzene to clean the production-line machinery that fills bottles for North America. Frederik Zimmer, managing director of Source Perrier, said that the machinery in question had been cleaned and repaired over the weekend. But in another news conference, Davis announced that he expected Perrier to be off the market for two to three months.

Such a long absence was seen by some marketing observers as potentially devastating to Perrier, despite its being the front-runner of the industry. Al Ries, chairman of a consulting firm and well-known business writer, was quoted in a *Wall Street Journal* article as saying: "If I were Perrier, I would make a desperate effort to reduce that time as much as possible, even if I had to fly it in on 747s from France."[4]

Without doubt, competitors were salivating at a chance to pick up market share of the $2.2 billion annual U.S. sales. Major competitors included Evian and Saratoga, both owned by BSN of France, and San Peligrino, an Italian import. In 1989, PepsiCo had begun test marketing H_2 OH!, and in January 1990, Adolph Coors Company introduced Coors Rocky Mountain Sparkling Water. The Perrier absence was expected to accelerate their market entry.

Despite competitive glee at the misfortune of Perrier, some in the industry were concerned. They feared that consumers would forsake bottled water altogether, with its purity now being questioned. Would the public be as willing to pay a substantial premium for any bottled brand? See the following Information Box for a discussion of the relationship between *price* and *quality*.

Worldwide Recall

A few days later, the other shoe fell. After reports of benzene being found in Perrier bottles in Holland and Denmark, on February 14, Source Perrier expanded its North American recall to the rest of the world, and acknowledged that all production lines for its sparkling water had been contaminated in recent months by tiny amounts of benzene.

At a news conference in Paris, company officials acknowledged for the first time that benzene occurs naturally in Perrier water, and that the current problem came about because workers failed to replace filters designed to remove it. This was a critical reversal of previous statements that the water was tainted only because an employee mistakenly used cleaning fluid containing benzene to clean machinery. Zimmer even went further, revealing that Perrier water naturally contains several gases, including benzene, that have to be filtered out.

The company insisted that its famous spring was unpolluted. But now questions were being raised about this and about contradictory statements made about the problem. For example, how widespread was the contamination? Was benzene a naturally

---

[4] Alix M. Freedman and Thomas R. King, "Perrier's Strategy in the Wake of Recall," *Wall Street Journal* (February 12, 1990), p. B1.

INFORMATION BOX

IS QUALITY BEST JUDGED BY PRICE?

We as consumers today have difficulty in judging the quality of competing products. With their complex characteristics and hidden ingredients, we cannot rely on our own expertise to determine the best. So, what sources of information can we use? We can rely on our past experiences with the brand; we can be swayed by our friends and neighbors; we might be influenced by advertising and salespeople (but more and more we become skeptical of their claims); we can study *Consumer Reports* and other consumer information publications. But all of these sources are flawed in that the experience and information usually is dated, and is a limited sample—usually of one—so that we can seriously question how representative the experience is.

Most people judge quality by price: the higher the price, the better the quality. But such a price/quality perception sets us up. While it may be valid, it also may not be. With the publicity about the impurity of Perrier, we are brought to the realization that paying many times the price of tap water gives us no assurance of better quality, as measured by purity.

Is a price/quality misperception mostly limited to bottled water, do you think? How about liquor? Designer clothes? Perfume?

occurring phenomenon, or does it represent man-made pollution? Suspicions were tending toward the man-made origin. While benzene occurs naturally in certain foods, it is more commonly found as a petroleum-based distillate used in many manufacturing processes.

Particularly surprising was the rather nonchalant attitude of Perrier executives. Zimmer, the president, even suggested that "all this publicity helps build the brand's renown."[5]

Ronald Davis was quick to point out that the company did not have to recall its entire 70-million-bottle U.S. inventory. After all, health officials both in the U.S. and France had noted that the benzene levels found in Perrier did not pose any significant health risk. The major risk really was to the image of Perrier: it had gone to great lengths to establish its water as naturally pure. And while not particularly dangerous, it was certainly not naturally pure—as all the world was finding out from the publicity about it. Add to this the undermining of the major attraction of bottled water that it was safer than ordinary tap water, and the recall and subsequent publicity assumed more ominous proportions. See the following Issue Box, Are Bottled Water Claims Bunk?

THE COMEBACK

It took until mid-July before Perrier was again widely available in the United States; this was five months rather than the expected three months. Still, Davis was confident

[5] Alix M. Freedman and Thomas R. King, "Perrier Expands North American Recall to Rest of Globe," *Wall Street Journal* (February 15, 1990), p. B1.

ISSUE BOX

ARE BOTTLED WATER CLAIMS BUNK?[6]

The bottled water industry came under serious attack in April 1991. As if the Perrier massive recall was not enough, now a congressional panel with wide media coverage accused the Food and Drug Administration of "inexcusably negligent and complacent oversight of the bottled-water industry." Despite its high price, the panel said, bottled water may be less safe than tap water. The panel noted that although consumers pay 300 to 1,200 times more for bottled water than for tap water, 25 percent of all bottled water comes from public drinking water sources. For example:

Lithia Springs Water Company touts its "world's finest" bottled mineral water as "naturally pure" and recommends its special Love Water as an "invigorator" before bedtime. Yet, it was found to be tainted with bacteria.

Artisia Waters, Inc., promotes its "100% pure sparkling Texas Natural Water." But it comes from the same underground sources that San Antonio uses for its municipal water supply.

Furthermore, the FDA released a list of twenty-two bottled-water recalls because of contaminants such as kerosene and mold. For the most part, these went unnoticed by consumers, being overshadowed by the Perrier recall.

At issue: Are we being hoodwinked?

Debate two positions: (1) the bottled-water industry really is a throwback to the snake-oil charlatans of the last century; and (2) a few unscrupulous or careless bottlers are denigrating the image of the entire industry, an industry that is primarily focused on health and purity.

that Perrier's sales would return to 85 percent of normal by the end of 1991. Actually, he was more worried about short supply than demand. He was not sure the one spring in Vergeze, France, would be able to replace the world's supply before the beginning of 1991.

Davis's confidence in the durability of the demand stemmed from his clout with retailers, where the brand does a majority of its business. He believed the brand's good reputation, coupled with the other brands marketed by Perrier that had replaced some of the supermarket space relinquished by Perrier, would bring quick renewal. To help this, he wrote letters to 550 CEOs of retail firms, pledging heavy promotional spending. The marketing budget was increased from $6 million to $25 million for 1990, with $16 million going into advertising and the rest into promotions and special events. A highly visible discount strategy was instituted, which included a buy-two, get-one-free offer. Supermarket prices had dropped, with bottles now going

[6] Examples are taken from Bruce Ingersoll, "FDA Finds Bunk in Bottled-Water Claims," *Wall Street Journal* (April 10, 1991), p. B1.

for $0.89 to $0.99, down from $1.09 to $1.19. To win back restaurant business, a new fifty-two-member sales force supplemented distributor efforts. However, a setback of sorts was the Food and Drug Administration order to drop the words "naturally sparkling" from Perrier labels.

Still, a recent consumer survey indicated that 84 percent of Perrier's U.S. drinkers intended to buy the product again.[7] Davis could also take heart from the less than aggressive actions of his competitors during the hiatus. None appeared to have strongly reacted, although most improved their sales considerably. The smaller competitors proved to be short of marketing money and bottling capacity, and apparently were fearful that a beleaguered Perrier would negatively affect the overall market. Big competitors, such as PepsiCo and Coors, who were introducing other bottled waters, somehow also appeared reluctant to move in aggressively.

CONSEQUENCES

By the end of 1990, however, it was clear that Perrier was not regaining market position as quickly and completely as Davis had hoped. Now more aggressive competitors were emerging. Some, such as Saratoga, La Croix, and Quibell, had experienced major windfalls in the wake of the recall. Evian, in particular, a nonsparkling water produced by the French firm BSN S.A. was the biggest winner. Through aggressive marketing and advertising it had replaced Perrier by the end of 1990 as the top-selling imported bottled water.

Perrier's sales had only reached 60 percent of pre-recall levels, and its share of the imported bottled-water market had sunk to 20.7 percent from the 44.8 percent of one year earlier. While the Perrier Group of America expected to report a sales gain for 1990 of 3.7 percent, this was largely because of the strong performance of such domestic brands as Calistoga and Poland Spring.

Particularly worrisome for Davis was the slow return of Perrier to bars and restaurants, which formerly accounted for about 35 percent of its sales. A sampling of comments of restaurant managers, as reported in such prestigious papers as the *Wall Street Journal* and *Washington Post*, were far from encouraging. For example:

> The manager of the notable Four Seasons restaurant in New York City said his patrons had begun to shift to San Pellegrino: "I think Perrier is finished," he said. "We can write it off."[8]

> The general manager of Spago restaurant in Los Angeles said: "Now consumers have decided that other brands are better or at least as good, so Perrier no longer holds the monopoly on water." And Spago no longer carries Perrier.[9]

> Le Pavillon restaurant in Washington, D.C., switched to Quibell during the recall, and has not gone back to Perrier. "Customers still ask for Perrier, but it's a generic term like Kleenex, and customers aren't unhappy to get a substitute.[10]

[7] Sellers, "Perrier Plots," p. 278.

[8] Freedman and King, "Perrier's Strategy," p. B3.

[9] Alix M. Freedman, "Perrier Finds Mystique Hard to Restore," *Wall Street Journal* (December 1, 1990), p. B1.

[10] Lori Silver, "Perrier Crowd Not Taking the Waters," *Washington Post* (July 4, 1990), p. 1.

Evian

David Daniel, thirty-four, was Evian's U.S. CEO since June 1988. He joined the company in 1987 as the first director of marketing at a time when the American subsidiary was a two-person operation. By 1990 there were 100 employees.

Daniel came from PepsiCo, and his background was marketing. He saw Evian's sphere to be portable water that is good for you, a position well situated to capitalize on the health movement. He was particularly interested in broadening the distribution of Evian, and he sought out soft-drink and beer distributors, showing them that their basic industries were only growing at 1 to 3 percent a year, while bottled water was growing at over 10 percent per year. In 1989, Evian sales doubled to 65 million, with $100 million in sight for 1990. The attractiveness of such growth to these distributors was of no small moment.

Daniel made Evian the most expensive water on the market. He saw the price as helping Evian occupy a certain slot in the consumer's mind—remember the price/quality perception discussed earlier. For example, at a fancy grocery in New York's West Village, a one liter bottle of Evian sold for $2.50; the city charges a fraction of a penny for a gallon of tap water[11]—a lot of perceived quality in that. This type of pricing along with the packaging that made Evian portable—plastic nonbreakable bottles and reusable caps—were seen as keys in the selling of bottled water.

Then, late in 1990, Evian benefited greatly from the Persian Gulf War, with free publicity from several newspapers and from all three national TV networks: GIs were shown gulping water from Evian bottles.

ANALYSIS

Was the massive recall overkill, or was it a prudent necessity? Did it show a concerned corporate citizen, or rather a panicked executive? Were consumers impressed with the responsibleness of the company, or were they more focused on its carelessness? These questions are all directed at the basic impact of the recall and the subsequent actions and admissions: Was it to have favorable, neutral, or unfavorable public reactions?

Perrier did *not* have to recall its product. It was a North Carolina county laboratory that first noticed the excessive amounts of benzene in Perrier and reported its findings to the state authorities. The state agriculture and health departments did not believe that a recall was necessary, but they did insist on issuing a health advisory, warning that Perrier should not be consumed until further tests could be made. It was the state's plan to issue the health advisory that was reported to Davis on the afternoon of the critical day, February 9. He announced the recall later that same day.

We are left to wonder. Perhaps a full and complete recall was not needed. Perhaps things could have been worked out entirely satisfactorily with less drastic

[11] Seth Lubove, "Perched Between Perrier and Tap," *Forbes*, (May 14, 1990), p. 120.

measures. Given that a recall meant a three- to five-months' absence from the marketplace, should it not have been the action of last resort?

But let us consider Davis's thought processes on that ill-fated afternoon in February. He did not know the source of the problem; he certainly had no reason to suspect that it emanated from the spring in southern France or that it was a worldwide problem. He probably considered it of less magnitude. Perhaps he thought of the total North American recall as a gesture showing the concerned thinking of the management of this product that had developed such a reputation of health and purity and, yes, status. Only with the experience after the fact do we know the error of this decision: that it was to result in an absence up to five months from the hotly competitive market; that it was to result in revelations of far more serious implications than a simple employee error or even a natural occurrence largely beyond the company's control.

So, perhaps Davis's drastic decision was fully justified and prudent. But it turned out to be confounded by circumstances he did not envision.

A lengthy complete absence from the marketplace is a catastrophe of rather monumental proportions—all the more so for a product that is habitually and frequently consumed, in Perrier's case, sometimes several times daily. Such an absence forces even the most loyal customers to establish new patterns of behavior, in this case switching brands. Once behavior becomes habituated, at least for some people, a change back becomes less likely. This is especially true if the competitive offerings are reasonably similar and acceptable. Anything that Perrier could have done to lessen the time away from the market would have been desirable—regardless of expense.

Perhaps the biggest problem for Perrier concerned the false impressions, and even outright deception, that the company had conveyed regarding the purity of its product. Now, in the wake of this total recall and the accompanying publicity, all was laid bare. Company officials in France had to own up that the contamination had occurred "in recent months," and not suddenly and unexpectedly on February 9.

But more than this, under intense pressure from the media to explain what caused the problem, Source Perrier ultimately conceded that its water does not bubble up pure, already carbonated and ready to drink, from its renowned spring in southern France. Instead, contrary to the image that it had spent tens of millions of dollars to promote, the company extracts the water and carbon dioxide gas separately, and must pipe the gas through charcoal filters before combining it mechanically with the water to give the fizz. Without the filters, Perrier water would contain benzene and, even worse, would taste like rotten eggs.

Finally, the public relations efforts were flawed. Source Perrier officials issued a confusing series of public statements and clarifications. Early on, the company tried to maintain the mystique of Perrier by concealing information about the cause of the contamination and by blaming it on a mistake by cleaning personnel in using an oily rag, which could have contained some benzene, to wipe equipment used for bottles to be shipped to the United States, when the spokespeople knew the problem was more fundamental than that.

An aura of nonchalance was conveyed by corporate executives and reported in the press. This was hardly in keeping with a serious problem having to do with the possible safety of customers. Furthermore, Source Perrier relied mainly on media reports to convey information to consumers. Misinformation and rumors are more likely with this approach to public relations than in a more proactive strategy of direct company advertisement and statements.

The reputation of Perrier was on the ropes. And top management seemed unconcerned about the probability of severe public image damage. See the following Information Box for a discussion of ignoring possible image damage.

UPDATE

Despite occasional publicity about the "ripoff" of the bottled-water industry—the exorbitant prices for water little better than tap water—the public's demand has been ever growing. In 2001, soft-drink sales were flat, but bottled-water sales were up 11.5 percent, continuing the double-digit rate of the last decade. Bottled water was now a $5.2 billion industry and in line to surpass coffee and tea and become second in liquid consumption sales only to soft drinks. More than 900 brands of bottled water were on the market. With the marketing clout of major firms, Pepsi's Aquafina and Coke's Dasani were becoming U.S. market leaders. This boom reflected a

INFORMATION BOX

IGNORING POSSIBLE NEGATIVE IMAGE CONSEQUENCES

We can identify several factors that induce a firm to ignore public image considerations until sometimes too late. First, a firm's public image often makes a nonspecific impact on company performance. The cause-and-effect relationship of a deteriorating image is virtually impossible to assess, at least until and unless image problems worsen. Image consequences may be downplayed because management is unable to single out the specific profit impact.

Second, an organization's image is not easily and definitively measured. Although some tools are available for tracking public opinion, they tend to be imprecise and of uncertain validity. Consequently, image studies are often spurned or given short shrift relative to more quantitative measures of performance.

Third, it is difficult to determine the effectiveness of image-building efforts. While firms may spend thousands, and even millions, of dollars for institutional and image-building advertising, measures of the effectiveness of such expenditures are inexact and also of questionable validity. For example, a survey may be taken of attitudes of a group of people before and after the image-building campaign is run. Presumably if a few more people profess to be favorably disposed toward the company after the campaign than before, this is an indication of its success. But an executive can question how much this really translates into sales and profits.

Given the near impossibility of measuring the effectiveness of image-enhancing promotion, how do you account for the prevalence of institutional advertising, even among firms that have no image problems?

remarkable turnabout from 1980 when sales of Perrier fizzy water were mostly limited to upscale restaurants.

Critical studies still found the product no cleaner or safer than big-city tap water, and still found a third of the bottles sampled were contaminated by synthetic chemicals, bacteria, and arsenic. Of the average $1.50 spent for a bottle of water, 90 percent went for bottling, packaging, marketing, retailing, and other expenses. The industry in defense claimed that the federal Centers for Disease Control had never found a U.S. outbreak of disease or illness linked to bottled water.[12]

LATEST ON PERRIER

Perrier was purchased in 1992 by Nestlé, the world's largest food company. Nestlé, headquartered in Vevey, Switzerland, has more than 500 factories and 230,000 employees worldwide, and produces such brands as Nestlé chocolate, Nescafe coffee, Stouffer's frozen foods, Contadina pastas, and Nestea iced tea products. Perrier, in the Nestlé Waters division, is just one bottled water brand among seventy brands worldwide. This division is the world's largest bottled water company, although in the last few years, Coca-Cola and Pepsi are making serious inroads in the market share position of Nestlé in the United States (see the Update in Chapter 12 on Coca-Cola and Pepsi for the latest in this bottled water battleground).

WHAT CAN BE LEARNED?

Exiting a market for several months or more poses critical risks, particularly for a habitually consumed product. To allow new habits to be established and new loyalties to be created not only among consumers but also dealers may be impossible to fully recover from. This is especially true if competing products are comparable, and if competitors are aggressive in seizing the preferred opportunity. Since a front-runner is a target anyway, abandoning the battlefield simply invites competitive takeover.

Deception discovered and grudgingly admitted destroys a mystique. No mystique is forever. Consumer preferences change, competitors become more skilled at countering, or perhaps a firm becomes complacent in its quality control or innovative technology. These conditions act to nibble away at a mystique and eventually destroy it. As in the case of Perrier, where long-believed images of a product, its healthfulness and purity, are suddenly revealed to be false—that the advertising was less than candid and was even deceptive—then any mystique comes tumbling down and is unlikely to ever be regained. This scenario can only be avoided if the publicity about the deception or misdeed is not widespread.

---

[12] Lance Gay, "Bottlers Tap Profits from Designer Water," Scripps Howard reported in *Cleveland Plain Dealer*, September 11, 2001, pp. A1 and A8.

But, with a popular product such as Perrier, publicity reaches beyond business journals to the popular press. Such is the fate of large, well-known firms.

A price/quality misperception strongly exists. Without doubt, most consumers judge quality by price: the higher the price, the higher the quality. Is a $2.50 liter of Evian better quality than a gallon of tap water costing a fraction of a cent? Perhaps. But is it a hundred times better? And yet many people embrace the misconception that price is the key indicator of quality, and are consequently taken advantage of every day.

An industry catering to health is particularly vulnerable to a few unscrupulous operators. We, the general public, are particularly vulnerable to claims for better health, beauty, and youthfulness. It is human nature to reach out, hopefully, for the false promises that can be made about such important personal concerns. We become gullible in our desire to find ways to change our condition. And so we have become victims of quacks and snake-oil charmers through the ages. Governmental agencies try to exercise strong monitoring in these areas, but budgets are limited, and all claims cannot be investigated. As recent congressional scrutiny has revealed, the bottled-water industry had long been overlooked by governmental watchdogs. Now this is changing, thanks at least partly to the Perrier recall.

Should an organization have a crisis management team? Perrier did a poor job in its crisis management. Would a more formal organizational unit devoted to this have handled things better, instead of leaving it to top executives unskilled in handling catastrophes? The issue can hardly be answered simply and all-inclusively. Crises occur rarely; and a serious crisis may never happen to a particular organization. A crisis team then would have to be composed of executives and staff who have other primary responsibilities. And their decisions and actions under fire may be no better than a less formal arrangement. For severe crises—and Perrier's was certainly that—top executives who bear the ultimate responsibility therefore have to be the final decision makers. Some will be cooler under fire than others, but this usually cannot be fully ascertained until the crisis occurs. More desirable for most organizations would seem to be contingency plans, with plans formulated for various occurrences, including the worst scenarios. With such action plans drawn up under more normal conditions, better judgments are likely to result.

CONSIDER

Can you think of additional learning insights?

QUESTIONS

1. How could the public relations efforts of Perrier have been better handled?
2. Discuss the desirability of Perrier's price-cutting during its comeback.
3. Whom do you see as the primary customers for Perrier? For Evian? For other bottled waters? Are these customers likely to be enduring in their commitment to bottled water?

4. Why do you think the big firms, such as Coca-Cola, PepsiCo, and Coors, have been so slow and unaggressive in entering the bottled-water market?

5. Are we being hoodwinked by bottled-water claims and images?

6. "The success of bottled water in the United States, unlike the situation in many countries of the world where bottled water is often essential for good health, attests to the power of advertising." Evaluate this statement.

7. Is the consumer appeal of bottled water largely attributable to an image developed of sophistication and status?

HANDS-ON EXERCISES

1. Put yourself in the position of Ronald Davis on the afternoon of February 9, 1990. The first report of benzene found by a Carolina lab has just come in. What would you do? Be as specific as you can, and describe the logic behind your decisions.

2. How would you attempt to build up or resurrect the mystique of Perrier after the recall?

TEAM DEBATE EXERCISE

Debate the issue of extreme measures (a massive recall) undertaken in a product safety situation versus more moderate reactions (a modest recall). Consider as many aspects of this issue as you can, and make educated judgments of various probable consumer and governmental reactions.

INVITATION TO RESEARCH

What is the popularity of bottled water today? Has it increased or decreased since these events described? Has Perrier regained market position? Where are the biggest markets for bottled water? Who are the biggest players in this industry today?

CHAPTER FIVE

Al Dunlap Savages Scott
Paper and Sunbeam

Al Dunlap was hired in July 1996 by two large Sunbeam investors to turn Sunbeam around. He had gained a reputation as a turnaround artist extraordinaire, most recently from his efforts at Scott Paper. His philosophy was to cut to the bone, and the press frequently called him "Chainsaw Al." But he met his comeuppance with Sunbeam. In the process, his philosophy as well as his character came under bitter attack. But was his strategy for managing crises all that bad?

ALBERT J. DUNLAP

Dunlap wrote an autobiography, *Mean Business: How I Save Bad Companies and Make Good Companies,* describing his business philosophy and how it had evolved. The book became a best seller. He grew up in the slums of Hoboken, New Jersey, the son of a shipyard worker, and was imbued with the desire to make something of himself. He played football in high school and graduated from West Point. A former army paratrooper, he was known as a quick hitter, a ruthless cost cutter, a tough boss. But he got results, at least in the short term.

In 1983, Dunlap became chief executive of Lily Tulip Co., a maker of disposable cups that was heavily in debt after a buyout. Dunlap quickly exhibited the management philosophy that was to make him famous. He slashed costs, decimating the headquarters staff, closing plants, and selling the corporate jet. When he left in the mid-1980s, the company was healthy. In the latter 1980s, Dunlap became the number-one operations man for Sir James Goldsmith, a notorious raider of corporations. Dunlap was involved in restructuring Goldsmith's acquisitions of Crown-Zellerbach and International Diamond. In 1991, he worked on a heavily debt-laden Australian conglomerate, Consolidated Press Holdings. Two years later, after his "chainsaw approach," Consolidated Press was 100 divisions lighter and virtually free of debt.

By now Dunlap was a wealthy man, having made close to $100 million on his various restructurings. Still, at fifty-six, he was hardly ready to retire. When the board of Scott Paper heard that he was available, they wooed him, even purchasing his $3.2 million house in Florida to free him up to relocate.

53

SCOTT PAPER—A SICK COMPANY— AND DUNLAP'S RESULTS

An aged Scott Paper was reeling in the early 1990s. Per share earnings had dropped 61 percent since 1989 on flat sales growth. In 1993, the company had a $277 million loss.

Part of the problem stemmed from Scott's commercial paper division, S. D. Warren. In 1990, the company spent to increase capacity at Warren. Unfortunately, the timing could not have been worse. One of the worst industry slumps since the Great Depression was just beginning. Three subsequent "restructurings" had little positive effect.

Table 5.1 shows the decline in sales from 1990 through 1993. Table 5.2 shows the net income and loss during these four years. Of even more concern was Scott's performance relative to the major competitors Procter & Gamble and Kimberly-Clark during these four years. Table 5.3 shows the comparisons of profits as a percent of sales, with Scott again showing up most poorly. Undoubtedly this was a company needing fixing.

In characteristic fashion, Dunlap acted quickly once he took over as chief executive officer on April 19, 1994. That same day, to show his confidence and commitment, he invested $2 million of his own money in Scott. A few months later, after the stock had appreciated 30 percent, he invested another $2 million.

TABLE 5.1   Sales of Scott, 1990–1993 (billions)

1990	$3.9
1991	3.8
1992	3.9
1993	3.6
Total change, 1990–1993	(7.7%)

Source: Company annual reports.

Commentary: The company's deteriorating sales come at a time of great economic growth and advancing revenues for most firms.

TABLE 5.2   Net Income of Scott and Percent of Sales, 1990–1993

	(millions)	% of sales
1990	$148	3.8%
1991	(70)	(1.8)
1992	167	4.3
1993	(277)	(7.7)

Source: Company annual reports.

Commentary: The company's erratic profit picture, culminating in the serious loss of 1993, deserved deep concern, which it received.

TABLE 5.3 Profit as a Percentage of Sales: Scott, Kimberly-Clark, and Procter & Gamble, 1990–1993

	1990	1991	1992	1993
Scott	3.8%	(1.8%)	4.3%	(7.7%)
P&G	6.6	6.6	6.4	(2.1)°
Kimberly-Clark	6.8	7.5	1.9	7.3

Source: Company annual reports.

° Extraordinary charges reflecting accounting changes.

Commentary: Scott again shows up badly against its major competitors, both in the low percentage of earnings to sales and their severe fluctuations into earnings losses.

Only hours on the job, Dunlap offered three of his former associates top positions in the company. On the second day, he disbanded Scott's powerful management committee. On the third day, he fired nine of the eleven highest ranking executives. To complete his blitzkrieg, on the fourth day he destroyed four bookshelves crammed with strategic plans of previous administrations.

Can such drastic and abrupt changes be overdone? Should change be introduced more slowly and with more reflection? See the Issue Box "How Soon to Introduce Drastic Changes" on the following page for a discussion of this.

At the annual meeting in June, barely two months after assuming command, Dunlap announced four major goals for the first year. First, he vowed to divest the company of nonstrategic assets, most notably S. D. Warren, the printing and publishing papers subsidiary that had received major expansion funding only a few years before. Second, he would develop a core team of accomplished senior managers. Third, Scott was to be brought to "fighting trim" through a one-time-only global restructuring. Last, he promised to develop new strategies for marketing Scott products around the world.

In one of the largest relative restructurings in corporate America, more than 11,000 positions out of a total of 25,900 worldwide were eliminated. This included 71 percent of the headquarters staff, 50 percent of the salaried employees, and 20 percent of the production workers. Such draconian measures certainly cut costs. But were they overdone? Might such cuts potentially have detrimental long-term consequences? Please see the Issue Box "How Deep to Cut?" for a discussion of this.

In addition to cutting staff, Dunlap sought to reduce other costs, including outsourcing some operations and services. If these could be provided cheaper by other firms, then they should be farmed out. Dunlap announced that with the restructuring completed by year-end, pre-tax savings of $340 million were expected.[1]

By late fall of 1994, Dunlap's plans to divest the company of nonstrategic assets bore fruit. S. D. Warren was sold for $1.6 billion to an international investment group. Other asset sales generated more than $2 billion. Dunlap was able to lower debt by $1.5 billion and repurchase $300 million of Scott stock. This led to the credit rating being upgraded.

[1] *The New Scott 1994 Annual Report,* p. 5.

ISSUE BOX

HOW SOON TO INTRODUCE DRASTIC CHANGES?

Some new administrators believe in instituting major changes as quickly as possible. They reason that an organization is expecting this and is better prepared to make the adjustments needed than it ever will be again. Such managers are often referred to as gunslingers who "shoot from the hip." Other managers believe in moving more slowly, gathering more information, and taking action only when all the pros and cons can be weighed. But sometimes such delays can lull an organization into a sense of false calm, and make for even more trauma when the changes eventually come.

Relevant to the issue of moving swiftly or slowly is the health of the entity. If a firm is sick, in drastic need of help, we would expect a new manager to move more quickly and decisively. A firm doing well, although perhaps not as well as desired, reasonably should not require such drastic and abrupt disruption.

It has always baffled me how a fast-acting executive can acquire sufficient information to make the crucial decisions of who to fire and who to retain and what operations need to be pruned and which supported—all within a few days. Of course, operating statistics can be studied before formally taking charge. But the causes of the problems or successes—the whys—can hardly be understood so soon.

Boards, investors, and creditors want a fast turnaround. Waiting months before taking action to fix a sick company is not acceptable. However, not all companies are easily fixable. For example, Borden, a food and chemical conglomerate, has gone through the fifth restructuring in six years, with little improvement. But maybe Borden needed an Albert Dunlap, the person with a clear vision and a willingness to clean house. And, yes, a supportive board.

Do you think Dunlap acted too hastily in his initial sweeping changes? Playing the devil's advocate (one who takes an opposing view for the sake of debate), support a position that he did indeed act far too hastily.

The results of Dunlap's efforts were impressive indeed. Second-quarter earnings rose 71 percent; third-quarter earnings increased 73 percent, the best quarterly performance for Scott in four years. Fourth-quarter earnings were 159 percent higher than in 1993, establishing an all-time record. For the whole year, net income increased 82 percent over the previous year, and the stock price performance since Dunlap took over stood at the top one percent of major companies traded on the New York Stock Exchange.[2] Still, the cost-slashing was not helping market share. In the fiscal year ended April 2, 1995, Scott's bath-tissue sales in key U.S. markets slipped 1 percent, while in paper towels, Scott lost 5.2 percent.[3]

On July 17, 1995, Dunlap's efforts to make Scott an attractive acquisition candidate were capped by Kimberly-Clark's $7.38 billion offer for the firm. In the process,

[2] *Ibid.*, p. 6.

[3] Joseph Weber and Paula Dwyer, "Scott Rolls Out a Risky Strategy," *Business Week,* May 22, 1995, p. 45.

ISSUE BOX

HOW DEEP TO CUT?

Bloated bureaucratic organizations are the epitome of inefficiency and waste, whether in business corporations or in governmental bodies, including school systems. Administrative overhead might even exceed actual operating costs. But remedies can be overdone, they can go too far. In Scott's case, was the axing of 11,000 employees out of 25,900 overdone?

Although we are not privy to the needed cost/productivity records, we can raise some concerns. Did the massive layoffs go well beyond fat and bloat into bone and muscle? If so, future operations might be jeopardized. Another concern ought to be: Does an organization owe anything to its loyal and long-standing employees, or should they simply be considered pawns in the pursuit of maximizing profits? Where do we draw the line between efficiency and responsibility to faithful employees? And even to the community itself?

You may want to consider some of these questions and issues. They are current in today's downsizing mindset.

Dunlap himself would be suitably rewarded, leaving far richer than after any of his seven previous restructuring efforts. But Dunlap insisted, "I am still the best bargain in corporate America."[4]

THE SUNBEAM CHALLENGE

Sunbeam was a maker of blenders, electric blankets, and gas grills. These old-line products had shown little growth, and revenues and profits languished. After Dunlap's well-publicized turnaround success at Scott, it was not surprisingly he was courted for the top job at Sunbeam, and he entered the fray with gusto.

The day he was hired, Sunbeam stock rose 50 percent, "on faith." It eventually rose 300 percent. With his customary modus operandi Dunlap terminated half of Sunbeam's 12,000 employees and cut back its product offerings. Gone were such items as furniture and bed linens, and efforts were concentrated on things like grills, humidifiers, and kitchen appliances. In 1996, he took massive write-offs amounting to $338 million, of which almost $100 million was inventory.

In 1997, it looked like Dunlap was accomplishing another of his patented "miracles." Sales were up 22 percent to $1.168 billion, while income had risen from a loss of $196 million the previous year to a gain of $123 million in 1997. For stockholders this translated into earnings per share of $1.41 from a $2.37 loss in 1996.

Table 5.4 shows the trend in revenues and income of Sunbeam through 1997.

[4] Joann S. Lublin and Steven Lipin, "Scott Paper's 'Rambo in Pin Stripes' Is on the Prowl for Another Company to Fix," *Wall Street Journal*, July 18, 1995, p. B1.

Table 5.4   Trend of Sunbeam Revenues and Income 1991–1997 (in millions)

	1991	1992	1993	1994	1995	1996	1997
Revenues	886	967	1,066	1,198	1,203	964	1,168
Net Income	47.4	65.6	88.8	107.0	50.5	−196.0	123.0

Sources: Company annual reports.

Commentary: Dunlap came on the scene in July 1996, the year that Sunbeam incurred $196 million in losses. The $123 million profit for 1997 showed a remarkable and awesome recovery, and would seemingly make Dunlap a hero with his slash-and-burn strategy. Unfortunately, a reaudit did not confirm these figures. The inaccurate figures were blamed on questionable accounting, including prebooking sales and incorrectly assigning costs to the restructuring. The auditors said the company overstated its loss for 1996, and overstated profits for 1997. The revised figures showed a loss of $6.4 million for 1997, instead of the $123 million profit. (*Sources:* Martha Brannigan, "Sunbeam Audit to Repudiate '97 Turnaround," *Wall Street Journal*, October 20, 1998, p. A3; "Audit Shows Sunbeam's Turnaround Really a Bust," *Cleveland Plain Dealer*, October 21, 1998, pp. 1C, 2C.)

In October 1997, barely a year on the job, Dunlap announced that the turn-around was complete and that he was seeking a buyer for Sunbeam. Stockholders had much to be pleased about. From a low of $12 a share in 1996, the price had risen to $50. Unfortunately, there was a serious downside to this, as Dunlap was soon to find: The high price for Sunbeam stock took it out of the range for any potential buyer; $50 gave a market capitalization of $4.6 billion, or four times revenues, a multiple reserved for only a few of the premier companies. So for the time being, the stock-holders were stuck with Dunlap.

Since he was not successful in selling the company, Dunlap went on a buying spree. He began talking about his "vision," with such words as "We have moved from constraining categories to expanding categories. Small kitchen appliances become kitchen appliances. We'll move from grills to outdoor cooking. Healthcare moves from just a few products to a broad range of products."[5]

Dunlap bought Coleman Company, Signature Brands and its Mr. Coffee, and First Alert for an aggregate of approximately $2.4 billion in cash and stock. Part of this was financed with $750 million of convertible debentures, as well as $60 million of accounts receivable that were sold to raise cash. Critics maintained he had paid too much for these, especially the $2.2 billion for money-losing Coleman. The effect of these acqui-sitions on Sunbeam's balance sheet was sobering if any stockholders looked closely.

When Dunlap took over Sunbeam, though it was performing poorly, it had only $200 million in debt. By 1998, Sunbeam was over $2 billion in debt, and its net worth had dropped from $500 million to a negative $600 million.[6]

---

[5] As quoted in Holman W. Jenkins, Jr., "Untalented Al? The Sorrows of a One-Trick Pony," *Wall Street Journal*, June 24, 1998, p. A19.

[6] Matthew Schifrin, "The Unkindest Cuts," *Forbes*, May 4, 1998, p. 45.

THE DEBACLE OF 1998, AND THE DEMISE OF DUNLAP

The first quarter of 1998 showed a complete reversal of fortunes from the turnaround of the previous year. Revenues were down and a first-quarter loss was posted of $44.6 million—all this far below expectations. Sunbeam's stock price fell by more than half, from $53 to $25. By midsummer it was to reach a low of $4.62.

Dunlap conceded that he and top executives had concentrated their attention too much on "sealing" the acquisitions of Coleman and the two smaller companies, allowing underlings to offer "stupid, low-margin deals" on outdoor cooking grills. He pointed to glitches with new products, a costly recall, and even El Niño. "People don't think about buying outdoor grills during a storm," he said. "Faced with sluggish sales, a marketing executive offered excessive discounts," he further said. More job cuts were promised, through eliminating one-third of the jobs at the newly acquired companies.[7]

On Monday, June 15th, after deliberating over the weekend, Sunbeam's board abruptly fired Al Dunlap, having "lost confidence in his ability to carry out the long-term growth potential of the company."[8] Now a legal fight ensued as to what kind of severance package, if any, Dunlap deserved as a consequence of his firing. A severance package for Dunlap would be "obscene—an obscenity on top of an obscenity, capitalism gone crazy," said union leader Michael Cavanaugh.[9] Other comments were reported in the media; a sampling is in the following Information Box.

Allegations of Fraud

At the end of a three-month audit after Dunlap's departure, auditors discovered accounting irregularities that struck down the amazingly high reported profits for 1997, the first full year of Dunlap's leadership. Rather than a turnaround, the good results came from improper accounting moves that adversely affected 1996 and 1998 results. The restated numbers showed that Sunbeam actually had a small operating loss in 1997, while 1996 showed a modest profit.

On May 15, 2001, the SEC formally charged that Dunlap and some of his executives broke security laws to make Sunbeam look healthier and more attractive for a buyer. This was done by fraudulently shifting revenue to inflate losses under the old management and boosting income to create the false impression of the rapid turnaround in financial performance for 1997. Furthermore, revenue was increased in 1997 at the expense of future results by inducing retail customers to sell merchandise more quickly than normal, a practice known as channel stuffing. By the next year, the company was getting desperate to hide its mounting financial problems and misrepresented its performance and prospects in quarterly reports, bond offerings material, press releases, and statements to stock analysts. Dunlap denied any involvement or

[7] James R. Hagerty and Martha Brannigan, "Sunbeam Plans to Cut 5,100 Jobs as CEO Promises Rebound from Dismal Quarter," *Wall Street Journal,* May 12, 1998, pp. A3, A4.

[8] Martha Brannigan and James Hagerty, "Sunbeam, Its Prospects Looking Ever Worse, Fires CEO Dunlap," *Wall Street Journal,* June 15, 1998, pp. A1, A14.

[9] Martha Brannigan and Joann S. Lublin, "Dunlap Faces a Fight Over His Severance Pay," *Wall Street Journal,* June 16, 1998, p. B3.

INFORMATION BOX

THE POPULARITY OF "CHAINSAW" AL DUNLAP

Not surprising, the slashing policy of Dunlap did not bring him a lot of friends, even though he may have been admired in some circles. The following are some comments reported in the press immediately after his firing:

> He finally got what he's been doing to a lot of people. It was a taste of his own medicine. (union representative)
>
> I'm happy the son-of-a-bitch is fired. (former supervisor)
>
> Somebody at that company finally got some sense. (small-town mayor)
>
> I couldn't think of a better person to deserve it. It tickled me to death. We may need to have a rejoicing ceremony. (small-town mayor)
>
> I guess the house of cards came tumbling down ... when you reduce your workforce by 50 percent, you lose your ability to manage. (former plant manager)

Is there a lesson to be learned from such comments as these? Perhaps it is that the human element in organizations and communities needs to be considered.

Taking a devil's advocate position (one who takes an opposing viewpoint for the sake of argument and full discussion), defend Dunlap's philosophy.

Sources: Thomas W. Gerdel, "Workers at Glenwillow Plant Cheer Firing of 'Chainsaw' Al," *Cleveland Plain Dealer,* June 16, 1998, 2C; "No Tears for a Chainsaw," *Wall Street Journal,* June 16, 1998, p. B1.)

knowledge of such matters and that any accounting changes by the auditors were "judgment calls" on matters subject to interpretation.[10]

With the company forced to restate financial results for eighteen months, it filed for bankruptcy protection in February 2001.

In early September 2002, Dunlap agreed to settle the suit by the SEC by paying $500,000 and agreeing never to be an officer or director of another public company. He neither admitted nor denied the SEC's claim that he masterminded the accounting fraud. A month earlier, Dunlap also paid $15 million in a settlement of a class-action suit filed by shareholders for their losses due to Sunbeam's fraudulent business practices.[11] All thoughts of a severance package for Dunlap after his firing were long forgotten.

---

[10] Martha Brannigan, "Sunbeam Slashes Its 1997 Earnings in Restatement," *Wall Street Journal,* October 21, 1998, p. B23.

[11] Jill Barton, Associated Press, as reported in "Sunbeam's 'Chain Saw Al' to Pay $500,000 Judgment," *Cleveland Plain Dealer,* September 5, 2002, p. C1.

The SEC came to believe there was funny accounting also at Scott Paper when Dunlap was running it. But this suspicion came at the height of the Enron furor, and the SEC had bigger game to pursue.[12]

ANALYSIS

Was Dunlap's Management Style of "Slash and Burn" Appropriate?

We see conflicting evidence in the Scott and Sunbeam cases. Without doubt, Dunlap achieved his goal to make Scott an attractive acquisition candidate, and thus reward shareholders and himself (although suspicions later arose that the sterling results may have been tainted). That he did this so quickly seemed at the time a strong endorsement of his strategy for turning around sick companies—simply decimate the organization, sell off all ancillary units, cut costs to the bone, and virtually force the company into increased profitability.

The flaw with this reasoning is that it tends to boost short-term performance at the expense of the longer term. Morale and dedication of surviving employees are destroyed. Vision and innovative thinking may be impaired since the depleted organization lacks time and commitment to deal effectively with more than day-to-day basic operations.

Dunlap's strategy backfired with Sunbeam. When he couldn't sell the company after manipulating the performance statistics for 1997, he was left with a longer-term management challenge, and was by no means up to this. It is ironic that the reputation for turning around sick companies acted against him with Sunbeam. Investors were so confident of his ability to quickly turn around the company that they bid the price up so high no other firm would buy it. And they were stuck with Dunlap.

Did the Adversity Require Such Drastic Changes?

Sales of both Scott and Sunbeam were flat, with profit performance deteriorating. Stock prices were falling counter to a bull market and investors were disillusioned. Did such situations call for draconian measures?

Neither company was in danger of going belly-up. True, they both were off the growth path, but their brands continued to be well regarded by consumers. On the other hand, many firms become too bureaucratic, burdened with high overhead and chained to established policies and procedures. Such organizations desperately need paring down, eliminating bloated staff and executive levels, and, not the least, curbing the red tape that destroys flexibility and creativity.

The best answer lies in moderation, cutting the deadwood, but not bone and muscle. The worst scenario is to cut with little investigation and reflection. This cost-cutting climate may degenerate to the extent that worthy operations and individuals are cut regardless of their merit and future promise. We would expect better long-term performance in an organization that is not decimated with shattered morale.

---

[12] Floyd Norris, *New York Times,* as reported in "Fraud Surrounded 'Chainsaw Al', Yet Little Was Done," *Cleveland Plain Dealer,* September 8, 2002, p. G3.

Dunlap quickly sold off the S. D. Warren unit of Scott, and this added $1.6 billion to Scott coffers. Previous Scott management had invested heavily in what seemed a reasonable diversification into commercial paper, only to encounter an unexpected industry downturn. How could this have been predicted? Was Warren worth keeping? Research and investigation might have found that it was.

Creeping Bureaucracy

Bureaucratic excesses often come about after years of reasonable success and viability. The following Information Box discusses the bureaucratic type of organization.

Bureaucracy seemed to have been rampant at Scott. After all, Dunlap eliminated 71 percent of the headquarters staff and four bookshelves crammed with strategic plans of previous administrations. Too many administrators and staff people bring higher overhead costs than leaner competitors, thus placing the firm at a competitive disadvantage. Some pruning needed to be done.

Was the same thing true with Sunbeam? Perhaps not to the same extent, although without more specific information we cannot know for sure. We can suspect, however, that Dunlap, caught up in his success at Scott, simply transferred his strategy to Sunbeam with no consideration of their differences. We might call this "slashing by formula," and it suggests a rigid mindset devoid of flexibility or compassion.

Paying Too Much for Acquisitions

With Sunbeam, Dunlap made three questionable acquisitions, and burdened the firm with several billions of dollars of debt. In particular, the $2.2 billion paid for money-losing Coleman seemed another of Dunlap's "shooting from the hip" decisions. Such questionable research in acquisitions decisions followed the pattern of his personnel-slashing decisions and the quick sale of S. D. Warren. Furthermore, the reckless accumulation of debt for these acquisitions almost suggests a masochistic mindset. Or did Dunlap think that if the share price now dropped drastically, the firm would become attractive for an acquisition?

Detection of Fraud Destroys Any Perception of Management Competence

Dunlap apparently had a long history of manipulating records to make himself look better, as we will further see in the following section. This fraud pales in comparison with the massive misdeeds of Enron, Tyco, WorldCom, and others, simply because Dunlap's were much smaller firms, but it can no more be condoned than those of the bigger firms. Dunlap could yet face jail time, should the SEC decides to turn its attention to less publicized cases.

LATER DEVELOPMENTS

Dunlap's exploits brought turmoil to the executive-search industry. It seems major search firms checking his employment history prior to being hired by Sunbeam failed to uncover that he had been fired from two previous positions. He was terminated at

INFORMATION BOX

THE BUREAUCRATIC ORGANIZATION

The bureaucratic organization is a natural consequence of size and age. Its characteristics include the following:

- A clear-cut division of labor
- A strict hierarchy of authority
- Staffing by technical competence
- Formal rules and procedures
- Impersonal approaches to decision making[13]

Although a well-structured organization would appear to be best in many circumstances, it tends to be too rigid. It relies heavily on rules and procedures and as a result is often slow to adapt to change. Red tape usually predominates, as do many layers of hierarchy, an abundance of staff, and overspecialization. Consequently, creativity and initiative are stifled, and communication between upper management and lower operations is cumbersome and often distorted. Perhaps even more serious, a bureaucratic organization, with its entrenched administrators and staff positions, has a built-in high overhead that makes it difficult to compete against low-cost competitors.

A bureaucratic organization does not have to be inevitable as a firm attains large size and dominance, as shown in Table 5.5: a firm can still mold itself as an adaptive organization. But the temptation is otherwise.

TABLE 5.5   Contrasts of Bureaucratic and Adaptive Organizations

Organizational Aspects	Bureaucratic	Adaptive
Hierarchy of authority	Centralized	Decentralized
Rules and procedures	Many	Few
Division of labor	Precise	Open
Spans of control	Narrow	Wide
Coordination	Formal and impersonal	Informal and personal

Can you identify the type of person who tends to work best in a bureaucracy? The one who performs worst in this setup?

Max Phillips & Sons in 1973 after only seven weeks. Three years later, in 1976, he was fired as president of Nitec Paper Corp. under circumstances of alleged fraud involving misstated profits, a situation not unlike his departure from Sunbeam.

---

[13] This section is adapted from John R. Schermerhorn, Jr., *Management*, 6th ed. (New York: Wiley, 1999), pp. 75, 223.

While these episodes took place twenty years before the recruiting for Scott Paper and Sunbeam and were apparently overlooked because of his supposedly strong track record in recent years, still significant and pertinent omissions in Dunlap's job history were not caught by search firms supposedly conducting thorough background checks. Along the way, Dunlap erased both jobs from his employment history, and no one who checked his background discovered the omissions.[14]

WHAT CAN BE LEARNED?

How to jumpstart a languid organization. Can we find any keys to stimulating an organization not performing up to potential? Or maybe even to inspire it to perform beyond its potential? The challenge is not unlike that of motivating a discouraged and downtrodden athletic team to rise up and have faith in itself and recommit itself to quality of performance.

In both athletics and business, the common notion is that personnel changes have to be made. Dunlap introduced the idea of severe downsizing. But this is controversial, and in view of Dunlap's problems with Sunbeam, now almost discredited. So how much should be cut, how quickly should changes be made and how sweeping should they be, and what kind of information is most vital in making such decisions? Furthermore, there is the question of morale and its importance in any restoration.

We find more art than science in this mighty challenge of restoration. In particular, the right blend or degree of change is crucial. Let us look at some considerations:

- How much do we trim? In most revival situations, some pruning of personnel and operations is necessary. But how much is too much, and how much is not enough? Is an ax always required for a successful turnaround? One would hope not. Certainly those personnel who are not willing to accept change may have to be let go. And weak persons and operations that show little probability of improvement need to be pruned, just as the athlete who can't seem to perform up to expectations may have to be let go. Still, it is often better to wait for sufficient information as to the "why" of poor performance, before assigning blame for the consequences.

- How long do we wait? Mistakes can be made both in taking action before all the facts are known and in waiting too long. If the changemaker procrastinates for weeks, an organization that at first was psychologically geared to major change might find it more traumatic and disruptive.

- What should be the role of strategic planning? Major actions should hardly be taken without some research and planning, but strategic plans too often delay change implementation. They tend to be the products of a fumbling

---

[14] Joann S. Lublin, "Search Firms Have Red Faces in Dunlap Flop," *Wall Street Journal*, July 17, 2001, pp. B1, B4: Floyd Norris, "Uncovering Lost Years of Sunbeam's Fired Chief," *New York Times*, reported in *Cleveland Plain Dealer*, July 17, 2001, pp. C1,C4.)

bureaucracy and of some abdication of responsibility. (Despite the popularity of strategic planning, it often is a vehicle for procrastination and blame-dilution: e.g., "I simply followed the strategy recommendations of the consultants.") Dunlap had an aversion to strategic planning, seeing this as indicative of a top-heavy bureaucratic organization. Perhaps he was right on this, when it is carried to an extreme. But going into an organization and heedlessly slashing positions without due regard for the individuals involved and the potential is akin to "shooting from the hip," with little regard for careful aiming. Then there is the matter of morale.

- How much weight should be given to morale?. Major restructuring usually is demoralizing to the organizations involved. The usual result is massive layoffs and forced retirements, complete reassignment of people, traumatic personnel and policy changes, and destruction of accustomed lines of communication and authority. This is hardly conducive to preserving stability and morale and any faint spark of teamwork. (You may want to look ahead to Chapter 17 and the Continental Air case for how Gordon Bethune achieved an amazing revitalization of employee morale.)

Moderation is usually best. Much can be said for moderation, for choosing the middle position, for example, between heavy cost-cutting and little cost-cutting. Of course, the condition of the firm is a major consideration. One on the verge of bankruptcy, unable to meet its bills, needs drastic measures promptly. But the problems both of Scott and Sunbeam were by means so serious. More moderate action could have been taken.

It is better to view the restoration challenge as a time for building rather than tearing down. This focuses attention more on the longer view than on short-term results that may come back to haunt the firm, as well as the changemaker, like Dunlap.

Periodic housecleaning produces competitive health. In order to minimize the buildup of dead wood, all aspects of an organization periodically ought to be objectively appraised. Weak products and operations should be pruned, unless solid justification exists for keeping them. Such justification might include good growth prospects or complementing other products and operations or even providing a desired customer service. In particular, staff and headquarters personnel and functions should be scrutinized, perhaps every five years, with the objective of weeding out the redundant and superfluous. Most important, these "axing" evaluations should be done objectively, with decisive actions taken where needed. While some layoffs may result, they might not be necessary if suitable transfers are possible.

CONSIDER

Can you add any other learning insights?

QUESTIONS

1. "Periodic evaluations of personnel and departments aimed at pruning cause far too much harm to the organization. Such 'axing' evaluations

should themselves be pruned." Argue this position as persuasively as you can.

2. Now marshal the most persuasive arguments for such "axing" evaluations.

3. Describe a person's various stages of morale and dedication to the company as it goes through a restructuring, with massive layoffs expected and realized, but with the person finding himself or herself one of the survivors. How, in your opinion, would this affect productivity and loyalty?

4. Is it likely that any decades-old organization will be bloated with excessive bureaucracy and overhead? Why or why not?

5. What decision guides should be used to determine which divisions and subsidiaries are to be divested or sold?

6. What arguments would you make in a time of restructuring for keeping your particular business unit? Which are likely to be most persuasive to an administration committed to a program of heavy pruning?

HANDS-ON EXERCISES

1. You are one of the nine high-ranking executives fired by Dunlap his third day on the job. Describe your feelings and your action plan at this point. (If you want to make some assumptions, state them specifically.)

2. You are one of the two high-level executives kept by Dunlap as he sweeps into office. Describe your feelings and your likely performance on the job.

3. You are one of the three outsiders brought into Scott vice-presidential jobs by Dunlap. You have worked for him before and must have impressed him. Describe your feelings and your likely performance on the job. What specific problems, if any, do you foresee?

TEAM DEBATE EXERCISE

It is early 1996. The board of Sunbeam is considering bringing in a turnaround team. One is the team of Dunlap, which argues for major and rapid change. Another team under consideration is Clarence Ripley's, who advocates more modest immediate changes. Array your arguments and present your positions as persuasively as possible. Attack the recommendations of the other side as aggressively as possible. We are talking about millions of dollars in fees and compensation at stake for the winning team.

INVITATION TO RESEARCH

What is Dunlap up to after being fired by the Sunbeam board in mid-1998? Has he gracefully retired or is he running scared pending legal charges? Is he still fighting for severance pay? Who replaced Dunlap, and how well is he doing? Are his policies much different from Dunlap's?

CHAPTER SIX

The Classic Masterpiece in Crisis Management: Johnson & Johnson's Tylenol Scare

*I*n one of the greatest examples of superb crisis management, James Burke, CEO of Johnson & Johnson, in 1982 handled a catastrophe that involved loss of life in the criminal and deadly contamination of its flagship product, Tylenol. The company exhibited what has become a model for corporate responsibility to customers, regardless of costs.

PRELUDE

It was September 30, 1982. On the fifth floor of the Johnson & Johnson (J&J) head-quarters in New Brunswick, New Jersey, Chairman James E. Burke was having a quiet meeting with President David R. Clair. The two liked to hold such informal meetings every two months to talk over important but nonpressing matters that they usually did not get around to in the normal course of events. That day both men had reason to feel good, for J&J's sales and earnings were up sharply and the trend of business could hardly have been more promising. They even had time to dwell on some nonbusiness matters that sunny September morning.

Their complacency and self-satisfaction did not last long. Arthur Quill, a member of the executive committee, burst into the meeting. Consternation and anguish flooded the room as he brought word of cyanide deaths in Chicago that were connected to J&J's most important and profitable product, Extra-Strength Tylenol capsules.

THE COMPANY

Johnson & Johnson manufactures and markets a broad range of health care products in many countries of the world. Table 6.1 shows the various categories of products and their percent of total corporate sales. In 1981, J&J was number 68 on the *Fortune* 500 list of the largest industrial companies in the United States, and it had sales of $5.4 billion. It was organized into four industry categories: professional, pharmaceutical, industrial, and consumer. The professional division included products

TABLE 6.1   Contribution to Total Johnson & Johnson Sales of Product Categories, 1983

Product Classification	Sales (millions)	Percent of Total Company Sales
Surgical and First-Aid Supplies	$1,268	21%
Pharmaceuticals	1,200	20
Sanitary Napkins and Tampons	933	16
Baby Products	555	9
Diagnostic Equipment	518	9
Tylenol and Variants	460	8
Other (includes hospital supplies, dental products, contraceptives)	1,039	17
Total	$5,973	100%

Source: "After Its Recovery, New Headaches for Tylenol," *Business Week* (May 14, 1984), p. 137.

such as ligatures, sutures, surgical dressings, and other surgery-related items. The pharmaceutical division included prescription drugs, and the industrial area included textile products, industrial tapes, and fine chemicals.

The largest division was the consumer division, consisting of toiletries and hygienic products such as baby care items, first aid products, and nonprescription drugs. These products were marketed primarily to the general public and distributed through wholesalers and directly to independent and chain retail outlets.

Through the years, J&J had assiduously worked to cultivate an image of responsibility and trust. Its products were associated with gentleness and safety—for all customers, from babies to the elderly. The corporate sense of responsibility fully covered the products and actions of any firms that it acquired, such as McNeil Laboratories.

THE PRODUCT

The success of Tylenol, an acetaminophen-based analgesic, in the late 1970s and early 1980s had been sensational. It had been introduced in 1955 by McNeil Laboratories as an alternative drug to aspirin, one that avoided aspirin's side effects. In 1959, Johnson & Johnson had acquired McNeil Laboratories, and the company ran it as an independent subsidiary.

By 1974, Tylenol sales had grown to $50 million at retail, primarily achieved through heavy advertising to physicians. A national consumer advertising campaign, instituted in 1976, proved very effective. By 1979, Tylenol had become the largest selling health and beauty aid in drug and food mass merchandising, breaking the eighteen-year domination of Procter & Gamble's Crest toothpaste. By 1982, Tylenol had captured 35.3 percent of the over-the-counter analgesic market. This was more than the market shares of Bayer, Bufferin, and Anacin combined. Table 6.2 shows the competitive positions of Tylenol and its principal competitors in this analgesic market.

TABLE 6.2   **Market Shares of Major Brands—
Over-the-Counter Analgesic Market, 1981**

Brand	Percent of Market
Tylenol	35.3
Anacin	13.0
Bayer	11.0
Excedrin	10.1
Bufferin	9.0

Source: "A Death Blow for Tylenol?" *Business Week* (October 18, 1982), p. 151.

Total sales of all Tylenol products went from $115 million in 1976 to $350 million in 1982, a whopping 204 percent increase in a highly competitive market. As such, Tylenol accounted for 7 percent of all J&J sales. More important, it contributed 17 percent of all profits.

Then catastrophe struck.

THE CRISIS

On a Wednesday morning in late September 1982, Adam Janus had a minor chest pain, so he purchased a bottle of Extra-Strength Tylenol capsules. He took one capsule and was dead by midafternoon. Later that same day, Stanley Janus and his wife also took capsules from the same bottle—both were dead by Friday afternoon. By the weekend four more Chicago-area residents had died under similar circumstances. The cause of death was cyanide, a deadly poison that can kill within fifteen minutes by disrupting the blood's ability to carry oxygen through the body, thereby affecting the heart, lungs, and brain. The cyanide had been used to contaminate Extra-Strength Tylenol capsules. Dr. Thomas Kim, chief of the critical care unit of Northwest Community Hospital in Arlington Heights, Illinois, noted, "The victims never had a chance. Death was certain within minutes."[1]

Medical examiners retrieved bottles from the victims' homes and found another ten capsules laced with cyanide. In each case the red half of the capsule was discolored and slightly swollen, and its usual dry white powder had been replaced with a gray substance that had an almond odor. One of the capsules had 65 mg of cyanide—a lethal does is considered to be 50 mg.

The McNeil executives learned of the poisonings from reporters calling for comment about the tragedy—calls came from all the media, and then from pharmacies, doctors, hospitals, poison control centers, and hundreds of panicky consumers. McNeil quickly gathered information on the victims, causes of deaths, lot numbers

[1] Susan Tifft, "Poison Madness in the Midwest," *Time* (October 11, 1982), p. 18.

on the poisoned Tylenol bottles, outlets where they had been purchased, dates when they had been manufactured, and the route they had taken through the distribution system.

After the deaths were linked to Tylenol, one of the biggest consumer alerts ever took place. Johnson & Johnson recalled batches and advised consumers not to take any Extra-Strength Tylenol capsules until the mystery had been solved. Drugstores and supermarkets across the country pulled Tylenol products from their shelves; it soon became virtually impossible to obtain Tylenol anywhere.

Those tracking down the mysterious contamination quickly determined that the poisoning did not occur in manufacturing, either intentionally or accidentally. The poisoned capsules had come from lots manufactured at both McNeil plants. Therefore, the tampering had to have happened in Chicago, since poisoning at both plants at the same time would have been almost impossible. The FDA suspected that someone unconnected with the manufacturer had bought the Tylenol over the counter, inserted cyanide in some capsules, then returned the bottles to the stores. Otherwise, the contamination would have been widespread, and not only in the Chicago area.

At this point, Johnson & Johnson was virtually cleared of any wrongdoing, but the company was stuck with having one of its major products publicly associated with poison and death, no matter how innocent it was. Perhaps the task of coping with the devastating impact of the tragedy would have been easier for Johnson & Johnson if the perpetrator were conclusively identified and caught. This was not to be, despite a special task force of 100 FBI agents and Illinois investigators who chased down more than 2,000 leads and filed 57 volumes of reports.[2]

COMPANY REACTION

Johnson & Johnson decided to elevate the management of the crisis to the corporate level and a game plan developed that company executives hoped would ensure eventual recovery. The game plan consisted of three phases: Phase I was to figure out what had actually happened; Phase II was to assess and contain the damage; and Phase III was to try to get Tylenol back into the market.

The company that had always tried to keep a low profile now turned to the media to provide it with the most accurate and current information, as well as to help it prevent a panic. Twenty-five public relations specialists were recruited from Johnson & Johnson's other divisions to help McNeil's regular staff of fifteen. Advertising was suspended at first. All Tylenol capsules were recalled—31 million bottles with a retail value of more than $100 million. Through advertisements promising to exchange tablets for capsules, through 500,000 telegrams to doctors, hospitals, and distributors, and through statements to the media, J&J hoped to demystify the situation.

With proof that the tampering had not occurred in the manufacturing process, the company moved into Phase II. Financially it experienced immediate losses

---

[2] "Tylenol Comes Back as Case Grows Cold," *Newsweek* (April 25, 1983), p. 16.

amounting to over $100 million, the bulk coming from the expense of buying unused Tylenol bottles from retailers and consumers and shipping them to disposal points. The cost of sending the telegrams was estimated at $500,000, and the costs associated with expected product liability suits were expected to run in the millions.

Of more concern to the management was the impact of the poisoning on the brand itself. Many predicted that Tylenol as a brand could no longer survive. Some suggested that Johnson & Johnson reintroduce the product under a new name to give it a fresh start and thus rid itself of the devastated brand image.

Surveys conducted by Johnson & Johnson about a month after the poisonings seemed to buttress the death of Tylenol as a brand name. In one survey 94 percent of the consumers were aware that Tylenol was involved with the poisonings. Although 87 percent of these respondents realized that the maker of Tylenol was not to blame for the deaths, 61 percent said they were not likely to buy Tylenol in the future. Even worse, 50 percent of the consumers said they would not use the Tylenol tablets either. The only promising result from the research was that 49 percent of the *frequent* users answered that they would eventually use Tylenol.[3]

The company found itself in a real dilemma. It wanted so much to keep the Tylenol name; after all, the acceptance had been developed by years of advertising. Now, was it all to be destroyed in a few days of adversity? On the one hand, if J&J brought Tylenol back too soon, before the hysteria had subsided, the product could die on the shelves. On the other hand, if the company waited too long to bring the product back, competitors might well gain an unassailable market share lead. The marketing research results were not entirely acceptable to Johnson & Johnson executives. One manager expressed the company's doubts: "The problem with consumer research is that it reflects attitudes and not behavior. The best way to know what consumers are really going to do is put the product back on the shelves and let them vote with their hands."[4] But what was the right timing?

Johnson & Johnson decided to rebuild the brand by focusing on the frequent users and then to expand to include other consumers. It hoped that a core of loyal users would want the product in both its tablet and capsule forms. In order to regain regular user confidence, J&J ran television commercials informing the public that the company would do everything it could to regain their trust. The commercials featured Dr. Thomas Gates, medical director of McNeil, urging consumers to continue to trust Tylenol: "Tylenol has had the trust of the medical profession and 100 million Americans for over twenty years. We value that trust too much to let any individual tamper with it. We want you to continue to trust Tylenol."[5]

Johnson & Johnson also tried to encourage Tylenol capsule users to switch to tablets, which are more difficult to sabotage. In an advertising campaign it offered to exchange tablets for capsules at no charge. In addition it placed 76 million coupons in Sunday newspaper ads good for $2.50 toward the purchase of Tylenol.

[3] Thomas Moore, "The Fight to Save Tylenol," *Fortune* (November 29, 1982), p. 48.
[4] *Ibid.,* p. 49.
[5] Judith B. Gardner, "When a Brand Name Gets Hit by Bad News," *U.S. News & World Report* (November 8, 1982), p. 71.

Finally, it designed a tamper-resistant package to prevent the kind of tragedy that occurred in Chicago. Extra-strength capsules were now sold only in new triple-sealed packages. The flaps of the box were glued shut and were visibly torn apart when opened. The bottle's cap and neck were covered with a tight plastic seal printed with the company name, and the mouth of the bottle was covered with an inner foil seal. Both the box and the bottle were labeled, "Do Not Use If Safety Seals Are Broken." This triple-seal package cost an additional 2.4 cents per bottle, but Johnson & Johnson hoped it would instill consumer confidence in the safety of the product and spur sales. In addition the company offered retailers higher-than-normal discounts—up to 25 percent on orders.

Consumers who said they had thrown away their Tylenol after the scare were given a toll-free number to call, and they received $2.50 in coupons too—in effect, a free bottle, since bottles of twenty-four capsules or thirty tablets sold for about $2.50.

Over 2,000 salespeople from all Johnson & Johnson domestic subsidiaries were mobilized to persuade doctors and pharmacists to again begin recommending Tylenol tablets to patients and customers. This was similar to the strategy initially used when the product was introduced some twenty-five years before.

The Outcome

Immediately after the crisis, J&J's market share plunged from 35.3 percent of the pain reliever market to below 7 percent. Competitors were quick to take advantage of the situation. Upjohn Company and American Home Products Corporation were seeking Food and Drug Administration permission to sell an over-the-counter version of ibuprofen, a popular prescription pain reliever. Upjohn also granted marketing rights for its brand, Nuprin, to Bristol-Myers Co., maker of Bufferin, Excedrin, and Datril. Upjohn's prescription brand, Motrin—a stronger formulation than Nuprin—was generating some $200 million in 1982, making Motrin the company's biggest-selling drug. And lurking in the wings was mighty Procter & Gamble Company (P&G), the world's heaviest advertiser. P&G was launching national ads for Norwich aspirin and was test-marketing a coated capsule containing aspirin granules.

Yet, there were some encouraging signs for J&J. When *Psychology Today* polled its readers regarding whether Tylenol would survive as a brand name, 92 percent thought Tylenol would survive the incident. This figure corresponded closely with the results of another survey conducted by Leo Shapiro, an independent market researcher, just two weeks after the deaths occurred, in which 91 percent said they would probably buy the product again.

Psychology Today tried to get at the roots of such loyalty and roused comments such as these:

A twenty-three-year old woman wrote that she would continue to use Tylenol because she felt that it was "tried and true."

A sixty-one-year old woman said that the company had been "honest and sincere."

And a young man thought Tylenol was an easy name to say.[6]

---

[6] Carin Rubenstein, "The Tylenol Tradition," *Psychology Today* (April 1983), p. 16.

Such survey results presaged an amazing comeback: J&J's conscientious actions paid off. By May 1983, Tylenol had regained almost all the market share lost the previous September; its market share reached 35 percent, which it held until 1986, when another calamity struck.

New industry safety standards had been developed by the over-the-counter drug industry in concert with the Food and Drug Administration for tamper-resistant packaging. Marketers under law had to select a package "having an indicator or barrier to entry, which if breached or missing, can reasonably be expected to provide visible evidence to the consumer that the package has been tampered with or opened."[7] Despite toughened package standards, in February 1986, a Westchester, New York, woman died from cyanide-laced Extra-Strength Tylenol capsules. The tragedy of three-and-a-half years before was being replayed. J&J immediately removed all Tylenol capsules from the market and offered refunds for capsules consumers had already bought.

Now the company made a major decision. It decided no longer to manufacture any over-the-counter capsules because it could not guarantee their safety from criminal contamination. Henceforth, the company would market only tablets and so-called caplets, which were coated and elongated tablets that are easy to swallow. This decision was expected to cost $150 million. The president explained: "People think of this company as extraordinarily trustworthy and responsible, and we don't want to do anything to damage that."[8]

By July 1986, Tylenol had regained most of the market share lost in February, and it now stood at 32 percent.

THE INGREDIENTS OF CRISIS MANAGEMENT

Johnson & Johnson was truly a management success in its handling of the Tylenol problem. It overcame the worst kind of adversity, that in which human life was lost in using one of its products, and a major product at that. Yet, in only a few months it recouped most of its lost market share and regained its public image of corporate responsibility and trust. What accounted for the success of J&J in overcoming such adversity?

We can identify five significant factors:

1. Keeping communication channels open
2. Taking quick, corrective action
3. Keeping faith in the product
4. Protecting the public image at all costs
5. Aggressively bringing back the brand

Effective communication has seldom been better done. Rapport must be gained with the media, to enlist their support and even their sympathy. Alas, this is

---

[7] "Package Guides Studied," *Advertising Age* (October 18, 1982), p. 82.

[8] Richard W. Stevenson, "Johnson & Johnson's Recovery," *New York Times* (July 5, 1986), pp. 33–34.

not easily done, for the press is inclined to sensationalize, criticize, and take sides against the big corporation. Johnson & Johnson gained the needed rapport through corporate openness and cooperation. In the disaster's early days it sought good two-way communication, with the media furnishing information from the field while J&J gave full and honest disclosure of its internal investigation and corrective actions. Important for good rapport, company officials need to be freely available and open to the press. Unfortunately, this goes against most executives' natural bent so that a spirit of antipathy often is fostered.

When product safety is in jeopardy, quick corrective action must be taken, *regardless* of the cost. This usually means immediate recall of the affected product, and this can involve millions of dollars. Even if the fault lies with only an isolated batch of products, a firm may need to recall them all since public perception of the danger likely will transfer to all units of that brand.

Johnson & Johnson kept faith with its product and brand name, despite the counsel of experts who thought the Tylenol name should be abandoned because public trust could never be regained. Of course, the company was not at fault: There was no culpability, no carelessness. The cause was right. Admittedly, in keeping faith with a product there is a thin line between a positive commitment and recalcitrant stubbornness to face up to any problem and accept any blame. But J&J's faith in Tylenol was justified, and without it the company would have had no chance of resurrecting the product and its market share.

Johnson & Johnson strove to protect its public image of being a socially responsible and caring firm. The following Information Box discusses *social responsibility* and presents the J&J credo regarding this. It is interesting to note that this credo is still prominently positioned in company annual reports ten years later. If there was to be any chance for a fairly quick recovery from adversity, this public image had to be guarded, no matter how beset it was. With the plight of Tylenol well known, with corrective actions prompt and thorough, many people were thus assured that safety was restored. We should note here that for the public image to be regained under adverse circumstances, the corrective actions must be well publicized. Public relations efforts and good communication with the media are essential for this. And, again, it helps when the fault of the catastrophe is clearly not the firm's.

A superb job was done in aggressively bringing back the Tylenol brand. In so doing, coordination was essential. Efforts to safeguard the public image had to be reasonably successful, the cause of the disaster needed to be conclusively established, the likelihood of the event ever happening again had to be seen as virtually impossible. Then aggressive promotional efforts could fuel the recovery.

Johnson & Johnson's efforts to come back necessarily focused on correcting the problem. Initially it designed a tamper-resistant container to prevent the kind of tragedy that had occurred in Chicago. Extra-strength capsules were now to be sold only in new triple-sealed packages. When another death occurred in 1986, the company dropped capsules entirely and offered Tylenol only in tablet form.

With the safety features in place, J&J then used heavy promotion. This included consumer advertising, with the theme of safety assurance and company social responsibility. J&J offered to exchange capsules for tablets at no charge. It

---

INFORMATION BOX

SOCIAL RESPONSIBILITY AND THE JOHNSON & JOHNSON'S CREDO REGARDING IT

We can define social responsibility as the sense of responsibility a firm has for the needs of society, over and above its commitment to maximizing profits and stockholders interests. The following credo of J & J illustrates the wide circle of corporate social responsibility that more and more firms are beginning to accept.

Johnson & Johnson's Credo[9]

We believe our first responsibility is to the doctors, nurses, and patients, to mothers and all others who use our products and services. In meeting their needs everything we do must be of high quality. We must constantly strive to reduce our costs in order to maintain reasonable prices. Customers' orders must be serviced promptly and accurately. Our suppliers and distributors must have an opportunity to make a fair profit.

We are responsible to our employees, the men and women who work with us throughout the world. Everyone must be considered as an individual. We must respect their dignity and recognize their merit. They must have a sense of security in their jobs. Compensation must be fair and adequate, and working conditions clean, orderly, and safe. Employees must feel free to make suggestions and complaints. There must be equal opportunity for employment, development, and advancement for those qualified. We must provide competent management, and their actions must be just and ethical.

We are responsible to the communities in which we live and work and to the world community as well. We must be good citizens—support good works and charities and bear our fair share of taxes. We must encourage civic improvements and better health and education. We must maintain in good order the property we are privileged to use, protecting the environment and natural resources.

Our final responsibility is to our stockholders. Business must make a sound profit. We must experiment with new ideas. Research must be carried on, innovative programs developed and mistakes paid for. New equipment must be purchased, new facilities provided, and new products launched. Reserves must be created to provide for adverse times. When we operate according to these principles, the stockholders should realize a fair return.

"Such statements are only pious platitudes. Social responsibility requires more than lip service." How would you answer this?

---

offered millions of newspaper coupons good for $2.50 toward the purchase of Tylenol. Retailers were also given incentives to back Tylenol through discounts, advertising allowances, and full refunds for recalled capsules with all handling costs paid. These efforts, directed to consumers and retailers alike, bolstered dealer confidence in the resurgence of the brand.

[9] From a company recruiting brochure and annual reports.

UPDATE

Johnson & Johnson has been an enduring growth company, with sales reaching $36 billion in 2003, and profits $6.6 billion. It ranks as the largest and most diversified health care company in the world. Its products now range from blockbuster prescription drugs, to professional products such as sutures, surgical accessories, and catheters, to a wide list of consumer products such as Tylenol, bandages, and toiletries.

With this broad product mix, how important is Tylenol to J&J today? In 1997, $1.3 billion, or almost 6 percent, came from Tylenol. (In 1982, at the time of the contamination, Tylenol contributed 8 percent of the $5.9 billion total company sales.) J&J heavily promoted Tylenol to maintain this prominence. In 1997, for example, the company's domestic ad budget for Tylenol was estimated at $250 million, more than Coca-Cola spent for Coke.[10]

WHAT CAN BE LEARNED?

Any company's nightmare is having its product linked to death or injury. Such a calamity invariably results in fear and loss of public confidence in the product and the firm. At worst, such disaster can kill a company, as happened with some canned-food firms whose products were contaminated with the deadly botulism toxin. The more optimistic projections would have a firm losing years of time and money it had invested in a brand, with the brand never able to regain its former robustness. In the throes of the catastrophe, J&J executives grappled with the major decision of abandoning the brand at the height of its popularity or keeping it. The decision could have gone either way. Now with hindsight, we know that the decision not to abandon was unmistakably correct, but at the time it was recklessly courageous.

Faced with a catastrophe, a brand may still be saved, but cost might be staggering. J&J successfully brought back Tylenol, but it cost hundreds of millions of dollars. The company's size at the time, over $5 billion in sales from a diversified product line, enabled it to handle the costs without jeopardy. A smaller firm would not have been able to weather this, especially without a broad product line.

Whenever product safety is an issue, the danger of lawsuits must be reckoned with. In the absence of corporate neglect, the swift constructive reaction, and the fact that the company could hardly have anticipated a madman, J&J escaped the worst scenario regarding litigation. Still, hundreds of millions of dollars in lawsuits were filed. Such suits accused J&J of failing to package Tylenol in a tamper-proof container, and the legal expenses of defending were high. The threat of litigation must be a major consideration for any firm. Even if the organization is relatively blameless, legal costs can run into the millions, and no one can predict the decisions of juries.

---

[10] Thomas Easton and Stephen Herrera, "J&J's Dirty Little Secret," *Forbes* (January 12, 1998), p. 44.

Copycat crimes are a danger. Although other firms in an industry stand to gain an advantage in a competitor's crisis, they and firms in related industries need to be alert for copycat crimes. By November, a month after the deaths, the Food and Drug Administration had received more than 270 reports of chemicals, pills, poisons, needles, pins, and razor blades in everything from food to drinks to medications. Fortunately, no deaths resulted from these incidents. But FDA Commissioner Hayes worried: "My greatest fear is that because of the notoriety of the case and the financial damage to the company, someone else will take out his or her grudges on a product and do something similar."[11] Actually, the Tylenol case was not the first time products had been deliberately contaminated. Eyedrops, nasal sprays, milk of magnesia, foods, and cosmetics have all been targets of tampering. An Oregon man was sentenced to twenty years in prison for attempting to extort diamonds from grocery chains by putting cyanide in food products on their shelves.

A firm can come back from extreme adversity with good crisis management. Certainly, one of the major things we can learn from this case is that it is possible to come back from extreme adversity. Before the Tylenol episode, most experts did not realize this. The general opinion was that severe negative publicity resulted in such an image destruction that recovery could take years. The most optimistic predictions were that Tylenol might recover to about a 20 to 21 percent market share in a year; the pessimistic predictions were that the brand would never recover and should be abandoned.[12] Actually, in eight months, Tylenol had regained almost all of its market share, to a satisfactory 35 percent. For such a recovery, a firm has to manifest unselfish concern, quick corrective action, and unsparing spending, and it must have a good public image before the catastrophe.

Contingency planning can aid crisis management. Although not all crisis possibilities can be foreseen, or even imagined, many can be identified. For example, contingency plans for worse-case scenarios can be developed for the possibility of food and medicine tampering or the loss of major executives in an accident of some sort. Sometimes in such planning, precautionary moves may become evident for minimizing the potential dangers. For example, with food and medicine tampering, different containers and sealed bottle tops might virtually eliminate the danger. And with executive accidents, many firms have a policy that key executives not fly on the same flight or ride in the same car.

CONSIDER

Can you think of other learning insights?

QUESTIONS

1. Did J&J move too far in recalling all Extra-Strength Tylenol capsules? Would not a sufficient action have been to recall only those in the Chicago area, thus saving millions of dollars? Discuss.

---

[11] "Lessons That Emerge from Tylenol Disaster," *U.S. News & World Report* (October 18, 1982), p. 68.

[12] "J&J Will Pay Dearly to Cure Tylenol," *Business Week* (November 20, 1982), p. 37.

2. How helpful do you think the marketing research results were in the decision on keeping the Tylenol name?

3. "We must assume that someone had a terrible grudge against J&J to have perpetrated such a crime." Discuss.

4. "J&J's 'recovery' has to be attributed to the fact that some evil person was to blame, and not J&J. The situation would not have worked out so well if J&J had major culpability." Discuss.

5. Assuming that J&J was at least partially to blame in not having adequate security, for example, should it have revised its crisis plan, and if so, how? Support your position.

6. Compare and contrast the handling of the Tylenol crisis with that of Perrier in a previous chapter. What learning insights can you suggest for the handling of these two crises?

HANDS-ON EXERCISES

1. Assume this scenario: It has been established that the fault of the contamination was accidental introduction of cyanide at a company plant. Now, how will you, as CEO of J&J, direct your recovery strategy? Give your rationale.

2. Assume this scenario: It has been established that the fault of the contamination was deliberate introduction of cyanide by a disgruntled employee. This person had a serious grievance about sexual harassment, and such grievances in the past had always been downplayed. The publicity about this has leaked out. Now, as CEO, what would you do?

TEAM DEBATE EXERCISE

Debate both sides of the burning issue at the height of the crisis of keeping the Tylenol name and trying to recoup it, or abandoning it. You must not use the benefit of hindsight for this exercise.

INVITATION TO RESEARCH

Can you find any instances of J&J not always having been a good citizen with superb customer concern? If so, investigate and draw conclusions about J&J's enviable position as a role model. Are there any learning insights?

PART TWO

RISKS IN
MERGER MANIA

CHAPTER SEVEN

Snapple: Overspending for an Acquisition

*I*n late 1994, Quaker Oats CEO William D. Smithburg bought Snapple Beverage Company for $1.7 billion. Many thought he had paid too much for this maker of non-carbonated fruit-flavored drinks and iced teas. But in a similar acquisition eleven years before, he had outbid Pillsbury to buy Stokely–Van Camp, largely for its Gatorade, then a $90 million sports drink. Despite criticisms of that purchase, Gatorade went on to become a billion-dollar brand, and Smithburg was a hero. He was not to be a hero with Snapple.

THE COMPANY, QUAKER OATS

Quaker Oats had nearly $6.4 billion in fiscal 1995 sales, of which $1.7 billion was from foreign operations. Its brands were generally strong in particular grocery products and beverage areas. In hot cereals, generations had used Quaker oatmeal, and it was still the number-three selling brand in the overall cereal category. Quaker's ready-to-eat cereals included Cap'n Crunch and Life brands. The firm was a leading competitor in the fast-growing rice cake and granola bar categories, and also in rice and pasta with its Rice-A-Roni, Pasta Roni, and Near East brands. Other products included Aunt Jemima frozen products, French toast, pancake mixes, and syrups; Celeste frozen pizza; as well as grits, tortilla flour, and corn meal.

With the purchase of Snapple, sales of its beverage operation would approach $2 billion or about one-third of total corporate sales. Gatorade alone accounted for $1.3 billion worldwide in fiscal 1995 and growth continued with sales in the United States increasing 7 percent over the previous year, while overseas the gain was a whopping 51 percent. In order to help pay for the Snapple acquisition, several mature but still moneymaking units were divested, including pet foods and chocolates.

THE SNAPPLE ACQUISITION

The Snapple brand had a modest beginning in 1972 in Brooklyn, New York, and its beverages were initially sold to health-food stores. As the healthy lifestyle became popular among certain segments of the general public, Snapple's sales for a time increased as much as 60 to 70 percent a year, especially in the Northeast and West

Coast. In 1992, it was purchased for $27.9 million by Boston-based Thomas H. Lee Co., which took the now-trendy brand public and built it up to almost $700 million in sales.

Unlike Gatorade, however, Snapple faced formidable competitors, including Coke's Fruitopia and Pepsi's joint venture with Lipton, which used low prices to capture 31 percent of the iced-tea market. Snapple's growth rate had turned to declines by December 1994 when, in an outpouring of supreme confidence in his own judgment, Smithburg bought Snapple for $1.7 billion. Before long, many said he had paid about $1 billion too much. Table 7.1 shows the quarterly sales results of Snapple since June 1993 before the acquisition, and after the acquisition.

William Smithburg

At the time of the purchase, Smithburg was fifty-six-years old, but looked younger. He liked to wear suspenders stretched tightly over muscular shoulders that he had developed from years of tournament handball. He had been CEO at Quaker Oats since 1981 and had evolved from a flashy boy wonder to a seasoned executive. He was also a fitness buff, and perhaps this colored his zeal for products like Gatorade and Snapple.

His interest in fitness developed as a result of a childhood bout with polio. While he recovered with no permanent damage, the experience shaped his life: "As soon as I started to walk and run again, I said, 'I have to stay healthy,' and it just became part of my life."[1] In his long tenure as CEO, that passion shaped Quaker, too. The company developed extensive fitness programs, including a heavily subsidized health club at headquarters. Quaker's product line, also, had increasingly emphasized low-fat foods compatible with the healthy lifestyle.

Indicative of Smithburg's personality, after graduating from DePaul University in 1960 with a BS degree in economics and marketing, he defied his father by

TABLE 7.1 Snapple's Sales Growth, 1993–1996

	Sales Growth (in millions)							
	1993	%	1994	%	1995	%	1996	%
1st quarter			$134		$112	–12%		
2nd quarter	$130		243	+87%	200	–18%	$180	–10%
3rd quarter	203		191	– 6%				–20%
4th quarter	118		105	–11%				

Source: 1995 Quaker Annual Report, and various 1996 updates.

Note: While we do not have complete information for all the quarters, still the negative sales since the second quarter of 1994—before the Snapple acquisition—can be readily seen: Every quarter since then has seen losses from the same quarter the preceding year.

[1] Greg Burns, "Crunch Time At Quaker Oats," *Business Week* (September 23, 1996), p. 72.

quitting his first job only three days later. He decided to enroll in Northwestern's business school.

With an MBA in hand he joined the Leo Burnett ad agency, and later, McCann Erickson. After five years of ad agency experience, he went to Quaker as brand manager for frozen waffles in 1966. There it took him ten years to become executive vice president of U.S. grocery products, Quaker's biggest division. Five years later in 1981 he became CEO, and was named chairman two years after that.

The same year he became chairman, he acquired Stokely–Van Camp, overbidding Pillsbury's $62-per-share bid with a $77 offer, which carried a price tag of $238 million. His own investment banker considered this too steep, and critics in the business press abounded. But Smithburg had done his homework, and his intuition was prescient. He recognized the potential in Stokely's Gatorade, a sport drink meant to replenish lost salts and fluids of athletes. "I'd been drinking Gatorade myself, and I knew the product worked."[2] A $90 million brand in 1983, by 1996 this was a $1.3 billion brand and held 80 percent of the growing sport-drink market.

Somehow, Smithburg did not do his homework well with Snapple, despite its seeming similarity to Gatorade.

Rationale for the Snapple Purchase

Snapple was the largest acquisition in Quaker's history. The *Quaker Oats 1995 Annual Report* discussed the rationale for this purchase and the "growth opportunity it offers to shareholders":

> Snapple appeals to all ages with its incomparable flavor variety in premium iced teas and juice drinks. Current sales are concentrated in the Northeast and West Coast. So, the rest of the country presents fertile territory for developing the brand. Because of its excellent cold-channel distribution, the Snapple brand has taught us a great deal about reaching consumers outside our traditional grocery channels. We can apply this knowledge to Gatorade thirst quencher, thereby enhancing its availability as well.[3]

So, Smithburg saw great opportunity to expand distribution of Snapple geographically from its present regional concentration. He thought it had wide appeal and that it could enhance sales of the already highly successful Gatorade.

Snapple beverages held good regional market positions in both the premium ready-to-drink tea and single-serve juice-drink categories. It was seemingly well positioned if consumer preferences continued to shift to all-natural beverages—and away from highly carbonated, artificially flavored, and chemically preserved soft drinks.

Apparently not the least of the reasons for Smithburg's infatuation with Snapple was that it had a "sexy aura," even though problems were already emerging when he bought it. He liked to contrast it with Quaker's pet food: Pet food "was a dead, flat business with five or six big companies beating their brains out in it."[4] So, it was not

[2] *Ibid.*, p. 74.
[3] *Quaker Oats 1995 Annual Report*, p. 6.
[4] Burns, p. 74.

surprising that the pet food business, which had been acquired less than nine years before, was sold a few months after Snapple was acquired.

Other speculations as to why Smithburg chased Snapple, besides misreading the growth potential, were that he wanted to make Quaker, which was a hotly rumored acquisition candidate, less vulnerable to a takeover. Some even speculated that Smithburg became bored with Quaker and sought the excitement of a splashy deal.[5]

PROBLEMS

One would think that Snapple's resemblance to Gatorade would bring instant compatibility and efficiencies in marketing the two brands. After all, with the proven success of Gatorade, Quaker had become the third-largest beverage company, after only Coca-Cola and Pepsi. And, like Gatorade, Snapple was a flavored, noncarbonated drink. Surely this was a compatible marriage.

But this was not the case. Only after it bought Snapple did Quaker fully realize that both Snapple's production and distribution systems were completely different from Gatorade's.

Quaker's production and distribution of Gatorade was state of the art. Its computers were closely integrated with those of its largest distributors and automatically kept these distributors well stocked, but not overstocked, with Gatorade.

The advertising of Gatorade was also markedly different. Several hundred million dollars a year was spent for Gatorade, with highly successful ads featuring Chicago Bulls star, Michael Jordan (Jordan was also a personal friend of Smithburg). Snapple's advertising, on the other hand, had run out of steam and was notably ineffective.

The production, distribution, and marketing efforts of Snapple at the time of the purchase were haphazard. Bottling was contracted to outsiders, and this resulted in expensive contracts for excess capacity when demand slowed. Snapple's 300 distributors delivered directly to stores; Gatorade's distributors delivered to warehouses. Quaker's efforts to consolidate the two distribution systems only created havoc. It tried to take the supermarket accounts away from Snapple distributors and give them to Gatorade, directing that the Snapple people concentrate on convenience stores and mom-and-pop retailers. Not surprising, Snapple distributors refused this downsizing of their operations. Eventually, Quaker backed down. But efforts at creating coordination and distribution efficiencies for 1995 were seriously delayed.

At the same time, Quaker failed to come up with a new business plan for Snapple in time for the peak 1995 season, which began in April. Tim Healy, president of a Snapple distributor in Chicago, noted, "there was no marketing plan, no initiatives, and no one to talk to [at Quaker]."[6]

The result was that 1995 sales of Snapple fell 9 percent, and there was a $100 million loss.

---

[5] *Ibid.*

[6] Scott McMurray, "Drumming Up New Business: Quaker Marches Double Time to Put Snap Back in its Snapple Drink Line," *U.S. News & World Report* (April 22, 1996), p. 59.

CORRECTIVE EFFORTS, 1996

As the dismal results of 1995 became widely publicized, Quaker faced the urgent need to vindicate the purchase of Snapple and somehow resurrect its failing fortunes. To aid the distributors, the company streamlined operations to reduce from two weeks to three days the time it took to get orders from bottlers to distributors. To do so, it coordinated its computers with the top fifty distributors, who represented 80 percent of Snapple's sales, so that it could replenish their inventory automatically, the way it was doing with Gatorade.

The company also introduced some packaging and product changes that it hoped would be more appealing both to dealers and to customers. It brought out thirty-two- and sixty-four-ounce plastic bottles of Snapple for families, along with twelve-packs and four-packs in glass bottles. It reduced the number of flavors from fifty to thirty-five and made taste improvements in some of the retained flavors. At the same time seasonal products were introduced, such as cider tea for Halloween.

To develop distributor enthusiasm, a two-day meeting had been held in San Diego. Quaker brought in comedian Bill Cosby to entertain and General Norman Schwarzkopf to motivate with a stirring speech on leadership. Then distributors were told that highly visible Snapple coolers would be placed in supermarkets, convenience stores, and schools—just like Coke and Pepsi.[7]

The weakness in the 1995 advertising also received, hopefully, corrective action. Quaker enlisted the creativity of Spike Lee, who had designed hyperkinetic TV commercials for Nike. While the campaign kept Snapple's "Made from the best stuff on earth," the new ads focused on Snapple's hope to become America's third choice in soft drinks, behind Coke and Pepsi, with such slogans as, "We want to be No. 3," and "Threedom = freedom." The goal of the advertising campaign, Smithburg explained, was to maintain Snapple's "funky" image while broadening its appeal beyond the East and West Coast markets.[8]

Still, sales languished. In late July, a huge nationwide sampling campaign was undertaken. In a $40 million effort, millions of bottles of the fruit-juice and ice-tea lines were given away during the height of the selling season, hopefully to spur consumer interest regardless of cost.

RESULTS OF 1996 EFFORTS

Unfortunately, the results of the summer giveaways were dismal. Instead of gaining market share during the important summer selling months, Snapple lost ground.

Snapple tea sales fell 14 percent, and juice sales fell 15 percent. This compared poorly with industry tea sales, which also dropped, but only 4 percent, and industry juice sales, which fell 5 percent during a particularly cool summer in the Northeast.[9]

---

[7] Zina Moukheiber, "He Who Laughs Last," *Forbes* (January 1, 1996), p. 42.

[8] *Ibid.*, p. 60.

[9] "Snapple Continues to Lose Market Share Despite Big Giveaway," *Wall Street Journal* (October 8, 1996), p. B9.

Relentless media scrutiny even found fault with the way in which Snapple was being given away. One critic observed the sampling at a New Jersey concert in which sixteen-ounce cans were handed out only twenty feet from the entrance in front of signs prohibiting food or drink beyond the gate. Most people barely had time to taste the drink before throwing it away. Furthermore, "for its brand undermining efforts, Quaker gets no consumer research either. Solution: In exchange for the self-serve sample, ask a few short ... questions."[10]

The reputation of Smithburg was being eroded, his early success with Gatorade not enough to weather more current adversity. Online, cybercritics assailed him. In conference calls with financial analysts, he was peppered with barbed questions about this $600 million beverage for which he paid $1.7 billion. "Even my dad," Smithburg laughed, "he says, 'What are you doing with Snapple?'"[11]

Under pressure, Smithburg cast off president and chief operating officer Philip Marineau, whom he had been grooming as heir apparent for many years. This departure was widely interpreted to be the result of Snapple's failure to justify its premium pricing, with Marineau the scapegoat. Nine months later, Donald Uzzi was replaced as president of Quaker's North America beverages unit. His successor was Michael Schott, former vice president of sales of Nantucket Nectars, a small, privately held drink maker.

Some critics assumed that Smithburg's job was in jeopardy, that he could not escape personal blame for the acquisition snafu. Still, the past success of Smithburg with Gatorade continued to sustain him. The board of directors remained supportive, although they denied him any bonus for 1995. What made the continued loyalty of the board more uncertain was Quaker's stock price, which had fallen 10 percent since just before the acquisition, even as the Standard & Poor's 500-stock index had climbed to new highs.

If Snapple could not be revitalized, Smithburg had several options regarding it. All of these, of course, would be admissions of defeat and that a major mistake was made in acquiring Snapple. Any one of them might cost Smithburg his job.

One option would be to spin off the ailing Snapple to shareholders, perhaps under the wing of the booming Gatorade. Smithburg was no stranger to such maneuverings since he had divested retail, toy, and pet-food operations in his years as CEO. An outright sale could probably only be made at bargain-basement prices and would certainly underscore the billion-dollar mistake of Smithburg's purchase. A less extreme option would be to draw back from attempts to make Snapple a national brand, and keep it as a regional brand in the Northeast and West Coast where it was well entrenched.

Perseverance

By early 1997, Smithburg still had not given up on Snapple. Quaker Oats announced it was pumping $15 million into a major four-month sweepstakes promotion for Snapple's

---

[10] Gabe Lowry, "They Can't Even Give Snapple Away Right," *Brandweek* (September 30, 1996), p. 16.

[11] Burns, p. 71.

diet drinks, this to start right after the new year when consumers might be more concerned with undoing the excesses of the holiday season and when competitors would be less likely to advertise chilled drinks in cold weather. The theme was to be "Escape with Taste," and among other winners would be fifty grand-prize trips to the refurbished Doral Resort and Spa in Miami. If the campaign developed any momentum, it should carry over to a retooled image campaign planned immediately afterward in the spring.

This promotion was the first from new president Mike Schott, and it built on one product category that managed to grow 16 percent in convenience stores during the previous summer, even as core juices and teas slid drastically. The promotion plan was well received by distributors: "This one [promotion] is wonderfully thought out," one distributor said. "Diet drinks in the first quarter? It's a no-brainer."[12]

Since being named the brand's president late in the year, Schott had been visiting distributors to build up relations, offer greater support, and dispel rumors that Snapple was going to retrench to a regional brand. Still, Snapple's sales and profits showed no rebound.

On March 27, 1997, Smithburg finally threw in the towel; he sold the ailing Snapple to Nelson Peltz, chief executive of the smallish Triarc Cos., owner of RC Cola and Arby's restaurants. The price was shockingly low, only $300 million, or just over half of Snapple's $550 million in sales—this for a brand for which Smithburg had paid $1.7 billion only three years before. The founder of Snapple, Leonard Marsh, who had previously sold his controlling interest, said that "they stole the company."[13]

Undoubtedly, Quaker was desperate to sell the money-draining Snapple, but at such a fire-sale price? As it turned out, the company had few options. Major suitors, such as PepsiCo, Coca-Cola, and Procter & Gamble, only wanted to consider a Snapple purchase along with Gatorade, Smithburg's crown jewel and most profitable brand.

On April 24, 1997, The *Wall Street Journal* reported that Quaker Oats had posted a $1.11 billion quarterly loss reflecting the final resolution of the Snapple affair, and that William Smithburg was stepping down. "Many investors have been asking for a long time why he hasn't stepped aside sooner," said one food-industry analyst.[14]

ANALYSIS

Beyond doubt, the price paid for Snapple was wildly extravagant. Demand was slumping, distribution inefficiencies had surfaced, and the advertising had run out of steam. We can understand Smithburg's reasoning that he had bought Gatorade at a high price and turned it into a winner. Why shouldn't he do the same thing with Snapple? The price paid for Gatorade, $238 million for sales of $90 million at the time, was roughly comparable to the $1.7 billion for Snapple sales of almost $700 million.

[12] Gerry Khermouch, "Snapple Diet Line Gets $15 mil Push," *Brandweek* (November 4, 1996), p. 1.

[13] I. Jeanne Dugan, "Will Triarc Make Snapple Crackle?" *Business Week* (April 28, 1997), p. 64.

[14] Michael J. McCarthy, "Quaker Oats Posts $1.11 Billion Quarterly Loss," *Wall Street Journal* (April 24, 1997), pp. A3, A12.

But we can surely fault Smithburg for not demanding that his subordinates analyze more thoroughly the compatibility of the two operations. There should have been no surprises after the sale that the distribution systems of Gatorade and Snapple were not compatible and maybe could not be made so. Furthermore, it seems only reasonable to expect for a purchase of this magnitude that adequate research and planning would also have been done concerning the promotional efforts of Snapple, whether they were adequate for the coming year or whether changes needed to be made, and, if so, what changes. Should not stockholders expect that rather solid business plans would be in place before the acquisition was finalized by Quaker? Without such, the decision to let go of $1.7 billion seems rather like decision making by hunch and intuition. Perhaps it was.

The spinning of wheels in 1996, after the disastrous 1995, suggests that Smithburg had fallen prey to the decision-making error called *escalating commitment.* This is a resolution to increase efforts and resources to pursue a course of action that is *not* working, to be unable to "call it quits."[15]

See the following Information Box for advice by John Schermerhorn on not being trapped in an escalation commitment.

INFORMATION BOX

HOW TO AVOID THE ESCALATION TRAP

When should we call it quits, admit the mistake, and leave the scene as gracefully as possible, amid the cries of critics and the debris of sunk costs in a hopeless cause, and even embarrassment and shame and possible ouster by a board of directors tormented by irate investors? John Schermerhorn offers these guidelines to avoid staying in a lost cause too long:[16]

1. Set advance limits on your involvement in a particular course of action, and stick to them.
2. Make your own decisions; others may also be prone to escalation.
3. Carefully consider why you are continuing this course of action; unless there are sufficient reasons to continue, don't.
4. Consider the costs of continuing, and the savings in costs as a reason to discontinue.
5. Be on guard for escalation tendencies, especially where a big commitment has already been made.

Do you think Drucker's idea of an escalating commitment and Schermerhorn's suggestions for avoiding it have any downsides? In other words, when do you call it quits?

---

[15] Peter F. Drucker, "The Global Economy and the Nation-State," *Foreign Affairs,* vol. 76 (September–October 1997), pp. 159–171.

[16] John R. Schermerhorn, Jr., *Management,* 6th ed. (New York: Wiley, 1999), p. 67.

You can imagine how the big commitment that had already been made for Snapple would have stimulated the escalating commitment to the fullest: "We have too much invested for this to fail."

If the product life cycle of Snapple had peaked before the Quaker purchase, this would account for the inability of Quaker management to reverse the downward trend of sales and profits. But such a possibility should surely have been considered before the acquisition decision. (See the following Information Box for a discussion of the product life cycle.)

One would think that the best minds in a major corporation, and any outside consultants used, should have been able to bring Snapple to more healthy national

---

INFORMATION BOX

THE PRODUCT LIFE CYCLE

Just as people and animals do, products go through stages of growth and maturity—that is, life cycles. They are affected by different competitive conditions at each stage, ranging often from no competition in the early stages to intense competition later on. We can recognize four stages in a product's life cycle: introduction, growth, maturity, and decline.

Figure 7.1 depicts three different product life cycles. Number 1 is that of a standard item in which sales take some time to develop and then eventually begin a slow decline. Number 2 shows a life cycle for a product in which a modification of the product or else the uncovering of a new market rejuvenates the product so that it takes off on a new cycle of growth (the classic examples of this are Listerine, originally sold as a mild external antiseptic, and Arm & Hammer Baking Soda, which was repositioned as a deodorizer). Number 3 shows the life cycle for a fad item or one experiencing rapid technological change and intense competition. Notice its sharp rise in sales and the abrupt downturn.

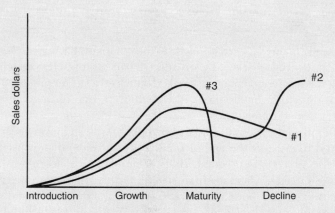

Figure 7.1 The product life cycle.

(Continues)

THE PRODUCT LIFE CYCLE *(Continued)*

Which life cycle most closely represented Snapple at the time of the acquisition? Snapple was definitely on a downward trend, which began the summer before Quaker purchased it, and this downward trend continued and even accelerated through 1995 and 1996. (See Table 7.1.) This suggests that Snapple had reached the maturity stage of its life cycle. As an admittedly trendy product, its curve in the worst scenario would resemble stage 3, the fad. An optimistic scenario would see a stage-2 curve, with strong efforts in 1997 bringing a rejuvenation. Perhaps the more likely life cycle is something akin to stage 1, with a slow downturn continuing for a lengthy period while aggressive efforts fail to stem the decline in an environment of more intense competition and less eager demand.

Do you agree with this prognosis? Why or why not?

and international sales, or at least to a more profitable situation, even if the product life cycle had become less favorable. But in high-stake, near-crisis situations, prudent judgment may be abandoned as money is flung about in desperate efforts to turn things around. Often such merely aggravates the situation, as was the case with the expensive and poorly planned $40 million sampling effort and the $15 million sweepstakes program.

Finally, it is worth emphasizing again that in the acquisition quest, extensive homework should be done. These are *major* decisions. Hundreds of millions of dollars, even billions, are at stake if an unwise acquisition has to be divested a few years later. In addition, there is the management time taken up with a poorly performing product line at the expense of other responsibilities.

UPDATE

Quaker's Gatorade remained a great strength of the company, having an estimated 78 percent of the sport-drink market. This made Quaker an attractive acquisition. In 2000, Coca-Cola was interested in buying Quaker, but faced a sticker price of $16 billion that its board of directors, among them Warren Buffett, one of the country's most astute investors, decided to reject.

Just a few months later, PepsiCo bid $14.02 billion, which Quaker accepted. The deal was expected to close by the end of June 2001, but federal antitrust enforcers continued to raise objections. Federal Trade Commission concern was that this merger would give Quaker's Gatorade brand even greater dominance once it became part of Pepsi's powerful distribution network. Coca-Cola's Powerade brand share was only 15 percent of the sport-drink market, while Pepsi's All-Sport, which the company agreed to sell, was a distant third. Opponents of the deal argued that it would enable Pepsi to gain too much clout with retailers, particularly convenience stores where

Gatorade and other Pepsi products such as Mountain Dew were already strong. FTC approval was still pending, although the deal had already been approved by several foreign regulators, including the European Union's antitrust authority.[17]

WHAT CAN BE LEARNED?

The illusion of compatibility. Bad acquisition decisions—in which the merger or acquisition turns out to be a mistake—often result from miscalculating the mutual compatibility of the two operations. Expectations are that consolidating various operations will result in significant cost savings. For example, instead of two headquarters' staffs, these can be reduced perhaps to a beefed-up single one. Sometimes even certain aspects of production can be combined, allowing some facilities to be closed for greater cost efficiencies. Computer operations, sales forces, and distribution channels might be combined. But for these combinations and consolidations to be feasible, the two operations essentially should be compatible.

As we saw in the case, the distribution channels of Snapple and Gatorade were not compatible, and efforts to consolidate brought serious rancor from those who would be affected. Quaker had failed to do its homework and probe deeply enough to determine the real depth of compatibility, not merely assuming compatibility because of product similarities.

Certainly we see many acquisitions and mergers of dissimilar operations: These are called *diversifications.* Some of these have little or no compatibility, and may not provide significant opportunities for reducing costs. Instead, they may be made because of perceived growth opportunities, to lessen dependence on mature products, to smooth out seasonality, and so on. Unfortunately, many of these dissimilar diversifications prove to be disappointing, and are candidates for divestiture some years later.

The acquisition contest. Once an acquisition candidate is identified, negotiations sometimes become akin to an athletic contest: Who will win? Not infrequently, several firms may be drawn to what they see as an attractive would-be acquisition, and a bidding war commences. Sometimes management of the takeover firm strongly resists. So, the whole situation evolves into a contest, almost a game. And aggressive executives get caught up in this game and sometimes overreach themselves in their struggle to win. No matter how attractive a takeover firm might be, if you pay way too much for it, this was a bad buy.

The paradox of perseverance: When do we give up? We admire people who persevere despite great odds: the student who continues with school even though family and work commitments may drag it out for ten years or more; the athlete

---

[17] John R. Wilke and Betsy McKay, "PepsiCo Cites FTC for Further Delay of Quaker Deal," *Wall Street Journal* (June 11, 2001), p. B6.

who never gives up; the author who has a hundred rejection slips, but still keeps trying. So, how long should we persevere in what seems totally a losing cause? Isn't there such a thing as futility and unrealistic dreams, so that constructive efforts should be directed elsewhere? The enigma of futility has even been captured in classic literature with Don Quixote, the "Man from LaMancha," tilting his lance at windmills.

The line is blurred between perseverance and futile stubbornness, the escalating commitment of Peter Drucker. Circumstances vary too much to formulate guidelines. Still, if a direct assault continues to fail, perhaps it is time to make an end run.

When should a weak product be axed? Weak products tend to take up too much management, sales force, and advertising attention, efforts that could better be spent making healthy products better and/or developing replacements. Publicity about such products may even cause customer misgivings and tarnish the company's image. This suggests that weak and/or unprofitable products or divisions ought to be gotten rid of, provided that the problems are enduring and not a temporary aberration.

Not all weak products should be pruned, however; rationale for keeping them may be strong. In particular, the weak products may be necessary to complete a line to benefit sales of other products. They may be desirable for customer goodwill. Some weak products may enhance the company's image or prestige. Although such weak products make no money in themselves, still their intrinsic value to the firm may be substantial. Other weak products may merely be unproven, too new in their product life cycle to have become profitable; in their growth and maturity stage they may contribute satisfactory profits. Finally, possibly a new business strategy will rejuvenate the weak product. That is the hope, and the proffered justification for keeping a weak product when its demise is overdue.

So, where did Snapple fit into this theoretical discussion? The only justification for procrastination would seem to be that business strategy alternatives to turn around the brand had not been exhausted. In the meantime, the image of Quaker Oats in the eyes of investors, and the reflection of this in stock prices, was being savaged.

Be cautious with possible fad product life cycles. With hindsight, we can classify Snapple's popularity as a short-term phenomenon. But it was heady and contagious while it lasted. Snapple transformed iced tea into a new-age product by avoiding the need for preservatives and adding fruit flavors and introducing innovative wide-mouth, sixteen-ounce bottles. It also used Howard Stern, with his cult following, as its spokesman.

The public offering of stock in 1993 was sensational. The original offering price was to be $14, but this was raised to $20; in the first day of trading the stock closed at $29. Two years later, Quaker paid $1.7 billion for a company whose founders paid just $500 to acquire the name. But the euphoric life cycle was turning down, and the cult following was distracted by imitators, such as Arizona Iced Tea, Mystic, and Nantucket Nectars, as well as Coke and Pepsi through alliances with Nestea and Lipton.

Perhaps what can be learned is that product life cycles are unpredictable, especially where they involve fad or cult followers who may be as fickle as the wind, and where imitation is easy. To bet one's firm on such an acquisition can be risky indeed. But in truth, Smithburg had faced a similar situation with Gatorade, and won big. The moral: Decision making under uncertainty can be a crap game. But prudence suggests a more cautious approach.

CONSIDER

Can you think of any other learning insights?

QUESTIONS

1. Why do you think the great Snapple giveaway was ineffective?
2. Do you think Snapple could have been turned around? Why or why not?
3. Do you think the premium retail price for Snapple was a serious impediment? Why or why not?
4. "Pouring more money into a lost cause is downright stupid. Smithburg has got to go." Discuss.
5. "This isn't a case where a guy has gone from a genius to a dummy. Who's better at running the company?"[18] Discuss this statement.
6. "What's all the fuss about? Snapple is doing great on our college campus. It's a success, man." Do you agree? Why or why not?
7. Do you drink Snapple? If not, why not? Is so, how often, and how well do you like it?
8. Do you think Snapple should have been sold for $300 million? Why or why not?

HANDS-ON EXERCISES

Before

1. A major decision is at hand. You are a vice president of the beverage operation at Quaker. William Smithburg is proposing the acquisition of Snapple for some huge sum. Before this decision is made, you have been asked to array any contrary arguments to this expensive acquisition, in other words, to be a devil's advocate (one who takes a contrary position for the sake of argument and clarification of opposing views). What concerns would you raise, and how would you defend them?

[18] Investor quote in Burns, p. 74.

After

2. It is late 1996. You are the assistant to Michael Schott, who has just been named president of Snapple. He asks you to formulate a strategic plan for resurrecting Snapple for 1997. What do you propose? Be as specific as you can, and be prepared to defend your recommendations.

TEAM DEBATE EXERCISE

The acquisition of Snapple is accomplished. Now begins the assimilation. A major debate has ensued regarding whether Snapple should be consolidated with Gatorade, or whether it should remain an independent entity. Debate the two positions as persuasively as possible. Be sure to identify any assumptions made.

INVITATION TO RESEARCH

What is the situation with Snapple and with Smithburg today? Has Snapple prospered under its new ownership? Is Smithburg running any company? Has Quaker been acquired, and, if so, by whom and at what price?

CHAPTER EIGHT

DaimlerChrysler: Blatant Misrepresentation

It was supposed to be so right, almost a merger made in heaven, some said at the beginning. Chrysler was the smallest but since 1994 the most efficient U.S. auto producer, with the highest profit margin. Now its productivity and innovative strength would be blended with the prestige of Daimler's legendary Mercedes-Benz. Furthermore, Chrysler during one of its periodic crises had sold off its international operations to help raise needed money, and this merger would increase international exposure in a big way and mate it with a rich partner. The instigator, Jürgen Schrempp of Daimler, was lauded for his intentions of building a new car company that would have global economies of scale.

Of course, there were two cultures involved, German and American. But in the executive offices, decision making would be shared, with Chrysler's CEO, Robert Eaton, being a co-chairman with Schrempp.

So in November 1998, this merger of "equals" was finalized. And the s____ hit the fan.

CHRYSLER BEFORE THE MERGER

During the previous several decades, Chrysler had had a spotted history.

Some said Lee Iacocca performed a miracle at Chrysler. He became president of an almost-moribund firm in November 1978. It was so bad he turned to Washington to bail out the company, and obtained federal loan guarantees of $1.5 billion to help it survive. By 1983, Iacocca had brought Chrysler to profitability, and then to a strong performance for the next four years. He paid back the entire loan seven years before it was due. Like a phoenix, the reeling number-three automaker had been given new life and respectability. Some said Iacocca should be president of the United States, that his talents were needed in the biggest job of all.

Iacocca turned to other interests in the latter half of the decade, and by 1988, the company was hurting again. To a large extent the new problems reflected capital deprivation: Sufficient money had not been invested in new car and truck designs.

This lack of funds was the result of a 1987 acquisition of American Motors Corporation (AMC). The crown jewel of this buyout was the Jeep line of sport-utility vehicles that appealed to younger, more affluent buyers than the older, lower-income customers of Chrysler. Still, Chrysler found itself saddled with the substantial inefficiencies that had bedeviled AMC.

An aging Iacocca again turned his full attention back to the car business, now seven years after retiring his company's horrendous bank debt. He staked company resources on four high-visibility cars and trucks: a minivan, the Jeep Grand Cherokee, LH sedans, and a full-size pickup. Fearful that the company might not survive until the new models came out, especially if a recession were to occur before then, Iacocca instituted a far-reaching austerity program, which cut $3 billion from the company's $26 billion annual operating costs.

By 1992, the company was riding high. Iacocca retired on December 31, 1992, with a job well done. As he said on TV, "When it's your last turn at bat, it sure is nice to hit a home run."[1] Robert Eaton, formerly with GM of Europe, replaced Iacocca as Chrysler chairman.

As it moved to the millennium, Chrysler prospered because of a combination of innovative designs, segment-leading products, and rising sales throughout the auto industry. See Table 8.1 for the sales and net profit statistics of these golden years for Chrysler relative to its two U.S. competitors, General Motors and Ford.

AFTER THE MERGER

Seldom has a merger turned out worse, and so quickly. Perhaps because of morale problems and too much attention given to smoothing relations between Detroit and Stuttgart, the bottom line of Chrysler was wracked. Or maybe the problems at Chrysler had been latent, below the surface, and only needed the disruption of a massive takeover to emerge. Or could the problems have been triggered by an unwise dictation by the company's German master?

On November 16, 1998, Daimler-Benz issued an additional $36 billion of its stock to buy Chrysler. This when added to the $48 billion value of its existing stock brought total market value of DaimlerChrysler to $84 billion. Early in December 2000, barely two years later, a collapsing DaimlerChrysler stock had a market value of only $39 billion, less than Daimler alone was worth before the deal.

Chrysler was bleeding money. During the second half of 2000, Chrysler lost $1.8 billion and went through $5 billion in cash, this at a time when GM and Ford were still doing well.

By 2000, Eaton was long gone, along with nine other top Chrysler executives, including the renowned designer, Thomas Gale. Then in November 2000, Eaton's successor, James Holden, a Canadian, the last high-level non-German remaining, was also given the ax. His replacement was Daimler executive Dieter Zetsche, forty-seven, a tall German with a walrus mustache. Zetsche brought with him Wolfgang Bernhard, thirty-nine, an intense young man, an engineer with an MBA from Columbia

---

[1] Alex Taylor III, "U.S. Cars Come Back," *Fortune* (November 16, 1992), p. 85.

TABLE 8.1 Sales and Profit Comparisons, Big Three U.S. Automakers, 1993–1998 (millions of dollars)

	1993	1994	1995	1996	1997	1998
Ford						
Sales	108,521	128.439	137,137	146,991	153,637	144,416
Net Profit	2,529	5,308	4,139	4,371	6,920	6,579
	2.3%	4.1%	3.0%	3.0%	4.5%	4.5%
GM						
Sales	138,220	154,951	168,829	164,069	173,168	161,315
Net Profit	2,466	5,659	6,933	4,668	5,972	3,662
	1.8%	3.7%	4.1%	2.8%	3.4%	2.3%
Chrysler						
Sales	43,600	52,235	53,195	61,397	61,147	NA
Net Profit	(2,551)	3,713	2,025	3,529	2,805	NA
	(5.9)%	7.1%	3.8%	5.7%	4.6%	

Sources: Company public records. NA=Not applicable because of merger with Daimler.

Commentary: After a poor year in 1993—a $2.5 billion loss—Chrysler really bounced back, making a profit of $3.7 billion, which was over 7 percent of sales, far above that of its two major competitors. Chrysler continued the strong showing with multibillion-dollar profits from 1994 on. In 1995, its 3.8 percent profit was well above Ford, but slightly less than GM; in 1996 and 1997 its profit margin again was the best. While we do not have specific figures in 1998, we know that this was also a good year. The collapse came in 1999.

Note: These are total company sales, the bulk of which are autos/trucks. But with nonvehicle diversifications, the sales will be somewhat overstated for autos/trucks.

who was a stickler for cost-cutting, as chief operating officer. It could have been worse: Zetsche could have brought a big team from Germany instead of only one other man. Still, indignation surfaced at this putting German executives in top positions at this old American firm—a firm that had played an important part in defeating the Germans in World War II.

Eaton and the rest of the Chrysler hierarchy had found to their dismay that this was not a merger of equals, despite Chairman Schrempp's 1998 statements to the contrary not only to Chrysler top management but also to the SEC (Securities and Exchange Commission), and the inclusion of the Chrysler name in the corporation name. In reality, Chrysler had become only a division of Daimler. In interviews with the media, Schrempp admitted that such subjugation of Chrysler had always been his intention, this a duplicity of no small moment.[2]

Later we will analyze why the merger so quickly proved a disaster, at least in the short and intermediate term. In the longer term, maybe: maybe not.

[2] For example, "A Deal for the History Books: The Auto Takeover May Be Remembered for All of the Wrong Reasons," *Newsweek* (December 11, 2000), p. 57.

Jürgen Schrempp

DaimlerChrysler Chairman, Jürgen Schrempp, a trim fifty-six, had an untarnished reputation going into the Chrysler merger. He began his career with Mercedes as an apprentice mechanic nearly forty years before, and had moved steadily upward. Now he acknowledged that he faced "outstanding" challenges with Chrysler. But he pointed out, "Five years ago in 1995, Daimler-Benz posted a loss of six billion marks [$3 billion]. We turned it around in a matter of two years. I think we have the experience and know-how to attend to matters, and if necessary we'll do that at Chrysler ... Our aim is to be the No. 1 motor company in the world."[3]

Still, there were those who thought he destroyed Chrysler, that "he didn't realize it was the people who counted, not the factories, which were old, or the sales and profits, which could come and go."[4] So, Schrempp either forced or encouraged key people to leave, and some would say these departures were of the heart and soul of Chrysler. His duplicity in misleading top Chrysler management and shareholders that this was to be a merger of equals could hardly be viewed as anything but ambitious conniving.

During the merger finalization, it was predicted that Chrysler would earn more than $5 billion in 2000, this being what it earned in 1998. In late 1999, however, Chrysler President James Holden reduced this prediction to only $2.5 billion because of having to spend billions retooling for new model introductions at a time when an economic slowdown seemed to be looming.

The reduced profit expectation coming so soon after the merger was unacceptable to Schrempp, and he pressured Chrysler to pump up earnings for the first half of the year by building 75,000 more cars and trucks than could readily be sold, with these quickly shipped to dealers. (The accepted accounting practice was to consider a car as revenue to Chrysler when it reached a dealer's lot, not when it was sold by the dealer.) As a result, Chrysler was just short of its $2.5 billion target in the first half of 2000.

Not surprisingly, the inventory buildup resulted in showrooms overflowing with old model minivans, just as new models began arriving in August. With car sales in general now slowing because of the economy, Chrysler had to cut prices even on popular minivans, and it was necessary to increase rebates up to $3,000 on the old models. These price cuts destroyed the profitability of Chrysler all the more since the company in its optimism after record profits in the 1990s had upgraded its cars and trucks, expecting to charge more for them. But with competition increasing and car pricing turning deflationary, such price hikes did not hold up, and this and the rebates severely affected profits in the third and fourth quarters. (See the following Information Box for a discussion of rebates.)

Schrempp Takes Action

With the huge losses in the second half of 2000, Schrempp sent Zetsche to Detroit with simple instructions: "My orders were to fix the place."[5] On his first day Zetsche

---

[3] Williams J. Holstein, "The Conquest of Chrysler," *U.S. News & World Report* (November 27, 2000), p. 54.

[4] Jerry Flint, "Free Chrysler!" *Forbes* (October 30, 2000), p. 132.

[5] Alex Taylor III, "Can the Germans Rescue Chrysler?" *Fortune* (April 30, 2001), p. 109.

INFORMATION BOX

REBATES

A rebate is a promise by a manufacturer to return part of the purchase price directly to the purchaser. The rebate is usually given to consumers, although it can be offered to dealers instead in the expectation that they will pass some or all of the savings along to consumers.

Obviously, the objective of a rebate is to increase sales by giving purchasers a lower price. But why not simply reduce prices? The rebate is used instead of a regular markdown or price reduction because it is perceived as being less permanent than cutting the list price. This can give more promotional push by emphasizing the savings off the regular price, but only for a limited time. Rebates can be effective in generating short-term business, but they may affect business negatively once the rebate has been lifted.

Do you see any dangers with rebates from the manufacturer's viewpoint? As a consumer, would you prefer a rebate to a price reduction, or does it make any difference?

fired the head of sales and marketing. Then in two months he developed a three-year turnaround plan. It called for cutting 26,000 jobs (29 percent of the workforce), reducing the cost of parts by 15 percent, and closing six assembly plants. Zetsche projected a breakeven point by 2002 and an operating profit of $2 billion in 2003.[6] This would still be well below the operating profit of Chrysler in 1993–1997, before the merger, as shown in Table 8.1.

His colleague from Stuttgart, Wolfgang Bernhard, organized engineers and procurement specialists into fifty teams to find ways to save money on parts. Suppliers were told to reduce prices by 5 percent as of January 2001, with a further 10 percent reduction over the next two years. Some companies such as Robert Bosch GmbH, the world's second-largest parts maker, and Federal Mogul, said they would not cut prices. Zetsche observed, "If they do not support us to get to the 15 percent, we have to consider that in our future decisions."[7]

Bernhard also focused attention on improving quality as a way to cut costs. In particular, the four-wheel drive trucks showed up poorly on quality surveys. The company began rigorously evaluating new models for quality while they were still in the design stage, so that parts or manufacturing processes could be changed before too much money had been committed.

Zetsche began to direct much of his attention to bringing back standout designs that Chrysler had been noted for in the 1990s. Of late, design and engineering

[6] *Ibid.*

[7] "Daimler Threatens to Drop Some Suppliers," Bloomberg News as reported in *Cleveland Plain Dealer* (February 28, 2001), p. 6C.

efforts, such as the 2001 minivan and the 2002 Ram, seemed more evolutionary than revolutionary, with leadership allowed to slip while Toyota and Honda became stronger competitors.

Despite increased competition, Zetsche had a unique asset that should help his company regain the edge: the prestige and competence of Mercedes-Benz technology. Mercedes previously had feared diluting its premium brand, but now it was directed to share components with Chrysler. New rear-wheel versions of the Chrysler Concorde and 300M coming out in 2004 and 2005, for example, were planned to make use of Mercedes electronics, transmissions, seat frames, and other parts. "If Zetsche can sprinkle some Mercedes magic on the Chrysler brand without damaging the premium status of Mercedes, Chrysler has a shot at doing well in the future."[8]

To his credit, Zetsche worked hard to overcome the anti-German feelings that initially followed his and Bernhard's arrival. To stem the potential brain drain, he persuaded many senior Chrysler executives to stay. And the drastic cutback of workers and closing of factories before long came to be viewed as necessary cost-cutting to keep the company viable. Even UAW President Steve Yokich endorsed these actions: "[Otherwise] I don't think there would be a Chrysler."[9]

Other Problems for Schrempp

Two other major problems confronted Schrempp. In October 2000, despite misgivings by Chrysler executives, he acquired 34 percent of Mitsubishi Motors, with the option to up that to 100 percent after three years. Hardly had the deal been finalized than Mitsubishi admitted it had misled consumers about product quality for decades. It also announced that losses for the last six months had nearly doubled. Schrempp reacted by installing a turnaround expert as chief operating officer at Mitsubishi and he was accompanied by dozens of Japanese-speaking Daimler executives. All the while the new chief executive, Takashi Sonobe, was quoted as saying that he, not the German team, remained in charge and that he saw no need for big changes. This was a contest of wills.[10]

DaimlerChrysler's Freightliner, the leading North American heavy-truck maker, was also struggling as the North American market hit one of the steepest slumps in a decade. After an aggressive growth policy that involved acquisitions of other truck makers and a heavy investment in a facility for reconditioning used trucks to sustain Freightliner's sale-buyback strategy, demand for new and used heavy trucks plummeted 50 percent, and prices fell sharply. It was expected that Schrempp would install a German national as head of this unit.[11]

---

[8] Detroit manufacturing consultant Ron Harbour, as reported in *Fortune* (April 30, 2001), p. 110.

[9] Taylor, p. 107.

[10] Holstein, "The Conquest of Chrysler."

[11] Joseph B. White, "Head of Truck Maker Freightliner Is Leaving Post," *Wall Street Journal* (May 25, 2001), p. A4.

PROGNOSIS

As of mid-2001, many observers were pessimistic of the probabilities of Schrempp resurrecting Chrysler any time soon. In the long term, perhaps; but they questioned whether creditors and shareholders would tolerate a long period of profit drain by Chrysler and low share prices for DaimlerChrysler stock. Rumors were that Deutsche Bank, DaimlerChrysler's largest shareholder, was getting ready to oust Schrempp, and that Chrysler would be broken up into smaller pieces and sold off.[12]

Still, friendly German banks and shareholders might be more patient than Wall Street. DaimlerChrysler was the first German company to be listed on the New York Stock Exchange, and such a listing subjected Schrempp to the impatience of the international financial markets and the markets' obsession with meeting quarterly earnings expectations. In an age of volatile markets, failure to meet such expectations often resulted in a company's stock price collapsing. This bothered Schrempp: "I don't think [it] is advantageous: focusing on quarterly results. It might well be that because we increase our spending, investment, whatever, for a very good reason, that I might occasionally miss what they [investors] expect from me."[13]

Schrempp could have another worry imperiling his job if Chrysler did not improve soon. The third largest holder of DaimlerChrysler stock was the Las Vegas takeover tycoon Kirk Kerkorian, a powerful man with a reputation for being easily offended. Rumors were that Schrempp did not make himself available to see Kerkorian, but instead went to his ranch in South Africa.[14]

Chrysler executives, much as they might dislike Schrempp, could be worse off if he should be ousted. Mercedes executives ruled in the headquarters at Stuttgart, and without Chrysler's main supporter, Schrempp, Chrysler could not be sure it would receive the resources needed to make a comeback. It could be broken up and sold, or left withering within DaimlerChrysler's empire.[15]

ANALYSIS

This case illustrates the downside of mergers and acquisitions, as will the next two cases.[16] The causes of these problems are diverse, although certain commonalities occur time and again.

We will examine the salient factors that led to the collapse of Chrysler soon after the merger under (1) those mainly Daimler's fault, (2) those Chrysler's fault, and (3) the externals that made the situation worse. Then we will examine this whole concept of a "merger of equals." Can there really be a merger of equals?

---

[12] "Can the Germans Rescue Chrysler?, pp. 106–107.

[13] Holstein, p. 69.

[14] Reported in "A Deal for the History Books," p. 57.

[15] See Robyn Meredith, "Batman and Robin," *Forbes* (March 5, 2001), pp. 67, 68; and Jerry Flint, "Free Chrysler," *Forbes* (October 30, 2000), p. 132 for more discussion of these scenarios.

[16] We use the terms *mergers* and *acquisitions* somewhat similarly, but will consider *merger* as closer to the idea of equals coming together, while *acquisition* suggests a larger firm absorbing a smaller one.

Daimler's Contribution to the Problem

The Morale Factor

Different cultures are often involved when a merger or acquisition takes place, even among seemingly similar firms. For example, one business culture may be more conservative and the other aggressive and even reckless; one may be formal and the other informal; one culture may insist on standard operating procedures (SOPs) being followed, while the other may be far less restricted; one may be dominated by accountant or control mentalities, which emphasize cost analysis and rigidity of budgets, and the other by the sales mentality, which seeks maximum sales production and flexibility of operations even if expenses sometimes get out of line. Such differences impede easy assimilation.

This assimilation challenge for divergent corporate cultures becomes all the more difficult when different nationalities are involved, for example, Germanic versus American. National pride, and even prejudice, may complicate the situation.

It is hardly surprising that this mammoth merger of a proud German firm and an American firm with a long heritage should present morale problems. Especially with one party misled as to the sharing of leadership, the seeds were laid for extreme resentment. Some of this resentment among rank-and-file workers could even go back to World War II.

But there were other obstacles to a smooth melding of the two firms. Daimler had to adjust from being an old-line German firm to becoming a huge international firm confronted with a diversity of cultures. "The German instinct is for hierarchy, order, planning. Daimler executives use Dr. or Prof. on their business cards. Many wear dark three-piece suits. Chrysler, by contrast, was known for a freewheeling creativity."[17]

Chrysler's company culture had been highly successful in the very recent past, as shown in Table 8.1 and in Table 8.2, which presents the gain in market share or competitive position during the 1990s. This rather unrestrained-by-rules culture seemed to many to be the key to innovative thinking and technical leadership. With the merger it was not only being challenged but repudiated and supplanted by Germans who little appreciated the contributions of designers like Bob Lutz, who came up with products customers wanted that were not engineered at great cost and research. "The daring and imagination of the old Chrysler [is] buried under German management."[18]

Schrempp's Major Blunder

A miscalculation by Schrempp little more than a year after the merger was to have drastic consequences. His order to produce and ship out 75,000 more older-model vehicles than could reasonably be sold before the new models came out, thus beefing up sales and profits for the first half of the year, resulted in huge imbalances of inventories in the last half and destroyed year-2000 results as well as the early months of

---

[17] Holstein, p. 56.
[18] Flint, p. 132.

TABLE 8.2   Chrysler's Market Share of the Big Three U.S. Automakers, 1991–1998

	Chrysler's Sales Percentage of U.S. Car/Truck Automakers
1991	12.2
1992	13.7
1993	15.0
1994	15.6
1995	14.8
1996	16.5
1997	15.8
1998	NA

Sources: Calculated from publicly reported sales figures; 1998 figures not applicable due to merger in November.

Commentary: The improvement in Chrysler performance in the middle and late 1990s is clearly evident. Market share improvement of even 0.05 percent translates into a gain in competitive position. And here we see a gain of more than 4.0 percent in 1996 and 3.6 percent in 1997. You can see how the improving performance of Chrysler in the latter years of the 1990s would be attractive to Daimler.

2001. This overproduction was perhaps the trigger that brought Chrysler its huge losses and even jeopardized the soundness of Schrempp's acquisition decision.

Chrysler's Contribution

Arguments could be raised that Chrysler had grown fat and inefficient after its years of success in the last half of the 1990s, that it was on the verge of a drastic decline in profits even if Daimler had not come on the scene to stir things up. By 1999, Chrysler showrooms were saddled with aging models, including the important minivans that were in their fifth year. While still the leader in minivan sales, Chrysler was losing market share to competitors with newer models, including the Honda Odyssey.

The prosperity of Chrysler in the mid-1990s may have reflected not so much inspired management as a combination of good luck factors: innovative designs and segment-leading products, yes, but also rising sales throughout the auto industry and a groundswell of demand for high-profit minivans and pickup trucks. Maybe the success of those years paved the way for the disaster that came shortly after Daimler took over. The great demand for vehicles like the Ram pickup truck, Jeep Grand Cherokee, and Dodge Durango brought a heady confidence that these good times would be lasting. Accordingly, Chrysler projected market share to increase to 20 percent by 2005, far above anything ever attained before. (See Table 8.2 for market share achievements during the heady days in the 1990s. You can see from this that attaining a 20 percent market share was not very close.) So Chrysler spent heavily on refurbishing plants and buying new equipment. It went from having the fewest workers per point of market share in 1996 to the most by 1999. It was spending money extravagantly and its entrepreneurial culture was operating unchecked. "The company lost its purpose and lost its direction," former chief engineer François Castaing said.[19]

The uncontrolled entrepreneurial culture led to poor communication and coordination, with each team buying its own components such as platforms and parts for the different cars, and thus not taking advantage of economies of scale. For example, the Durango and the Jeep had different windshield wipers, and Chrysler's five teams specified three different kinds of corrosion protection for the rolled steel used to reinforce plastic bumper surfaces.[20]

Other lapses of good judgment included continuing production of old-model minivans as it was switching production to the new one, thus flooding the market. This yielding to the pressure of Schrempp was, as we have seen earlier, a major factor in the disastrous 2000 results. Could Chrysler executives have protested more vigorously? The practice of the old management to introduce new models in batches rather than spreading them over several years brought a feast or famine situation: very good years, and rather bad years in between.

External Factors

Certainly the merger was consummated at a time when the auto industry, and the economy in general, was on the threshold of a downturn. Chrysler apparently miscalculated such an eventuality, spending heavily for costlier models just before demand turned down, and its brands were not strong enough to command higher premiums from customers. By early 2001, Chrysler was outspending all other major automakers on rebates and other incentives.

Chrysler also seemed to be oblivious to the threat of competitors during its golden years. Despite this heavy use of incentives, Chrysler lost market share for the first three months of 2001: a 14.2 percent market share versus 15.1 percent for the same three months in 2000.

Can There Really Be a Merger of Equals?

In reality there is seldom a merger of equals. Unless the two parties actually recapitalize themselves with new stock—and this is seldom done—there is always an acquirer and an acquiree. Even if both parties to the merger have equal seats on the board of directors, still the acquiring firm and its executives are more dominant. Even if the name of the new, combined firm is completely changed, this does not assure a merger of equals. For example, in a well-publicized merger "of equals" in 2000 between Bell Atlantic and GTE, the name *Verizon* was created. But no one was fooled: Bell Atlantic was in charge. Furthermore, there can be no true merger of equals if one firm owns more of

---

[19] As quoted in "Can the Germans Rescue Chrysler?", p. 109.
[20] *Ibid.*

the consolidated stock (usually reflecting its larger size) than the other, and this is almost always the case. Daimler was certainly the larger firm in this merger, having paid $36 billion for Chrysler while its own shares just before the merger had a market value of about $48 billion.

How important is this merger of equals to the executives of acquired firms? Apparently to many it is not of major consequence as long as they get a good price for their stake, or as long as they believe the acquiring firm will honor their importance. Occasionally a merger negotiation will fall apart over the issue of who will be in charge. Take the example of Lucent and Alcatel of France, two of the world's biggest makers of communications equipment: At the last minute on May 29, 2001, Henry B. Schacht, chairman of Lucent, called off the merger talks. "It started to feel more like an acquisition than a merger," one of the Lucent participants explained. They could not accept the probability that Alcatel would be in charge.[21]

UPDATE

At the beginning of 2002, Chrysler reported it had lost a staggering $2 billion in 2001, and this brought a new wave of criticism of the merger—after all, it was four years after the deal. For the first years after the merger, Mercedes closely guarded its parts and designs for fear of eroding the Mercedes mystique. Now headquarters in Stuttgart, Germany, finally began forcing its far-flung operations to begin working together. In the Spring of 2003, Chrysler introduced two models that reflected more German engineering: the Pacifica, a cross between a station wagon and an SUV; and the Crossfire, a sleek sports car. Waiting in the wings were an LX sedan and an SUV called the Magnum. Headquarters also began bringing engineers from its Mitsubishi subsidiary to Stuttgart in order to integrate some ideas for smaller cars.[22] High time that assimilation efforts should begin, in this now five year merger.

A trial was to begin December 1, 2003, on a lawsuit brought by billionaire investor Kirk Kerkorian, who claimed he was deceived about the 1998 merger of Daimler-Benz and Chrysler. Kerkorian is seeking $3 billion in damages. He contended that he and other investors were misled into thinking the combination was a "merger of equals." Such a merger would be more acceptable to U.S. antitrust officials and to Chrysler shareholders; it would also avoid paying a $10 billion takeover premium. CEO Jürgen Schrempp and Chief Financial Officer Manfred Gentz would be testifying.[23] At long last, this questionable "merger of equals" would be tested in the courts.

[21] For more details, see Seth Schiesel, *New York Times*, reported in *Cleveland Plain Dealer* (June 3, 2001), p. 1H.

[22] Neal E. Boudette, "At Daimler Chrysler, a New Push to Make Its Units Work Together," *Wall Street Journal*, March 12, 2003, pp. A1 and A15.

[23] "DaimlerChrysler CEO Will Testify in Lawsuit," Bloomberg News, as reported in *Cleveland Plain Dealer*, November 25, 2003, p. C2.)

WHAT CAN BE LEARNED?

Mergers are no panacea. For years, in recurrent cycles of exuberance and caution, businesses have tried to solve the problem of growth with mergers and acquisitions. What you didn't have you could acquire, faster and better than developing it yourself, so the reasoning went. The term *synergy* became widely used, especially in the 1980s, to tout the great benefits and advantages of such mergers and acquisitions. (The following Information Box describes in more detail this concept of synergy.)

Wall Street dealmakers, investment bankers, and lawyers reap the bonanza from merger activities, but many of these mergers do not work out as well as expected, and some are even outright disasters, as we will examine in two other cases in Part II.

We have seen the cultural conflict in the DaimlerChrysler merger. But this is just one of the things that can go wrong. Many acquisition seekers are so eager to get the target company because it has strength in market share or access to strategic technologies, or because it will make their firm so much bigger in its industry (with

INFORMATION BOX

SYNERGY

Synergy results from creating a whole that is greater than the sum of its parts, that can accomplish more than the total of individual contributions. In an acquisition, synergy occurs if the two firms, when combined, are more efficient, productive, and profitable than they were as separate operations before the merger. Sometimes this is referred to as $2 + 2 = 5$.

How can such synergy occur? If duplication of efforts can be eliminated, if operations can be streamlined, if economies of scale are possible, if specialization can be enhanced, if greater financial, technical, and managerial resources can be tapped or new markets made possible—then a synergistic situation is likely to occur. Such an expanded operation should be a stronger force in the marketplace than the individual single units that existed before.

The concept of synergy is the rationale for mergers and acquisitions. But sometimes combining causes the reverse: negative synergy, where the consequences are worse than the sum of individual efforts. If friction arises between the entities, if organizational missions are incompatible, if the new organizational climate creates fearful, resentful, and frustrated employees, then synergy is unlikely, at least in the short and intermediate term. Furthermore, if because of sheer optimism or an uncontrolled acquisitive drive more is paid for the acquisition than it is really worth, then we have a grand blunder. Could that have been the case with the Chrysler acquisition, in addition to the culture problem?

Do you think a typical committee or group has more synergy than the same individuals working alone? Why or why not?

all the glamour and prestige of large size for the executives involved) that they are prepared to pay well, and often too much. Funds for such borrowing are usually readily available, heavy debt has income tax advantages, and profits may be distributed among fewer shares so that return on equity is enhanced. But all too often the best of the acquired human assets are soon sending out resumes to prospective new employers, and the assimilation and effective consolidation of the two enterprises may be years away. Furthermore, acquiring companies may be left with mountains of debt from overambitious mergers and acquisitions, thus greatly increasing the overhead to cover with revenues before profits can be realized.

Cultural differences should be considered in mergers and acquisitions. These differences—in perceptions, in customs, in ways of doing things, in prejudices—often are not given enough heed. The acquiring firm expects to bulldoze its culture on the acquired firm (despite how this may affect pride and willingness to cooperate). As we saw with the Daimler merger with Chrysler—in reality a merger of unequals—arrogance and resentments surfaced.

Should the acquiring company express its dominance quickly, or should it try to be as soothing as possible? Morale will probably not be salvaged in a soothing takeover, but there can be serious problems with this approach also. We will see in Chapter 20, Maytag's English adventure, that permitting an acquisition's nationals to continue operating with little control can be a disaster waiting to happen.

How much can you trust? Both parties to a merger negotiation may express a commitment to equality. But such lip service may prove a façade. Even if executive positions are as evenly balanced as possible, one person may be a more dominant personality than the other, perhaps by dint of bigger stock ownership. Consequently, the merger of equals becomes in name only, with any equal standing of the acquired firm existing only at the convenience of the acquirer.

Another way to bring together two companies. There is another way to bring together the strengths of two companies without the huge costs and without the morale and coordination problems of mergers and acquisitions. Strategic alliances, also called partnering, are increasingly being used by companies seeking to stimulate growth. See the following Information Box.

The danger of cannibalization. Cannibalization occurs when a new product takes away sales from an existing product. This is likely to occur whenever a new product is introduced, but flooding the market with the old product just before a new model introduction, as Daimler pressured Chrysler to do, is asking for headaches, and worse. DaimlerChrysler found that it took both massive rebates of the old models and well as substantial price reductions of the new ones to move the inventory—all of this destructive to profitability. The same scenario had confronted computer makers and other firms at the cutting edge of new technology. When do you let go the old model without jeopardizing sales in the interim?

We do not advocate stopping production of the older model when the new model is first announced. But it seems judicious to reduce production in the months after the announcement. Then if the newer, technologically advanced model should be more attractive, shouldn't it command a higher price than the

INFORMATION BOX

STRATEGIC ALLIANCES

Some are calling this the most powerful trend to sweep American business in a century. Strategic alliances can take many forms—outsourcing, information sharing, Web consortia, joint marketing. The most extreme is a corporate partnership "wherein two proudly independent companies together spawn a new company in many ways independent of its parents." Indicative of the importance attached to this alternative to mergers and acquisitions (M&As) by major firms is the creation of a new major executive position by Coca-Cola: President of New Business Ventures, with Steven Heyer as the first outsider to be brought in as an operating president in more than twenty years. He was president of Turner Broadcasting Systems. One of his first actions was to meld Coke's noncarbonated beverages into a new joint venture with Procter & Gamble's snacks, such as Pringles chips and drinks. This partnership would start off with sales of $4 billion.

Of an estimated 10,000-plus new strategic alliances formed in 2000 were such major firms as IBM, Kmart, Wal-Mart, Pfizer, Eli Lilly, Dow Chemical, Xerox, Cisco, Microsoft, AOL, and Intel, as well as many young companies.

Critics of such partnerships raise the objection that they are likely to dissolve into disruptive squabbles in the absence of a hierarchical corporate structure. Do you think this is the Achilles heel of such new business structures? If so, is this downside worse than the negatives of M&As?

Sources: Matthew Schifrin, "Partners or Perish," *Forbes* (May 21, 2001), pp. 26–28; and James W. Michaels, "Don't Buy, Bond Instead," *Forbes* (May 21, 2001), p. 20.

older version? DaimlerChrysler's problems in 2000 were aggravated in that the new models were not so much technologically superior, as having expensive options that some buyers found not worth the extra money.

Let us not denigrate the desirability of cannibalizing. As products are improved, they should be brought to the marketplace as soon as possible, and not held back because there may be some cannibalization. The temptation to hold back is there, especially when the new product may have a lower profit margin than the product it is supplanting, perhaps because of competition and higher costs. Invariably, the firm that restrains an innovation because of fear of cannibalizing a high-profit product winds up making the arena attractive for competitors to gain an advantage. *Fear of cannibalization should not impede innovation.*

CONSIDER

Can you think of other learning insights?

QUESTIONS

1. Do you think Schrempp was wise to replace the top Chrysler executives? Why or why not?

2. How could Chrysler boss Robert Eaton have been so naive as to permit himself to be ousted from power in a negotiation that he actively campaigned for and accepted? Do you see any way he might have protected his position in the merger?

3. How specifically can a firm protect itself from the extreme risks of cannibalization?

4. Do you think the cultural problems could have been largely avoided in this merger? How?

5. Dieter Zetsche was sent from Stuttgart headquarters to fix all-American Chrysler, after a disastrous year 2000. On his first day in Detroit he fired the head of sales and marketing. Discuss the advisability of such a quick action, considering as many ramifications and justifications as possible.

6. Evaluate the desirability of rebates rather than regular markdowns or price cuts.

7. Do you personally think the use of Mercedes parts in Chrysler vehicles would diminish the prestige of the Mercedes brand? Would it help Chrysler that much?

8. Do you think good times can ever be lasting in the auto industry? Why or why not?

HANDS-ON EXERCISES

1. You are one of Chrysler's largest suppliers of certain parts. You are shocked at the decree by the new management of Chrysler that you must cut your prices by 5 percent immediately, and another 10 percent within two years. What do you do now? Discuss and evaluate as many courses of action as you can. You can make some assumptions, but be specific.

2. Place yourself in the position of Robert Eaton, CEO of Chrysler before the merger, and now "co-chairman" with Jürgen Schrempp. You have just been told that your services are no longer needed, that the co-chairman position has been abolished. What do you do at this point? Try to be specific and support your recommendations.

3. You are Steve Yokich, president of the United Auto Workers. You had initially endorsed the plans of Dieter Zetsche to cut costs severely, including laying off 26,000 workers and closing six plants. You had been convinced that such downsizing was necessary to save Chrysler. Now many of your union members are storming about such arbitrary cuts. They are castigating you for supporting these plans, and you may be ousted. Discuss your actions.

TEAM DEBATE EXERCISES

1. In this case we have the great controversy of German top executives replacing American ones. Debate the desirability of such replacements versus keeping most of the American incumbents. I would suggest dividing into two groups, with one being as persuasive as possible in arguing for bringing in fresh blood from German headquarters, and the other strongly contesting this. Be prepared to attack your opponents' arguments, and defend your own.

2. Debate the desirability of mergers and acquisitions versus strategic alliances or partnerships. You may need to do some research on these two alternatives. Consider the pros and cons and debate their desirabilities under different situations, such as size of firms, technological differences, and so on.

INVITATION TO RESEARCH

What is the situation with DaimlerChrysler today? Has the DaimlerChrysler stock bounced back to values before the merger? Are Chrysler cars and trucks gaining market share? Is Jürgen Schrempp still Chairman? Is Zetsche still heading up the Chrysler operation?

CHAPTER NINE

Newell Rubbermaid:
A Sour Acquisition

John McDonough, CEO of Newell, specialized in buying small marginal firms and improving their operations. In ten years he had bought seventy-five such firms and polished them by eliminating underperforming products, employees, and factories and by stressing customer service. This format began to be called "Newellizing." It is hardly surprising that most of the acquisitions had strong brand names, but mediocre customer service. Rubbermaid fit this mode, though it was by far the biggest acquisition and would nearly double Newell's sales.

Rubbermaid, manufacturer and marketer of high-volume, branded plastic and rubber consumer products and toys, had been a darling of investors and academicians alike. For ten years in a row, it placed in the *Fortune* survey of "America's Most Admired Corporations," and it was No. 1 in both 1993 and 1994. It was ranked as the second most powerful brand in a Baylor University study of consumer goodwill, and received the Thomas Edison Award for developing products to make people's lives better. Under CEO Stanley Gault, Rubbermaid's emphasis on innovation often resulted in a new product every day, thereby helping the stock routinely to return 25 percent annually.

Surprisingly, by the middle 1990s, Rubbermaid began faltering, partly because of inability to meet the service demands of Wal-Mart, a major customer. Rubbermaid stock plummeted 40 percent from the 1992 high, leaving it ripe for a takeover. Newell Company acquired Rubbermaid on March 24, 1999, expecting to turn it around. But then Newell had to wonder...

THE ACQUISITION AND WOLFGANG SCHMITT

Former Rubbermaid CEO Wolfgang Schmitt felt a cloak of apprehension settling over him in May 1999. It was only two months after the merger with Newell had been completed, and things were not going as he expected.

Schmitt had become CEO a year after the legendary Stanley Gault retired in 1991. Gault had returned in 1980 to his home town of Wooster, Ohio (Rubbermaid

111

headquarters), after more than thirty-one years with the General Electric Company, to helm Rubbermaid. During Gault's tenure, Rubbermaid stock split four times to the delight of stockholders. It was a tough act to follow.

Schmitt often thought about this, but he was certainly a worthy successor to Gault. He had spent all his working life with Rubbermaid after graduating in 1966 from Otterbein College in Westerville, Ohio (about sixty miles from Wooster), with a degree in economics and business administration. A recruiter visiting the campus convinced him to join the rapidly growing Rubbermaid. Schmitt started as a management trainee, and in twenty-seven years worked his way up the corporate ranks to become chairman of the board and chief executive officer in 1993. He was proud of this accomplishment, and thought his experience must be an inspiration to young people in the company: Any one of them could dream of becoming CEO, with hard work and loyalty. A significant highlight of his professional life came when he was invited back to Otterbein in November 1997 to inaugurate its Distinguished Executive Lecture Series.

During Schmitt's reign, Rubbermaid reached $2 billion in sales in 1994. When it celebrated its seventy-five-year anniversary a year later, Schmitt set the company's sights on $4 billion in sales for the turn of the century. To do this, he knew it had to become a truly global company, and he instigated four foreign acquisitions that year.

He was an effective CEO; he knew he was. When the Newell Company, a slightly larger multinational firm, expressed an interest in merging, Schmitt thought he owed it to his stockholders, and to himself, to pursue this. After all, the two firms' houseware and hardware products and marketing efforts were compatible, and their combination would result in a $7-billion-a-year consumer products giant. Aiding Schmitt's decision to merge was a nice severance guarantee of $12 million after taxes in addition to his stock options. While Newell's CEO John McDonough would assume the CEO position of the merged corporation, Schmitt was to be a vice chairman and would work closely with McDonough to ensure the smooth merger and to help mold the new company.

Now, barely two months later, Schmitt had been shunted aside. He did not have an office at headquarters, his name was not listed on a new report of the seven highest-paid executives, and he was not even included in the list of directors reported to the Securities and Exchange Commission (SEC). He couldn't help feeling betrayed about no longer having a role in the operations of the company, after he had been so instrumental in bringing about the merger. At fifty-five years of age, he still had many productive years left. More than this, there was the principle of the thing: This was like a kick in the teeth.

But he was not alone. Three of Rubbermaid's five division presidents—the five divisions were Home Products, Little Tykes, Graco-Century, Curver, and Commercial Products—had already been replaced since the merger. Furthermore, in the Home Products division, only two of the top eight executives were still there.

NEWELL'S ASSESSMENT OF RUBBERMAID

If John McDonough of Newell was so unhappy with current Rubbermaid management and operations, why did he buy Rubbermaid in the first place—and for $6.3 billion, more than two times current sales? At a shareholders' meeting a few months after the acquisition, McDonough tried to explain. He told them that Rubbermaid was a troubled company, but that once it was pulled into the revered operations of Newell, it could be great again.[1]

The shareholders were told that although jobs were being cut, the operations would be stronger in the long run. As a strength, McDonough noted that Rubbermaid commanded 94 percent brand loyalty and generated great customer traffic in stores. But Rubbermaid executives needed to slash unnecessary costs, introduce robotics, and reduce product variety. For example, was it really necessary to have dozens of the same type of wastebasket?

Still, McDonough saw poor customer service as the biggest deficiency of Rubbermaid, the most unacceptable aspect of its operation, and the one that Newell could most easily correct. After all, Newell had achieved a 98.5 percent on-time delivery rate in dealings with Wal-Mart. He would see that Rubbermaid was brought up to this same performance standard.

Rubbermaid's Customer Service Problems

Perhaps a declining commitment to customer service dated back to the retirement of Gault, though Schmitt would likely dispute that. Customer service can erode without being obvious to top management. While some customers complain, many others simply switch their business to competitors. Still, Rubbermaid's lapses in customer service should have been obvious for years. After all, Wal-Mart was not tolerant with vendors who did not meet its standards. When McDonough's people began digging deeper into Rubbermaid's operations, they found that the company wasn't even measuring customer service. This deficiency is almost the kiss of death when dealing with major retailers.

Up to the mid-1990s, about 15 percent of Rubbermaid's $2 billion-plus revenues came from Wal-Mart. Rubbermaid had had an impressive earnings growth of at least 15 percent a year to go along with 20 percent operating margins, much of this due to the generous space Wal-Mart gave its plastic and rubber products. This was to change abruptly.

In 1995, Wal-Mart refused to let Rubbermaid pass on much of its higher raw material costs, and began taking shelf space away and giving it to smaller competitors who undersold Rubbermaid. This resulted in a major earnings drop (see Table 9.1) that forced Rubbermaid to shut nine facilities and cut 9 percent of its 14,000 employees. "When you hitch your wagon to a star, you are at the mercy of that star."[2]

Wal-Mart not only complained about poor deliveries but began taking more drastic action. Each day Wal-Mart gives suppliers such as Newell a two-hour time slot in which their trucks can deliver orders placed twenty-four hours before. Should the supplier miss the deadline, it pays Wal-Mart for every dollar of lost margin. Now such a fast replenishment of orders required that factories be tied in with Wal-Mart's computers. Rubbermaid began installing software to do this in 1996 and had spent $62 million by

[1] Teresa Dixon Murray, "Newell Details Its Plans for Rubbermaid," *Cleveland Plain Dealer*, May 27, 1999, p. 1C.

[2] Matthew Schifrin, "The Big Squeeze," *Forbes*, March 11, 1996, p. 46.

Table 9.1 Rubbermaid Sales and Earnings, 1992–1997

	1992	1993	1994	1995	1996	1997
Sales (in billions)	$1.81	$1.96	$2.17	$2.34	$2.35	$2.40
Net earnings (in millions)	184.0	211.0	228.0	59.0	152.0	143.0
Earnings as percentage of sales	10.2%	10.8%	10.5%	2.5%	6.5%	6.0%
Earnings per share	1.15	1.32	1.42	0.38	1.01	0.95

Source: Company reports

Commentary: This six-year comparison of sales and the various profit indicators show rather starkly the decline in fortunes of Rubbermaid beginning in 1995. Sales remained practically static from 1995 on, although admittedly they were not growing very robustly in the three years before. The lack of growth occurred during a period of unprecedented national economic prosperity.

The earnings comparisons show up worse. While acceptable earnings growth occurred up to 1995, they greatly worsened beginning in 1995. Not only were net earnings figures drastically reduced, but they showed little sign of recouping, even though there was some improvement from the bottom of 1995. Of course, net earnings as a percent of sales and per share also drastically declined from what they were in 1992–1994. Rubbermaid's major problems with Wal-Mart occurred in 1995.

1999, but still was often not achieving even 80 percent on-time delivery service. This was unacceptable to Wal-Mart, and returns and fines for poor service rose to 4.4 percent of sales in 1998.[3] Finally, Wal-Mart purged most of its stores of Rubbermaid's Little Tikes toy line, giving the space to a competitor, Fisher-Price. See the following Information Box for a discussion of the power of a giant retailer and the demands it can make.

Wal-Mart had such a high regard for the customer service of Newell that, upon hearing of the impending merger with Newell, Wal-Mart again began carrying Little Tikes toys. McDonough vowed to get Rubbermaid's on-time delivery rate of 80 percent up to Newell's 98.5 percent, and he began ripping out Rubbermaid's computer system and writing off the entire $62 million. In addition, McDonough claimed to be able to squeeze $350 million of costs out of Rubbermaid, which would double its operating income.[4]

AFTER THE MERGER

Newell did not quickly turn around and Newellize Rubbermaid, and stockholders were shocked and disappointed. In a time of rising stock prices, Newell Rubbermaid's shares plunged 20 percent in one day in September 1999 as the now-giant consumer goods firm warned that third-quarter earnings would fall short of expectations. This was only the latest in a string of negatives, and Newell Rubbermaid's stock was to lose almost half of its value since the Rubbermaid acquisition in March. It blamed lower-than-expected sales of Rubbermaid's plastic containers and Little Tikes toys. Still, company officials maintained that "the integration process remains on plan."[5]

[3] Murray, p. 3C.

[4] Michelle Conlin, "Newellizing Rubbermaid," *Forbes*, May 31, 1999, p. 118.

[5] James P. Miller, "Newell Rubbermaid Shares Fall 20% as an Earnings Short Fall Is Predicted," *Wall Street Journal*, September 7, 1999, p. A4.

INFORMATION BOX

THE DEMANDS OF A GIANT RETAILER

Giant retailers, especially the big discount houses, stand in a power position today relative to their vendors. Part of this power lies in their providing efficient access to the marketplace—imagine the problems of a large consumer goods manufacturer in trying to deal with thousands of small retailers rather than the few big firms that dominate their markets. These giant firms can account for 50 percent and more of many manufacturers' sales. However, if such a major customer is lost or not completely satisfied, a vendor's viability could be in jeopardy.

Retailers like Wal-Mart make full use of their power position. Take paying of invoices, for example. Many vendors give a 2 percent discount if bills are paid within ten days instead of thirty. Wal-Mart routinely pays its bills closer to thirty days and still takes the 2 percent discount. Wal-Mart has also led in "partnering" with its vendors. This "partnering" really means that vendors have to pick up more of the inventory management and merchandising costs associated with Wal-Mart stores, with most of these costs incurred in providing fast replenishment so that the stores can maintain lean stocks without losing customer sales through stockouts.

So-called slotting fees are common in the supermarket industry, with manufacturers paying to get their products on store shelves. It is estimated that some $9 billion annually changes hands in private, unwritten deals between grocery retailers and food and consumer goods manufacturers.[6]

The following is an example of a slotting fee stipulation of a supermarket chain:

Effective January 1, 1996
Our slotting fee is... $2,500
An item authorized will remain authorized for a minimum of six months (as
long as the basic cost does not go up substantially). Just as a reminder, many
times it is the slotting fee that determines whether we authorize an item or not.

With the coercive power of a big retailer, a vendor is practically forced to meet their demands no matter what the cost.

Do you think a big manufacturer, such as Coca-Cola, can be coerced by a big retailer? Why or why not? What might determine the extent of retailer coercion? Can a manufacturer coerce a retailer?

A month later, coinciding with a Wal-Mart announcement that it was expanding vigorously in Europe, Newell Rubbermaid said it would focus on expanding overseas to serve domestic retailers who are moving abroad. The company had been getting a quarter of its sales outside the United States. "Our customers are going international," McDonough said. "We have the opportunity to follow them. It's a

[6] John S. Long, "Specialty Items to Drive New Market," *Cleveland Plain Dealer,* October 6, 1999, p. 4F.

once-in-a-lifetime opportunity."[7] The company also maintained that it had sharply reduced the number of late shipments of Rubbermaid products and expected to have 98 percent of orders shipped on time either in the present quarter or next.[8]

Was this a wise merger? Did Newell pay too much for a faltering Rubbermaid? It was hardly likely in the first year of a merger that management would admit that it might have made a mistake. But stockholders were betting with their money. Meantime, Wolfgang Schmitt pondered his exile and the erosion of value of his stock options.

Disappointment

John McDonough resigned as CEO in November 2000, after Newell Rubbermaid cut profit forecasts three times in the year after the Rubbermaid acquisition. Joseph Galli, a "master marketer," as *Forbes* proclaimed him, and the first outsider in the company's ninety-nine-year history, became the chief executive in January 2001.

Newell needed a rescuer. McDonough, whose forte was buying underperforming companies and Newellizing them, had met his match. This was the third year of flat or falling profits. For 2001, sales were off 2.4 percent and net income down 42 percent, with share prices reflecting this. The $6 billion purchase of Rubbermaid, its biggest deal, had brought Newell to its knees, and Rubbermaid remained the sickest division.

Joseph Galli

In nineteen years at Black & Decker, the now forty-three-year-old Galli had built a reputation as a marketing wunderkind, a brand builder. He was running the company's crown jewel, the DeWalt brand, a high-margin line of power tools for skilled tradesmen and consumer do-it-yourselfers. Galli recruited teams of college graduates, dubbed "swarm teams," to be supermissionary salespeople hawking the DeWalt brand not only at store openings but at union halls and Nascar races as well (see the Information Box on the following page).

Galli brought amazing growth to DeWalt, pushing $60 million in sales in 1992 to more than $1 billion by 1999, in the process providing 64 percent of the company's $4.6 billion sales. By age thirty-eight, Galli was the second-highest-paid executive at Black & Decker and in line for the top position—except that the CEO was not ready to step down anytime soon.

Galli left to be president of Amazon.com, staying only a year, then became chief of VerticalNet for 167 days. Some were calling him a tumbleweed, but conceded that if anybody could add sizzle to an unpretentious product line of such things as mop buckets, toilet brushes, and plastic containers, he might be the best.[9]

Galli spent his first three months at Newell Rubbermaid traveling the world and meeting every manager he could. His predecessor, John McDonough, was a diabetic

---

[7] "Newell Rubbermaid to Resume Acquisitions, Expand Overseas," *Cleveland Plain Dealer*, October 6, 1999, p. 2C.

[8] *Ibid.*

[9] Bruce Upbin, "Rebirth of a Salesman," *Forbes*, October 1, 2001, pp. 95–104.

INFORMATION BOX

MISSIONARY SALESPEOPLE

Missionary, or supporting, salespeople do not normally try to secure orders. They are used by manufacturers to provide specialized services and create goodwill and more dealer push. They work with dealers, perhaps to develop point-of-service displays, train dealer salespeople to do a better job of selling the product, provide better communication and rapport between distributor and manufacturer, and in general, aggressively promote the brand. They are particularly important in selling to self-service outlets, such as supermarkets and discount stores, where with no retail clerks selling to customers, displays, shelf space, and in-stock conditions have to be the selling tools.

Galli's supermissionaries, or swarm teams, are small armies of energetic college recruits who also work Nascar races, trade shows, new store openings and the like. A typical supermissionary is given the use of a new Ford Explorer Sport Trac, a territory of fourteen Wal-Marts, and a mission: Make sure Newell's pens, bowls, buckets, and blinds are neatly displayed, priced right, and piled high in prominent spots.[10]

Evaluate this statement: "Good customer service doesn't do you much good, but poor customer service can kill you."

whose leg was amputated in 1999 and who spent almost all his time at company headquarters in Beloit, Wisconsin; in his first six months, Galli spent just thirty-six hours there.

Newell hadn't run a national ad campaign on television in three years. In 2000, the firm spent 0.7 percent of sales on research and development. (Even conservative Colgate spent 2 percent on the innovation of adding a new color of dish detergent.) Sales of the Rubbermaid unit had declined every year since 1998, and were now at $1.8 billion. No-name rivals were taking business away in major retailers such as Wal-Mart, Home Depot, Target, and Bed Bath & Beyond.

Galli tripled spending on new product development for Rubbermaid. He promoted the brand on prime-time TV for the first time in three years with a budget of $15 million, more than was spent in the previous ten years combined. He also budgeted $40 million for swarm teams of well-paid college grads to push Newell Rubbermaid products at mass retailers, as they had done so successfully with power tools at Black & Decker.[11] Galli made his first acquisition in November 2002—buying American Saw and Manufacturing Co., thus expanding into the hand-tool and power-tool market that he knew so well.[12] Could it be that Newell Rubbermaid was on the verge of a turnaround?

---

[10] Upbin, p. 100.

[11] *Ibid.*, p. 104.

[12] "Newell Rubbermaid To Buy American Saw in $450 Million Deal," *Wall Street Journal,* November 25, 2002, p. B6.

ANALYSIS

This case illustrates not only the risks of dealing with behemoth customers, but also the rewards if you can satisfy their demands. After all, in better days Newell Rubbermaid prepared to follow Wal-Mart to Europe and be a prime supplier of its stores there. But a vendor has to have the commitment and ability to meet stringent requirements. If a twenty-four-hour delivery cycle is demanded, the vendor must achieve this regardless of costs. If selling prices are to be pared to the bone, efficiency must somehow be jacked up and production costs pruned, or else profitability may have to be sacrificed even to the point of extreme concern. Otherwise, the vendor can be replaced.

The alternative? To be content with far less revenues from a host of smaller accounts, or else to have such a brand name as to be partly insulated from price competition. Rubbermaid thought it had this, due to its public accolades of past years. Perhaps this contributed to its apathy regarding its delivery service. But Wal-Mart hardly was impressed with the superiority of this brand's products that cost more than alternative suppliers and could not be delivered on time.

But note that improving service and shortening replenishment time is not easily or cheaply done. Rubbermaid spent $62 million on computer technology to enable it to meet Wal-Mart's demands, but it was not enough. Better control of warehouse inventories and production schedules is essential. The vendor will need to carry more of the inventory burden traditionally assumed by the retailer and incur additional expenses and investment for more manpower and trucks and other equipment. Perhaps the most damning indictment of Rubbermaid's service deficiencies was how long these continued without being corrected. The problem initially surfaced in 1995, but by 1999, on-time deliveries had still not improved appreciably. What was Rubbermaid top management doing all this time? Wolfgang Schmitt can hardly escape the blame that in almost five years he had not corrected this serious problem with his most important customer.

The eagerness to merge that we saw in this case, by both McDonough of Newell and Schmitt of Rubbermaid, may not always be in the best interests of shareholders, and certainly not of employees. Communities also suffer, as plants are closed and headquarters moved. It may even not be in the best interest of the executives involved, as Schmitt realized to his dismay—despite taking home a sizable severance package. But is this enough to make up for losing the power and prestige of a top management position, and all the perks that go with it? And what if the value of the stock in the severance package crashes, as Schmitt found to his further dismay? And McDonough in his holdings?

In this era of merger mania, a more sober appraisal is needed by many firms. Not all mergers are in the best interests of both parties. Too many times a firm pays too much to acquire another firm, as we saw in Chapter 7 where Quaker Oats bought Snapple for $1.7 billion and three years later got rid of it for $300 million. Frequently the glowing prospects of synergy do not work out. (See "Information Box: Synergy" in Chapter 8 for a discussion of the allure and pitfalls of synergy in a merger.)

When an acquisition finally turns out to be unwise, especially where too much is paid for the acquired firm, the conclusion may be that someone fumbled the homework, that the research and investigation of the firm to be acquired was hasty, biased, or downright incompetent. Admittedly, in some cases several suitors may be bidding for the same acquisition candidate, and this then becomes a contest: Who will make the winning bid? The only beneficiaries to such a situation—besides the consultants, lawyers, and investment bankers—are the shareholders of the firm to be acquired.

UPDATE

Early in 2003, Galli announced plans to move the headquarters of Newell Rubbermaid from the "cornfields surrounding the hometown of Freeport, Illinois" to Atlanta, "the city of the future," as Galli depicted it. He thought moving would be a signal that big changes were happening inside and out. He saw that the key to a new image was being in a city that symbolized change and innovation. It didn't hurt that Atlanta offered a sweet deal, potentially giving the company up to $25 million in breaks and $1.3 million in cash for land and equipment purchases, as well as some tax relief.[13]

WHAT CAN BE LEARNED?

Customer service is vital in dealing with big customers. We saw in this case the consequences of not being able to meet the service demands of Wal-Mart. A vendor's very viability may depend on somehow gearing up to meet the service expectations. This should be a top priority if such a customer is not to be lost. Correcting the situation should be a matter of weeks or months, and not years.

The well-known brand name does not always compensate for higher prices or poor service when dealing with big retailers. Generally we think of a well-respected brand name as giving the vendor certain liberties, of insulating the vendor at least somewhat from vicious price competition, and even excusing the vendor from some service standards such as prompt and dependable delivery. After all, a respected brand name gives an image of quality, which lesser brands do not have, and an assured body of loyal customers.

Well, Wal-Mart's dealings with Rubbermaid before the merger certainly disprove that notion.

How can this be? It still becomes a matter of power position. Not having Rubbermaid, or Little Tikes toys, was hardly damaging to Wal-Mart with its eager alternative suppliers. But the loss of Wal-Mart, even only the partial loss of being given less shelf space, was serious for Rubbermaid.

The positive aspects of organizational restructuring for acquisitions are mixed. The idea of restructuring generally means downsizing. Some assets or corporate divisions may be sold off or eliminated, and the remaining organization thereby streamlined. This usually means lay-offs, plant closings, and headquarters relocations. In Rubbermaid's case, the small Ohio town of Wooster faced the loss of its

---

[13] Peralte C. Paul and Patti Bond, Cox News, as reported in "Out With the Old," *Cleveland Plain Dealer,* March 8, 2003, pp. C1, C3.

headquarters and some 3,000 jobs. Of course, management's defense always is that while jobs are being cut, the operations will be stronger in the long run. Perhaps; but not always.

Where an organization has become fat and inefficient with layers of bureaucracy, some pruning of personnel and operations is necessary. But how much is too much, and how much is not enough? Certainly those personnel who are not willing to accept change may have to be let go. Weak persons and operations that show little probability of improvement need to be cut, just as the athlete who can't perform up to expectations can hardly be carried. Still, it is usually better to wait for sufficient information as to the "why" of poor performance before assigning blame for unsatisfactory operational results. (You may want to review Chapter 5 and the Scott Paper and Al Dunlap case for the worst-case scenario here.)

Periodic housecleaning produces competitive health. In order to minimize the buildup of deadwood, all aspects of an organization ought to be objectively appraised periodically. Weak products and operations should be pruned, unless solid justification exists for keeping them. Such justification might include good growth prospects or complementing other products and operations or even providing a desired customer service. In particular, staff and headquarters personnel and functions should be scrutinized, perhaps every five years, with the objective of weeding out the redundant and superfluous. Most important, these evaluations should be done objectively, with decisive actions taken where needed. While some layoffs may result, they might not be necessary if suitable transfers are possible.

Going back to Rubbermaid, the five-year-long tolerance of little improvement in customer service was inexcusable, and one would think that heads should roll (as undoubtedly some did, and quickly, when Newell took over).

Is there life without Wal-Mart for a big mass market consumer goods manufacturer? Can such a large manufacturer be strong and profitable without selling to the giant retailers? Certainly other distribution channels are available in reaching consumers, such as smaller retailers, different types of retailers, wholesalers, and the Internet. For smaller manufacturers some of these are viable alternatives to Wal-Mart, Target, Kmart, and the various large department store corporations.

Newell and Rubbermaid's products were diversified but still geared to rather pedestrian household and hardware consumer use, hardly the grist to create a fashion or fad demand. A limited distribution strategy such as through boutiques would hardly produce the sales volume needed. Only the megaretailers could provide the mass distribution and sales volume needed. Of course, Wal-Mart was not the only large retailer, but it was the biggest. Kmart, Target, and the chain department stores were alternatives. But these tended to be just as demanding as Wal-Mart. This suggests that somehow the demands of giant retailers had to be catered to, regardless of costs or inclinations for firms like Newell and Rubbermaid.

Missionary salespeople can be a good enhancement of customer service in dealing with large retailers. Many vendors are realizing this today, and such sales-support staff are frequently used to provide the service, rapport, and feedback desirable in dealing with these most important clients. The vendor that provides the best such support may well win out over competitors. Furthermore, such missionaries may alert the vendor to emerging problems or competitive situations that need to be countered. Where they are swarm teams like Galli's, they can be a powerful tool in winning the battle for shelf space.

CONSIDER

Can you add any additional learning insights?

QUESTIONS

1. "Periodic evaluations of personnel and departments aimed at pruning deadwood cause far too much harm to the organization. Such 'axing' evaluations should themselves be pruned." Argue this position as persuasively as you can.

2. Now gather your most persuasive arguments for such "axing" evaluations.

3. How do you account for Rubbermaid's inability to improve its delivery service to Wal-Mart? What factors do you see as contributing to this on-going deficiency?

4. Do you think Newell acted too hastily in discharging Schmitt and other top executives so soon after the merger? Why or why not?

5. Do you think Wal-Mart and the other large retailers are going too far in their demands on their suppliers? Where would you draw the line?

6. Stanley Gault's strategy of trying to introduce a new product every day was lauded as the mark of a successful firm permeated with innovative thinking. Do you agree with this?

7. Is it likely that a decades-old organization, such as Rubbermaid, would be bloated with excessive bureaucracy and overhead? Why or why not?

HANDS-ON EXERCISES

1. Be a devil's advocate (one who argues a contrary position). You have been asked by several concerned board members to argue against the avid "Newellizing" policy of John McDonough at the next board meeting. Marshall as many contrary or cautionary arguments as you can and present them as persuasively, yet as tactfully, as you can.

2. You are one of the three divisional presidents fired by McDonough in the first two months of the merger. Describe your feelings and your action plan at this point. (If you want to make some assumptions, state them specifically.)

3. You are a vice president of Rubbermaid, reporting to Wolfgang Schmitt in 1995. The first serious complaints have surfaced from Wal-Mart concerning unacceptable delivery problems. Schmitt has ordered you to look into the complaints and prepare a course of action. Be as specific as you can on how you would approach this and what recommendations you would make.

TEAM DEBATE EXERCISE

It is early 1998. The demands of Wal-Mart are intensifying, and Newell is making overtures to acquire Rubbermaid. Debate these two courses of action in this turnabout year for Rubbermaid: (1) We must gear up to meet Wal-Mart's demands, even though estimated costs of complying are $300 million in a new computer network and other capital and operating costs, versus (2) It is better to sacrifice the increasingly dictatorial Wal-Mart account and seek alternative distribution.

INVITATION TO RESEARCH

What is Wolfgang Schmitt doing after being ousted from an active role with Newell Rubbermaid? Have Newell Rubbermaid's fortunes improved under Galli's management?

CHAPTER TEN

Hewlett-Packard's Merger With Compaq Computer: A Model of Success?

In July 1999, Hewlett-Packard, the world's second-biggest computer maker, chose Carly Fiorina to be its CEO. Thus she became the first outsider to take the reins in HP's sixty-year history. Never before had the company ever filled any top jobs with outsiders, and now this. Fiorina now became one of only three women to head a *Fortune* 500 company.

Three years later in May 2002, Fiorina engineered the biggest merger in high-tech history, with Compaq Computer. To do so she had to convince government regulators in the United States and Europe that this merger was not anti-competitive. She also had to get stockholder approval in the face of bitter opposition by Walter Hewlett, son of cofounder Bill Hewlett. She even had to survive a court challenge by Hewlett, who claimed she misled stockholders into voting for the merger.

By August 2003, it looked like the massive merger and the differing cultures was being well assimilated—unlike the problems of many mergers, including the other ones discussed in this Part II. Was HP to be the model, a paragon, for bringing together two organizations?

CARLY FIORINA

Carleton "Carly" Fiorina disappointed her father, a federal court judge and law professor, by dropping out of law school after one semester at UCLA. (The name Carleton was a tradition started in the Civil War when her father's family lost all the men named Carleton. In remembrance, each descendant named either a son Carleton or a daughter Cara Carleton. Carly is the ninth Cara Carleton since the Civil War.)

Before dropping law, Fiorina earned a BA in medieval history and philosophy from Stanford University in 1976. She received a MBA in marketing from the University of Maryland in 1980, and a MS from MIT's Sloan School.

She was forty-four years old when chosen for the CEO post at Hewlett-Packard, after nearly twenty years at AT&T and Lucent Technologies. At Lucent, she spearheaded the spin-off from AT&T in 1996, overseeing the company's initial public offering and the marketing campaign that positioned Lucent as an Internet company.

In 1998, she became president of Lucent's global service-provider business, a $19 billion operation that sold equipment to the world's largest telephone companies.

Fiorina is known for having a "silver tongue and an iron will," being articulate and persuasive. She has a personal touch that inspires intense loyalty, even giving such things as balloons and flowers to employees who land big contracts. Her coddling of customers at Lucent was legendary, as were her sales and marketing skills.[1]

Still, how did a student of philosophy and medieval history succeed in being the winning candidate for CEO by HP's search committee? Each member of the committee listed twenty qualities they would like to see in the new CEO. Then they boiled these down to four essential criteria: the ability to conceptualize and communicate sweeping strategies, the operations savvy to deliver on quarterly financial goals, the power to bring urgency to an organization, and the management skills to drive a nascent Internet vision throughout the company. Fiorina was selected from 300 potential candidates.[2] She would be the first outsider in the company's history to be CEO; indeed, no other outsiders had even been high-level executives. See the following Issue Box for a discussion of promoting from within.

THE HEWLETT-PACKARD COMPANY

HP was founded by Stanford University classmates Bill Hewlett and Dave Packard in 1938. They invented their company's first product in a tiny Palo Alto, California,

ISSUE BOX

SHOULD WE PROMOTE FROM WITHIN?

A heavy commitment to promoting from within, as had long characterized HP, is sometimes derisively called "inbreeding." The traditional argument against this stand maintains that an organization with such a policy is not alert to needed changes, that it is enamored with the status quo, "the way we have always done it." Proponents of promotion from within talk about the motivation and great loyalty, as well as team spirit, that it engenders, with every employee knowing that he or she has a chance of becoming a high-level executive.

The opposite course of action—that is, heavy commitment to placing outsiders in important executive positions—plays havoc with the morale of trainees and lower-level executives and destroys the sense of continuity and loyalty. A middle ground seems preferable: filling many executive positions from within, promoting this idea to encourage both the achievement of current executives and the recruiting of trainees, and at the same time bringing the strengths and experiences of outsiders into the organization.

Do you think there are particular circumstances in which one extreme or the other regarding promotion policy might be best? Discuss.

[1] Peter Burrows, with Peter Elstrom, "HP's Carly Fiorina: The Boss," *Business Week Online,* August 2, 1999.
[2] *Ibid.*

garage. It was an audio oscillator, an electronic test instrument for sound engineers. One of their first customers was Walt Disney Studios, which purchased the oscillators to develop and test an innovative sound system for the movie *Fantasia*. From 1938 to 1978 Hewlett and Packard built a company that became a model for thousands of subsequent Silicon Valley enterprises. In so doing, they created an informal egalitarian culture where brilliant engineers could flourish. Their emphasis on teamwork and respect for coworkers was dubbed the "HP Way."

From 1978 to 1992, John Young directed HP into becoming a major computer company, something AT&T, Honeywell, RCA, and other first-generation electronics companies never were able to do. But Young's efforts to consolidate HP's independent units bogged the company down in bureaucracy.

From 1992 to 1999, Lew Platt, a well-liked engineer who had joined the firm in 1966, guided HP through its growth in the mid-1990s, but he encountered difficulties when PC prices and sales in Asia plummeted in the late 1990s. By now, HP had become a staid company, but one with deep engineering roots and old-fashioned dependability.

THE SITUATION WHEN CARLY FIORINA TOOK OVER

"Some might say we're stodgy, but no one would say this company doesn't have a shining soul," Fiorina said when she took over.[3] HP had had no major breakthrough product since the inkjet printer in 1984. And the "HP Way" had evolved into a bureaucratic, consensus-style culture, somehow not conducive to being in the forefront in a time of rapid technological innovations.

A bloated bureaucracy seems a concomitant of many old successful organizations. We encounter others in this book, such as Sunbeam, Scott Paper, and Boeing. Examples abound of the bureaucracy run amok that had developed at HP. The company had 130 different product groups. When retailer Best Buy wanted to buy some computer products, fifty HP salespeople showed up to push their units' goods. When a vice president at HP wanted an operational change, thirty-seven different internal committees had to approve it.[4]

The dearth of new products went along with the cumbersome bureaucracy and the many different product groups. Managers often were reluctant to invest in new ideas for fear of missing their sales goals. If the proposed new product did not seem assured of healthy profits, or might cannibalize or take away business from existing products, it was not considered further.

The crown jewel of HP's arsenal of products was its printer business, which it had dominated since the 1980s. Ink and toner refills brought HP some $10 billion annually, 15 percent of total revenues. The profitability of these refills enabled the company to sell printers at low prices, much as Gillette sells its razors for bare-bones prices but makes huge profits on the sales of blades.

In 1998, with revenue growth slowing to the low single digits, CEO Platt began to act more decisively in combating the malaise. He hired McKinsey & Co. consultants to

---

[3] Burrows and Elstrom, "HP's Carly Fiorina: The Boss."

[4] Examples cited in Burrows and Elstrom, "HP's Carly Fiorina: The Boss."

explore restructuring, which led to the spin-off of HP's $8 billion test-and-measurement division, which had little relevance to the faster-growing computer and printer businesses. Platt put his own job on the line, suggesting the board hire a new CEO. This led to Fiorina's hiring.

FIORINA'S ACTIONS

The Merger with Compaq

Fiorina began searching for a big deal soon after becoming CEO. HP and Compaq agreed to the rough outline of a merger in June 2001, then spent four months planning it before the formal announcement. But she could hardly have expected the controversy of the ensuing merger battle, in which Walter Hewlett, an HP board member, first voted in favor of the deal and then waged a bitter and public campaign against it. He voted his family's 24 percent of the ballots against the merger, and it passed by only three percentage points. Not content with this defeat, Hewlett sued, charging that Fiorina and HP had illegally manipulated the vote, but he was unsuccessful and the merger went ahead.

What might have led to serious divisiveness among the organization and particularly the higher executive staff, and made Fiorina's job difficult at best, had more of the opposite effect. While some had initially resented her as an outsider who didn't understand the "HP Way," now most united behind their controversial new leader. "None of us anticipated the conflict. Carly was characterized as someone who destroyed the soul of HP, and we were her willing accomplices," Susan Bowick, HP's personnel chief said as she seethed.[5] Still, we would expect that many employees would resist change, knowing that Fiorina's arrival most likely heralded substantial changes and jobs lost. See the following Information Box for a discussion of resistance to change.

Forcing the Integration with Compaq

The planning and tradeoffs that went into merging the two firms may prove to be a model for other successful mergers. One month after the merger announcement, and before it had been officially approved, executives and staff from both firms met to resolve the thousands of issues involved in bringing a smooth integration. These ranged from what product lines to keep to which pension plan to use. The group started with almost 100 employees and grew to 2,500 by the merger's completion. Of the fifteen highest-ranking executives, ten were to come from HP and five from Compaq.

When the books of both organizations were opened, striking contrasts became evident: HP lost $100 million per quarter on an industry-standard product called NetServer, but made money on a proprietary model; Compaq had the reverse problem. HP's personal computer (PC) sales were mostly from retail, while Compaq had a

[5] Quentin Hardy, "We Did It," *Forbes*, August 11, 2003, p.80.

INFORMATION BOX

RESISTANCE TO CHANGE

People as well as organizations have a natural reluctance to embrace change. Change is disruptive. It can destroy accepted ways of doing things and familiar authority-responsibility relationships. It makes people uneasy because their routines will likely be disrupted, and their interpersonal relationships with subordinates, coworkers, and superiors may well be modified. Positions that were deemed important before the change may be downgraded or even eliminated. And persons who view themselves as highly competent in a particular job may be forced to assume unfamiliar duties.

Resistance to change can be combatted by good communication with participants about forthcoming changes. Without such communication, rumors and fears can assume massive proportions. Acceptance of change can be facilitated if managers involve employees as fully as possible in planning the changes, solicit and welcome their participation, and are assured that their own positions will not be impaired, only changed. Gradual rather than abrupt changes also make a transition smoother, as participants can be initially exposed to the changes without drastic upheavals.

In the final analysis, however, needed changes should not be delayed or canceled because of their possible negative repercussions on the organization. If change is necessary, it should be initiated. Individuals and organizations can adapt to change, although it may take some time.

The worst change an employee may face is layoff. And when no one knows when the next layoff will occur or who will be affected, morale and productivity may both be devastated. Discuss how managers might handle the necessity of upcoming layoffs.

profitable Web-based business. One company got a better deal from Microsoft on Windows, while the other did better with chips from Intel—and these small percentage differences amounted to billions of dollars.

The decision was made early that only one of the two companies' practices in the various areas could be allowed to survive in the new organization, and these changes would not be delayed. The choices involved jobs; the more consolidation, the more jobs lost. For examples: the HP Jornada handheld was dropped in favor of the Compaq iPAQ; the HP money-losing HP NetServer was killed and Compaq's rival Proliant line kept; Compaq's consumer PC business was axed in favor of the HP business; HP's corporate PC business was killed and Compaq's kept. Table 10.1 shows how the various product categories of the two firms were meshed.

The companies' four incompatible e-mail systems were consolidated into one, connecting 215,000 PCs and 49,000 other devices. Before the merger, HP and Compaq had more than 1,000 locally set policies on such things as rebates for customers and dental coverage for employees. These were unified into a single set of rules for 160 countries.

Table 10.1: How HP and Compaq Meshed

Servers
  HP servers made money on Unix, not Linux. Compaq made money on Linux, not Unix.

Commercial PCs
  Compaq made money. HP lost.

Consumer PCs
  HP made money. Compaq lost. (In order to maximize retail shelf space, HP closed the Compaq commercial line, but kept the brand.)

Printers
  HP was the world leader. Compaq contracted it out.

Handhelds
  Compaq's iPAQ won over HP's money-losing Jornada.

Software
  Compaq had software for individual servers to work harder. HP had software to manage big groups of servers.

Direct sales over the Internet
  Compaq had a $500 million engine. HP needed one.

Headquarters
  Compaq's Houston base was closed. HP stayed in Palo Alto, California.

Sources: Company; and Quentin Hardy, "We Did It," *Forbes,* August 11, 2003, p. 80.

Commentary: We can see from this meshing of the various products and systems that there was not major duplication. In most areas, where one was weak, the other was strong. The weak one then was eliminated or absorbed. This probably accounted for Fiorina's success in getting the merger approved by U.S. and European antitrust regulators.

Cost Cutting through Greater Efficiencies

Opportunities for cost cutting abounded. For examples:

- The old HP spent $140 million a year for printing documents, manuals, and brochures, with estimates that $50 million of these were unused; expenditures for the combined giant were now reduced to $130 million, with only $10 million of estimated waste.

- HP's manufacturing costs in the first year of the merger were down 26 percent. All HP's vendors were organized into just five supply chains, and most suppliers were connected to HP via the Internet and got consumption data and replenished orders automatically, for a saving of $1 billion. Inventory was sliced from forty-eight days' supply to forty days, thereby freeing up $1.2 billion in working capital.

- Accounts receivable were shrunk by four days, and the faster customer payments freed up $800 million.

- 17,000 jobs were eliminated after the merger.

Through these and other cost savings from the complex merger, Fiorina was able to cut $3.5 billion in annual costs—a billion more and a year earlier than promised.[6]

New Products and New Business

In the first full year after the merger, the results were impressive. Some 3,000 new patents had been racked up and 367 new products introduced, The patents spanned every part of the technology complex, from print technology to molecular computing. HP gained market share in key categories, and won a ten-year, $3 billion outsourcing deal with Procter & Gamble. Combined sales to Disney have more than doubled since 2001. HP built technology for Walt Disney World's newest ride, Mission: Space, and wireless headsets that explained the theme park in five languages.

The sales and profit quarterly results for fiscal 2002 are shown in Table 10.2. The first two quarters reflect the figures for the two companies before the merger, the last two quarters are after the merger. The last quarter's figures, ending October 31, 2002, made Carly Fiorina particularly proud: "During the fourth quarter of fiscal 2002, we returned to profitability after incurring nearly $3 billion in significant restructuring and other acquisition related charges, which led to an overall operating loss of $2.5 billion in the third fiscal quarter. The charges were primarily for eliminating redundant positions and offices around the world, in-process research and development, and employee retention bonuses incurred in accordance with the acquisition-integration plans we drew up in the first half of the year."[7]

On the basis of HP's apparent success in its merger with Compaq, Fiorina began pitching to corporate America that you have to consolidate and you have to cut, and

Table 10.2: Quarterly HP Results Before and After the Merger

For Fiscal Year Ended October 31, 2002 (millions)

	Before Merger		After Merger	
	Jan. 31	April 30	July 31	Oct. 31
Net revenue	$11,383	$10,621	$16,536	$18,048
Earnings (loss) from operations	625	414	(2,476)	425

Source: Hewlett-Packard company reports.

Commentary: You can see from this profit realized for the fourth quarter ended October 31, 2002, that Fiorina had reason to feel that the merger had been well orchestrated and the two firms rather quickly integrated. The big loss in the third quarter reflected the extraordinary expenses and write-offs due to the merger, and these were now behind the company as it looked to 2003 and beyond.

[6] *Ibid.*, pp. 76–82.

[7] *HP 2002 Annual Report*, CEO Carly Fiorina's Statement, January 31, 2003, p. 25.

we can help you do it because we have done it ourselves. HP portrayed itself as The Greatest Case Study Ever Told.

In merging its systems with Compaq's, HP could boast that it had erected a single communications network linking more than a quarter million PCs and handhelds; it handled 26 million e-mails a day. It also cut the number of software applications used from 7,000 to 5,000, and of components bought from 250,000 to 25,000.

We can perform similar miracles for you, Fiorina and her colleagues told such clients as General Electric, the Department of Homeland Security, and the Walt Disney Company, as well as many smaller firms. HP called its approach "adaptive enterprise," using new technology and smarter consulting to help organizations lower their overhead. HP guaranteed in written contracts that its adaptive model would save 15 to 30 percent in operating costs. HP claimed its own information-technology budget fell 24 percent after the merger by making use of this adaptive approach.

The Threat of IBM

HP's most awesome competitor to its services and consulting business was IBM. IBM called its approach "on-demand computing," and it was well equipped to dominate this market. While IBM's annual revenue was only $9 billion more than HP's $72 billion, the market value of its stock at $142 billion was more than twice HP's. IBM made huge profits, more than double HP's, even though IBM employed more than twice as many people. IBM was already a major factor in higher-profit services, while HP still got most of its revenue from such hardware as printers, servers, and PCs, many of these barely covering their costs. In a recent quarter, for example, HP's $5 billion PC business had a profit margin of only 0.4 percent. Furthermore, IBM had several years up on HP in promoting its business consulting services, part of its $36.3 billion global services unit. And it could boast that it also recently slashed $3 billion in costs by selling off three factories, shifting manufacturing to cheaper locations such as China and Ireland, and simplifying product designs. In the process IBM reduced inventories by a third, cut suppliers by half, and found other economies such as packaging PCs in cheaper cardboard boxes and recycling components from old mainframes.[8] Table 10.3 shows selected comparisons between IBM and HP.

Still, HP could claim one of the fastest and most effective mergers in all of business, and by far the biggest in the computer industry. It saw its adaptive model as a technology and strategy that could be sold to other firms contemplating mergers and strategic changes. The first big test was a $3 billion Procter & Gamble contract, for which the bidding specifications ran 10,000 pages. HP was the underdog against the likes of IBM and Electronic Data Services. But it won the contract on the first round, selling the potential cost savings, data virtualization, and new across-the-company roles for 2,000 Procter & Gamble technicians that it agreed to involve in the deal. IBM claimed that HP took a big future loss on the Procter & Gamble contract to get a trophy win. "It's good news to hear that," said HP veteran Ann Livermore, who ran the services business. "They're still underestimating our capabilities."[9]

---

[8] Daniel Lyons, "Back on the Chain Gang," *Forbes,* October 13, 2003, pp. 114, 116.
[9] Hardy, "We Did It," p. 82.

Table 10.3: IBM and HP Selected Comparisons, 2002

	IBM	HP
Sales (000,000)	81,186	63,082
Profits (000,000)	8,060	(680)
Assets (000,000)	96,484	72,093
Annual cash flow	$13.8 bil.	$4.8 bil.
Annual R&D	about $5 bil.	about $4 bil.
Total patents	38,000	19,000
Patents in past year	3,288	3,000
Size of sales army	35,000	21,750

Sources: "The Top 500 Companies in America," *Forbes,* April 14, 2003, p. 144; and Quentin Hardy, "We Did It," *Forbes,* August 11, 2003, p. 82.

Commentary: HP with the Compaq merger approaches the size of IBM in sales and in assets. The loss in income is hardly a true comparison with IBM because of the nonrecurring expenses of the merger. HP shows surprising strength in R&D spending and in patents in the past year. But its much lower cash flow is an impediment against IBM, and the sales staff is far smaller.

With this win, selling moved into high gear at HP. See the following Information Box for a discussion of the importance of selling at all levels of an organization.

IS THE "SUCCESSFUL" MERGER A DONE DEAL?

For a while, skeptics of the HP merger with Compaq appeared to be proven wrong. CEO Fiorina impressed analysts with cost cuts faster and deeper than they had ever imagined. She unveiled a host of new consumer products and a new vision. Investors were willing to attribute anemic revenue growth to the deep recession in technological spending.

As the economy and stock market began to improve in 2003, HP stock flirted with a fifty-two-week high of $24 a share until August 20, the day after HP announced it had missed its third-quarter earnings expectations because of slack European markets, which accounted for 40 percent of company sales, plus price-cutting in personal computers and weakness in HP's enterprise businesses. The stock slid 11 percent on this news.

Dell was the big culprit affecting HP's computer sales, and it had turned in a strong quarter, by contrast. HP failed to raise PC prices fast enough to keep pace with such components as computer memory. It also missed the boat in forecasting sales for flat-panel computer screens, and had to use expensive air freight to meet the demand. Then Dell announced it was cutting prices of its business computers by 22 percent.[10]

Fiorina planned to excite consumers, who had been steadier customers than corporate clients—consumer-related sales comprised 30 percent of total HP sales—with 150 new products in time for the 2003 back-to-school and Christmas seasons. HP was also testing a "store-in-store" concept at consumer electronics retailers, such as

[10] Quentin Hardy, "HP Slips Up," *Forbes,* September 15, 2003, p. 42.

INFORMATION BOX

IMPORTANCE OF SELLING AT ALL LEVELS

Whether you are working for a small or a big company, whether you are the lowest employee, or a professional sales rep, or a high-level corporate executive, or even the CEO, you should always be selling—to employees, customers, your bosses, Wall Street. Maybe you don't even realize it, but what you're really selling is yourself, although it may more ostensibly be a product, the company, or an idea.

Carly Fiorina certainly sold herself to those who could make her CEO—she was, after all, chosen from 300 other candidates. And she sold herself to the organization, if not to Walter Hewlett, so that they accepted her and were motivated far beyond what they had been.

Including Fiorina, each of HP's fifteen highest-ranking executives became a seller as well as a manager, calling on up to fifteen major customer accounts. For example, Peter Blackmore, a former Compaq top executive who ran the $11 billion-a-year large computer business, spent almost every weekday on a HP jet calling on major accounts, and also managed sales reps who brought in as much as $400 million a year each. "The thing you have to learn is the sheer scale of all this. Wherever you are, you have to get each process implanted right, or it won't work. People watch you all the time, your body language—you can't have an off day," he says. But Blackmore further expounds, "It's worth the exhaustion. It took IBM eight years to get their act together. We're going to beat them in two or three."

Do you agree with this assessment of the importance of selling at all levels in an organization? Can you think of some exceptions?

Sources: Adapted from Carol Hymowitz, "Business Leaders List Books That Inspire and Inform Their Work," *Wall Street Journal,* October 14, 2003, p. B1; and Quentin Hardy, "We Did It," *Forbes,* August 11, 2003, pp. 80, 82.

Circuit City. The HP area within these larger retailers would emphasize how all the HP products can work together, with assortments well beyond just PCs and printers, as for example media-center PCs that link home entertainment and computers together. But adding to HP's worries, Dell recently announced that it would cut prices on its personal computers and network servers. Sales for HP's personal-systems division, which included notebooks and desktops, rose 4.5 percent in the third quarter, but the division remained unprofitable.

Printers and ink refills have long carried HP, with rising sales and profits. Yet the enterprise-systems group, which generated about 20 percent of total revenue, remained the last of HP's four main businesses to still be in the red as fiscal 2003 drew to a close. The turnaround of the systems group, which made server computers, storage devices, and related software used by large corporations and agencies, was plagued by competition from Dell and IBM and by slow tech spending by corporate customers. Unless this could quickly be turned around, it would represent a continuing black mark on the controversial $19 billion Compaq purchase, which was partly undertaken to repair the enterprise business.[11]

Whether the merger with Compaq is a model of how to best handle mergers will have to be determined after more concrete and growing earnings results are established.

ANALYSIS

Unlike the other mergers we have seen in Part II, HP's merger with Compaq would seem an unqualified success, even if the combined company still faced profitability problems in its environment. After all, despite being larger now, it still faced formidable competitors, particularly IBM and Dell Computer. The boom in corporate spending for high tech had ended and the long-term growth prospects for the industry no longer seemed robust, while a number of marginal firms were on the ropes. With the merger, HP was poised to take full advantage of a revival of corporate interest, and a continuation and perhaps regeneration of consumer interest from new appealing products. All the while, the high-profit ink refill market was still dominated by HP, despite threatened incursions by Dell. (See Chapter 18 for the case on Dell Computer.)

We can identify these major ingredients of this successful merger:

First of All, It Was Not a Hostile Acquisition

Both parties believed coming together would strengthen the resulting firm, making it a bigger power in the market and bringing substantial cost savings.

Thorough and Objective Planning of the Merger

For four months before the merger was even announced, a top-level committee was studying the feasibility and planning for the integration of the two organizations. After the approval of the merger, months more of detailed preparation were involved. All conceivable problems or stumbling points were identified and resolved, with prompt implementation once the merger was officially approved.

Involvement of Executives and Staffs of Both Firms

The study group began with not quite 100 employees and had 2,500 by the merger's completion. Top level executives and staffs of both firms participated, in apparently a spirit of equality and objectivity, and many stayed with the new organization.

Redundancies Were Avoided at All Costs

Early disagreements or indecisions were curbed by HP strategist Robert Napier. "Every business decision triggers an IT [information technology] event," he declared. Such would force the new HP to rejigger its systems, which would be costly and time consuming. So the commitment was made to pick just one of the two companies' products and practices and make it law. The new merger mantra became: "Adopt and go."[12]

[11] For more details, see Amy Tsao, "Carly Fiorina's Next Big Challenge," *Business Week Online*, August 22, 2003; and Pui-Wing Tam, "Man on the Hot Seat at HP's Struggling Enterprise Unit," *Wall Street Journal*, August 19, 2003, pp. B1, B5.

[12] Hardy, "We Did It," p. 81.

Compatibility and Congeniality Were Sought

Fiorina joined the rather close-knit HP as an outsider, and had to strive to gain acceptance. The bitter merger battle with Walter Hewlett served to unite most of the organization behind Fiorina. The goodwill apparently carried over with the acceptance of Compaq employees as part of the HP team, even though some 17,000 jobs were eliminated because of redundancies.

Fiorina admitted that one of the toughest aspects of the integration was the reduction of workforce through a combination of layoffs, early retirements, and attrition. "Although layoffs are never easy, we worked hard to conduct this process with dignity and compassion, recognizing the many contributions our employees had made during their careers."[13]

WHAT CAN BE LEARNED?

Don't rush into the merger or acquisition. We have already seen in earlier cases the major blunders when firms spent billions of dollars for acquisitions without careful research and reasoned judgment. Sometimes it seems that CEOs are throwing around shareholders' money for a crap shoot. Sometimes it seems they get so caught up in the acquisitions game, especially if another firm is also interested in the acquisition, that a bidding war drives up prices beyond the reasonable.

Enough time should be taken to ensure what is a fair price and where the limit should be. Enough research needs to be done to prevent surprises. Ideally, the investigation should go beyond the numbers and records—the quantitative data—and look for qualitative from employees, customers, suppliers. For example, does the firm and its brands have a good reputation, a so-so one, or a negative one? Such information can hardly be gained in just a few weeks.

Organizational compatibility is important. While complete compatibility is hardly possible, especially in hostile acquisitions, it should be a major factor in the decision. Compatibility encompasses not only personnel in the two organizations and any cultural differences that may affect assimilation, but also products, distribution channels, ways of doing business, and a number of other factors. We have seen lack of compatibility in the other cases in this section, and the nasty surprises that came from this.

Redundancies should be identified and decisions made about them. We saw in this case superb attention given to identifying redundant products and operations and the decisions to remove these duplications. Sometimes HP's product or way of doing things was eliminated; other times Compaq's. The issues were already being decided before the merger was even announced. Such efforts brought profitable integration of the merger within a year.

One major argument for a merger is that two firms can thereby streamline separate operations by combining their various entities into one. For example, two

[13] *HP's 2002 Annual Report*, p. 23.

separate sales forces might be combined into one; similarly with such staff departments as information technology, human resources, and the like. Therefore, total costs should be less than they would be with two separate firms.

However, if the matter of redundancy is not quickly resolved, any cost benefits of the merger are delayed. Sometimes the result of a poorly researched merger is an indigestible mass. We have seen this in the three cases of Part II.

Assumptions should be defended. It is easy when caught up in the merger game, especially in a bidding war, to assume all kinds of optimistic things, such as a synergy that does not exist, a compatibility that can never be achieved, a sales potential that is not to be realized. Optimistic assumptions have no place in merger decisions. So much money is involved and so much executive and staff time will be needed that the bad merger decision can torment the firm and its shareholders for years to come, as we have seen before. Objectivity and conservative projections seem called for.

Top management should insist that assumptions and their reasoning be defended, at least as much as possible in an uncertain future. It might be prudent to consider a worst-case scenario: What if…? The use of a devil's advocate—one who takes an opposing position for the sake of bringing out all aspects of a particular course of action—can often be very worthwhile, yet is so seldom utilized.

A charismatic leader can energize an organization. Carly Fiorina proved to be a charismatic leader. Even though new to the HP organization, she was quickly able to motivate employees and managers to jump-start the innovation machine, to escape the staid and bureaucratic culture that had crept into the organization in recent years. She was able to get key people in both firms to enthusiastically support the Compaq merger and to work together to make it work. Mergers can succeed without charisma, but it helps if enthusiasm and commitment can be instilled.

CONSIDER

Can you think of other learning insights?

QUESTIONS

1. We noted the four criteria the HP search committee for the new CEO proposed. Do you think "human relations skills" should have been a fifth? Why or why not? Can you think of other criteria that might have been added?

2. "Tradition has no place in corporate thinking today." Discuss this statement.

3. Giant organizations are often plagued with cumbersome bureaucracies. Discuss how this tendency could be prevented as an organization grows to large size over many years.

4. Playing a devil's advocate, present the case against the Compaq merger. (You may want to research the arguments raised by Walter Hewlett in his aggressive campaign against the merger.)

5. "HP is gouging the consumer in charging such high prices for its ink refill cartridges. Sure, it's a high-profit item, but such profits cross the line and are obscene." Discuss.

6. Do you think the 17,000 jobs lost in the merger was laudatory, or should it be condemned? What would swing your opinion?

7. Should all redundancies be eliminated? Can you think of any that might be worth continuing?

HANDS-ON EXERCISES

1. You have been asked by Carly Fiorina to draw up a rationale for eliminating 17,000 jobs. She wants this to be as tactful and persuasive as possible.

2. Be a devil's advocate and argue against the elimination of 17,000 jobs.

3. Michael Dell, founder and CEO of Dell Computer, has his sights set on invading HP's lucrative printer and ink refill business. As an advisor to Carly Fiorina, what action, if any, would you recommend HP undertake to thwart Dell's incursion? Be prepared to support your recommendations.

TEAM DEBATE EXERCISES

1. The search committee for a new CEO is seriously considering Carly Fiorina. Based on the information in the case, debate the controversy: Should we hire this outsider, or look for someone else among our 300 candidates?

2. In the planning for the implementation of the merger, it has been proposed that all redundancies should be eliminated, that any commonalities of products and practices be resolved by axing one and combining into the other. Debate this draconian proposal.

INVITATION TO RESEARCH

1. How has HP's operating performance fared in fiscal year 2004 and beyond? Has the stock price risen above the low to middle 20s?

2. Is the business press in general extolling Carly Fiorina, or has it turned critical?

3. Whatever happened to Walter Hewlett?

PART THREE

PLANNING

CHAPTER ELEVEN

Euro Disney: Bungling a Successful Format

With high expectations, Euro Disney opened just outside Paris in April 1992. Success seemed ensured. After all, the Disneylands in Florida, California, and, most recently, Japan were all spectacular successes. But somehow all the rosy expectations became a delusion. The opening results cast even the future continuance of Euro Disney into doubt. How could what seemed so right be so wrong? What mistakes were made?

PRELUDE

Optimism

Perhaps a few early omens should have raised some cautions. Between 1987 and 1991, three $150 million amusement parks had opened in France with great fanfare. All had fallen flat, and by 1991 two were in bankruptcy. Now Walt Disney Company was finalizing its plans to open Europe's first Disneyland early in 1992. This would turn out to be a $4.4 billion enterprise sprawling over 5,000 acres twenty miles east of Paris. Initially it would have six hotels and 5,200 rooms, more rooms than the entire city of Cannes, and lodging was expected to triple in a few years as Disney opened a second theme park to keep visitors at the resort longer.

Disney also expected to develop a growing office complex, one only slightly smaller than France's biggest, La Defense, in Paris. Plans also called for shopping malls, apartments, golf courses, and vacation homes. Euro Disney would tightly control all this ancillary development, designing and building nearly everything itself, and eventually selling off the commercial properties at a huge profit.

Disney executives had no qualms about the huge enterprise, which would cover an area one-fifth the size of Paris itself. They were more worried that the park might not be big enough to handle the crowds:

My biggest fear is that we will be too successful.

139

I don't think it can miss. They are masters of marketing. When the place opens it will be perfect. And they know how to make people smile—even the French.[1]

Company executives initially predicted that 11 million Europeans would visit the extravaganza in the first year alone. After all, Europeans accounted for 2.7 million visits to the U.S. Disney parks and spent $1.6 billion on Disney merchandise. Surely a park in closer proximity would draw many thousands more. As Disney executives thought more about it, the forecast of 11 million seemed most conservative. They reasoned that since Disney parks in the United States (population of 250 million) attract 41 million visitors a year, then if Euro Disney attracted visitors in the same proportion, attendance could reach 60 million with Western Europe's 370 million people. Table 11.1 shows the 1990 attendance at the two U.S. Disney parks and the newest Japanese Disneyland, as well as the attendance/population ratios.

Adding fuel to the optimism was the fact that Europeans typically have more vacation time than do U.S. workers. For example, five-week vacations are commonplace for French and German employees, compared with two to three weeks for U.S. workers.

The failure of the three earlier French parks was seen as irrelevant. Robert Fitzpatrick, Euro Disneyland's chairman, stated, "We are spending 22 billion French francs before we open the door, while the other places spent 700 million. This means we can pay infinitely more attention to details—to costumes, hotels, shops, trash baskets—to create a fantastic place. There's just too great a response to Disney for us to fail."[2]

TABLE 11.1 Attendance and Attendance/Population Ratios, Disney Parks, 1990

	Visitors	Population	Ratio
	(millions)		
United States			
Disneyland (Southern California)	12.9	250	5.2%
Disney World/Epcot Center (Florida)	28.5	250	11.4%
Total United States	41.4		16.6%
Japan			
Tokyo Disneyland	16.0	124	13.5%
Euro Disney	?	310[a]	?

Source: Euro Disney, *Amusement Business Magazine.*

[a] Within a two-hour flight.

Commentary: Even if the attendance/population ratio for Euro Disney is only 10 percent, which is far below that of some other theme parks, still 31 million visitors could be expected. Euro Disney "conservatively" predicted 11 million the first year.

[1] Steven Greenhouse, "Playing Disney in the Parisian Fields," *New York Times* (February 17, 1991), Section 3, 1, 6.

[2] Greenhouse, "Playing Disney," 6.

Nonetheless, a few scattered signs indicated that not everyone was happy with the coming of Disney. Leftist demonstrators at Euro Disney's stock offering greeted company executives with eggs, ketchup, and "Mickey Go Home" signs. Some French intellectuals decried the pollution of the country's cultural ambiance with the coming of Mickey Mouse and company: They called the park an American cultural abomination. The mainstream press also seemed contrary, describing every Disney setback "with glee." And French officials in negotiating with Disney sought less American and more European culture at France's Magic Kingdom. Still, such protests and bad press seemed contrived, unrepresentative, and certainly not predictive. Company officials dismissed the early criticism as "the ravings of an insignificant elite."[3]

The Location Decision

In the search for a site for Euro Disney, Disney executives examined 200 locations in Europe. The other finalist was Barcelona, Spain. Its major attraction was warmer weather, but its transportation system was not as good as that around Paris, and it lacked level tracts of land of sufficient size. The clincher for the Paris decision was its more central location. Table 11.2 shows the number of people within two to six hours of the Paris site.

The beet fields of the Marne-la-Vallee area were the choice. Being near Paris seemed a major advantage, since Paris was Europe's biggest tourist draw. And France was eager to win the project to help lower its jobless rate and also to enhance its role as the center of tourist activity in Europe. The French government expected the project to create at least 30,000 jobs and to contribute $1 billion a year from foreign visitors.

To entice the project, the French government allowed Disney to buy up huge tracts of land at 1971 prices. It provided $750 million in loans at below-market rates, and it spent hundreds of millions of dollars on subway and other capital improvements for the park. For example, Paris's express subway was extended out to the park; a thirty-five-minute ride from downtown cost about $2.50. A new railroad station for

TABLE 11.2 Number of People Within 2–6 Hours of the Paris Site

Within a 2-hour drive	17 million people
Within a 4-hour drive	41 million people
Within a 6-hour drive	109 million people
Within a 2-hour flight	310 million people

Source: Euro Disney, *Amusement Business* magazine.

Commentary: The much more densely populated and geographically compact European continent makes access to Euro Disney much more convenient than it is in the United States.

[3] Peter Gumbel and Richard Turner, "Fans Like Euro Disney But Its Parent's Goofs Weigh the Park Down," *Wall Street Journal* (March 10, 1994), p. A12.

the high-speed Train a Grande Vitesse was built only 150 yards from the entrance gate. This enabled visitors from Brussels to arrive in only ninety minutes. And when the English Channel tunnel opened in 1994, even London was only three hours and ten minutes away. Actually, Euro Disney was the second largest construction project in Europe, second only to construction of the English Channel tunnel.

Financing

Euro Disney cost $4.4 billion. Table 11.3 shows the sources of financing in percentages. The Disney Company had a 49 percent stake in the project, which was the most that the French government would allow. For this stake it invested $160 million, while other investors contributed $1.2 billion in equity. The rest was financed by loans from the government, banks, and special partnerships formed to buy properties and lease them back.

The payoff for Disney began after the park opened. The company receives 10 percent of Euro Disney's admission fees and 5 percent of the food and merchandise revenues. This is the same arrangement as Disney has with the Japanese park. But in the Tokyo Disneyland, the company took no ownership interest, opting instead only for the licensing fees and a percentage of the revenues. The reason for the conservative position with Tokyo Disneyland was that Disney money was heavily committed to building the Epcot Center in Florida. Furthermore, Disney had some concerns about the Tokyo enterprise. This was the first non-American and the first cold-weather Disneyland. It seemed prudent to minimize the risks. But this turned out to be a significant blunder of conservatism, because Tokyo became a huge success, as the following Information Box discusses in more detail.

Special Modifications

With the experiences of the previous theme parks, and particularly that of the first cold-weather park in Tokyo, Disney construction executives were able to bring state-of-the-art refinements to Euro Disney. Exacting demands were placed on French

TABLE 11.3 Sources of Financing for Euro Disney (percent)

Total to Finance: $4.4 billion	100%
Shareholders equity, including $160 million from Walt Disney Company	32
Loan from French government	22
Loan from group of 45 banks	21
Bank loans to Disney hotels	16
Real estate partnerships	9

Source: Euro Disney.

Commentary: The full flavor of the leverage is shown here, with equity comprising only 32 percent of the total expenditure.

INFORMATION BOX

THE TOKYO DISNEYLAND SUCCESS

Tokyo Disneyland opened in 1983 on 201 acres in the eastern suburb of Urazasu. It was arranged that an ownership group, Oriental Land, would build, own, and operate the theme park with advice from Disney. The owners borrowed most of the $650 million needed to bring the project to fruition. Disney invested no money but receives 10 percent of the revenues from admission and rides and 5 percent of sales of food, drink, and souvenirs.

Although the start was slow, Japanese soon began flocking to the park in great numbers. By 1990 some 16 million a year passed through the turnstiles, about one-fourth more than visited Disneyland in California. In fiscal year 1990, revenues reached $988 million with profits of $150 million. Indicative of the Japanese preoccupation with things American, the park serves almost no Japanese food, and the live entertainers are mostly American. Japanese management even apologizes for the presence of a single Japanese restaurant inside the park: "A lot of elderly Japanese came here from outlying parts of Japan, and they were not very familiar with hog dogs and hamburgers."[4]

Disney executives were soon to realize the great mistake they made in not taking substantial ownership in Tokyo Disneyland. They did not want to make the same mistake with Euro Disney.

Would you expect the acceptance of the genuine American experience in Tokyo to be indicative of the reaction of the French and Europeans? Why or why not?

construction companies, and a higher level of performance and compliance resulted than many thought possible to achieve. The result was a major project on time, if not completely on budget. In contrast, the Channel tunnel was plagued by delays and severe cost overruns.

One of the things learned from the cold-weather project in Japan was that more needed to be done to protect visitors from such weather problems as wind, rain, and cold. Consequently, Euro Disney's ticket booths were protected from the elements, as were the lines waiting for attractions and even the moving sidewalk from the 12,000-car parking area.

Certain French accents—and British, German, and Italian accents as well—were added to the American flavor. The park has two official languages, English and French, but multilingual guides are available for Dutch, Spanish, German, and Italian visitors. Discoveryland, based on the science fiction of France's Jules Verne, is a new attraction. A theater with a full 360-degree screen acquaints visitors with a sweep of European history. And, not the least modification for cultural diversity, Snow White speaks German, and the Belle Notte Pizzeria and Pasticceria are right next to Pinocchio.

---

[4] James Sterngold, "Cinderella Hits Her Stride in Tokyo," *New York Times* (February 17,1991), p. 6.

Disney had foreseen that it might encounter some cultural problems. This was one of the reasons for choosing Robert Fitzpatrick as Euro Disney's president. He is American but speaks French, knows Europe well, and has a French wife. However, he was unable to establish the rapport needed and was replaced in 1993 by a French native. Still, some of his admonitions that France should not be approached as if it were Florida fell on deaf ears.

RESULTS

As the April 1992 opening approached, the company launched a massive communications blitz aimed at publicizing the fact that the fabled Disney experience was now accessible to all Europeans. Some 2,500 people from various print and broadcast media were lavishly entertained while being introduced to the new facilities. Most media people were positively impressed with the inauguration and with the enthusiastic spirit of the staffers. These public relations efforts, however, were criticized by some for being heavy-handed and for not providing access to Disney executives.

As 1992 wound down after the opening, it became clear that revenue projections were, unbelievably, not being met. But the opening turned out to be in the middle of a severe recession in Europe. European visitors, perhaps as a consequence, were far more frugal than their American counterparts. Many packed their own lunches and shunned the Disney hotels. For example, a visitor named Corine from southern France typified the "no spend" attitude of many: "it's a bottomless pit," she said as she, her husband, and their three children toured Euro Disney on a three-day visit. "Every time we turn around, one of the kids wants to buy something."[5] Perhaps investor expectations, despite the logic and rationale, were simply unrealistic.

Indeed, Disney had initially priced the park and the hotels to meet revenue targets and had assumed demand was there, at any price. Park admission was $42.25 for adults—higher than at the American parks. A room at the flagship Disneyland Hotel at the park's entrance cost about $340 a night, the equivalent of a top hotel in Paris. It was soon averaging only a 50 percent occupancy. Guests were not staying as long or spending as much on the fairly high-priced food and merchandise. We can label the initial pricing strategy at Euro Disney as *skimming pricing.* The Information Box on the following page discusses skimming and its opposite, penetration pricing.

Disney executives soon realized they had made a major miscalculation. Whereas visitors to Florida's Disney World often stayed more than four days, Euro Disney—with one theme park compared to Florida's three—was proving to be a two-day experience at best. Many visitors arrived early in the morning, rushed to the park, staying late at night, then checked out of the hotel the next morning before heading back to the park for one final exploration.

The problems of Euro Disney were not public acceptance (despite the earlier critics). Europeans loved the place. Since the opening it attracted just under 1 million visitors a month, thus easily achieving the original projections. Such patronage made it Europe's biggest paid tourist attraction. But the large numbers of frugal patrons did

[5] "Ailing Euro Disney May Face Closure," *Cleveland Plain Dealer* (January 1, 1994), E1.

INFORMATION BOX

SKIMMING AND PENETRATION PRICING

A firm with a new product or service may be in a temporary monopolistic situation. If there is little or no present and potential competition, more latitude in pricing is possible. In such a situation (and, of course, Euro Disney was in this situation), one of two basic and opposite approaches may be taken in the pricing strategy: skimming or penetration.

Skimming is a relatively high-price strategy. It is most tempting where the product or service is highly differentiated because it yields high per-unit profits. It is compatible with a quality image. But it has limitations. It assumes a rather inelastic demand curve, in which sales will not be appreciably affected by price. And if the product or service is easily imitated (which was hardly the case with Euro Disney), then competitors are encouraged because of the high profit margins.

The penetration strategy of low prices assumes an elastic demand curve, with sales increasing substantially if prices can be lowered. It is compatible with economies of scale, and it discourages competitive entry. The classic example of penetration pricing was the Model T Ford. Henry Ford lowered his prices to make the car within the means of the general public, expanded production into the millions, and in so doing realized new horizons of economies of scale.

Euro Disney correctly saw itself in a monopoly position; it correctly judged that it had a relatively inelastic demand curve with customers flocking to the park regardless of rather high prices. What it did not reckon with was the shrewdness of European visitors: Because of the high prices they shortened their stay, avoided the hotels, brought their own food and drink, and bought only sparingly the Disney merchandise.

What advantages would a lower price penetration strategy have offered Euro Disney? Do you see any drawbacks?

not come close to enabling Disney to meet revenue and profit projections and cover a bloated overhead.

Other operational errors and miscalculations, most of these cultural, hurt the enterprise. A policy of serving no alcohol in the park caused consternation in a country where wine is customary for lunch and dinner. (This policy has since been reversed.) Disney thought Monday would be a light day and Friday a heavy one and allocated staff accordingly, but the reverse was true. It found great peaks and valleys in attendance: The number of visitors per day in the high season could be ten times the number in slack times. The need to lay off employees during quiet periods came up against France's inflexible labor schedules.

One unpleasant surprise concerned breakfast. "We were told that Europeans don't take breakfast, so we downsized the restaurants," recalled one executive. "And guess what? Everybody showed up for breakfast. We were trying to serve 2,500 breakfasts at 350-seat restaurants. The lines were horrendous."[6]

[6] Gumbel and Turner, "Fans Like Euro Disney," A12.

Disney failed to anticipate another demand, this time from tour bus drivers. Restrooms were built for fifty drivers, but on peak days 2,000 drivers were seeking the facilities. "From impatient drivers to grumbling bankers, Disney stepped on toe after European toe."[7]

For the fiscal year ending September 30, 1993, the amusement park had lost $960 million, and the future of the park was in doubt (as of December 31, 1993, the cumulative loss was 6.04 billion francs, or $1.03 billion). Walt Disney made $175 million available to tide Euro Disney over until the next spring. Adding to the problems of the struggling park were heavy interest costs. As depicted in Table 11.3, against a total cost of $4.4 billion, only 32 percent of the project was financed by equity investment. Some $2.9 billion was borrowed primarily from sixty creditor banks, at interest rates running as high as 11 percent. Thus, the enterprise began heavily leveraged, and the hefty interest charges greatly increased the overhead to be covered from operations. Serious negotiations began with the banks to restructure and refinance.

ATTEMPTS TO RECOVER

The $960 million lost in the first fiscal year represented a shortfall of more than $2.5 million a day. The situation was not quite as dire as these statistics would seem to indicate. Actually, the park was generating an operating profit, but nonoperating costs were bringing it deeply into the red.

Still, operations were far from satisfactory, although they were becoming better. It had taken twenty months to smooth out the wrinkles and adjust to the miscalculations about demand for hotel rooms and the willingness of Europeans to pay substantial prices for lodging, meals, and merchandise. Operational efficiencies were slowly improving.

By the beginning of 1994, Euro Disney had been made more affordable. Prices of some hotel rooms were cut—for example, at the low end, from $76 per night to $51. Expensive jewelry was replaced by $10 T-shirts and $5 crayon sets. Luxury sitdown restaurants were converted to self-service. Off-season admission prices were reduced from $38 to $30. And operating costs were reduced 7 percent by streamlining operations and eliminating over 900 jobs.

Efficiency and economy became the new watchwords. Merchandise in stores was pared from 30,000 items to 17,000, with more of the remaining goods being pure U.S. Disney products. (The company had thought that European tastes might prefer more subtle items than the garish Mickey and Minnie souvenirs, but this was found not so.) The number of different food items offered by park services was reduced more than 50 percent. New training programs were designed to remotivate the 9,000 full-time permanent employees, to make them more responsive to customers and more flexible in their job assignments. Employees in contact with the public were given crash courses in German and Spanish.

Still, as we have seen, the problem had not been attendance, although the recession and the high prices had reduced it. Some 18 million people passed through the turnstiles in the first twenty months of operation. But they were not spending money

[7] *Ibid.*

as people did in the U.S. parks. Furthermore, Disney had alienated some European tour operators with its high prices, and it diligently sought to win them back.

Management had hoped to reduce the heavy interest overhead by selling the hotels to private investors. But the hotels had an occupancy rate of only 55 percent, making them unattractive to investors. Although the recession was a factor in such low occupancy rates, a significant part of the problem lay in the calculation of lodging demands. With the park just thirty-five minutes from the center of Paris, many visitors stayed in town. About the same time as the opening, the real estate market in France collapsed, making the hotels unsalable in the short term. This added to the overhead burden and confounded the business plan forecasts.

While some analysts were relegating Euro Disney to the cemetery, few remembered that Orlando's Disney World showed early symptoms of being a disappointment. Costs were heavier than expected, and attendance was below expectations. But Orlando's Disney World turned out to be one of the most profitable resorts in North America.

PROGNOSIS

Euro Disney had many things going for it, despite the disastrous early results. In May 1994, a station on the high-speed rail running from southern to northern France opened within walking distance of Euro Disney. This should help fill many of the hotel rooms too ambitiously built. The summer of 1994, the 50th anniversary of the Normandy invasion, brought many people to France. Another favorable sign for Euro Disney was the English Channel tunnel's opening in 1994, which potentially could bring a flood of British tourists.

Furthermore, the recession in Europe was bound to end, and with it should come renewed interest in travel. As real estate prices become more favorable, hotels can be sold and real estate development around the park spurred.

Even as Disney Chairman Michael Eisner threatened to close the park unless lenders restructured the debt, Disney increased its French presence, opening a Disney store on the Champs Elysees. The likelihood of a Disney pullout seemed remote, despite the posturing of Eisner, since royalty fees could be a sizable source of revenues even if the park only breaks even after servicing its debt. With only a 3.5 percent increase in revenues in 1995 and a 5 percent increase in 1996, these could yield $46 million in royalties for the parent company. "You can't ask, 'What does Euro Disney mean in 1995?' You have to ask, 'What does it mean in 1998?'"[8]

ANALYSIS

Euro Disney, as we have seen, fell far short of expectations in the first twenty months of its operation, so far short that its continued existence was even questioned. What went wrong?

[8] Lisa Gubernick, "Mickey N'est pas Fini," *Forbes* (February 14, 1994), p. 43.

External Factors

A serious economic recession that affected all of Europe undoubtedly was a major impediment to meeting expectations. As noted before, it adversely affected attendance —although still not all that much—but drastically affected spending patterns. Frugality was the order of the day for many visitors. The recessions also affected real estate demand and prices, thus saddling Disney with hotels it had hoped to sell at profitable prices to eager investors to take the strain off its hefty interest payments.

The company assumed that European visitors would not be greatly different from those visitors, foreign and domestic, of U.S. Disney parks. Yet, at least in the first few years of operation, visitors were much more price conscious. This suggested that those within a two- to four-hour drive of Euro Disney were considerably different from the ones who traveled overseas, at least in spending ability and willingness.

Internal Factors

Despite the decades of experience with the U.S. Disney parks and the successful experience with the new Japan park, Disney still made serious blunders in its operational planning, such as the demand for breakfasts, the insistence on wine at meals, the severe peaks and valleys in scheduling, and even such mundane things as sufficient restrooms for tour bus drivers. It had problems in motivating and training its French employees in efficiency and customer orientation. Did all these mistakes reflect an intractable French mindset or a deficiency of Disney management? Perhaps both. But Disney management should have researched all cultural differences more thoroughly. Further, the park needed major streamlining of inventories and operations after the opening. The mistakes suggested an arrogant mindset by Disney management: "We were arrogant," concedes one executive. "It was like 'We're building the Taj Mahal and people will come—on our terms.'"[9]

The miscalculations in hotel rooms and in pricing of many products, including food services, showed an insensitivity to the harsh economic conditions. But the greatest mistake was taking on too much debt for the park. The highly leveraged situation burdened Euro Disney with such hefty interest payments and overhead that the breakeven point was impossibly high, and it even threatened the viability of the enterprise. See the Information Box on the following page for a discussion of the important inputs and implications affecting breakeven, and how these should play a role in strategic planning.

Were such mistakes and miscalculations beyond what we would expect of reasonable executives? Probably not, with the probable exception of the crushing burden of debt. Any new venture is susceptible to surprises and the need to streamline and weed out its inefficiencies. While we would have expected such to have been done faster and more effectively from a well-tried Disney operation, European, and particularly French and Parisian, consumers and employees showed different behavior and attitude patterns than expected.

The worst sin that Disney management and investors could make would be to give up on Euro Disney and not to look ahead two to five years. A hint of the future

---

[9] Gumbel and Turner, "Fans Like Euro Disney," A12.

INFORMATION BOX

THE BREAKEVEN POINT

A breakeven analysis is a vital tool in making go/no-go decisions about new ventures and alternative business strategies. This can be shown graphically as follows:

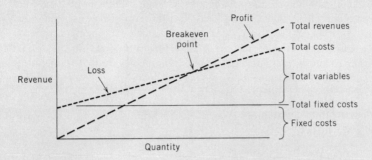

Below the breakeven point, the venture suffers losses; above it, the venture becomes profitable.

Let us make a hypothetical comparison of Euro Disney with its $1.6 billion in high interest loans (some of these as high as 11 percent) from the banks, and what the situation might be with more equity and less borrowed funds.

For this example, let us assume that other fixed costs are $240 million, that the average interest rate on the debt is 10 percent, and that average profit margin (contribution to overhead) from each visitor is $32. Now let us consider two scenarios: (a) the $1.6 billion of debt; and (b) only $0.5 billion of debt.

The number of visitors needed to break even are determined as follows:

$$\text{Breakeven} = \frac{\text{Total fixed costs}}{\text{Contribution to overhead}}$$

Scenario (a): Interest = 10% ($1,600,000,000) = $160,000,000
     Fixed costs = Interest + $240,000,000
            = 160,000,000 + 240,000,000
            = $400,000,000

$$\text{Breakeven} = \frac{\$400,000,000}{\$32} = 12,500,000 \text{ visitors needed to breakeven}$$

Scenario (b) Interest = 10% (500,000,000) = $50,000,000
     Fixed costs = 50,000,000 + 240,000,000
            = $290,000,000

$$\text{Breakeven} = \frac{\$290,000,000}{\$32} = 9,062,500 \text{ visitors needed to breakeven}$$

(Continues)

THE BREAKEVEN POINT *(Continued)*

Because Euro Disney expected 11 million visitors the first year, it obviously was not going to break even while servicing $1.6 billion in debt with $160 million in interest charges per year. The average visitor would have to be induced to spend more, thereby increasing the average profit or contribution to overhead.

In making go/no go decisions, many costs can be estimated quite closely. What cannot be determined as surely are the sales figures. Certain things can be done to affect the breakeven point. Obviously it can be lowered if the overhead is reduced, as we saw in s(but would probably affect total sales quite adversely). Promotion expenses can be either increased or decreased and affect the breakeven point, but they probably also have an impact on sales. Some costs of operation can be reduced, thus lowering the breakeven. But the hefty interest charges act as a lodestone over an enterprise, greatly increasing the overhead and requiring what may be an unattainable breakeven point.

Does a new venture have to break even or make a profit the first year to be worth going into? Why or why not?

promise was Christmas week of 1993. Despite the first year's $920 million in red ink, some 35,000 packed the park most days. A week later on a cold January day, some of the rides still had forty-minute waits.

POSTSCRIPT

On March 15, 1994, an agreement was struck aimed at making Euro Disney profitable by September 30, 1995. The European banks would fund another $500 million and make concessions such as forgiving eighteen months' interest and deferring all principal payments for three years. In return, Walt Disney Company agreed to spend about $750 million to bail out its Euro Disney affiliate. Thus, the debt would be halved, with interest payments greatly reduced. Disney also agreed to eliminate for five years the lucrative management fees and royalties it received on the sale of tickets and merchandise.[10]

The problems of Euro Disney were not resolved by mid-1994. The theme park and resort near Paris remained troubled. However, a new source for financing had emerged: A member of the Saudi Arabian royal family had agreed to invest up to $500 million for a 24 percent stake in Euro Disney. Prince Alwaleed had shown considerable sophistication in investing in troubled enterprises in the past. Now, his commitment to Euro Disney showed a belief in the ultimate success of the resort.[11]

Finally, in the third quarter of 1995, Euro Disney posted its first profit, some $35 million for the period. This compared with a year earlier loss of $113 million. By now, Euro Disney was only 39 percent owned by Disney. It attributed the turnaround

[10] Brian Coleman and Thomas R. King, "Euro Disney Rescue Package Wins Approval," *Wall Street Journal* (March 15, 1994), pp. A3, A5.

[11] Richard Turner and Brian Coleman, "Saudi to Buy as Much as 24% of Euro Disney," *Wall Street Journal* (June 2, 1994), p. A3.

partly to a new marketing strategy in which prices were slashed both at the gate and within the theme park in an effort to boost attendance, and also to shed the nagging image of being overpriced. A further attraction was the new "Space Mountain" ride that mimicked a trip to the moon.

However, some analysts questioned the staying power of such a movement into the black. In particular, they saw most of the gain coming from financial restructuring in which the debt-ridden Euro Disney struck a deal with its creditors to temporarily suspend debt and royalty payments. A second theme park and further property development were seen as essential in the longer term, as the payments would eventually resume.[12]

In August 1995, news broke of Walt Disney Company's proposed $10 billion acquisition of Capital Cities/ABC Inc. Experts said this would be an entertainment behemoth into the next century. Although many growth avenues were now possible, including great international growth in television programming and distribution such as ESPN and the Disney Channel, theme parks were considered very promising. Disney Chairman Michael Eisner announced possibilities of new theme parks in South America, possibly Brazil, as well as in Asia. He noted that Disney executives were scouring the globe looking for potential sites and partners in countries from Spain to China.[13]

In November 1997, *Forbes* magazine updated the situation with Euro Disney—although it had been renamed Disneyland Paris—under the provocative title, "Mickey's Last Laugh (Once Struggling Euro Disney Has Become a Favorite Tourist Destination in Europe)." The article noted that it had 11.7 million visitors in 1996, up from 8.8 million three years before. Cash flow margins had tripled since 1993, and even exceeded those of Tokyo Disneyland, the world's most popular park. The turnaround was credited to lower prices, the big new Space Mountain ride, and the 1994 restructuring that included the cash infusion from Prince Alwaleed.[14]

To the delight of the French government, plans were announced in 1999 to build a movie theme park, Disney Studios, next to the Magic Kingdom, to open in 2002. It was estimated that this expansion would attract an additional 4.2 million visitors annually, drawing people from farther afield in Europe. In 1998, Disneyland Paris had 12.5 million visitors, being France's number-one tourist attraction, beating out Notre Dame.

Also late in 1999, Disney and Hong Kong agreed to build a major Disney theme park there, with Disney investing $314 million for 43 percent ownership while Hong Kong contributed nearly $3 billion. Hong Kong's leaders expected the new park would generate 16,000 jobs when it opened in 2005, certainly a motivation for the unequal investment contributions.[15]

[12] Brian Coleman, "Euro Disney Posts Its First Profit, $35.3 Million for Its Third Quarter," *Wall Street Journal* (July 26, 1995), p. A9.

[13] Lisa Bannon, "Expanded Disney to Look Overseas for Fastest Growth," *Wall Street Journal* (August 2, 1995), p. A3.

[14] "Mickey's Last Laugh," *Forbes* (November 3, 1997), p. 16.

[15] "Hong Kong Betting $3 billion on Success of New Disneyland," *Cleveland Plain Dealer* (November 3, 1999), p. 2C; Charles Fleming, "Euro Disney to Build Movie Theme Park Outside Paris," *Wall Street Journal* (September 30, 1999), pp. A18, A21.

WHAT CAN BE LEARNED?

Beware the arrogant mindset, especially when dealing with new situations and new cultures. French sensitivities were offended by Disney corporate executives who often turned out to be brash, insensitive, and overbearing. A contentious attitude by Disney personnel alienated people and aggravated planning and operational difficulties. "The answer to doubts or suggestions invariably was, 'Do as we say, because we know best.'"[16]

Such a mindset is a natural concomitant to success. It is said that success breeds arrogance, but this inclination must be fought against by those who would spurn the ideas and concerns of others. For a proud and touchy people, the French, this almost contemptuous attitude by the Americans fueled resentment and glee at Disney miscues. It did not foster cooperation, understanding, or the willingness to smooth the process. One might almost speculate that had not the potential economic benefits to France been so great, the Euro Disney project might never have been approved.

Great success may be ephemeral. We often find that great successes are not lasting, that they have no staying power. Somehow the success pattern gets lost or forgotten or is not well rounded. Other times an operation grows beyond the capability of the originators. Hungry competitors are always in the wings, ready to take advantage of any lapse. As we saw with Euro Disney, having a closed mind to new ideas or to needed revisions of an old success pattern—the arrogance of success—makes expansion into different environments more difficult and even risky.

While corporate Disney has continued to have strong success with its other theme parks and its diversifications, competitors are moving in with their own theme parks in the United States and elsewhere. We may question whether this industry is approaching saturation, and we may wonder whether Disney has learned from its mistakes in Europe.

Highly leveraged situations are extremely vulnerable. During most of the 1980s, many managers, including corporate raiders, pursued a strategy of debt financing in contrast to equity (stock ownership) financing. Funds for such borrowing were usually readily available, heavy debt had income tax advantages, and profits could be distributed among fewer shares so that return on equity was enhanced. During this time a few voices decried the overleveraged situations of many companies. They predicted that when the eventual economic downturn came, such firms would find themselves unable to meet the heavy interest burden. Most lenders paid little heed to such lonesome voices and encouraged greater borrowing.

The widely publicized problems of some of the raiders in the late 1980s, such as Robert Campeau, who had acquired major department store corporations only to find himself overextended and unable to continue, suddenly changed some expansionist lending sentiments. The hard reality dawned that these arrangements were often fragile indeed, especially when they rested on

---

[16] Gumbel and Turner, "Fans Like Euro Disney," p. A1.

optimistic projections for asset sales, for revenues, and for cost savings to cover the interest payments. An economic slowdown hastened the demise of some of these ill-advised speculations.

Disney was guilty of the same speculative excesses with Euro Disney, relying far too much on borrowed funds and assuming that assets, such as hotels, could be easily sold off at higher prices to other investors. As we saw in the breakeven box, hefty interest charges from such overleveraged conditions can jeopardize the viability of the enterprise if revenue and profit projections fail to meet the rosy expectations.

Be judicious with the skimming price strategy. Euro Disney faced the classical situation favorable for a skimming price strategy. It was in a monopoly position, with no equivalent competitors likely. It faced a somewhat inelastic demand curve, which indicated that people would come almost regardless of price. So why not price to maximize per-unit profits? Unfortunately for Disney, the wily Europeans circumvented the high prices by frugality. Of course, a severe recession exacerbated the situation.

The learning insight from this example is that a skimming price assumes that customers are willing and able to pay the higher prices and have no lower-priced competitive alternatives. It is a faulty strategy when many customers are unable, or else unwilling, to pay the high prices and can find a way to experience the product or service in a modest way.

CONSIDER

Can you think of other learning insights from this case?

QUESTIONS

1. How could the company have erred so badly in its estimates of the spending patterns of European customers?

2. How could a better reading of the impact of cultural differences on revenues have been achieved?

3. What suggestions do you have for fostering a climate of sensitivity and goodwill in corporate dealings with the French?

4. How do you account for the great success of Tokyo Disneyland and the problems of Euro Disney? What are the key contributory differences?

5. Do you believe that Euro Disney might have done better if located elsewhere in Europe rather than just outside Paris? Why or why not?

6. "Mickey Mouse and the Disney park are an American cultural abomination." Evaluate this critical statement.

7. A deficiency in the planning was neglecting to win over European travel people, such as travel agents, tour guides, even bus drivers. How might this be corrected now?

HANDS-ON EXERCISES

Before

1. It is three months before the grand opening. As a staff assistant to the president of Euro Disney, you sense that the plans for high prices and luxury accommodations are ill-advised. What arguments would you marshal to persuade the company to offer lower prices and more moderate accommodations? Be as persuasive as you can.

After

2. It is six months after opening. Revenues are not meeting target, and a number of problems have surfaced and are being worked on. The major problem remains, however, that the venture needs more visitors and/or higher expenditures per visitor. Develop plans to improve the situation.

TEAM DEBATE EXERCISE

It is two years after the opening. Euro Disney is a monumental mistake, profitwise. Two schools of thought are emerging for improving the situation. One is to pour more money into the project, build one or two more theme parks, and really make this another Disney World. The other camp believes more investment would be wasted at this time, that the need is to pare expenses to the bone and wait for an eventual upturn. Debate the two positions.

INVITATION TO RESEARCH

Has the recent profitability of Euro Disney continued? Are expansion plans going ahead? Have other theme parks been announced?

CHAPTER TWELVE

Coca-Cola versus Pepsi: Move and Countermove

*I*ntense competition between Pepsi and Coca-Cola has characterized the soft-drink industry for over fifty years. In this chess game of giant firms, Coca-Cola ruled the soft-drink market throughout the 1950s, 1960s, and early 1970s. It outsold Pepsi by two to one. But this was to change. Then the chess game, or "war," switched to the international arena, and it became a "world war."

EARLY BATTLES, LEADING TO NEW COKE FIASCO
Pepsi Inroads, 1970s and 1980s

By the mid-1970s, the Coca-Cola Company was a lumbering giant. Performance reflected this. Between 1976 and 1978, the growth rate of Coca-Cola soft drinks dropped from 13 percent annually to a meager 2 percent. As the giant stumbled, Pepsi Cola was finding heady triumphs. First came the "Pepsi Generation." This advertising campaign captured the imagination of the baby boomers with its idealism and youth. This association with youth and vitality greatly enhanced the image of Pepsi and firmly associated it with the largest consumer market for soft drinks.

Then came another management coup, the "Pepsi Challenge," in which comparative taste tests with consumers showed a clear preference for Pepsi. This campaign led to a rapid increase in Pepsi's market share, from 6 to 14 percent of total U.S. soft-drink sales.

Coca-Cola, in defense, conducted its own taste tests. Alas, these tests had the same result—people liked the taste of Pepsi better, and market share changes reflected this. As Table 12.1 shows, by 1979 Pepsi was closing the gap on Coca-Cola, having 17.9 percent of the soft-drink market to Coke's 23.9 percent. By the end of 1984, Coke had only a 2.9 percent lead, while in the grocery store market it was now trailing by 1.7 percent. Further indication of the diminishing position of Coke relative to Pepsi was a study done by Coca-Cola's own marketing research department. This showed that, in 1972, 18 percent of soft-drink users drank Coke exclusively, while just

4 percent drank only Pepsi. In ten years the picture had changed greatly: Only 12 percent now claimed loyalty to Coke, while the number of exclusive Pepsi drinkers almost matched, with 11 percent. Figure 12.1 shows this change graphically.

What made the deteriorating comparative performance of Coke all the more worrisome and frustrating to Coca-Cola was that it was outspending Pepsi in advertising by $100 million. It had twice as many vending machines, dominated fountains, had more shelf space, and was competitively priced. Why was it losing market share? The advertising undoubtedly was not as effective as that of Pepsi, despite vastly more money spent. And this raises the question: How can we measure the effectiveness of advertising? See the following Information Box for a discussion.

TABLE 12.1 Coke and Pepsi Shares of Total Soft-Drink Market 1950s–1984

		1975		1979		1984	
	Mid-1950s Lead	% of Market	Lead	% of Market	Lead	% of Market	Lead
Coke	Better than 2 to 1	24.2	6.8	23.9	6.0	21.7	2.9
Pepsi		17.4		17.9		18.8	

Source: Thomas Oliver, *The Real Coke, The Real Story* (New York: Random House, 1986), pp. 21, 50; "Two Cokes Really Are Better Than One—For Now," *Business Week* (September 9, 1985), p. 38.

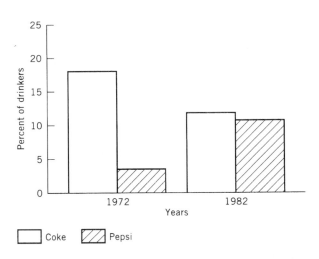

Figure 12.1 Coke versus Pepsi: Comparison of exclusive drinkers.

INFORMATION BOX

HOW DO WE MEASURE THE EFFECTIVENESS OF ADVERTISING?

A firm can spend millions of dollars for advertising, and it is only natural to want some feedback on the results of such an expenditure: To what extent did the advertising really pay off? Yet many problems confront the firm trying to measure this.

Most methods for measuring effectiveness focus not on sales changes but on how well the communication is remembered, recognized, or recalled. Most evaluative methods simply tell which ad is the best among those being appraised. But even though one ad may be found to be more memorable or to create more attention than another, that fact alone gives no assurance of relationship to sales success. A classic example of the dire consequences that can befall advertising people as a result of the inability to directly measure the impact of ads on sales occurred in December 1970.

In 1970, the Doyle Dane Bernbach advertising agency created memorable TV commercials for Alka-Seltzer, such as the "spicy meatball man," and the "poached oyster bride." These won professional awards as the best commercials of the year and received high marks for humor and audience recall. But in December, the $22 million account was abruptly switched to another agency. The reason? Alka-Seltzer's sales had dropped somewhat. Of course, no one will ever know whether the drop might have been much worse without these notable commercials.

So, how do we measure the value of millions of dollars spent for advertising? Not well; nor can we determine what is the right amount to spend, what is too much or too little.

Can a business succeed without advertising? Why or why not?

COCA-COLA TRIES TO BATTLE BACK

The Changing of the Guard at Coke

J. Paul Austin, chairman of Coca-Cola, was nearing retirement in 1980. Donald Keough, president of the American group, was expected to succeed him. But a new name, Roberto Goizueta, suddenly emerged.

Goizueta's background was far different from that of the typical Coca-Cola executive. He was not from Georgia (the company is headquartered in Atlanta), and was not even southern. Rather, he was the son of a wealthy Havana sugar plantation owner. He came to the United States at age sixteen, speaking virtually no English. By using the dictionary and watching movies, he quickly learned the language and graduated from Yale in 1955 with a degree in chemical engineering. Returning to Cuba, he went to work in Coke's Cuban research lab.

Goizueta's complacent life was to change in 1959 when Fidel Castro seized power. With his wife and three children he fled to the United States, arriving with $20. At Coca-Cola he became known as a brilliant administrator and in 1968 was brought to company headquarters; he became chairman of the board thirteen years later, in 1981. Donald Keough had to settle for being president.

In the new era of change, the sacredness of the commitment to the original Coke formula became tenuous and the ground was laid for the first flavor change in ninety-nine years.

Introducing a New Flavor for Coke

With the market-share erosion of the late 1970s and early 1980s, despite strong advertising and superior distribution, the company began to look at the soft-drink product itself. Taste was suspected as the chief culprit in Coke's decline, and marketing research seemed to confirm this. In September 1984, the technical division developed a sweeter flavor; in perhaps the biggest taste test ever, costing $4 million, 55 percent of 191,000 people approved it over both Pepsi and the original formula of Coke. Top executives unanimously agreed to change the taste and take the old Coke off the market.

But the results flabbergasted company executives. While some protests were expected, they quickly mushroomed; by mid-May calls were coming in at the rate of 5,000 a day, in addition to a barrage of angry letters. People were speaking of Coke as an American symbol and as a long-time friend who had suddenly betrayed them.

Anger spread across the country, fueled by media publicity. Fiddling with the formula for the ninety-nine-year-old beverage became an affront to patriotic pride. Even Goizueta's father spoke out against the switch and jokingly threatened to disown his son. By now the company began to worry about a consumer boycott against the product.

On July 11th, company officials capitulated to the outcry. They apologized to the public and brought back the original taste of Coke.

Roger Enrico, president of Pepsi-Cola, USA, gloated, "Clearly this is the Edsel of the '80s. This was a terrible mistake. Coke's got a lemon on its hand and now they're trying to make lemonade." Other critics labeled this the "marketing blunder of the decade."[1]

Unfortunately for Pepsi, the euphoria of a major blunder by Coca-Cola was short-lived. The two-cola strategy of Coca-Cola—it kept the new flavor in addition to bringing back the old classic—seemed to be stimulating sales far more than ever expected. While Coke Classic was outselling New Coke by better than two to one nationwide, for the full year of 1985 sales from all operations rose 10 percent and profits 9 percent. Coca-Cola's fortunes continued to improve steadily. By 1988, it was producing five of the top-ten selling soft drinks in the country, and now had a total 40 percent of the domestic market to 31 percent for Pepsi.[2]

---

[1] John Greenwald, "Coca-Cola's Big Fizzle," *Time*, July 22, 1985, pp. 48–49.

[2] "Some Things Don't Go Better with Coke," *Forbes*, March 21, 1988, pp. 34–35.

BATTLE SHIFTS TO INTERNATIONAL ARENA

Pepsi's Troubles in Brazil

Early in 1994, PepsiCo began an ambitious assault on the soft-drink market in Brazil. Making this invasion even more tempting was the opportunity to combat arch-rival Coca-Cola, already entrenched in this third-largest soft-drink market in the world, behind only the United States and Mexico.

The robust market of Brazil had attracted Pepsi before. Its hot weather and a growing teen population positioned Brazil to become one of the world's fastest-growing soft-drink markets, along with China, India, and Southeast Asia. But the potential still had barely been tapped. Brazilian consumers averaged only 264 eight-ounce servings of soft drinks a year, far below the U.S. average of about 800.[3]

Three times before over the previous twenty-five years, Pepsi had attempted to enter the Brazilian market with splashy promotional campaigns and different bottlers. Each of these efforts proved disappointing, and Pepsi had quickly dropped them and retreated from the field. In 1994 it planned a much more aggressive and enduring push.

A Super Bottler, Baesa, and Charles Beach

Buenos Aires Embotelladora SA, or Baesa, was to be the key to Pepsi's rejuvenated entry into Brazil. Baesa would be Pepsi's "superbottler," one that would buy small bottlers across Latin America, expand their marketing and distribution, and be the fulcrum in the drive against Coca-Cola. Charles Beach, the CEO of Baesa, was the person around whom Pepsi planned its strategy.

Beach, sixty-one, was a passionate, driven man, a veteran of the cola wars, but his was a checkered past. A Coca-Cola bottler in Virginia, he was indicted by a federal grand jury on charges of price fixing and received a $100,000 fine and a suspended prison sentence. He then bought Pepsi's small Puerto Rican franchise in 1987. Then, in 1989, Beach acquired the exclusive Pepsi franchise for Buenos Aires, Argentina—one of the most important bottling franchises outside the United States. By discounting and launching new products and packages, he caught Coke by surprise. In only three years he had increased Pepsi's market share in the Buenos Aires metro area from almost zero to 34 percent.[4]

With Pepsi's blessing, Beach expanded vigorously, borrowing heavily to do so. He bought major Pepsi franchises in Chile, Uruguay, and most importantly, Brazil, where he built four giant bottling plants. Pepsi worked closely with Baesa's expansion, providing funds to facilitate it.

However, they underestimated the aggressiveness of Coca-Cola. Their rival spent heavily on marketing and cold drink equipment for its choice customers. As a result Baesa was shut out of small retail outlets, those most profitable for bottlers. Goizueta, CEO of Coca-Cola, used his Latin American background to influence the

---

[3] Robert Frank and Jonathan Friedland, "How Pepsi's Charge into Brazil Fell Short of Its Ambitious Goals," *Wall Street Journal*, August 30, 1996, p. A1.

[4] Patricia Sellers, "How Coke Is Kicking Pepsi's Can," *Fortune*, October 28, 1996, p. 78.

Argentine president to reduce an onerous 24 percent tax on cola to 4 percent. This move strengthened Coke's position against Baesa, which in contrast to Coca-Cola was earning most of its profits from non-cola drinks.

By early 1996, Baesa's expansion plans—and Pepsi's dream—were floundering. The new Brazilian plants were running at only a third of capacity. Baesa lost $300 million for the first half of 1996, and PepsiCo injected another $40 million into Baesa.

On May 9, Beach was relieved of his position. Allegations now surfaced that Beach might have tampered with Baesa's books.[5] But PepsiCo's troubles did not end with the debacle in Brazil.

Intrigue in Venezuela

Brazil was symptomatic of other overseas problems for Pepsi. Roger Enrico, now CEO, had reasons to shake his head and wonder at how the gods seemed against him. But it was not the gods, it was Coca-Cola. Enrico had been on Coke's blacklist since he had gloated a decade before about the New Coke debacle in his memoir, *The Other Guy Blinked: How Pepsi Won the Cola Wars*. Goizueta was soon to gloat, "It appears that the company that claimed to have won the cola wars is now raising the white flag."[6]

The person Enrico thought was his close friend, Oswaldo Cisneros, head of one of Pepsi's oldest and largest foreign bottling franchises, suddenly abandoned Pepsi for Coca-Cola. Essentially, this took Pepsi out of the Venezuela market.

Despite close ties of the Cisneroses with the Enricos, little things led to the chasm. The closeness had developed when Enrico headed the international operations of PepsiCo. After Enrico left this position for higher offices at corporate headquarters, Oswaldo Cisneros felt that Pepsi management paid scant attention to Venezuela: "That showed I wasn't an important player in their future," he said.[7] Because Cisneros was growing older, he wanted to sell the bottling operation, but Pepsi was only willing to acquire 10 percent.

Coca-Cola wooed the Cisneroses with red-carpet treatment and frequent meetings with its highest executives. Eventually, Coca-Cola agreed to pay an estimated $500 million to buy 50 percent of the business.

Pepsi's Problems Elsewhere in the International Arena

Pepsi's problems in South America mirrored its problems worldwide. It had lost its initial lead in Russia, Eastern Europe, and parts of Southeast Asia. While it had a head start in India, this was being eroded by a hard-driving Coca-Cola. Even in Mexico its main bottler reported a loss of $15 million in 1995.

The contrast with Coca-Cola was significant. Pepsi still generated more than 70 percent of its beverage profits from the United States; Coca-Cola got 80 percent from overseas.[8]

[5] *Ibid.*, p. 79.
[6] *Ibid.*, p. 72.
[7] *Ibid.*, p. 75.
[8] Frank and Friedland, "How Pepsi's Charge into Brazil…," p. A1.

Table 12.2 shows the top ten markets for Coke and Pepsi in 1996 in the total world market. Coke had a 49 percent market share while Pepsi had only 17 percent, despite its investment of more than $2 billion since 1990 to straighten out its overseas bottling operations and improve its image.[9] With its careful investment in bottlers and increased financial resources to plow into marketing, Coke continued to gain greater control of the global soft-drink industry.

If there was any consolation for PepsiCo, it was that overseas business had always been far less important to it than to Coca-Cola, but this was slim comfort in view of the huge potential this market represented. Most of Pepsi's revenues were in the U.S. beverage, snack food, and restaurant businesses, with such well-known brands as Frito-Lay chips and Taco Bell, Pizza Hut, and KFC (Kentucky Fried Chicken) restaurants. But as a former Pepsi CEO was fond of stating, "We're proud of the U.S. business. But 95 percent of the world doesn't live here."[10] And Pepsi seemed unable to hold its own against Coke in this world market.

TABLE 12.2 Coke and Pepsi Shares of Total Soft-Drink Sales, Top Ten Markets, 1996

Markets	Market Shares	
	Coke	Pepsi
United States	42%	31%
Mexico	61	21
Japan	34	5
Brazil	51	10
East-Central Europe	40	21
Germany	56	5
Canada	37	34
Middle East	23	38
China	20	10
Britain	32	12

Source: Company annual reports, and Patricia Sellers, "How Coke is Kicking Pepsi's Can," *Fortune*, October 28, 1996, p. 82.

Commentary: These market share comparisons show the extent of Pepsi's ineptitude in its international markets. In only one of the top ten overseas markets is it ahead of Coke, and in some, such as Japan, Germany, and Brazil, it is practically a nonplayer.

[9] Robert Frank, "Pepsi Losing Overseas Fizz to Coca-Cola," *Wall Street Journal*, August 22, 1996, p. C2.
[10] *Ibid.*

COKE TRAVAILS IN EUROPE, 1999

The Trials of Douglas Ivester

In early 1998, Douglas Ivester took over as chairman and chief executive of Coca-Cola. Things seemed to go downhill from then on, but it was not entirely his fault. The first quarter of 1999 witnessed a sharp slowdown in Coca-Cola's North American business, at least partly due to price increases designed to overcome weakness resulting from overseas economic woes. While most analysts thought the sticker shock of higher prices would be temporary, some thought the company needed to be more innovative, needed to do more than offer supersize drinks.[11] Other problems emanated from a racial discrimination lawsuit, as well as Ivester's "brassy" attempts to make acquisitions such as Orangina and Cadbury Schweppes, angering overseas regulators and perhaps motivating them to make life difficult for Coke.

Such concerns paled before what was to come.

Contamination Scares

On June 8, 1999, a few dozen Belgian schoolchildren began throwing up after drinking Cokes. This was to result in one of the most serious crises in Coca-Cola's 113-year history. An early warning had seemingly been ignored when in mid-May the owner of a pub near Antwerp complained of four people becoming sick from drinking bad-smelling Coke. The company claimed to have investigated but found no problems.

The contamination news could not have hit at a worse time. Belgium was still reeling from a dioxin-contamination food scare in Belgian poultry and other foods, and European agencies were coming under fire for a breakdown in their watchdog responsibilities. Officials were inclined to be overzealous in their dealings with this big U.S. firm.

The problems worsened. Coca-Cola officials were meeting with Belgium's health minister, seeking to placate him, telling him that their analyses "show that it is about a deviation in taste and color" that might cause headaches and other symptoms, but "does not threaten the health of your child." In the middle of this meeting news came that fifteen additional students at a different school had gotten sick.[12]

It was thought that the contamination came from bottling plants in Antwerp and Ghent and from the Dunkirk plant that produced cans for the Belgium market. European newspapers were speculating that Coke cans were contaminated with rat poison.

Soon hundreds of sick people in France were blaming their illnesses on Coke, and France banned products from the Dunkirk plant. France and Belgium rebuffed Coca-Cola's urgent efforts to lift the ban, and scolded the company for not supplying enough information as to the cause of the problem. The setback left Coke out of the

---

[11] Nikhil Deogun, "Coke's Slower Sales Are Blamed on Price Increases," *Wall Street Journal,* March 31, 1999, pp. A3, A4.

[12] "Anatomy of a Recall: How Coke's Controls Fizzled Out in Europe," *Wall Street Journal,* June 29, 1999, p. A6.

market in parts of Europe because the company had badly underestimated how much explanation governments would demand before letting it back in business.

Not until June 17, did Belgium and France lift restrictions, and then only on some products; the bans were continued on Coca-Cola's Coke, Sprite, and Fanta. Then the Netherlands, Luxembourg, and Switzerland also imposed selective bans until health risks could be evaluated. Some 14 million cases of Coke products eventually were recalled in the five countries, and estimates were that Coke was losing $3.4 million per day in revenues. Case volume for the European division was expected to fall 6 to 7 percent from the previous year.[13] Summer, the peak soft-drink season, had arrived, and the timing of the scare could not have been worse.

The European Union requested further study as the health scare spread. At the same time, Coca-Cola and its local distributors launched an advertising campaign defending the quality of their products. The company blamed defective carbon dioxide, used for fizz, for problems at Antwerp. It also said the outside of cans made in Dunkirk were contaminated with a wood preservative during shipping. One company-commissioned study suggested that health problems were in the victim's heads. Meanwhile, the Ivory Coast seized 50,000 cans of Coke imported from Europe as a precautionary measure, though there was no evidence that anyone in the Ivory Coast had become ill by drinking imported Coke.

Problems continued to spread. All glass bottles of Bonaqua, a bottled water brand of Coca-Cola, were recalled in Poland because about 1,500 bottles were found to contain mold. This recall in Poland soon spread to glass bottles of Coke. Company officials believed the mold was caused by inadequate washing of returnable bottles. Barely a week later, the company recalled 180,000 plastic bottles of Bonaqua after discovering nonhazardous bacteria. Coca-Cola also had to recall some soft drinks in Portugal after small bits of charcoal from a filtration system were found in some cans.

Coca-Cola Finally Acts Aggressively

In the initial contamination episodes, Coca-Cola was accused of dragging its feet. Part of the problem in ameliorating the situation was the absence of an explanation by any top Coca-Cola officials. Ivester was criticized for this delay when he finally made an appearance in Brussels on June 18, ten days after the initial scare. He visited Brussels again four days later, meeting with the prime minister. Strenuous efforts to improve the company's image and public relations then began.

Ivester, in a major advertising campaign, apologized to Belgian consumers and explained "how the company allowed two breakdowns to occur." The ads showed his photograph along with these opening remarks, "My apologies to the consumers of Belgium; I should have spoken with you earlier." Ivester further promised to buy every Belgian household a Coke. A special consumer hotline was established, and fifty officials including several top executives were temporarily shifted from the Atlanta headquarters to Brussels.

[13] Will Edwards, "Coke Chairman Tries to Assure Europeans," *Cleveland Plain Dealer,* June 19, 1999, pp. 1C, 3C; and Nikhil Deogun, "Coke Estimates European Volume Plunged 6% to 7% in 2nd Quarter," *Wall Street Journal,* July 1, 1999, p. A4.

Five thousand delivery people then fanned out across the country offering a free 1.5 liter bottle of Coke's main brands to 4.37 million households. Around Belgium, Coke trucks and displays proclaimed, "Your Coca-Cola is coming back." In newspaper ads, the company explained its problems and noted it was destroying old products and using fresh ingredients for new drinks. A similar marketing strategy was planned for Poland, where two million free beverages were distributed to consumers.

PEPSI'S COMPETITIVE MANEUVERS NEAR THE MILLENNIUM

Pepsi's Role in Coke's European Problems

Some thought that Coca-Cola's problems should have been Pepsi's gain. Yet Pepsi did nothing to capitalize on the situation, did not gloat, did not increase advertising for its brand. Worldwide, Pepsi experienced some temporary gains in sales, most surprisingly in countries far removed from the scare—such as China. A Pepsi bottler in Eastern Europe probably expressed the prevailing company attitude when he observed that people were buying bottled water and juices instead of soda pop: "That's why we don't wish this stuff on anyone," he said, referring to the health scare.[14]

But Pepsi was not idle in Europe.

Pepsi's Antitrust Initiatives against Coca-Cola

In late July 1999, European Union officials raided offices of Coca-Cola and its bottlers in four countries in Europe—Germany, Austria, Denmark, and Britain—on suspicions that the company used its dominant market position to shut out competitors. Coming at a time when Coca-Cola was still trying to recover from the contamination problems, this was a cruel blow. All the more so since such alleged noncompetitive activities affected its plans to acquire some additional businesses in Europe.

The raids were expected to lead to a full-blown antitrust action against Coke. The major suspicion was that Coke was illegally using rebates to enhance its market share. The several types of rebates under investigation were rebates on sales that boosted Coke's market share at the expense of rivals, as well as rebates given to distributors who agreed to sell the full range of Coke products or to stop buying from competitors.

Coca-Cola's huge market share in most countries of Europe fed the concern. See Table 12.3 for Coke's market shares of the total soft-drink market in selected countries in Europe.

While the market share of Coke was being scrutinized by European antitrust officials, the investigation was sparked by a complaint—filed by Pepsi—that Coke was illegally trying to force competitors out of the market.

Pepsi also filed a complaint with Italian regulators, and they were quicker to act. A preliminary report found that Coca-Cola and its bottlers violated antitrust laws by abusing a dominant market position through practices such as discounts, bonuses,

TABLE 12.3 Coca-Cola's Market Share of Soft-Drink Market in Selected European Countries, 1998

France	59%
Spain	58
Germany	55
Central Europe	47
Italy	45
Nordic and Northern Eurasia	41
Great Britain	35

Source: Company published reports.

Commentary: The dominance of Coke in almost all countries of Europe, not surprisingly, makes it vulnerable to antitrust scrutiny.

and exclusive deals with wholesalers and retailers. The Italian regulators also said there was evidence that Coke had a "strategic plan" to remove Pepsi from the Italian market, one of the biggest in Europe, by paying wholesalers to remove Pepsi fountain equipment and replace it with Coke. At about this time, Australian and Chilean officials also began conducting informal inquiries in their markets.

Coca-Cola officials responded to the Italian report as follows: "We believe this is a baseless allegation by Pepsi and we believe that Pepsi's poor performance in Italy is due to their lack of commitment and investment there. As a result, they are attempting to compete with us in the courtroom instead of the marketplace."[15]

ANALYSIS

What Went Wrong with the New Coke Decision?

The most convenient scapegoat was the marketing research that preceded the decision. Yet Coca-Cola spent about $4 million and devoted two years to the marketing research. About 200,000 consumers were contacted during this time. The error in judgment was surely not from want of trying. But when we dig deeper into the research, some flaws become apparent.

Flawed Marketing Research

The major design of the marketing research involved taste tests by representative consumers. After all, the decision point was whether to go with a different flavored Coke, so what could be more logical than to conduct taste tests to determine acceptability of the new flavor, not only versus the old Coke but also versus Pepsi? The results were strongly positive for the new formula, even among Pepsi drinkers. This was a clear "go" signal.

[15] Betsy McKay, "Coke, Bottlers Violated Antitrust Laws in Italy, a Preliminary Report States," *Wall Street Journal*, August 13, 1999, p. A4.

With benefit of hindsight, however, some deficiencies in the research design merited concern. Research participants were not told that by picking one cola, they would lose the other. This proved to be a significant distortion: Any addition to the product line would naturally be far more acceptable than completely eliminating the traditional product would be.

While three to four new tastes were tested with almost 200,000 people, only 30,000 to 40,000 of these tried the specific formula for the new Coke. Research was geared more to the idea of a new, sweeter cola than that used in the final formula. In general, a sweeter flavor tends to be preferred in blind taste tests. This is particularly true with youths, the largest drinkers of sugared colas and the very group drinking more Pepsi in recent years. Interestingly, preference for sweeter-tasting products tends to diminish with use.[16]

Consumers were asked whether they favored change as a concept, and whether they would likely drink more, less, or the same amount of Coke if there were a change. But such questions could hardly prove the depth of feelings and emotional ties to the product.

Symbolic Value

The symbolic value of Coke was the sleeper. Perhaps this should have been foreseen. Perhaps the marketing research should have considered this possibility and designed the research to map it and determine the strength and durability of these values— that is, would they have a major effect on any substitution of a new flavor?

Admittedly, when we get into symbolic value and emotional involvement, any researcher is dealing with vague attitudes. But various attitudinal measures have been developed that can measure the strength or degree of emotional involvement.

Herd Instinct

Here we see a natural human phenomenon, the herd instinct: the tendency of people to follow an idea, a slogan, a concept, to "jump on the bandwagon." At first, new Coke appeared to be reasonably well accepted. But as more and more outcries were raised—fanned by the media—about the betrayal of the old tradition (somehow this became identified with motherhood, apple pie, and the flag), public attitudes shifted strongly against the perceived unworthy substitute. The bandwagon syndrome was fully activated. It is doubtful that by July 1985, Coca-Cola could have done anything to reverse the unfavorable tide. To wait for it to die down was fraught with danger— for who would be brave enough to predict the durability and possible heights of such a protest movement?

Could, or should, such a tide have been predicted? Perhaps not, at least regarding the full strength of the movement. Coca-Cola expected some protests. But perhaps it should have been more cautious, by considering a worst-case scenario in addition to what seemed the more probable, and by being better prepared for such a contingency.

---

[16] "New Cola Wins Round 1, but Can It Go the Distance?" *Business Week*, June 24, 1985, p. 48.

Pepsi's, and Later Coca-Cola's, International Problems

Pepsi's Defeats in South America

With hindsight we can identify many of the mistakes Pepsi made. It tried to expand too quickly in Argentina and Brazil, imprudently putting all its chips on a distributor with a checkered past instead of building up relationships more slowly and carefully. It did not monitor foreign operations closely enough or soon enough to prevent rash expansion of facilities and burdensome debt accumulations by affiliates. It did not listen closely enough to old distributors and their changing wants, and so lost Venezuela to Coca-Cola. Pepsi apparently did not learn from its past mistakes: Three times before it had tried to enter Brazil and had failed. Why the failures? Why was it not more careful to prevent failure the next time?

Finally, we can speculate that maybe Pepsi was not so bad, but rather that its major competitor was so good. Coca-Cola had slowly built up close relationships with foreign bottlers over decades. It was aggressive in defending its turf. Perhaps not the least of its strengths, at least in the lucrative Latin American markets, was a CEO who was also a Latino, who could speak Spanish and share the concerns and build on the egos of its local bottlers. In selling, this is known as a dyadic relationship, and it is discussed further in the following Information Box. After all, why can't a CEO do a selling job on a distributor and capitalize on a dyadic relationship?

INFORMATION BOX

THE DYADIC RELATIONSHIP

Sellers are now recognizing the importance of the buyer-seller interaction, a dyadic relationship. A transaction, negotiation, or relationship can often be helped by certain characteristics of the buyer and seller in the particular encounter. Research suggests that salespeople tend to be more successful if they have characteristics similar to their customers in age, size, and other demographic, social, and ethnic variables.

Of course, in the selling situation this suggests that selecting and hiring sales applicants most likely to be successful might require careful study of the characteristics of the firm's customers. Turning to the Pepsi/Coke confrontation in Brazil and Venezuela, the same concepts should apply and give a decided advantage to Coca-Cola and Roberto Goizueta in influencing government officials and local distributors. After all, in interacting with customers and affiliates, even a CEO needs to be persuasive in presenting ideas as well as handling problems and objections.

Can you think of any situations where the dyadic theory may not work?

Coca-Cola's Problems in Europe

Could Coca-Cola have handled the Belgian crisis better? With hindsight we see a flawed initial reaction. Still, the first incident of twenty-four schoolchildren getting ill and throwing up after drinking Coke seemed hardly a major crisis at the time. But crises often start slowly with only minor indications, and then mushroom to even catastrophic proportions. Eventually hundreds of people reported real or imagined illnesses from drinking the various Coca-Cola products.

The mistakes of Coca-Cola in handling the situation were (1) not taking the initial episodes seriously enough; (2) not realizing the intense involvement and skepticism of governmental officials, who demanded complete explanations of the cause(s) and were reluctant to lift bans; and (3) not involving Coca-Cola Chairman Douglas Ivester and other high-level executives soon enough. Allowing ten days to go by before his personal intervention was a long time for Ivester to let problems fester. Added to that, the quality-control lapses should not have been allowed to occur in the first place. Eventually, Ivester and Coke acted aggressively in restoring Coca-Cola, but lost revenues could not be fully recovered.

Of interest in this environment of moves and countermoves was Pepsi's restraint in not trying to take advantage of Coke's problems. This was not altruism but fear that the whole soft-drink industry would face decreased demand, so Pepsi did not want to aggravate the situation. Anyway, Pepsi saved its competitive thrusts for antitrust challenges.

With its great size and market-dominance visibility in country after country, Coca-Cola was vulnerable to regulatory scrutiny and antitrust allegations, especially when stimulated by its number one competitor, PepsiCo. Does this mean that it is dangerous for a firm to become too big? In certain environments, such as that facing a foreign firm in some European countries, this may well be the case. The firm then needs to tread carefully, tone down inclinations toward arrogance, and be subtle and patient in seeking acquisitions on foreign turf.

UPDATE

Faced with static or declining sales of flagship soft drinks—volume of Coca-Cola Classic fell 2 percent in 2002, while Pepsi's Cola volume dropped 4 percent—both firms looked for line extensions to boost overall sales. Vanilla Coke showed the most promise and Pepsi quickly followed with Pepsi Vanilla, although sales of these spin-offs dropped sharply after the novelty wore off.

Not surprising in view of slumping soda sales, both firms had moved aggressively into bottled water by 2003 as this became the fastest growing sector of the beverage industry. Americans, for example, consumed 60 percent more bottled water in 2002 than they did five years before; the increase was even greater in India and China. Furthermore, bottled water carried hefty markups. Pepsi's Aquafina became the leading brand and was enhanced by a multimillion-dollar promotional campaign, while Coke through acquisitions amassed such brands as Dannon, Evian, and Dasani. Nestlé was the industry leader with regional brands including Poland Spring and Deer Park. By summer 2003, competition among the major beverage companies became more intense as growth slowed and consumers leaned toward less-expensive, private-label brands. The result? A water price war. Some analysts would say it's about time that these exorbitant markups be curbed.[17]

WHAT CAN BE LEARNED?

Consumer taste is fickle. Taste tests are commonly used in marketing research, but I have always been skeptical of their validity. Take beer, for example. I know of few people—despite their strenuous claims—who can in blind taste tests unerringly identify which is which among three or four disguised brands of beer. We know that people tend to favor the sweeter in taste tests. But does this mean that a sweeter flavor will always win out in the marketplace? Hardly; something else is operating with consumer preference other than the fleeting essence of a taste—unless the flavor difference is extreme.

Brand image usually is a more powerful sales stimulant. Advertisers consistently have been more successful in cultivating a desirable image or personality for their brands or the types of people who use them, than by such vague statements as "better tasting."

Don't tamper with tradition. Not many firms have a 100-year-old tradition to be concerned with—or even twenty-five years or ten years. Most products have much shorter life cycles. No other product has been so widely used and so deeply entrenched in societal values and culture as Coke.

The psychological components of the great Coke protest make interesting speculation. Perhaps in an era of rapid change, many people wish to hang on to the one symbol of security or constancy in their lives—even if it's only the traditional Coke flavor. Perhaps many people found this protest to be an interesting way to escape the humdrum, by making waves in a rather harmless way, in the process seeing if a big corporation might be forced to cry "uncle."

One is left to wonder how many consumers would even have been aware of any change in flavor had the new formula been quietly introduced without fanfare. But, of course, the advertising siren call of "New" would have been muted.

So, do we dare tamper with tradition? In Coke's case the answer is probably not, unless done very quietly, but then Coke is unique.

Don't try to fix something that isn't broken. Conventional wisdom may advocate that changes are best made in response to problems, that when things are going smoothly the success pattern or strategy should not be tampered with. Perhaps. But perhaps not.

Actually, things were not going all that well for Coke by early 1985. Market share had steadily been lost to Pepsi for some years. So it was certainly worth considering a change, and the obvious one was a different flavor. I do not subscribe to the philosophy of "don't rock the boat." But Coke had another option.

---

[17] Sherri Day, *New York Times*, as reported in *Cleveland Plain Dealer*, "Water War," May 13, 2003, p. C2; Brian Steinberg, "Pepsi Puts Its Hopes on Plain Vanilla," *Wall Street Journal*, August 15, 2003, p. B4.

Don't burn your bridges. Coke could have introduced the new Coke, but kept the old one. Goizueta was concerned about dealer resentment at having to stock an additional product in the same limited space. Furthermore, he feared Pepsi emerging as the No. 1 soft drink due to two competing Cokes. This rationale was flawed, as events soon proved.

Consider the power of the media. Press and broadcast media are powerful influencers of public opinion. With new Coke, the media exacerbated the herd instinct by publicizing the protests. News seems to be spiciest when someone or something can be criticized or found wanting. We saw this fanning of protests in Coke's contamination problems in Europe, to the extent that some people came up with psychosomatic illnesses after drinking Coca-Cola products. The power of the media should not only be recognized but even be a factor in making decisions that may affect an organization's public image.

International growth requires tight controls. In Pepsi's problems with Baesa we saw the risks of placing too much trust in a distributor. One could question the selection of Charles Beach to spearhead the Pepsi invasion of Coke strongholds in South America. Prudence would dictate close monitoring of plans and performance, with major changes—in expansion planning, marketing strategy, and financial commitments—approved by corporate headquarters. In international dealings, the tendency is rather to loosen controls due to the distances, different customs and bureaucratic procedures, and unfamiliar cultures. We will see an extreme example of this in the Maytag case.

The human factor may be more important in international dealings. Rapport with associates and customers may be even more important in the international environment than domestically. The distances involved usually necessitate more decentralization and therefore more autonomy. If confidence and trust in foreign associates are misplaced, serious problems can result. Customers and affiliates may need a closer relationship with corporate management if they are not to be wooed away. Furthermore, in some countries the political climate is such that the major people in power must be catered to by the large firm wanting to do business in that country.

Sound crisis management requires prompt attention by top management. The chief executive is both an expediter and a public relations figure in crises, particularly in foreign environments. Ivester's delay in rushing to Belgium may have held up resolution of the crisis for several weeks, and it cost Coca-Cola millions in lost revenues. No other person is as well suited as the CEO to handle serious crises. Some sensitive foreign officials see lack of top management involvement as an affront to their country and are likely to express their displeasure in regulatory delays, calls for more investigations, and bad publicity toward a foreign firm. In the case of Coca-Cola, even though Ivester eventually made a conciliatory appearance, by that time some countries were receptive to antitrust allegations made by Pepsi against Coca-Cola.

CONSIDER

Can you think of other learning insights?

QUESTIONS

1. In the new Coke fiasco, how could Coca-Cola's marketing research have been improved? Be a specific as you can.

2. When a firm faces a negative press—as Coca-Cola did with the new Coke, and almost fifteen years later in Europe— what recourse does a firm have? Support your conclusions.

3. "If it's not broken, don't fix it." Evaluate this statement.

4. Do you think Coca-Cola engineered the whole scenario with the new Coke, including fanning initial protests, in order to get a bonanza of free publicity? Defend your position.

5. Critique Pepsi's handling of Baesa. Could it have prevented the South American disaster? If so, how?

6. With hindsight, how might Enrico, CEO of PepsiCo, have kept Cisneros, his principal bottler in Venezuela, in the fold instead of defecting to Coke?

7. How could Coca-Cola have lessened the chances of antitrust and regulatory scrutiny in Europe?

8. Do you think Pepsi can ever make big inroads in Coke's market share in Europe? Why or why not?

9. A big stockholder complains, "All this fuss over a few kids getting sick to their stomach. The media have blown this all out of proportion." Discuss.

HAND-ON EXERCISES

1. Assume that you are Robert Goizueta and that you are facing increased pressure in early July 1985 to abandon the new Coke and bring back the old formula. However, your latest marketing research suggests that only a small group of agitators are making all the fuss. Evaluate your options and support your recommendations to the board.

2. As a market analyst for PepsiCo, you have been asked to present recommendations to CEO Roger Enrico and the executive board for the invasion of Brazil's soft-drink market. The major bottler, Baesa, is already in place and waiting for Pepsi's final plans and objectives. You are to design a planning blueprint for the "invasion," complete with an estimated timetable.

3. You are a staff assistant to Ivester. It is 1998, and he has just assumed the top executive job with Coca-Cola. One of his first major decisions concerns raising soft-drink prices 5 percent to improve operating margins and make up for diminished revenues in a depressed European market. He wants you to provide pro and con information on this important decision.

TEAM DEBATE EXERCISES

1. "There is no way Pepsi can ever win the war with Coca-Cola. We are best off to try to hang on to what we have with soft drinks, and devote our efforts to diversify outside the soft-drink industry." Debate this issue: Should Pepsi essentially leave the battlefield to Coke and diversify, or should it continue to focus on the soft-drink core and try to win the cola war?

2. Debate Ivester's plan to distribute millions of free bottles of Coke products to people in Belgium and Poland. In particular, debate the costs versus benefits of this recovery strategy. Are the benefits likely to be worth the substantial cost?

INVITATION TO RESEARCH

What are the newest developments in the cola wars? Has Coke lost market share in Europe? Has Pepsi been able to make any inroads in Latin America? How do the two firms stack up in profitability? Have there been any innovations in this arena? How has the bottled-water battleground gone for the two rivals?

CHAPTER THIRTEEN

Philip Morris (Now Altria) Changes an Enduring Strategy

Cigarettes are among the world's most profitable consumer products. A cigarette "costs a penny to make, sell it for a dollar, it's addictive, and there's fantastic brand loyalty." So said master investor Warren Buffett as he unsuccessfully sought to take over RJR Nabisco, the tobacco conglomerate.[1] Perhaps because of its profitability, the morality of the business has long been suspect.

Criticisms have accelerated in recent years and bans widely imposed. Still, the tobacco industry remained stubbornly focused on its own best interests. That most critics saw tobacco's best interests as diametrically opposed to society's best interests mattered little to the industry as it aggressively struck back at critics.

In November 1998, a tobacco deal was agreed upon between the industry and forty-six states to settle state lawsuits filed to recover Medicaid money spent treating diseases related to smoking. Some said the industry got off far too easy, as this seemingly ended the largest-ever legal and financial threat to the industry.

Philip Morris has been the dominant player in this industry, the one most obdurate in self interest. Now its position seems to be changing as the environment has changed. But has it come too late for shareholders?

PAST CONTROVERSIAL STRATEGIES OF THE INDUSTRY

Targeting Minorities

Uptown

This new cigarette was packaged in a showy black-and-gold box and was the first cigarette aimed specifically at African American smokers. It followed the new strategy of tobacco companies to introduce new brands directed to specific groups, such as women. Now, using careful research and design, everything about Uptown was tailored to black consumers. The results were a surprise.

---

[1] "The Tobacco Trade: The Search for El Dorado," *Economist*, May 16, 1992, p. 21.

A storm of protests quickly ensued. Critics maintained that the marketing of Uptown represented a cold-blooded targeting of blacks, who already suffered a lung cancer rate 58 percent higher than whites. The protests even reached the office of Louis Sullivan, the Secretary of Health and Human Services. He quickly sided with the critics: "Uptown's message is more disease, more suffering, and more death for a group already bearing more than its share of smoking-related illness and mortality." He condemned "the attempts of tobacco merchants to earn profits at the expense of the health and well-being of our poor and minority citizens."[2]

Given the virulence of the protests, R. J. Reynolds abandoned the brand, bitterly decrying the negative attention being focused on it "by a few zealots." The critics had won, this time.

Dakota

Another new cigarette, also targeted to a specific group, was beset with controversy. Dakota was aimed at "virile females," non-college-educated women age 18–24 with blue-collar jobs. Critics of tobacco's relationship with lung cancer and heart disease were quick to attack this as a nefarious appeal to women.[3]

Another group was especially upset. In some Native American languages, *dakota* means "friend." Yet, to a group that already had high rates of smoking addiction, such a brand name seemed a betrayal.

Controversies over Tobacco Company Sponsorships

Following the 1971 federal ban on cigarette advertising on TV and radio, tobacco companies desperately sought other media to place their hundreds of millions of advertising dollars. By the early 1990s, serious questions were raised about their use of certain media, such as billboards, promoting smoking and alcohol in African American neighborhoods.

Advertising support of black publications by tobacco companies also came under fire, even though few other major firms were advertising in black media. Many small minority publications would have folded without the advertising dollars of tobacco companies.

Tobacco company support for minority organizations also began to be questioned. The National Association of Black Journalists turned down a Philip Morris donation: "We couldn't take money from an organization deliberately targeting minority populations with a substance that clearly causes cancer," said the group's president.[4]

The tobacco industry also liberally provided money to women's sports at a time when other money sources were virtually nonexistent. For example, Virginia Slims' funding brought women's tennis into prominence. The controversy concerning this is discussed in the following Issue Box.

---

[2] Ben Wildavsky, "Tilting at Billboards," *New Republic,* August 20, 1990, p. 19.

[3] Paul Cotton, "Tobacco Foes Attack Ads That Target Women, Minorities, Teens and the Poor," *Journal of the American Medical Association,* September 26, 1990, p. 1505.

[4] *Ibid.,* p. 1506.

ISSUE BOX

TOBACCO COMPANY SPONSORSHIP OF ATHLETIC EVENTS

Is it right to allow tobacco companies to sponsor certain athletic events? What seems like a simple question becomes far more complex when we consider tennis tournaments such as Virginia Slims. There is no longer any doubt that smoking causes serious damage to heart and lungs, yet tennis requires top physical fitness and aerobic capacity.

Such sponsorship had particular advantages from the industry's perspective. It created the false association of smoking with vitality and good health, and it directly targeted women. Philip Morris essentially was taking advantage of the inadequate funding of women's sports by making itself a strong presence in this sector.

So we have an unhealthy product sponsoring a prestigious athletic event for women, an event that at least in the early days, would probably not have been able to get started without such funding. Do we refuse this funding? Do we ban all cigarette promotions that appear to have some tie-in with health and fitness? Does the evil outweigh the good?

You are a feminist leader with convictions that women's athletic events should be promoted more strongly. The major funding for tennis and golf tournaments has been the tobacco industry, with no alternative major sponsors likely in the near future. Discuss your position regarding accepting such tobacco company sponsorships. Present your rationale as persuasively as you can.

The Old Joe Camel Controversy

In 1988, R. J. Reynolds stumbled upon a promotional theme for its slumping Camel brand. Using a sunglasses-clad, bulbous nosed cartoon camel that it called Joe, the company instituted a $75 million-a-year advertising campaign. It featured Joe in an array of macho gear and targeted the campaign to appeal to younger male smokers who had been deserting the Camel brand in droves.

The campaign was an outstanding success. In only three years, Camel's share of sales among the eighteen to twenty-four age group almost doubled, from 4.4 percent to 7.9 percent.

But the appeal of Old Joe went far beyond the target age group. It was found to be highly effective in reaching children under 13, who were enamored with the character. Six-year-olds in the United States recognized Joe Camel at a rate nearly equal to their recognition of Mickey Mouse. Children as young as three could even identify the cartoon character with cigarettes. Of even more concern to critics, Camel's share of the market of underage children who smoke was nearly 33 percent, up from less than 1 percent before the Old Joe campaign. See Table 13.1 for other results of the survey.

TABLE 13.1 **Survey Results of Knowledge and Attitudes Regarding Camel's Old Joe Advertisements**

	Students	Adults
Have seen Old Joe	97.7%	72.2%
Know the product	97.5	67.0
Think ad looks cool	58.0	39.9
Like Joe as a friend	35.0	14.4
Smokers who identify Camel as a favorite brand	33.0	8.7

Source: Data from the *Journal of the American Medical Association*, as presented in Walecia Konrad, " I'd Toddle a Mile for a Camel," *Business Week* (December 23, 1991), 34. The results are based on a survey of 1,055 students, ages twelve to nineteen years, and 345 adults, aged twenty-one to eighty-seven years.

Controversies over Billboard Advertising

Critics of Uptown initially focused on its billboard advertising in African American neighborhoods. They soon expanded their protests to cigarettes in general and to alcohol, and began painting over offending billboards. Their only recourse, they argued, was to use civil disobedience to attract attention to their cause.

Reverend Calvin O. Butts, III, fiery pastor of Harlem's Abyssinian Baptist Church, led his flock to paint signs with black paint to denote their Afrocentric perspective. Agitation against billboards spread beyond Harlem. In Dallas, County Commissioner John Wiley Price led a group that whitewashed twenty-five billboards and were arrested on misdemeanor charges. And Chicago priest Michael Pfleger was also arrested for painting billboards. Antismoking and antibillboard activists were having a field day.

Business began heeding the mounting pressure. In June 1990, the Outdoor Advertising Association of America, representing 80 percent of billboard companies, recommended voluntary limits on the number of billboards advertising cigarettes and alcohol near schools, places of worship, and minority neighborhoods.

Targeting Foreign Markets

With increasing restraints on cigarette advertising in the United States and diminishing per capita consumption of cigarettes, the industry turned to foreign markets. But criticisms and restraints surfaced there also.

At least as early as 1984, the Royal College of Physicians in the United Kingdom harshly denounced tobacco usage, stating that smoking killed 100,000 people a year in the U.K. alone. But the Royal College particularly condemned the lack of availability of low-tar cigarettes, "which are practically unknown in the Third World. Developed countries bear a heavy responsibility for the worldwide epidemic of smoking."[5] Most of Europe imposed some bans on advertising by 1991.

With Western Europe's mounting inhospitality to the industry, U.S. tobacco firms eagerly pushed into Asia, Africa, Eastern Europe, and the former Soviet Union.

[5] "Developing Countries: Governments Should Take Action Against Cigarettes before Too Many People Acquire the Potentially Lethal Habit," *New Scientist,* December 1, 1983, p. 42.

These were big markets and local cigarette makers were thought vulnerable to the aggressive efforts of U.S. firms.

Countries in the expanding sales area had few marketing or health labeling controls. In Hungary, for example, Marlboro cigarettes were even handed out to young fans at pop music concerts.[6]

ASSESSING THE CONTROVERSIES

Assessing Minority Targeting

Was R. J. Reynolds with its new Uptown brand an ogre, as critics claimed? Without question, inner-city African Americans had higher usage rates of tobacco and alcohol than their suburban counterparts. There was little doubt that the tobacco firms thought they had developed an effective targeting strategy with brands like Uptown. The dispute hinged on this: Are certain minority groups so susceptible to advertising that they need to be protected from potentially unsafe products?

Although proponents of controls argued that certain groups, such as young blacks, needed such protection, others saw that protection as paternalism. Even some black leaders decried the billboard whitewashing and the contentious preaching of certain ministers. Certainly, tempting people was hardly the same as oppressing them. After all, no one was forced to buy cigarettes and alcohol.

Regardless of the pro and con arguments concerning the susceptibility of inner-city youth to advertisements for unhealthy products, there was more validity to the claims of susceptibility when we consider the vulnerability of children to the attractive models found in most of these commercials and advertisements.

Finally, if legislation should be enacted to ban certain products from billboards, as was done with radio and TV advertising decades ago, where should the line be drawn? Should promotions in minority neighborhoods be banned for products that are economically extravagant, such as expensive athletic shoes? Or should promotions be banned for high-cholesterol foods that might cause high blood pressure, or for "muscle" cars that tempt reckless driving?

Assessing Joe Camel

Not surprisingly, criticism abounded after the American Medical Association's disclosure of the study that found Joe Camel so appealing to children. The basis for the concern, of course, was that the popular ads would encourage children to start smoking.

RJR would not yield. It denied that the ads were effective with children: "Just because children can identify our logo doesn't mean they will use the product."[7] It stoutly maintained its right to freedom of speech.

Some advertising people believed RJR's stubbornness was misguided: "By placing Old Joe as a freedom-of-speech issue instead of an unintentional marketing overshoot, [it] risks goading Congress into bans and restrictions on all tobacco advertising…

---

[6] "The Tobacco Trade: The Search for El Dorado," *Economist*, May 16, 1992, p. 23.
[7] "Old Joe Must Go," *Advertising Age*, January 13, 1992.

which would shift responsibility for tobacco products to the Food and Drug Administration [which] could regulate the tobacco industry into oblivion."[8] In 1997, without fanfare, RJR quit using the character.

See the following Issue Box for identification of more cigarette issues.

Assessing Tobacco's Push Overseas

A firm seems entitled to make all the profit it can. If certain markets are being severely constrained, should the firm not have the right to aggressively develop other markets? This is what the tobacco firms were doing.

The issue is clouded because while smoking is generally conceded to be hazardous to health, the consequences are a long time in coming. As long as many people are willing to take the risk, should the industry be so negatively judged?

When sophisticated and aggressive promotional efforts are directed to countries where consumers are more easily swayed and far more vulnerable to promotional blandishments, does our perception of what is ethical and what is undesirable change? *Should* it change?

THE SIEGE INTENSIFIES

Allegations of Rigging Nicotine Levels

A new threat arose to severely test the complacency of the tobacco industry: charges of long-time rigging of nicotine levels to ensure that smokers stay hooked. Adding fuel

---

ISSUE BOX

CONTROVERSIES ABOUT SMOKING

The controversies concerning cigarettes go beyond those detailed in this chapter. For example:

- Should smoking be restricted in the workplace? In restaurants? On airplanes?
- What about some firms not allowing employees to smoke even when they are not at work?
- Should the tobacco industry pay for employee suits concerning their "right to smoke"?
- Should nonsmokers be protected from passive smoke?
- In general, are the rights of smokers being violated?

Discuss, and even debate, these questions and any other smoking issues you come up with.

---

[8] Craig Stoltz, "RJR Appears Intent on Sticking with Old Joe to the Bitter End," *Adweek* Eastern Edition, March 23, 1992, p. 18.

to such allegations were Brown & Williamson Tobacco Corp. internal documents, including a fifty-four-page handbook, obtained by the *Wall Street Journal*, that indicated the tobacco companies had been adding ammonia-based compounds to their cigarettes. Such compounds essentially increase the potency of the nicotine a smoker actually inhales. The B & W documents asserted that Philip Morris's Marlboro, the top brand with a 30 percent share of the U.S. market at the time, may have been the first to use such ammonia technology. Regardless of who was the trailblazer, the practice seemingly had been widely emulated within the tobacco industry.[9]

Nicotine was viewed by most scientists as the active ingredient that caused cigarettes to be addictive. Anything that enhanced the delivery of this into the bloodstream, then, would increase the addictive potential. The industry would not admit this. It maintained that the ammonia compounds simply provided better flavor: "The primary purpose for using DAP [an ammonia additive] is to increase taste and flavor, reduce irritation, and to improve body." While admitting that this also increased nicotine delivery, a B & W spokesperson called this "an incidental effect."[10] And tobacco companies at that time still doggedly denied any links between cigarette smoking and heart disease, cancer, or other ailments.

But in 1996, newly disclosed documents suggested that Philip Morris, the nation's foremost tobacco company, had in place as far back as the 1970s, a system to hide and destroy potentially damaging data about smoking and health because of liability suits: "These documents appear to be further evidence of the industry's extraordinary effort to keep information secret. These are just the tip of the iceberg of evidence of document destruction."[11]

Repercussions

The industry was already under heavy fire before the latest revelations regarding the ammonia component. The increasing pressure, spearheaded by David Kessler, commissioner of the Food and Drug Administration (FDA), was a sharp contrast to the situation when he assumed office in 1990. Then, a few health coalitions were complaining about smoking, but that had been going on for decades. Few people in government paid any attention, mostly because the tobacco industry seemed invulnerable: It had the support of powerful tobacco-state congressmen, and it also had great monetary resources to provide for the finest legal arsenal and lobbying efforts.

Though perhaps not obvious to tobacco executives, the climate was subtly changing. In 1985, the Colorado ski resorts of Aspen and Vail banned smoking in restaurants. Other scattered bans followed. The slow trend abruptly accelerated in 1993 when the Environmental Protection Agency declared smoke a carcinogen. By the end of that year, 436 cities had smoking restrictions. Smoking came to be banned from all domestic air flights regardless of length.

[9] Alix M. Freedman, "Tobacco Firm Shows How Ammonia Spurs Delivery of Nicotine," *Wall Street Journal*, October 18, 1995, pp. A1 and A6.

[10] *Ibid.*, p.A6.

[11] Alix M. Freedman and Milo Geyelin, "Philip Morris Allegedly Hid Tobacco Data," *Wall Street Journal*, September 18, 1996, p. B11.

Even the courts were now joining the act. In addition to criminal investigations by the Justice Department in New York and Washington, thirteen other states were seeking reimbursement from the industry for the costs of treating smoking-related illnesses. More, the industry was facing eight class-action suits, filed by smokers claiming they became hooked while the industry concealed the addictive nature of its product. Dr. Kessler added the resources of the FDA to the struggle against cigarettes.

Previous defense strategies of the industry had always been that it was a smoker's free choice to smoke despite an "unproven" risk of lung cancer, so how dare the government interfere. Now Dr. Kessler, given the newest revelations about the ability of the industry to control nicotine with its powerful addictive hold, had a new strategy to present to Capitol Hill. Former Surgeon General C. Everett Koop exhorted him, "Do anything you can" to regulate tobacco. "The country is going to be behind you."[12]

On August 10, 1995, in the White House, President Clinton, with Dr. Kessler standing nearby, unveiled tough proposed regulations on cigarette marketing and sales. This marked the new FDA role against tobacco and one of the most aggressive federal moves ever against the industry.

Even the seemingly fertile overseas markets were rising against tobacco. An aggressive European ad campaign by Philip Morris backfired and had to be abandoned amid a barrage of lawsuits, complaints to regulators, and government criticism. The campaign had cited scientific studies to claim that second-hand smoke was not a meaningful health risk to nonsmokers. It even suggested that inhaling secondary smoke was less dangerous than eating cookies or drinking milk.[13]

The stakes were high, with Philip Morris's $11.4 billion in European tobacco sales in 1995. But resentment against the tobacco industry was rising by governments struggling to contain burgeoning healthcare costs.

Joe Camel was doing somewhat better in Argentina, despite intense criticism by antismoking activists. The first such advertising campaign in Latin America saw sales of the formerly marginal Camel brand shooting up 50 percent, a gain perhaps reflecting that Argentina had no national cigarette age limit.[14]

THE INDUSTRY FIGHTS BACK

The fight was on. Tobacco firms as well as the advertising industry attacked with lawsuits against the FDA, while tobacco-state legislators desperately worked to replace the proposed regulations with friendlier laws. In the first half of 1996, more than $15 million was spent for lobbying. More millions went to campaign donations to influence lawmakers, and additional millions to defend against lawsuits.[15]

---

[12] Laurie McGinley and Timothy Noah, "Long FDA Campaign And Bit of Serendipity Led to Tobacco Move," *Wall Street Journal*, August 22, 1995, p. A4.

[13] Martin Du Bois and Tara Parker-Pope, "Philip Morris Campaign Stirs Uproar in Europe," *Wall Street Journal*, July 1, 1996, p. B1.

[14] Jonathan Friedland, "Under Siege in the U.S., Joe Camel Pops Up Alive, Well in Argentina," *Wall Street Journal*, September 10, 1996, p. B1.

[15] "Tobacco Lobbyists Spend Millions," *Cleveland Plain Dealer*, September 9, 1996, p. 8A.

The tobacco industry had been notorious for defending its position aggressively and being confrontational. For example, the professor in Georgia whose study found that Joe Camel was almost as recognizable as Disney characters, thereby calling into question the tobacco industry's claims that their ads were not targeting children, became a target himself. The industry pressured the school administration to fire him. "The only protection he really had was tenure."[16] This saved his job.

Philip Morris had been the most aggressive player in attacking critics. In 1994, it sued the city of San Francisco, trying to overturn one of the nation's toughest anti-smoking ordinances. The ordinance had banned smoking in offices and would shortly also ban it in restaurants. Philip Morris sought to have the court declare the ordinance invalid and unenforceable.

Geoffrey Bible, chairman of Philip Morris, declared an all-out war on tobacco's enemies, with legal attacks and newspaper ads. "We are not going to be anybody's punching bag," he said. "When you are right and you fight, you win."[17] Bible had spent his career pushing Philip Morris around the world, and he practiced what he preached: smoking cigarettes and attacking all critics.

Those struggling to preserve the tobacco industry and its efforts to avoid regulation were by no means limited to cigarette producers. Tobacco was so ingrained in many sectors of our economy that many would suffer were it curbed—for example, local distributors, truckers, people who own and/or replenish vending machines, those involved with billboard ads for cigarettes, and the hundreds of thousands of vendors who saw cigarette sales as a major part of their total business, not to mention those tobacco growers in the southern states who could not countenance switching their crops to lower-yielding alternatives. Against the arguments that alternative employment would replace cigarette dependence, many looked back over decades of such dependence and cringed at the thought of losing it.

Results

Hopes that campaigns against smoking were becoming more effective were dispelled by a study published in the November 1998 *Journal of the American Medical Association.* The research, carried out at 116 four-year colleges, found 28 percent of college students smoking in 1997, up from 23 percent in 1994. The report concluded that this is a cause for national concern.[18]

In 1998, Philip Morris's share of the U.S. cigarette market passed 50 percent for the first time ever. In addition to its aggressive use of the Marlboro Man on billboards and magazine ads, it had a sales-incentive program called Retail Masters that rewarded retailers with payouts based on sales and display of Philip Morris cigarettes. This program was particularly effective with the rapidly expanding cigarette outlet stores, numbering some 5,800 by 1998, that sold nothing but cigarettes at 10 to 15 percent less

[16] Example cited in Maureen Smith, "Tenure," *University of Minnesota Update,* November 1995, p. 4.

[17] Suein L. Hwang, "Philip Morris's Passion to Market Cigarettes Helps It Outsell RJR," *Wall Street Journal,* October 30, 1995, p. A1.

[18] H. Wechsler et al, "Increased Levels of Cigarette Use Among College Students: A Cause for National Concern," *Journal of the American Medical Association,* Vol. 280, No. 19, November 18, 1998, pp. 1673–78.

than convenience stores because of generous manufacturer rebates and display fees. Other tobacco firms also had incentive programs but they were outmuscled by Philip Morris.

Overseas, Philip Morris captured nearly a quarter of the cigarette market in Turkey. It did this by enlisting help of influential people and lobbying heavily to eliminate the government's control of tobacco prices and distribution. Its prime bargaining chip was the promise that it would invest millions of dollars in the country. True to its word, Philip Morris opened a factory there in 1993, and expanded it into a $230 million facility. Now it could engineer cigarettes to appeal to Turkish tastes but with a stronger kick than local brands. Its salesmen, dressed as cowboys, spread across the country to 130,000 stores with a lavish in-store promotional and incentive plan. Of course, it advertised the Marlboro Man heavily, with cowboy scenes and panoramic vistas. In late 1996, pressured by antitobacco groups, Turkey's Parliament passed one of the strictest cigarette advertising bans in the world. Philip Morris got around this by omitting the word "Marlboro" in its ads and displays, but leaving the easily identifiable red chevron. The company also shrewdly noted that the ban did not cover all non-tobacco products and events, and so its Marlboro jeans and other paraphernalia became best sellers and potent promoters of the brand.

Tobacco companies found a new target market for future smokers in women in developing countries. To woo these potential users, they sponsored sporting and entertainment events geared to female audiences; they offered cigarettes with free crystal, designer scarves, and silk camisoles; they sent sample cigarettes as congratulatory gifts to new female college graduates. In the Philippines, a devoutly Catholic nation, calendars were even distributed featuring the Virgin Mary and other women saints praying over cigarette packs.[19]

THE TOBACCO DEAL

In spring 1997, new developments portended monumental changes for the tobacco industry in the United States. In late March, the solidarity of the industry was shaken as Liggett Group settled a lawsuit with twenty-two states, and in the process, finally admitted that smoking was addictive and caused cancer. Further information from Liggett showed that children were targeted for tobacco sales.

In April 1997, Philip Morris and RJR Nabisco began talks with attorneys general for twenty-five states suing to recover billions of dollars in public healthcare costs for sick smokers. The industry sought protection from all current and future litigation and was willing to contribute an amazing $300 billion over a twenty-five-year period to a settlement fund as well as making certain other concessions. When Congress took up ratifying the agreement in early 1998, it raised the price to $516 billion and cigarette makers were denied the legal immunity they sought in return. Not surprisingly, the industry did not accept this.

[19] Information for this section has been compiled from a number of sources including Yumiko Ono, "For Philip Morris, Every Store Is a Battlefield," *Wall Street Journal*, June 29, 1998, B1, B4; Suein L. Hwang, "How Philip Morris Got Turkey Hooked On American Tobacco," *Wall Street Journal*, September 11, 1998, pp. A1, A8; and Stephanie Stapleton, "Tobacco Targeting Third-World Women," *Cleveland Plain Dealer*, November 10, 1998, p. 3F.

In November 1998, a milder deal was negotiated, amounting to $206 billion spread over twenty-five years. Undoubtedly tobacco's position was bolstered by a major victory that Reynolds scored in a Florida state court on May 5, 1997, where a jury found that the firm was not responsible for the death of a three-pack-a-day smoker who died of lung cancer at age forty-nine. The trial had been closely watched as a bellwether for future litigation against the industry.

Forty-six states accepted the new deal. Four other states had already settled their individual suits for a total of $40 billion. The deal seemingly put an end to antismoking groups' hopes for a broader agreement that would combat teenage smoking and bring the industry under federal regulation.

THE BATTLE CONTINUED

As of August 1999, despite a stack of lawsuits and other actions filed against it, Philip Morris was still a very profitable company, bullying its competitors and outselling its nearest one, RJR, two to one. Despite a 70-cents-a-pack price hike to pay off forty-six states and their lawyers, demand was almost as big as ever. Not even a partial injunction granted in a lawsuit filed against Philip Morris by its competitors, alleging antitrust violations in its Retail Leaders sales-incentive program, could phase Philip Morris. It confidently planned to appeal the injunction. Meantime, with tens of millions of smokers on its computers, its "relationship marketing programs" were geared to keeping these dedicated smokers in the Philip Morris camp.

The situation was not as good for U.S. tobacco companies in international markets as the millennium neared. Not even in Asia, home to half of the billion smokers in the world, was the situation encouraging. In China, for example, the state-owned China National Tobacco Corp. had a virtual monopoly with a 200 percent import duty on cigarettes to go along with major distribution restrictions. Elsewhere in Asia, import duties and restraints brought slumping market shares to foreign firms, with their tobacco products not only hard to find and difficult to advertise and promote, but priced out of reach of most consumers. For Philip Morris, international tobacco sales were expected to decline 4 percent in 1999.

In the United States, suddenly the industry found that the legal battle was not over. On September 22, 1999, the Justice Department reopened the battle by filing a massive lawsuit claiming that forty-five years of industry deception about the dangers of cigarettes had contributed to the federal government's spending more than $20 billion a year to treat ill smokers.

On October 13, 1999, Philip Morris announced that it would spend about $100 million a year, or about 5 percent of its total ad budget, on a new TV campaign aimed at presenting a "friendlier public face." Antitobacco groups promptly criticized this as an attempt "to win court cases and stave off political change."[20]

---

[20] Compiled from these sources: Gordon Fairclough, "Philip Morris TV Ad Campaign Seeks to Repair Cigarette Maker's Image," *Wall Street Journal*, October 13, 1999, p. B16; David S. Cloud and Gordon Fairclough, "U.S. Sues Tobacco Makers in Massive Case," *Wall Street Journal*, September 23, 1999, pp. A3, A8; Seth Lubove, "Brand Power," *Forbes,* August 9, 1999, pp. 98–104; and Andrew Tanzer, "Where There's Smoke ...," *Forbes*, March 22, 1999, pp. 84–86.

ON THE ROPES

Louis Camilleri, forty-eight, took over as CEO from Geoffrey Bible in April 2002. He was a chain smoker, just like his predecessor (one wonders if being a chain smoker was one of the criteria for high executive positions). Things looked rosy now after the multibillion-dollar November 1998 settlement with states' attorneys general. Profit was growing and the threat of lawsuits had diminished. With Philip Morris's acquisition of Kraft Foods, it was decided to rename the company Altria Group, and play down the tobacco role.

By 2003, the situation had worsened for Philip Morris and for the other major players in the industry. Indicative of the hostile climate, now Camilleri could no longer even light up in his office because of a new ban on workplace smoking enacted by New York City; such bans seemed to be sweeping the country. Profit was being savaged due to a price war with upstart makers of deep-discount ciga-rettes. They had rushed into the market with names like Bronco, Ranger, Rave, and Hi-Val, as Philip Morris and its kind had kept raising prices to pay for the tobacco settlements and still make good profits to pay good dividends, while states were also raising excise taxes on cigarettes. By the end of 2002, the cut-rate smokes had already captured 10 percent of the market, versus 3 percent in 1998, and were growing fast.

On top of all this, an Illinois court had just awarded $10.1 billion in a class-action suit against Philip Morris. Despite the 1998 settlement, the risks of litigation were far from over. In an attempt to get the court to reconsider the immense award, Camilleri threatened to take the company into bankruptcy, which would stop its continuing payments to the states under the 1998 settlement.

Faced with these real and potential threats, Philip Morris decided on a massive strategy switch, one undreamed of ever before. It would try to make friends with the FDA in an effort to get the tobacco industry under government regulation. In doing so, this would make an alliance of longstanding bitter enemies, and bring together tobacco executives and anti-smoking advocates, northeastern and tobacco-state legislators, farmers, and urban liberals.

Philip Morris had always been in the vanguard opposed to government restrictions on the tobacco industry, for example, on cigarette advertising. But after the sweeping 1998 settlement of state lawsuits, it found that these restrictions resulted in protect-ing Marlboro's already well-established market share. FDA regulation would force the upstart firms to adhere to new standards for product manufacturing, thereby reducing their price advantage. The FDA could create new marketing rules, such as better disclosure of harmful ingredients, and even require nicotine levels to be reduced. Furthermore, government regulation ought to improve the image problems of the industry.

As of the end of 2003, this marriage with the FDA was no done deal. But Philip Morris had just about won over its tobacco farmers whose support was crucial in influencing their legislators.

It seemed that Philip Morris's self interest had become melded with that of the FDA. What a wonder!

In October 2003, RJR and Brown & Williamson, the second- and third-largest tobacco companies in the United States, agreed to merge into a new company to be called Reynolds American. It would have a 32 percent share of the market compared to Philip Morris's 49.6 percent. The deal was felt necessary to counter the increasingly perilous environment of multibillion-dollar lawsuits and competition from cheaper brands of cigarettes.[21]

WHAT CAN BE LEARNED?

Vigorously promoting a product seen by many as unsafe and even deadly is stupid in today's environment. This issue gets to the heart of the whole matter of tobacco production and marketing. Considered by practically all health experts as dangerous and, in the long run, life threatening, tobacco had long been protected by powerful governmental interests, but now such support has crumbled.

Even though the industry stubbornly admitted some health charges, it refused to soften its aggressiveness in promoting its products until very recently. Worse was its vigorous invasion of third-world countries, until these efforts faced such major obstacles in some countries that they had to be abandoned.

The industry has been huge with such allies and stakeholders as tobacco growers, processors, retailers, tax collectors, influential people in the halls of government, even the lowly paster of billboard ads. Not the least of the supporters of the industry have been the users themselves—though this now declines year by year. Loyal users tended to discount health dangers as being both far in the future and affecting only a minority of users. "And never me!" Still, it was easy for stakeholders to rationalize that any bad consequences were uncertain and that the good of profits and livelihoods outweighed any bad possibilities.

The increasing power of public opinion, of lawsuits in the billions of dollars, of now hostile regulators and Congress, have at last presented the tobacco industry with a new ballgame, one in which its old ways of denial and confrontation are no longer tolerated.

A firm in a vulnerable and changing industry must be prepared to adjust if it is to survive. In earlier days, the horse and buggy industry faced a major change with the coming of automobiles, and most firms in this industry could not adjust and failed. The tobacco industry now faces, not a change in technological innovation, but one of changing social mores. However, the tobacco companies are adjusting to the new business climate, by diversifying, changing their names, and modifying their tactics. The tobacco companies—surprisingly to many old-time tobacco executives and shareholders—can still be profitable, and now better citizens.

---

[21] Compiled from Associated Press, as reported in "Struggling Tobacco Titans Plan to Merge," *Cleveland Plain Dealer,* October 28, 2003, p. D3; George Fairclough, "Cheap Smokes Are Squeezing Big Tobacco," *Wall Street Journal,* November 14, 2002, pp. C1, C3; Vanessa O'Connell, "Why Philip Morris Decided to Make Friends with FDA," *Wall Street Journal,* Sept. 25, 2003, pp. A1, A12; and Gordon Fairclough and Vanessa O'Connell, "Altria's CEO Faces a Pack of Problems," *Wall Street Journal,* April 14, 2003, pp. B1, B9.

Even if it stays within the law, a firm's or industry's pursuit of its own best interests is not always compatible with society's best interests. This rationale that "if it's legal, it's ethical," supported tobacco efforts, whether Joe Camel, targeting naive consumers, foreign markets, or nicotine enhancement. No laws were directly violated by these actions, though many people would say they were reprehensible. So, do not laws reflect the majority views on what is moral and ethical? Critics would say that the absence of such laws regarding tobacco did not reflect prevailing majority views, but rather bowed to the positions of powerful minority interests.

Perhaps the real issue is whether a firm's best interests should take precedence over those of its customers and of society. Either position can be argued. On the one hand, should not a firm seek to foster a better corporate image and benefit both society and itself? Or should its priority be to maximize profitability to the benefit of management and stockholders regardless of outside critics? But management beware: In today's litigious environment, short-term profit-maximizing goals may not be in the long-term best interest of the firm.

A firm deludes itself if it thinks its public image is of no consequence as long as it has a loyal body of customers who support it. This was the enduring position of the tobacco industry: defiant of critics, secure in the loyalty of a sizable group of addicted customers, aided and abetted by powerful political interests whose constituents had an economic stake in the viability of the industry. For decades this mindset of disregard for the public image had successfully prevailed, despite the critics, including most of the medical profession.

Now, finally, the cigarette makers—and Philip Morris, the industry's most ardent defender—have come to realize that they were wrong to assume that the past can dictate the future and that attitudes and power positions would remain unchanged.

Perhaps it is high time they seek to develop a more healthy cigarette, even if this lessens the addiction and alienates diehards who demand their nicotine cocktail. The late-breaking news that Philip Morris is starting image-building advertising and even making overtures to the FDA for regulation suggests an about-face in recognizing the importance of public relations—if nothing else, to tone down jury awards. At the same time, these overtures to the FDA suggest a shrewd strategy to keep low-priced cigarette makers at bay.

In today's litigious environment, callousness regarding society's growing concerns may be courting disaster. The tobacco industry proudly boasted that it had never lost a lawsuit accusing it of responsibility for lung cancer and other physical ills and deaths. The industry had always successfully defended itself on the grounds of unproven charges of cigarette smoking contributing to such health hazards, and also on the grounds of individual choice and individual freedom. Now this defense has crumbled. Some at least would see that the industry capitulated in accepting the $206 billion tobacco deal. Others would say that it was the state attorneys general who capitulated in accepting a deal far milder than the 1997 one. Still, our litigious environment is doing what lawmakers in a pluralistic society with diverse agendas have been unable to do: bring the tobacco industry to heel. The day of reckoning may also be at hand for executives of other firms whose products and ways of doing business are contrary to the best interests of the general public.

CONSIDER

Can you propose other learning insights or ethical issues?

QUESTIONS

1. Do you actually think Joe Camel led youngsters to become smokers when they got older? Why or why not?

2. Do you have any problems with the idea of militant ministers leading their followers to whitewash offensive billboards? If not, is tearing down such billboards acceptable? Please discuss as objectively as possible.

3. Do you consider the proof adequate that cigarettes pose a substantial health threat and should be banned or tightly constrained? If you accept this position, should tobacco growers be allowed to continue growing such "unsafe" harvests without restraints?

4. Playing the devil's advocate (one who argues an opposing position for the sake of examining all sides), what arguments would you offer that cigarette manufacturers should be permitted complete freedom in targeting developing countries?

5. How do you weigh the relative merits of the tangible financial contributions the tobacco industry has made to various minority groups and media, against the negative health consequences of smoking?

6. What is the ethical difference between promoting cigarettes and promoting fatty, cholesterol-laden foods?

7. Do you agree with banning cigarettes from public buildings, workplaces, restaurants, airplanes, and so on? Why or why not?

8. Are the rights of nonsmokers being too highly emphasized? Do smokers have any rights?

HANDS-ON EXERCISES

1. You are the public relations spokesperson for Philip Morris. You have been ordered by Geoffrey Bible to plan a public relations campaign to overturn some of the banning of cigarettes. Be as specific and creative as you can. How successful do you think such efforts would be?

2. You have been asked by the executive committee of a major tobacco firm to draw up plans for changing the negative public image of the tobacco industry. The hope thereby is to defuse the probability of upcoming federal legislation

that would be detrimental, as well as curb the vulnerability to lawsuits. What do you propose? Be as specific as possible.

TEAM DEBATE EXERCISES

1. A great controversy is brewing in the executive offices of Philip Morris. One group led by CEO Bible is strongly in favor of aggressively attacking all critics and defending cigarettes with no holds barred. Still, there is another group supported by some prominent board members who believe the company and the industry should soften its stance. Debate the two sides of this issue.

2. Debate the issue: The rights of nonsmokers are being emphasized too much. Smokers have rights, too.

3. Debate the great $206 billion deal of the tobacco industry. Who won? Should the attorneys general have held stronger against the industry? (You may need to research the provisions of the final agreement with what might have been.)

INVITATION TO RESEARCH

1. What is the current situation regarding overseas incursions by U.S. tobacco companies?

2. Has the tobacco industry encountered any new criticisms?

3. Has the tobacco deal been advantageous to the industry?

4. Has smoking by college students changed since the JAMA report of 1998?

5. Is Geoffrey Bible still alive, or has he died of lung cancer?

6. Has Philip Morris succeeded in bringing regulation to the tobacco industry? If so, has this lessened the inroads of the discount smokes?

CHAPTER FOURTEEN

Vanguard: Success in Taking the Road Less Traveled

Vanguard Group has become the largest mutual fund family in the world, besting Fidelity Investments. While Fidelity had been increasing its fund assets about 20 percent a year, Vanguard was growing at 33 percent. Fidelity advertised heavily, while Vanguard did practically no advertising, spending a bare $8 million for a few ads to get people to ask for prospectuses. The Kaufmann Fund, one-hundredth Vanguard's size, spent that much for advertising, and General Mills spent twice as much just to introduce a new cereal, Sunrise.[1]

What is Vanguard's secret? How wise is it with such a consumer product to spurn advertising? The answer lies in the vision and steadfastness of John C. Bogle, the founder and now retired chairman.

JOHN BOGLE AND THE CREATION OF VANGUARD

In 1950, as a junior at Princeton, Bogle was groping for a topic for his senior thesis. He wanted a topic that no one had written about in any serious academic paper. In December 1949, he read an article in *Fortune* on mutual funds. At that time, all mutual funds were sold with sales commissions often 8 percent of the amount invested, and this was taken off the top as a front-end load. (This meant that if you invested $1,000, only $920 would be earning you money. Today we find no funds with a front-end load more than 6.5 percent, so there has been some improvement.) In addition, these funds had high yearly overheads or expense ratios. As Bogle thought about this, he wondered why funds couldn't be bought without salespeople or brokers and their steep commissions, and if growth could not be maximized by keeping overhead down.

Right after graduation he joined a tiny mutual fund, Wellington Management Company, and moved up rapidly. In 1965, at age thirty-five, he became the chief executive. Unwisely, he decided to merge with another firm, but the new partners turned out to be active managers (buying and selling with a vengeance), generating high overhead costs. The relationship was incompatible with Bogle's beliefs and in 1974 he was fired as chief executive.

[1] Thomas Easton, "The Gospel According to Vanguard," *Forbes* (February 8, 1999), p. 115.

He decided to go his own way and change the "very structure under which mutual funds operated" into a fund distribution company mutually owned by shareholders. The idea came from his Princeton thesis, and included such heresies as "reduction of sales loads and management fees," and "giving investors a fair shake" as the rock on which the new enterprise would be built. He chose the name "Vanguard" for his new company after the great victory of Lord Nelson over Napoleon's fleet with his flagship, *HMS Vanguard*. Bogle launched the Vanguard Group of Investment Companies on September 26, 1974, and he hoped "that just as Nelson's fleet had come to dominate the seas during the Napoleonic wars, our new flagship would come to dominate the mutual fund sea."[2]

But success was long in coming. Bogle brought out the first index fund the next year, a fund based on the Standard & Poor's 500 Stock Price Index, and named it Vanguard 500 Index Fund. It was designed to mirror the market averages, and thus required minimal management decisions and costs. It flopped initially. Analysts publicly derided the idea, arguing that astute management could beat the averages every time, though they ignored the costs of high-priced money managers and frequent trading.

At the millennium, twenty-five years later, this Vanguard flagship fund that tracks the 500 stocks on the Standard & Poor's Index had more than $75 billion in assets and had beat 86 percent of all actively managed stock funds in 1998, and an even higher percentage over the past decade. By early 2000, it overtook Fidelity's famed Magellan Fund as the largest mutual fund of all. The relative growth between Magellan and Vanguard's 500 Index is shown in Table 14.1.

The Vanguard family of funds had become the world's largest *no-load* mutual fund group, with 12 million shareholders and $442 billion in assets as of the beginning of 1999. Fidelity, *partly load and partly no-load,* had nearly $700 billion, but the gap was closing fast.

TABLE 14.1   Relative Growth Comparisons of the Two Largest Mutual Funds

	Assets (millions $)		5-Year Gain
	6/30/94	6/30/99	(percent)
Fidelity Magellan	$33,179	$97,594	194.2%
Vanguard 500 Index	8,443	92,644	997.3

Source: Company reports.

Commentary: Especially notable is the tremendous growth of Vanguard's 500 Index Fund in the last five years, growing from $8 billion in assets to over $92 billion.

---

[2] John C. Bogle, *Common Sense on Mutual Funds* (New York: Wiley, 1999), pp. 402–403.

Bogle, the Messiah

A feature article in the February 8, 1999, issue of *Forbes* had this headline:

> The Gospel According to Vanguard—How do you account for the explosive success of that strange business called Vanguard? Maybe it isn't really a business at all. It's a religion.[3]

Bogle's religion was low-cost investing and service to customers. He believed in funds being bought and not sold, thus, no loads or commissions to salespeople or brokers. Customers had to seek out and deal directly with Vanguard. The engine was frugality with the investor-owner's best interests paramount. This was not advertised, not pasted on billboards, but the gospel was preached in thousands of letters to shareholders, editors, Securities and Exchange Commission members, and congressmen. Bogle made many speeches, comments to the news media, and appearances on such TV channels as CNBC, and wrote two best-selling books. With his gaunt face and raspy voice, he became the zealot for low-cost investing, and the major critic of money managers who trade frenetically, in the process running up costs and tax burdens for their investors. As the legions of loyal and enthusiastic clients grew, word-of-mouth from past experiences, and favorable mentions in business and consumer periodicals such as *Forbes*, the *Wall Street Journal, Money,* and numerous daily newspapers, as well as TV stations, brought a groundswell of new and repeat business to Vanguard.

Bogle turned seventy in May 1999, and was forced to retire from Vanguard's board. The new chairman, John J. Brennan, forty-four, seemed imbued with the Bogle philosophy, and with vision. He said, "We're a small company, and we haven't begun to explore our opportunities, yet." He noted that there's Europe and Asia, to say nothing of the trillions of dollars held in non-Vanguard funds. "It's humbling."[4]

GREAT APPEAL OF VANGUARD

Performance

Each year *Forbes* presents "Mutual Funds Ratings" and "Best Buys." The Ratings list the hundreds of mutual funds that are open end, that is, can be bought and sold at current net asset prices.[5] The Best Buys are those select few that *Forbes* analysts judged to "invest wisely, spend frugally, and you get what you pay for," and that perform best in shareholder returns over both up and down markets. Vanguard equity and bond funds dominate *Forbes's* Best Buys:

> Of forty-three U.S. *equity* funds listed in the various categories, twelve are Vanguard funds.

> Of seventy *bond* funds, twenty-seven are Vanguard.[6]

[3] Easton, p. 115.

[4] Easton, p. 117.

[5] A far smaller number of mutuals are closed-end funds that have a fixed number of shares and are traded like stocks. These generally have higher annual expenses, yet sell at a discount from net asset value. We will disregard these in this case.

[6] *Forbes* (August 23, 1999), pp. 128, 136–137.

Forbes explains that "the preponderance of Vanguard funds in our Best Buy Tables is a testament to the firm's cost controls ... Higher expenses, for most other fund families, are like lead weights. Why carry them?"[7] Table 14.2 shows representative examples of the substantially lower expenses of Vanguard funds relative to others on the Best Buy list.[8]

Looking at total averages, the typical mutual fund has an expense ratio of 1.24 percent of assets annually. The ratio for Vanguard's 101 funds is 0.28 percent, almost a full percentage point lower.[9]

How does Vanguard achieve such a low expense ratio? We noted before the reluctance to advertise at all; nor does it have any mass sales force. Its commitment has been to pare costs to the absolute minimum. But there have been other economies.

TABLE 14.2 Comparative Expense Ratios of Representative Mutual Funds

	Annual Expenses per $100
Balanced Equity Funds:	
Vanguard Wellington Fund	0.31
Columbia Balanced Fund	0.67
Janus Balanced Fund	0.93
Ranier Balanced Portfolio	1.19
Index Equity Funds:	
Vanguard 500 Index	0.18
T. Rowe Price Equity Index 500	0.40
Dreyfus S&P 500 Index	0.50
Gateway Fund	1.02
Municipal Long-Term Bonds:	
Vanguard High Yield Tax Exempt	0.20
Dreyfus Basic Muni Bond	0.45
Strong High Yield Muni Bond	0.66
High-Yield Corporate Bonds:	
Vanguard High Yield Corp.	0.29
Fidelity High Income	0.75
Value Line Aggressive Income	0.81
Ivesco High Yield	0.86

Source: Company records as reported in *Forbes Mutual Fund Guide*, August 23, 1999.

Commentary: The great cost advantage of Vanguard shows up very strikingly here. It is not a slightly lower expense ratio, but one that is usually three or four times lower than similar funds. Take, for example, the category of Index Equity Funds, where the goal is to simply track the Index averages, which suggests passive management rather than free-wheeling buying and selling. Yet, Vanguard's costs are far below the other funds; in one case, the Gateway fund is five times higher.

[7] *Ibid.*, p. 136.

[8] *Ibid.*, pp. 128, 137.

[9] Easton, p. 116.

Fidelity and Charles Schwab have opened numerous walk-in sales outposts. Certainly these bring more sales exposure to prospective customers. But are such sales promotion efforts worth the cost? Vanguard decided not. It had one sales outpost in Philadelphia, but closed it to save money.

Vanguard discouraged day traders and other market timers from in-and-out trading of its funds. It even prohibited telephone switching on the Vanguard 500 Index; redemption orders had to come by mail. Why such market timing discouragement? Frequent redemptions run up transaction costs, and a flurry of sell orders might impose trading costs that would have to be borne by other shareholders as some holdings might have to be sold.

Not the least of the economies is what Bogle calls passive investing, tracking the market rather than trying to actively manage the funds by trying to beat the market. The funds with the highest expense ratios are hedge funds and these usually are the most active traders, with heavy buying and selling. Yet, they seldom beat the market but squander a lot of money in the effort and burden shareholders with sizable capital gains taxes because of the flurry of transactions. Still, the common notion prevails

INFORMATION BOX

THE PRICE-QUALITY PERCEPTION REVISITED

We had a similar box in Chapter 4 on Perrier, and will have again in a later chapter. But the topic is worth further discussion. In the Perrier case, we considered whether high-priced bottled water was that much better than regular tap water or lower-priced bottled water, and concluded that it usually was not. The same thing applies to perfume, to beer and liquor, and to many other consumer products. "You get what you pay for" is a common perception, and its corollary is that you judge quality by price: The higher the price, the higher the quality. But this notion leads many consumers to be taken advantage of, and for top-of-the-line brands and products to command a higher profit margin than lower-priced alternatives. Admittedly, sometimes we are led to the more expensive brand or item for the prestige factor.

When it comes to money management, by no means do high fees mean better quality; the reverse is usually true. And prestige should hardly be a factor since we are not inclined to show off our investments like we might a new car. Does a high-overhead index fund deliver better performance than a cheap one, than Vanguard? Not at all. And hedge funds as we noted before seldom even beat the averages despite running up some of the highest expenses in the mutual fund industry. Looking at Table 14.2, which shows typical expense ratios of Vanguard and its competitors, are the other funds doing a better job than Vanguard with their expenses three to five times higher? No, because their high expense ratios take away from any performance advantage, even if frequent trading resulted in somewhat better gains, and that seldom is achieved.

If Vanguard advertised its great expense advantage aggressively to really get the word out, do you think it would win many more customers? Why or why not?

that more is better, that the more expensive car or service must be better than its less expensive alternative. See the following Information Box for another discussion of the price-quality perception.

Another factor also contributes to the great cost advantage of Vanguard. It is a mutual firm, organized as a nonprofit owned by its customers. Almost all other financial institutions, except TIAA-CREF (and we will discuss this shortly), have stock ownership with its heavy allegiance to profit maximization.

Customer Service

Many firms espouse a commitment to customer service. It is the popular thing to do, rather like motherhood, apple pie, and the flag. Unfortunately, pious platitudes do not always match reality. Vanguard's commitment to service seems to be more tangible.

Service to customers is often composed of the simple things, such as just answering the phone promptly and courteously, or responding to mail quickly and completely, or giving complete and unbiased information. Vanguard's 2,000 phone representatives are ready to answer the phone by the fourth ring. During a market panic or on April 15, when the tax deadline stimulates many inquiries, CEO John Brennan brings a brigade of executives with him to help man the phones. Vanguard works to make its monthly statements to investors as complete and easy-to-understand as possible, and it leads the industry in this.

The philosophy of a customer-service commitment was espoused by Bogle. "Our primary goal: to serve, to the best of our ability, the human beings who are our clients. To serve them with candor, with integrity, and with fair dealing. To be the stewards of the assets they have entrusted to us. To treat them as we would like the stewards of our own assets to treat us."

Bogle described a talk he gave to Harvard Business School in December 1997 on how "our focus on human beings had enabled Vanguard to become what at Harvard is called a 'service breakthrough company.' I challenged the students to find the term *human beings* in any book they had read on corporate strategy. As far as I know, none could meet the challenge. But 'human beingness' has been one of the keys to our development."[10]

Not the least of the consumer best interests has been a commitment to holding down taxable transactions for shareholders. Vanguard has led the industry with tax-managed funds aimed at minimizing the capital gains that confront most mutual fund investors to their dismay at the end of the year.

COMPETITION

Why is Vanguard's low-expense approach not matched by competitors? All the other fund giants that sell primarily to the general public are for-profit companies. Are they willing to sacrifice profits to win back Vanguard converts? Hardly likely. Are they willing

---

[10] Bogle, pp. 423, 424.

to reduce their hefty marketing and advertising expenditures? Again, hardly likely. Why? Because advertising, not word-of-mouth, is vital to their visibility and to seeking out customers.

TIAA-CREF

One potential competitor looms, another low-cost fund contender. TIAA-CREF, which manages retirement money for teachers and researchers, in 1997 launched six no-load mutual funds that are now open to all investors. The funds' annual expenses range from 0.29 percent to 0.49 percent, comparable with Vanguard's. A significant potential attraction over Vanguard is that each fund's investment minimum is just $250, compared with Vanguard's usual minimum of $3,000. As of late August 1999, the combined assets of the six TIAA-CREF funds was $1.5 billion, far less, of course, than the near–$500 billion of Vanguard.

TIAA-CREF is also run solely for the benefit of its shareholders, being another mutual, with the long-term aim of providing fund-management services at cost. Still, there is some doubt that expense ratios can be kept low, should the new funds fail to attract enough investors.

Is this a gnat against the giant Vanguard? Perhaps; however, the low investment requirement of only $250 should certainly attract cost-conscious investors who cannot come up with the $3,000 that Vanguard requires on most of its funds. Still, six fund choices versus the more than 100 of Vanguard is not very attractive yet. Efforts to be as tax-efficient as Vanguard are also unknown.

ANALYSIS

The success of Vanguard with its disavowal of most traditional business strategies flies in the face of all that we have come to believe. It suggests that heavy advertising expenditures may at least be questioned as not always desirable—and what a heresy this is. It suggests that relying on word-of-mouth and whatever free publicity can be garnered may sometimes be preferable to advertising. All you need is a superior product or service. It supports the statement that textbooks like to shoot down: "If you build a better mousetrap, people will come." Conventional wisdom maintains that without advertising to get the message out, this better mousetrap will fade away from lack of buyer knowledge and interest. But the planning of Bogle and Vanguard to tread a different path and not be dissuaded despite the critics illustrates a remarkable and enduring commitment first formulated almost three decades ago.

How do we reconcile Vanguard with the commonly accepted notion that communication is essential to get products and services to customers (except perhaps when selling solely to the government or to a single customer)?

Maybe we should not try to fit Vanguard into such traditional beliefs. Maybe it is the exception, the anomaly, in its seeming repudiation of them. Still, let us not be too hasty in this judgment.

I do not believe that Vanguard contradicts traditional principles of marketing and business strategy. Rather, it has revealed another approach to the communication component: the effective use of word-of-mouth publicity. If we have a distinctive product that can be *tangibly demonstrated* as superior in relative cost advantages to competitors, then demand may be stimulated without mass advertising. Word-of-mouth, enhanced or developed through formal publicity—from media, public appearances, and publications—can replace massive advertising expenditures of competitors. But is there a downside to all this?

Let us examine the role of word-of-mouth in more detail in the following Information Box.

INFORMATION BOX

THE POTENTIAL OF WORD-OF-MOUTH AND UNPAID PUBLICITY

Word-of-mouth advertising, by itself, is almost always frowned on by the experts. It is the sign of the marginal firm, one without sufficient resources, so they say, to do what is needed to get established. Such a firm is bound to succumb to competitors who are better managed and better resourced. The best they can say for word-of-mouth advertising is that if the firm can survive for an unknown number of years, and if it *really* has a superior product or service, then it might finally attain some modest success.

Compared to spending for advertising, word-of-mouth takes far longer to have any impact, and firms seldom have the staying power to wait years, so the belief holds. The best strategy would be to have both, with healthy doses of advertising to jumpstart the enterprise, and let favorable word-of-mouth reinforce the advertising.

As we have seen, Bogle and his Vanguard repudiated the accepted strategy, yet became highly successful. Still, it took time, even decades. As shown in Table 14.1, in 1994 after sixteen years the flagship Index 500 fund had reached $8 billion in assets; not bad, but far below the heavily advertised Magellan fund of Fidelity. The growth of the Index 500 fund has accelerated only in recent years. Would more advertising have shortened the period?

Bogle would maintain that such advertising would have destroyed the uniqueness of Vanguard by making its expenses like other funds. He would also likely contend that the favorable publicity enhanced the word-of-mouth influence of satisfied shareholders, and thus there was no need for expensive advertising. But in the early years of Vanguard it did not have much favorable publicity. On the contrary, it took experts a long time to admit that a low-expense fund with passive management could do as well or better than aggressively managed funds with a lot of buying and selling and big trading and marketing expenses.

So the success of Vanguard without much formal advertising attests to the success of word-of-mouth heavily seasoned by favorable free publicity. But was it too conservative, especially in the early years?

Do you think Vanguard should have advertised more, especially in its early days? Why or why not? If yes, how much more do you think it should have spent?

Vanguard illustrates a commendable application of an important marketing principle: the desirability of uniqueness or product differentiation. It differentiated itself from competitors in two respects: (1) its resolve and ability to bring out a low-priced product and at the same time one of good quality, and (2) its achievement of good customer service despite the low price.

Even today, after several decades of competitors seeing this highly effective strategy, Vanguard still is virtually unmatched in its uniqueness, except for one newcomer that is hardly a contender but could be a factor should Vanguard let down its guard and be tempted to seek more profits.

Prognosis—Can Vanguard Continue As Is?

Is it likely Vanguard can continue its success pattern without increasing advertising and other costs and becoming more like its competitors? Why should it change? It has become a giant with its low-cost strategy. The last decade saw a growing momentum created by favorable word-of-mouth and publicity that made the need for heavy advertising and selling efforts far less than in the early years. It took bravery, or audacity, in those early years not to succumb to the Lorelei beguilement that advertising and commission selling was the only viable strategy. Something would be lost if Vanguard were to change its strategy and uniqueness and become a higher-cost imitation of its competitors.

If Vanguard is so good, why are so many investors still doing business with the higher-cost competitors? We can identify four groups of consumers who are non-customers of Vanguard:

1. Those who have not studied the statistics and editorials of publications like *Forbes* and the *Wall Street Journal,* and are not aware of the Vanguard advantage.

2. Those who are naive in investing and content to let someone else—brokers or bankers—advise them and reap the commissions.

3. Those who are swayed by the massive advertisements of firms like Fidelity, Dreyfus, T. Rowe Price, and others.

4. Those who put their faith in the price-quality perception: the higher the price the higher the quality, with quality guaranteeing higher investor returns.

In addition to continued investments of its ardent customers, Vanguard should find potential in the gradual eroding of the commitment of these four consumer groups. Of course, the overseas markets also offer a huge and virtually untapped potential for Vanguard.

WHAT CAN BE LEARNED?

Marketing can be overdone. The success of Vanguard shows that marketing can be overdone. Too much can be spent for advertising, without realizing congruent benefits. Sales expenses and branch office overhead may get out of line. Yet, few firms think they dare reduce such costs lest they be competitively disadvantaged. For example, it is the brave executive who reduces advertising in the face of increases by competitors, though the results of the advertising may be impossible to measure with any accuracy.

Still, despite the success of Vanguard in downplaying advertising, one has to wonder how much faster the growth might have been by budgeting more dollars for selling, at least in the early years.

Can word-of-mouth do the job of advertising by itself? In Vanguard's case, word-of-mouth combined with favorable unpaid publicity from the media brought it to the largest mutual fund family in the industry. However, the time it took for word-of-mouth, even eventually with good publicity, to build demand has to be a negative. Without such favorable publicity, it would have taken far longer.

The benefits of frugality. There is far too much waste in most institutions, business and nonbusiness. Some waste comes from undercontrolled costs and such extravagances as lavish expense accounts and entertainment, and expenditures that do little to benefit the bottom line. Other factors may be a top-heavy bureaucratic organization saddled with layers of staff personnel, and/or too many debt payments due to heavy investments in plant and equipment or mergers. Heavy use of advertising may not always pay off enough to justify the expenditures, as we saw in Chapter 12 when Coca-Cola was outspending Pepsi by $100 million, but was still losing market share. In money management, trading costs may get far out of line.

Vanguard shows the benefit of austerity in greatly reduced expense ratios for its funds compared to competitors. At last, more and more astute investors are recognizing this unique cost advantage that gives not only a better return on their investment dollars but some of the best customer service in the industry.

The power of differentiation. Firms seek to differentiate themselves, to come up with products or ways of doing business that are unique in some respect compared with competitors. This is a paramount quest of business strategy and accounts for the massive expenditures for advertising. Too often such attempts to find uniqueness are fragile, not very substantial, and easily lost or countered by competitors. Sometimes, though, they can be rather enduring, as, for example, the quality-image perception perpetrated by advertisements featuring the lonely Maytag repairman, described in Chapter 20. If a firm can effectively differentiate itself from competitors, it gains a powerful advantage and may even be able to charge premium prices.

While Vanguard seemingly disregarded marketing, John Bogle found a powerful and enduring way to differentiate through low-cost quality products and superb customer service. For decades no competitor has been able to match this attractive uniqueness.

Beware placing too much faith in the price-quality relationship. We are drawn to judge quality by a product's price relative to other choices. Often this is justified, although the better quality may not always match the higher price. In other words, the luxury item may not be worth the much higher price, except for the significant psychological value that some people see in the prestige of a fine brand name. Unfortunately, there are some products and services where the higher price does not really reflect higher quality, better workmanship, better service, and the like. Then we are taken advantage of with this price-quality perception. Beware of always judging quality by price.

CONSIDER

Can you think of additional learning insights?

QUESTIONS

1. "The success of Vanguard is due to media exploitation of what would otherwise be a very ordinary firm." Discuss.

2. Why do you think people continue to buy front-end load mutual funds with 5–6 percent commission fees when there are numerous no-load funds to be had?

3. Do you think Bogle's shunning advertising was really a success, or was it a mistake?

4. Was Vanguard's failure to open walk-in sales outposts a mistake and an example of misplaced frugality? Why or why not?

5. What are the differences in passive and active fund management? How significant are these?

6. "Vanguard seems too good. There must be a downside." Discuss.

7. What is a service breakthrough company?

8. Can publicity ever take the place of massive advertising expenditures?

HANDS-ON EXERCISES

1. You are an executive assistant to John Brennan, the new CEO of Vanguard now that Bogle has retired. Brennan is thinking of judiciously adding some marketing and advertising expenditures to the paucity that Bogle had insisted on. He has directed you to draw up a position paper on the merits of adding some advertising and even some walk-in sales outposts such as other big competitors have already done.

2. You are John Brennan, CEO. It is 2005, and TIAA-CREF is turning out to be a formidable competitor, and is gaining fast on your first-place position in the industry. What actions would you take, and why? Discuss all ramifications of these actions that you can think of.

TEAM DEBATE EXERCISES

1. You are a member of the board of directors of Vanguard. John Bogle is approaching the retirement age as set forth in the company policies. However, he wants to continue as chairman of the board, even though he is willing to let Brennan assume active management. Debate the issue of whether to force Bogle to step down or bow to his wishes.

2. Debate the no-advertising policy of Bogle.

INVITATION TO RESEARCH

Is Vanguard still number one in the mutual fund industry? Has it increased its advertising expenditures? Has Brennan made any substantial changes?

PART FOUR

EXECUTING

CHAPTER FIFTEEN

Boeing Loses Industry Dominance to Airbus

$\mathbf{T}$he commercial jet business had long been subject to booms and busts: major demand for new aircraft and then years of little demand. By the second half of the 1990s, demand burgeoned as never before. Boeing, the world's leading producer of commercial airplanes, seemed in the catbird seat amid the worldwide surge of orders. This was an unexpected windfall, spurred by markets greatly expanding in Asia and Latin America at the same time that domestic demand, helped by deregulation and prosperity, boomed. In the midst of these good times, Boeing in 1997, incurred its first loss in fifty years.

During this same period, Airbus (Airbus Industrie), a European aerospace consortium, an underdog, began climbing toward its long-stated goal of winning 50 percent of the over-100-seat airplane market. The battle was all-out, no-holds-barred, and Boeing was blinking.

BOEING

Background of the Company

Boeing's is a fabled past. The company was a major factor in the World War II war effort, and in the late 1950s led the way in producing innovative, state-of-the-art commercial aircraft. It introduced the 707, the world's first commercially viable jetliner. In the late 1960s, it almost bankrupted itself to build a jetliner twice the size of any other then in service, while the critics predicted it could never fly profitably. But the 747 dramatically lowered costs and airfares and brought passenger comfort previously undreamed of in flying. In the mid-1990s, Boeing introduced the high technology 777, the first commercial aircraft designed entirely with the use of computers.

In efforts to reduce the feast-or-famine cycles of the commercial aircraft business, Boeing acquired Rockwell International's defense business in 1996, and in 1997 purchased McDonnell Douglas for $16.3 billion.

In 1997, Boeing's commercial aircraft segment contributed 57 percent of total revenues. This segment ranged from 125-passenger 737s to giant 450-500-seat 747s. In 1997, Boeing delivered 374 aircraft, up from 269 in 1996. The potential seemed enormous: Over the next twenty years, air passenger traffic worldwide was projected to rise 4.9 percent per year and airlines were predicted to order 16,160 aircraft to expand their fleets and replace aging planes.[1] As the industry leader, Boeing had 60 percent of this market. At the end of 1997, its order backlog was $94 billion.

Defense and space operations comprised 41 percent of 1997 revenues. This included airborne warning and control systems (AWACS), helicopters, B-2 bomber subcontract work, and the F-22 fighter, among other products and systems.

PROBLEMS WITH THE COMMERCIAL AIRCRAFT BUSINESS SEGMENT

Production Problems

Boeing proved to be poorly positioned to meet the surge in aircraft orders. Part of this resulted from its drastic layoffs of experienced workers during the industry's last slump, in the early 1990s. Though Boeing hired 32,000 new workers over eighteen months starting in 1995, the experience gap upped the risk of costly mistakes. Boeing had also cut back its suppliers in strenuous efforts to slash parts inventories and increase cost efficiency.

But Boeing had other problems. Its production systems were a mess. It had somehow evolved some 400 separate computer systems, and these were not linked. Its design system was labor intensive and paper dependent, and very expensive as it tried to cater to customer choices. A $1 billion program had been launched in 1996 to modernize and computerize the production process. But this was too late: The onslaught of orders had already started. (It is something of an irony that a firm that had the sophistication to design the 777 entirely by computers was so antiquated in its use of computers otherwise.)

Demands for increased production were further aggravated by unreasonable production goals and too many plane models. Problems first hit with the 747 Jumbo, and then with a new version of the top-selling 737, the so-called next-generation 737NG. Before long, every line was affected: the 757, 767, and 777. While Boeing released over 320 planes to customers in 1997 for a 50 percent increase over 1996, this was far short of the planned completion rate. For example, by early 1998 a dozen 737NGs had been delivered to airlines, but this was less than one-third of the forty supposed to have been delivered by then. Yet, the company maintained through September 1997 that everything was going well, that there was only a month's delay in the delivery of some planes.

Soon it became apparent that problems were much greater. In October, the 747 and 737 assembly lines were shut down for nearly a month to allow workers to catch up and ease part shortages. The *Wall Street Journal* reported horror stories of parts being rushed in by taxicab, of executives spending weekends trying to chase down needed parts, of parts needed for new planes being shipped out to replace defective

---

[1] *Boeing 1997 Annual Report.*

parts on an in-service plane. Overtime pay brought some assembly-line workers incomes over $100,000, while rookie workers muddled by on the line.[2]

Despite its huge order backlog, Boeing took a loss for 1997, the first in over fifty years. See Table 15.1 for the trend in revenues and net income from 1988 to 1998.

The loss mostly resulted from two massive write-downs. One, for $1.4 billion, arose from the McDonnell Douglas acquisition and in particular from its ailing commercial aircraft operation at Long Beach, California. The bigger write-off, $1.6 billion, reflected production problems, particularly on the new 737NG. Severe price competition with Airbus resulted in not enough profits on existing business to bring the company into the black. Production delays continued, with more write-downs on the horizon.

As Boeing moved into 1998, analysts wondered how much longer it would take to clear up the production snafus. This would be longer than anyone had been led to believe. Unexpectedly, a new problem arose for Boeing. Disastrous economic conditions in Asia now brought major order cancellations.

Customer Relations

Not surprisingly, Boeing's production problems resulting in delayed shipments had a serious impact on customer relations. For example, Southwest Airlines had to postpone adding service to another city because the ordered planes were not ready. Boeing

Table 15.1: Boeing's Trend of Revenues and Income, 1988–1998 (in millions)

	Revenue	Net Income
1988	16,962	614
1989	20,276	675
1990	27,595	1,385
1991	29,314	1,567
1992	30,184	1,554
1993	25,438	1,244
1994	21,924	856
1995	19,515	393
1996	22,681	1,095
1997	45,800	–177
1998	56,100	1,100

Source: Boeing Annual Reports

Commentary: Note the severity of the decline in revenues and profits during the industry downturn in 1993, 1994, and 1995. It is little wonder that Boeing was so ill-prepared for the deluge of orders starting in 1995. Then in an unbelievable incongruity, the tremendous increase in revenues in 1997 to the highest ever—partly reflecting the acquisitions—was accompanied by a huge loss.

[2] Frederic M. Biddle and John Helyar, "Behind Boeing's Woes: Clunky Assembly Line, Price War with Airbus," *Wall Street Journal*, April 24, 1998, p. A16.

paid Southwest millions of dollars of compensation for the delayed deliveries. Continental also had to wait for five overdue 737s.

Other customers switched to Boeing's only major competitor, Airbus Industrie, of Toulouse, France.

AIRBUS INDUSTRIE

Airbus had to salivate at Boeing's troubles. It was a distant second in market share to Boeing's 60 percent.

Now this was changing and Airbus could see achieving a sustainable 50 percent market share. See the Information Box: Importance of Market Share for a discussion of market share.

Background of Airbus

Airbus was founded in 1970 as a consortium that came to include companies of four countries: British Aerospace, DaimlerChrysler Aerospace (Germany), France's Aerospatiale, and Spain's Casa. Each of the partners supplied components such as wings and fuselages; the partners also underwrote the consortium's capital expenses (sometimes with government loans) and were prepared to cover its operating losses.

INFORMATION BOX

IMPORTANCE OF MARKET SHARE

The desire to surpass a competitor is a common human tendency, whether in sports or business. A measurement of performance relative to competitors encourages this desire and can be highly motivating for management and employees alike. Furthermore, market-share performance is a key indicator in ascertaining how well a firm is doing and in spotting emerging problems, as well as sometimes allaying blame. As an example of the latter, declining sales over the preceding year accompanied by a constant and improving market share can suggest that the firm is doing a good job, even though certain factors adversely affected the whole industry.

Market share is usually measured by (1) share of overall sales and/or (2) share relative to certain competitors, usually the top one or several in the industry. Of particular importance is trend data: Are things getting better or worse? If worse, why is this, and what needs to be done to improve the situation?

Since Boeing and Airbus were the only real competitors in this major industry, relative market shares became critical. The perceived importance of gaining, or not losing, market share led to severe price competition that cut into the profits of both firms, as will be discussed later.

How would you respond to the objection that market share data is not all that useful, since "it doesn't tell us what the problem really is"?

Can emphasizing market share be counterproductive? If so, why?

The organizational structure seemed seriously flawed. It was politicized, with the partners voting on major issues in proportion to their country's ownership stakes. From this fragmented leadership, public squabbles frequently arose, some very serious. For example, plans to produce a new 107-seat A318 were held up by the French company, which thought it was not getting its fair share of the production. Finances were also tangled with components supplied by the various countries charged to Airbus at suspiciously high prices.

The result was that in 1998, Boeing made $1.1 billion on sales of $56.1 billion, while Airbus was losing $204 million on sales of $13.3 billion. Boeing accused Airbus of selling below cost in order to steal business from Boeing, and Airbus blamed Boeing for the same thing.

The competition between the two companies became increasingly bitter after 1996. In that year Boeing and several Airbus partners discussed a joint development of a superjumbo. The talks ended when they could not agree on a single design. But Airbus suspected Boeing was not sincerely interested in this collaboration, that its main purpose in the talks was to stall Airbus's plans.

Airbus went ahead with its plans, while Boeing pooh-poohed the idea of such a huge plane.

Airbus Chairman Noel Forgeard

A slight Frenchman with a cheery disposition, Noel Forgeard, age fifty-two, joined the consortium in 1998 from Matra, a French aerospace manufacturer. He came with several major goals: to centralize decision-making, to impose sensible bookkeeping, and to make Airbus consistently profitable. The task was not easy. For example, plans to build the world's largest airplane, code-named A3XX, were even threatened by disagreements over where it would be assembled. Both the French and the German companies thought it should be produced in their country. Forgeard stated, "The need for a single corporate entity is well recognized. Everybody here is focused on it."[3] Still, while the need for reorganizing into something like a modern corporation was evident to most executives, the major partners were divided over how to proceed.

The World's Largest Plane

The A3XX was designed as a double-decker plane that could carry 555 passengers comfortably—137 more than a Boeing 747-400 (it could even carry 750 people on routes around Asia where people did not care as much about seating comfort). It was expected to fly by 2004, with prices starting somewhat over $200 million. Development costs could reach $15 billion, so essentially the A3XX was a bet-the-company project with an uncertain outlook, much as was Boeing's 747 thirty years before. Airbus expected to get 40 percent of the plane's development costs from suppliers such as Sweden's Saab, 30 percent from government loans arranged by its partners, and the rest from its own resources.

---

[3] Alex Taylor II, "Blue Skies for Airbus," *Fortune,* August 2, 1999, p. 103.

The huge financing needed for this venture could hardly be obtained without a corporate reorganization, one that would provide a mechanism for handling internal disputes among the various partner countries, not the least of which was where the plane would be assembled. So, Forgeard had necessity on his side for reorganizing. But the A3XX faced other issues and concerns.

Should a Plane Like the A3XX Even Be Built?

Boeing's publicly expressed opinion was that such a plane would never be profitable. "Let them launch it," said one Boeing official, with a hint of malice.[4] Boeing took the position that consumers want frequent, nonstop flights, such as Southwest Airlines had brought to prominence with its saturation of city-pair routes with frequent flights. An ultralarge aircraft would mean far less frequency.[5]

Airbus, meantime, surveyed big airlines and discerned enough interest in a superjumbo to proceed. It also consulted with more than sixty airports around the world to determine whether such a big plane would be able to take off and land easily. Weight is critical to these maneuvers, and Airbus pledged that the A3XX would be able to use the same runways as the 747 because of a new lightweight material. Instead of regular aluminum, the planes would use a product called Glare, made of aluminum alloy and glass-fiber tape.

Airbus promised ambitious plans for passenger comfort in this behemoth. It built a full-size, 237-foot mockup of the interior to show prospective customers, and enlisted 1,200 frequent flyers to critique the cabin mockup. To reduce claustrophobia, the designers added a wide staircase between upper and lower decks. Early plans also included exercise rooms and sleeping quarters fitted with bunk beds.

Airbus claimed that the 555-seat A3XX would be 15 percent cheaper to operate per seat-mile than Boeing's 747. Boeing maintained this was wildly optimistic. United Airlines' Frederick Brace, vice president of finance, also expressed doubts: "The risk for Airbus is whether there's a market for A3XX. The risk for an airline is: Can we fill it up? We have to be prudent in how we purchase it."[6]

Competitive Position of Airbus

Airbus was well positioned to supply planes to airlines whose needs Boeing couldn't meet near term. Some thought it was even producing better planes than Boeing.

United Airlines chose Airbus's A320 twinjets over Boeing's 737s, saying passengers preferred the Airbus product. Several South American carriers also chose A320s over the 737, placing a $4 billion order with Airbus. For 1997, Airbus hacked out a 45 percent market share, the first time Boeing's 60 percent market share had eroded.

The situation worsened drastically for Boeing in 1998. US Airways, which had previously ordered 400 Airbus jets, announced in July that it would buy thirty more. But the biggest defection came in August when British Airlines announced plans to

---

[4] Steve Wilhelm, "Plane Speaking," *Puget Sound Business Journal,* June 18, 1999, p. 112.

[5] *Ibid.*

[6] Taylor, "Blue Skies for Airbus," p. 108.

buy fifty-nine Airbus jetliners and take options for 200 more. This broke its long record as a Boeing-loyal customer. The order, worth as much as $11 billion, would be the biggest victory of Airbus over Boeing.[7]

Beyond the production delays of Boeing, Airbus had other competitive strengths. While it had less total production capability than Boeing (235 planes versus Boeing's 550), the Airbus production line was efficient and the company had done better in trimming its costs. This meant it could go head to head with Boeing on price. And price seemed to be the name of the game in the late 1990s. This contrasted with earlier days when Boeing rose to world leadership with performance, delivery, and technology more important than cost. "They [the customers] do not care what it costs us to make the planes," Boeing Chairman and Chief Executive Philip Condit admitted. With airline design stabilized, he saw the airlines buying planes today as chiefly interested in how much carrying capacity they could buy for a buck.[8]

Increasingly passengers were grousing about the cramped interiors of planes designed for coast-to-coast trips, and the dearth of lavatories to accommodate 126 to 189 passengers on long flights. Passenger rage appeared to be cropping up more and more. *Forbes* magazine editorialized that "the first carrier that makes an all-out effort to treat passengers as people rather than oversized sardines will be an immense money-maker."[9]

Boeing's new 737-700s and 737-800s were notorious for giving customer comfort low priority. Airbus differentiated itself from Boeing by designing its A320 150-seat workhorse with a fuselage 7.5 inches wider than Boeing's, thus adding an inch to every seat in a typical six-across configuration.

In the first four months of 1999, Airbus won an amazing 78 percent of orders. US Airways Chairman Stephen Wolf, whose airline had ordered 430 Airbus planes since 1996, said, "Airbus aircraft offer greater flexibility for wider seats, more overhead bin space, and more aisle space—all important in a consumer-conscious business."[10]

A Donnybrook

An interesting marketing brawl occurred in mid-1999 that was indicative of the intensity of this airliner war. Boeing won a $1.9 billion order for ten of its 777 jetliners from Singapore Airlines. This in itself would not have raised eyebrows, but there was more to it. As a condition, Boeing agreed to purchase for resale seventeen Airbus A340-300 jets from Singapore Airlines, which would allow the airline to phase out these Airbus planes.

Airbus officials claimed that Boeing had agreed to unprofitable terms out of desperation to close a 777 sale agreement and that this signaled a new price war involving trade-ins to provide a discount rather than direct price cutting. Boeing crowed that the carrier's decision to eliminate the competing version of the A340 from its fleet was a victory for Boeing.[11]

[7] "British to Order Airbus Airliners," *Cleveland Plain Dealer,* August 25, 1998, p. 6C.

[8] Howard Banks, "Slow Learner," *Forbes,* May 4, 1998, p. 54.

[9] "Plane Discomfort," *Forbes,* September 6, 1999, p. 32.

[10] Taylor, "Blue Skies for Airbus," p. 104.

[11] Jeff Cole, "Airbus Industrie Charges Boeing Is Inciting Price War in Asian Deal," *Wall Street Journal,* June 21, 1999, p. A4.

A month later, still stung by the marketing move of Boeing, and in an effort to thwart it, Airbus announced that it would not provide its standard support services for the jets it sold to Singapore Airlines if Boeing bought and resold them. Such a countermove could prove costly to Boeing. On the other hand, Boeing was likely to offer the jets first to airlines with fleets of the same planes, several of whom had already expressed interest. Refusing to provide support service would put Airbus in the position of denying support for a small number of planes within the fleet of a major customer. Move and countermove, this.[12]

WHO CAN WE BLAME FOR BOEING'S TROUBLES?

Was It CEO Philip Condit?

Philip Condit became chief executive in 1996, just in time for the emerging problems. He had hardly assumed office before he was deeply involved in the defense industry's merger mania, first buying Rockwell's aerospace operation and then McDonnell Douglas. Condit later admitted that he probably spent too much time on these acquisitions, and not enough time on watching the commercial part of the operation.[13]

Condit's credentials were good. His association with Boeing began in 1965 when he joined the firm as an aerodynamics engineer. The same year, he obtained a design patent for a flexible wing called the sailwing. Moving through the company's engineering and managerial ranks, he was named CEO in 1996 and chairman in 1997. Along the way, he earned a master's degree in management from the Massachusetts Institute of Technology in 1975, and in 1997 a doctorate in engineering from Science University of Tokyo, where he was the first Westerner to earn such a degree.

Was Condit's pursuit of the Rockwell and McDonnell Douglas mergers a major blunder? While analysts did not agree on this, prevailing opinion was more positive than negative, mostly because these businesses could smooth the cyclical nature of the commercial sector.

Interestingly, in the face of severe adversity, no heads rolled, as they might have in other firms. See the Issue Box: Management Continuity During Adversity.

Were the Problems Mostly Due to Internal Factors?

The airlines' unexpected buying binge, which was brought about by worldwide prosperity fueling air travel, maybe should have been anticipated. However, even the most prescient decision maker probably would have missed the full extent of this boom. For example, orders jumped from 124 in 1994 to 754 in 1996. With hindsight we know that Boeing made a grievous management mistake in trying to bite off too much, by promising expanded production and deliveries that were wholly unrealistic. We know what triggered such extravagant promises: trying to keep ahead of arch-rival Airbus.

---

[12] Daniel Michaels, "Airbus Won't Provide Support Service for Jets It Sold to Singapore Air if Boeing Resells Them," *Wall Street Journal,* July 28, 1999, p. A17.
[13] Banks, "Slow Learner," p. 56.

ISSUE BOX

MANAGEMENT CONTINUITY DURING ADVERSITY: WHAT IS BEST FOR MAXIMUM EFFECTIVENESS?

Management shake-ups during adversity can range from practically none to widespread head-rolling. In the first scenario, a cooperative board is usually necessary, and it helps if the top executives control a lot of stock. But the company's problems will probably continue. In the second scenario, at the extreme, wielding a mean ax with excessive worker and management layoffs can wreck havoc on a company's morale and longer-term prospects.

In general, neither extreme—complacency or upheaval—is good. A sick company usually needs drastic changes, but not necessarily widespread bloodletting that leaves the entire organization cringing and sending out resumes. But we need to further define *sick*. At what point is a company so bad off it needs a drastic overhaul? Was Boeing such a sick company? Would a drastic overhaul have quickly changed things? Certainly Boeing management had made some miscalculations, mostly in the area of too much optimism and too much complacency, but these were finally recognized.

Major competitor Airbus was finally aggressively attacking, and that certainly had something to do with Boeing's problems. Major executive changes and resignations might not have helped.

How do you personally feel about the continuity of management at Boeing during these difficult times? Should some heads have rolled? What criteria would you use in your judgment of whether to roll heads or not?

Huge layoffs in the early 1990s contributed to the problems of gearing up for new business. An early-retirement plan had been taken up by 9,000 of 13,000 eligible people. This was twice as many as Boeing expected, and it removed a core of production-line workers and managers who had kept a dilapidated system working. New people could not be trained or assimilated quickly enough to match those lost.

Boeing had begun switching to the Japanese practice of lean inventory management that delivers parts and tools to workers precisely as needed so that production costs can be reduced. Partly due to this change, and to the early 1990s downturn, Boeing's supplier base changed significantly. Some suppliers quit the aviation business; others had suffered so badly in the slump that their credit was affected and they were unable to boost capacity for the suddenly increased business. The result was serious parts shortages.

Complicating production problems was Boeing's long-standing practice of customizing. Because it permitted customers to choose from a host of options, Boeing was fine-tuning not only for every airline, but for every order. For example, it offered the 747's customers thirty-eight different pilot clipboards and 109 shades of the color white.[14] Such tailoring added significantly to costs and production time. This perhaps

[14] John Greenwald, "Is Boeing Out of Its Spin?" *Time*, July 13, 1998, p. 68.

was acceptable when these costs could be easily passed on to customers in a more leisurely production cycle, but it was far from maximizing efficiency. With deregulation, fare wars made extreme customizing archaic. Boeing apparently got the message with the wide-bodied 777, designed entirely by computers. Here, choices of parts were narrowed to standard options, such as car makers offer in their transmissions, engines, and comfort packages.

Cut-rate pricing between Boeing and Airbus epitomized the situation by the mid-1990s. Then, costs became critical if a firm was to be profitable. In that climate, Boeing was so obsessed with maintaining its 60 percent market share that it fought for each order with whatever price it took. Commercial airline production had some-how become a commodity business, with neither Boeing nor Airbus having products all that unique to sell. Innovation seemed disregarded, and price was the only factor in getting an order. So, every order became a battleground, and prices might be slashed 20 percent off list in order to grab all the business possible.[15] And Boeing did not have the low-cost advantage over Airbus.

Such price competition worked to the advantage of the airlines, and they grew skillful at gaining big discounts from Boeing and Airbus by holding out huge contracts and negotiating hard.

The cumbersome, cost-inefficient production systems of Boeing became a burden in this cost-conscious environment. While some of the problems could be attributed to computer technology not well applied to the assembly process, others involved organizational myopia regarding even such simple things as a streamlined organization and common parts. For example, before recent changes the commercial group had five wing-design groups, one for each aircraft program. It now has one. Another example cited in *Forbes* tells of different tools needed in the various plane models to open their wing access hatches.[16] Why not use the same tool?

There is a paradox in Boeing's dilemma. Its 777 was the epitome of high technology and computer design, as well as efficient production planning. Yet, much of the other production was mired in a morass with supplies, parts management, and produc-tion inefficiency.

Harry Stonecipher, former CEO of McDonnell Douglas before the acquisition and then president and chief operating officer of Boeing, cited arrogance as the mind-set behind Boeing's problems. He saw this as coming from a belief that the company could do no wrong, that all its problems came from outside, and that business as usual would solve them.[17]

The Role of External Factors

Adding to the production and cost-containment difficulties of Boeing were increased regulatory demands. These came not only from the U.S. Federal Aviation Administration, but also from the European Joint Airworthiness Authority (a loose grouping of regulators from more than twenty European countries). The first major

---

[15] Biddle and Helyar, "Behind Boeing's Woes ...," A1, A16.

[16] Banks, "Slow Learner," p. 60.

[17] Bill Sweetman, "Stonecipher's Boeing Shakeup," *Interavia Business & Technology*, September 1998, p. 15.

consequence of this increased regulatory climate concerned the new 730NG. Boeing apparently thought it could use the same over-the-wings emergency exits as it had on the older 737. But the European regulators wanted a redesign. They were concerned that the older type of emergency exits would not permit passengers in the larger version of the plane to evacuate quickly enough. So Boeing had to design two new over-the-wing exits on each side. This was no simple modification since it involved rebuilding the most crucial aspect of the plane. The costly refitting accounted for a major part of the $1.6 billion write-down Boeing took in 1997.

Europe's Airbus Industrie had made no secret of its desire to achieve parity with Boeing and have 50 percent of the international market for commercial jets. This mindset led to the severe price competition of the latter 1990s as Boeing stubbornly tried to maintain its 60 percent market share even at the expense of profits. While its total production capacity was somewhat below that of Boeing, Airbus had already overhauled its manufacturing process, and was better positioned to compete on price. Airbus's competitive advantage seemed stronger with single-aisle planes, those in the 120–200 seat category, mostly 737s of Boeing and A320s of Airbus. But this accounted for just 43 percent of the $40 billion expected to be spent on airliners in 1998.[18]

The future was something else. Airbus placed high stakes on a superjumbo successor to the 747, with seating capacity well beyond that of the 747. Such a huge plane would operate from hub airports such as New York City's JFK. Meantime, Boeing staked its future on its own 767s and 777s, which could connect smaller cities around the world without the need for passenger concentration at a few hubs.

Have you ever heard of a firm complaining of too much business? Probably not, but then we're confronted with Boeing's immersion in red ink, caused by trying to cope with too many orders. However, Boeing's feast of too much business abruptly ended. Financial problems in Asia brought cancellations and postponements of orders and deliveries.

In October 1998, Boeing disclosed that thirty-six completed aircraft were sitting in company storage areas in the desert, largely because of canceled orders. By December 1998, Boeing warned that its operations could be hurt by the Asian situation for as long as five years, and it announced that an additional 20,000 jobs would be eliminated and production cut 25 percent.[19] Of course, it didn't help that Airbus was capitalizing on Boeing's production difficulties by wresting orders from the stable of Boeing's long-term customers, nor that Airbus planned a 30 percent production increase for 1999.

Later Developments

By 2001, the competition between Airbus and Boeing continued unabated. Airbus had gone ahead with its superjumbo A3XX, now named the A380, with delivery to start in 2006 for a list price of $239 million. In its standard configuration, the world's largest passenger jet would carry 555 passengers between airport hubs. With delivery still five years

[18] Banks, "Slow Learner," p. 60.

[19] Frederick M. Biddle and Andy Pasztor, "Boeing May Be Hurt Up to 5 Years by Asia," *Wall Street Journal*, December 3, 1998, p. A3.

away, Airbus already had orders for seventy-two of the jumbos, and expected to reach the 100 milestone early in 2002. It would break even with 250 of the wide bodies.

In March 2001, Boeing scrapped plans for an updated but still smaller 747-X project. Instead it announced plans for a revolutionary delta-winged "Sonic Cruiser," carrying 150 to 250 passengers higher and faster than conventional planes. The savings in time would amount to fifty minutes from New York City to London, and almost two hours between Singapore and London. Further time savings would come from the plane flying to point-to-point destinations, bypassing layovers at such congested hubs as London and Hong Kong. Delivery was expected in 2007 or 2008.

Both companies had undergone major organizational changes. As of January 1, 2001, Airbus was no longer a four-nation consortium, but now an integrated company with centralized purchasing and management systems. Operations were streamlined toward bottom-line responsibilities.

Boeing had previously diversified itself away from so much dependence on commercial aircraft through its acquisitions of Rockwell's aerospace and defense business, McDonnell Douglas, Hughes Space & Communications, and several smaller companies. Boeing expected that within five years more than half its revenues would come from new business lines, including financing aircraft sales, providing high-speed Internet access, and managing air-traffic problems.[20]

Everything changed with 9/11.

The airline industry's woes that began with 9/11 intensified in 2002. By late that year two major carriers, US Airways and United, were in bankruptcy, and other airlines—with the exception of a few discount carriers, notably Southwest and JetBlue—were experiencing horrific losses. Airlines were placing no new orders and even reneging on accepting delivery of previously ordered planes. Boeing's jet production fell to half of what it had been a year earlier, and forecasts for 2003 and 2004 were little better.

In this environment, the competition between Airbus and Boeing for winning the few customers still buying became even more fierce and was influenced almost entirely by price. The biggest prize was capturing the 120-plane order from British budget carrier easyJet, and this customer milked its power position to the utmost, repeatedly sending Boeing and Airbus back to improve their offers.

During the aviation slump in the early 1990s, Boeing had beefed up its order backlog by selling at steep discounts, only to find itself in a serious bind in 1997 when it could not keep up with the built-up demand, and production costs skyrocketed. Now, Boeing refused to follow Airbus into unprofitable terrain, and Airbus got the easyJet order. Though Airbus claimed it was not selling its planes at a loss, many people in the industry thought otherwise.

In late December 2002, Boeing announced it was shelving the ambitious development program for its high-speed Sonic Cruiser. In talks with potential customers to gauge interest in such a plane in this post-9/11 environment, few expressed any

---

[20] Compiled from such sources as David J. Lynch, "Airbus Comes of Age with A-380," *USA Today,* June 21, 2001, pp. 1B, 2B; J. Lynn Lunsford, Daniel Michaels, and Andy Pasztor, "At Paris Air Show, Boeing-Airbus Duel Has New Twist," *Wall Street Journal,* June 15, 2001, p. B4.

interest; most wanted a replacement plane that would be cheaper to operate than existing ones. So, Boeing began changing its focus to developing a new 250-seat plane that would be 20 percent cheaper to operate than existing jetliners.[21]

UPDATE

The competition between Boeing and Airbus continued in 2003. For the first time, Airbus was expected to deliver more planes than Boeing that year. It already had ninety-five orders for its A380 superjumbo jet seating 550 passengers that should enter service in 2006, very close to its declared milestone point of 100. Furthermore Airbus thought it detected an opening for it to sell to the U.S. military. A $20 billion deal for Boeing to supply the U.S. Air Force with 100 modified 767 jetliners for midair refueling was in jeopardy as politicians criticized the agreement as being unfavorable to U.S. taxpayers and smacking of corporate welfare because of no competitive bidding.

Meanwhile, Boeing announced that it would stop making its twin-engine 757 because of waning interest. It was in preliminary planning for a new model, called the 7E7, a long-range jet that would seat 200–250 and be 20 percent cheaper to own and operate than other planes. This could enter service around 2008.

Boeing has not had a new model since 1995, and badly needs a success with the new 7E7. While military business has been booming, the company has suffered serious setbacks elsewhere. It has taken financial charges on its slow-selling single-aisle 717, and has also written off $2.4 billion of its commercial satellite and launch business.

But Boeing achieved profitability by revamping assembly lines, contracting out fabrication of parts, and laying off 32,000 workers since 9/11. Union leaders claimed the result was an aging skilled workforce and rock-bottom morale.[22]

WHAT CAN BE LEARNED?

Beware the "king of the hill", three-C's mind-set. Firms that have been well entrenched in their industry and that have dominated for years tend to fall into a particular mind-set that leaves them vulnerable to aggressive and innovative competitors.

The "three C's" are detrimental to a frontrunner's continued success:

- Complacency
- Conservatism
- Conceit

[21] J. Lynn Lunsford, "Boeing to Drop Sonic Cruiser, Build Plane Cheaper to Operate," *Wall Street Journal*, December 19, 2002, p. B4; Daniel Michaels and J. Lynn Lunsford, "Airbus is Awarded easyJet Order for 120 New Planes Over Boeing," *Wall Street Journal*, October 15, 2002, pp. A3, A6; and Scott McCartney and J. Lynn Lunsford, "Skies Darken for Boeing, AMR and UAL as Aviation Woes Grow," *Wall Street Journal*, October 17, 2002, pp. A1, A9.

[22] J. Lynn Lunsford, "Boeing, Losing Ground to Airbus, Faces Key Choice," *Wall Street Journal*, April 21, 2003, pp. A1, A8; J. Lynn Lunsford, "Boeing May Risk Building New Jet," *Wall Street Journal*, October 15, 2003, pp. A1, A13; and Daniel Michaels, "Airbus Sees Military-Sales Opening," *Wall Street Journal*, September 15, 2003, p. A8.

Complacency is smugness—a complacent firm is self-satisfied, content with the status quo, no longer hungry and eager for innovative growth. Conservatism, when excessive, characterizes a management that is wedded to the past, to the traditional, to the way things have always been done. Conservative managers see no need to change because they believe nothing is different today (e.g., "Our 747 jumbo jet is the largest that can be profitably used"). Finally, conceit further reinforces the myopia of the mind-set: conceit regarding current and potential competitors. The beliefs that "we are the best" and "no one else can touch us" can easily permeate an organization that has dominated its industry for years. Usually the three Cs insidiously move in at the highest levels and readily filter down to the rest of the organization.

Stonecipher, former CEO of McDonnell Douglas and then president of Boeing, admitted to company self-confidence bordering on arrogance. The current problems of Boeing should have destroyed any vestiges of the three Cs mindset. But the former "king of the hill" position may be lost.

Growth must be manageable. Boeing certainly demonstrated the fallacy of attempting growth beyond immediate capabilities in a growth-at-any-cost mind-set. The rationale for embracing great growth is that firms "need to run with the ball" if they ever get that rare opportunity to suddenly double or triple sales. But there are times when a slower, more controlled growth is prudent.

Risks lie on both sides as businesses reach for these opportunities. When a market begins to boom and a firm is unable to keep up with demand without greatly increasing capacity and resources, it faces a dilemma: (1) Stay conservative in fear that the opportunity will be short-lived, but thereby abdicate some of the growing market to competitors, or (2) Expand vigorously to take full advantage of the opportunity, but risk being overextended and vulnerable should the potential suddenly fade. Regardless of the commitment to a vision of great growth, a firm must develop an organization and systems and controls to handle it, or find itself in the same morass as Boeing, with quality control problems, inability to meet production targets, alienated customers, and costs far out of line. And not the least, having its stock price savaged by Wall Street investors while its market share tumbles. Growth must not be beyond the firm's ability to manage it.

Downsizing has its perils. Boeing presents a sobering example of the risks of downsizing in this era when downsizing is so much in fashion. With incredibly bad timing, Boeing encouraged many of its most experienced and skilled workers and supervisors to take early retirement just a few years before the boom began. Boeing found out the hard way that it could replace bodies, but not the skills needed to produce the highly complex planes under severe deadlines for output. The company would have been better off to have maintained a core of experienced workers during the downturn rather than lose them forever. It would have been better to have suffered with higher labor costs during the lean times, disregarding management's typical attitude of paring costs to the bone during such times. Yet, when we look at Table 15.1 and see the severe decreases of revenues and income in 1993, 1994, and lasting well into 1995, we can appreciate the dilemma of Boeing's management.

Problems of competing entirely on price. Price competition almost invariably leads to price-cutting and even price wars to win market share. In such an environment, the lowest-cost, most efficient producer wins.

More often, all firms in an industry have rather similar cost structures, and severe price competition hurts the profits of all competitors without bringing much additional business. Any initial pricing advantage is quickly matched by competitors unwilling to lose market share. In this situation, competing on nonprice bases has much to recommend it. Nonprice competition emphasizes uniqueness, perhaps in some aspects of product features and quality, perhaps through service and quicker deliveries or maybe better quality control. A firm's reputation, if good, is a powerful nonprice advantage.

Usually new and rapidly growing industries face price competition as marginal firms are weeded out and more economies of operation are developed. The more mature an industry, the greater likelihood of nonprice competition since cutthroat pricing causes too much hardship to all competitors.

Certainly the commercial aircraft industry was mature, and much has been made of airlines being chiefly interested in how much passenger-carrying capacity they can buy for the same buck, and of their pitting Airbus and Boeing against each other in bidding wars.[23] Nonprice competition badly needed to be reinstated in this industry. At that point, Airbus appeared to be doing a better job of finding uniqueness, with its passenger-friendly planes and its charting new horizons with the superjumbo.

The synergy of mergers and acquisitions is suspect. The concept of synergy says that a new whole is better than the sum of its parts. In other words, a well-planned merger or acquisition should result in a better enterprise than the two separate entities. Theoretically, this would seem possible since operations can be streamlined for more efficiency and since greater management and staff competence can be brought to bear as more financial and other resources are tapped; or in Boeing's case, since the peaks and valleys of commercial demand could be countered by defense and space business.

Unfortunately, as we have seen in other cases, such synergy often is absent, at least in the short and intermediate term. More often such concentrations incur severe digestive problems—problems with people, systems, and procedures—that take time to resolve. Furthermore, greater size does not always beget economies of scale. The opposite may in fact occur: an unwieldy organization, slow to act, and vulnerable to more aggressive, innovative, and agile smaller competitors. The siren call of synergy is often an illusion.

The acquisitions of McDonnell Douglas and Rockwell may work out well for Boeing. But their assimilation came at a most troubling time for Boeing. The Long Beach plant of McDonnell Douglas alone led to a massive $1.4 billion write-off, and contributed significantly to the losses of 1997. Less easily calculated, but certainly a factor, was the management time involved in coping with these new entities.

---

[23] For example, Banks, "Slow Learner," p. 54.

CONSIDER

Can you think of additional learning insights?

QUESTIONS

1. Do you think Boeing should have anticipated the impact of Asian economic difficulties long before it did?

2. If it had more quickly anticipated the drying up of the Asian market for planes, could Boeing have prevented most of the problems that confronted it? Discuss.

3. Do you think top management at Boeing should have been fired after the disastrous miscalculations in the late 1990s? Why or why not?

4. A major stockholder grumbles, "Management worries too much about Airbus, and to hell with the stockholders." Evaluate this statement. Do you think it is valid?

5. What do you see for Boeing three to five years down the road? For Airbus?

6. Do you think it likely that Boeing will have to contend with new competitors over the next ten years? Why or why not?

7. Discuss synergy in mergers. Why does synergy so often seem to be lacking despite expectations?

8. You are a skilled machinist for Boeing and have always been quite proud of participating in the building of giant planes. You have just received notice of another lengthy layoff, the second in five years. Discuss your likely attitudes and actions.

9. How wise do you think it was for Airbus to "bet the company" on the super-jumbo A380, the world's largest jet?

10. Do you think Airbus's more passenger-friendly planes give it a significant competitive advantage? Why or why not? Discuss as many aspects of this as you can.

HANDS-ON EXERCISES

Before

You are a management consultant advising top management at Boeing. It is 1993 and the airline industry is in a slump, but early indications are that things will improve greatly in a few years. What would you advise that might have prevented the problems Boeing faced a few years later? Be as specific as you can, and support your recommendations as to practicality and probable effectiveness.

After

1. It is late 1998, and Boeing has had to announce drastic cutbacks, with little improvement likely before five years, and Boeing's stock has collapsed and

Airbus is charging ahead. What do you recommend now? (You may need to make some assumptions; if so, state them clearly and keep them reasonable.)

2. Be a devil's advocate (one who argues an opposing position to assure that all aspects of a course of action are considered): Amass all the arguments and rationale you can for Boeing to continue developing the high-speed Sonic Cruiser.

3. Be a devil's advocate: You are a union leader and the 32,000 layoffs after 9/11 appall you. Array all the arguments you can muster for Boeing to reconsider such massive layoffs. Be as persuasive as you can.

TEAM DEBATE EXERCISES

1. A business columnist writes: Boeing could "have told customers 'no thanks' to more orders than its factories could handle. ...It could have done itself a huge favor by simply building fewer planes and charging more for them."[24] Debate the merits of this suggestion.

2. Debate the controversy of Airbus Chairman Forgeard's decision to go for broke with the A380 superjumbo. Is the risk/reward probability worth such a mighty commitment? Debate as many pros and cons as you can, and also consider how much each should be weighted or given priority consideration.

INVITATION TO RESEARCH

1. What is the situation with Boeing today? Has it recovered its profitability? How is the competitive position with Airbus?

2. What is the situation with the A380 of Airbus? Is it still an on-going project with delivery scheduled for 2006?

3. How has 9/11 affected the fortunes of the two companies? Has it changed the competitive picture?

[24] Holmana W. Jenkins Jr., "Boeing's Trouble: Not Enough Monopolistic Arrogance," *Wall Street Journal*, December 16, 1998, p. A23.

CHAPTER SIXTEEN

Harley Davidson: Success Through a Mystique

*I*n the early 1960s, a staid and unexciting market was shaken up, was rocked to its core, by the most unlikely invader. This intruder was a smallish Japanese firm that had risen out of the ashes of World War II, and was now trying to encroach on the territory of a major U.S. firm, a firm that had in the space of sixty years destroyed all of its U.S. competitors, and now had a solid 70 percent of the motorcycle market.

Yet, almost inconceivably, in half a decade this market share was to fall to 5 percent, and the total market was to expand many times over what it had been for decades. A foreign invader had furnished a textbook example of the awesome effectiveness of carefully crafted marketing efforts. In the process, this confrontation between Honda and Harley Davidson was a harbinger of the Japanese invasion of the auto industry.

Eventually, by the late 1980s, Harley was to make a comeback. But only after more than two decades of travail and mediocrity.

THE INVASION

Sales of motorcycles in the United States were around 50,000 per year during the 1950s, with Harley Davidson, Britain's Norton and Triumph, and Germany's BMW accounting for most of the market. By the turn of the decade, Honda began to penetrate the U.S. market. In 1960, less than 400,000 motorcycles were registered in the United States. While this was an increase of almost 200,000 from the end of World War II, fifteen years before, it was far below the increase in other motor vehicles. But by 1964, only four years later, the number had risen to 960,000; two years later it was 1.4 million; and by 1971 it was almost 4 million.

In expanding the demand for motorcycles, Honda instituted a distinctly different strategy. The major elements of this strategy were lightweight cycles and an advertising approach directed toward a new customer. Few firms have ever experienced such a shattering of market share as did Harley Davidson in the 1960s. (Although its market share declined drastically, its total sales remained nearly constant, indicating that it was getting none of the new customers for motorcycles.)

Reaction of Harley Davidson to the Honda Threat

Faced with an invasion of its staid and static U.S. market, how did Harley react to the intruder? They did not react! At least not until far too late. Harley Davidson considered themselves the leader in full-size motorcycles. While the company might shudder at the image tied in with their product's usage by the leather jacket types, it took solace in the fact that almost every U.S. police department used its machines. Perhaps this is what led Harley to stand aside and complacently watch Honda make deep inroads into the American motorcycle market. The management saw no threat in Honda's thrust into the market with lightweight machines. The attitude was exemplified in this statement by William H. Davidson, the president of the company and son of the founder:

> Basically, we don't believe in the lightweight market. We believe that motorcycles are sport vehicles, not transportation vehicles. Even if a man says he bought a motorcycle for transportation, it's generally for leisure-time use. The lightweight motorcycle is only supplemental. Back around World War I, a number of companies came out with lightweight bikes. We came out with one ourselves. They never got anywhere. We've seen what happens to these small sizes.[1]

Eventually Harley recognized that the Honda phenomenon was not an aberration, and that there was a new factor in the market. The company attempted to fight back by offering an Italian-made lightweight in the mid-1960s. But it was far too late; Honda was firmly entrenched. The Italian bikes were regarded in the industry to be of lower quality than the Japanese. Honda, and toward the end of the 1960s other Japanese manufacturers, continued to dominate what had become a much larger market than ever dreamed.

AFTERMATH OF THE HONDA INVASION: 1965–1981

In 1965, Harley Davidson made its first public stock offering. Soon after, it faced a struggle for control. The contest was primarily between Bangor Punta, an Asian company, and AMF, an American company with strong interests in recreational equipment including bowling. In a bidding war, Harley Davidson's stockholders chose AMF over Bangor Punta, even though the bid was $1 less than Bangor's $23 a share offer. Stockholders were leery of Bangor's reputation of taking over a company, squeezing it dry, and then scrapping it for the remaining assets. AMF's plans for expansion of Harley Davidson seemed more compatible.

But the marriage was troubled: Harley Davidson's old equipment was not capable of the expansion envisioned by AMF. At the very time that Japanese manufacturers—Honda and others—were flooding the market with high-quality motorcycles, Harley was falling down on quality. One company official noted that "quality was going down just as fast as production was going up."[2] Indicative of the depths of the problem at

[1] Tom Rowan, "Harley Sets New Drive to Boost Market Share," *Advertising Age* (January 29, 1973), pp. 34–35.
[2] Peter C. Reid, *Well Made in America—Lessons from Harley Davidson on Being the Best* (New York: McGraw-Hill, 1990), p. 10.

a demoralized Harley Davidson, quality-control inspections failed 50–60 percent of the motorcycles produced. This compared to 5 percent of Japanese motorcycles that failed their quality-control checks.

AMF put up with an average $4.8 million operating loss for eleven years. Finally, it called quits and put the division up for sale in 1981. Vaughan Beals, vice president of motorcycle sales, still had faith in the company: he led a team that used $81.5 million in financing from Citicorp to complete a leveraged buyout. All ties with AMF were severed.

VAUGHAN BEALS

Beals was a middle-aged Ivy Leaguer, a far cry from what one might think of as a heavy motorcycle aficionado. He had graduated from MIT's Aeronautical Engineering School, and was considered a production specialist.[3] But he was far more than that. His was a true commitment to motorcycles, personally as well as professionally. Deeply concerned with AMF's declining attention to quality, he achieved the buyout from AMF.

The prognosis for the company was bleak. Its market share, which had dominated the industry before the Honda invasion, now was 3 percent. In 1983, Harley Davidson would celebrate its eightieth birthday; some doubted it would still be around by then. Tariff protection seemed Harley's only hope. And massive lobbying paid off. In 1983, Congress passed a huge tariff increase on Japanese motorcycles. Instead of a 4 percent tariff, now Japanese motorcycles would be subject to a 45 percent tariff for the coming five years.

The tariff gave the company new hope, and it slowly began to rebuild market share. Key to this was restoring confidence in the quality of its products. And Beals took a leading role in this. He drove Harley Davidsons to rallies where he met Harley owners. There he learned of their concerns and their complaints, and he promised changes. At these rallies a core of loyal Harley Davidson users, called HOGs (for Harley Owners Group), were to be trailblazers for the successful growth to come.

Beals had company on his odyssey: Willie G. Davidson, grandson of the company's founder, and the vice president of design. Willie was an interesting contrast to the more urbane Beals. His was the image of a middle-age hippie. He wore a Viking helmet over his long, unkempt hair, while a straggly beard hid some of his wind-burned face. An aged leather jacket was compatible. Beals and Davidson fit in nicely at the HOG rallies.

THE STRUGGLE BACK

In December 1986, Harley Davidson asked Congress to remove the tariff barriers, more than a year earlier than originally planned. The confidence of the company had been restored and it believed it could now compete with the Japanese head to head.[4]

[3] Rod Willis, "Harley Davidson Comes Roaring Back," *Management Review* (March 1986), pp. 20–27.
[4] "Harley Back in High Gear," *Forbes* (April 20, 1987), p. 8.

Production Improvements

Shortly after the buyout, Beals and other managers visited Japanese plants both in Japan and Honda's assembly plant in Marysville, Ohio. They were impressed that they were being beaten not by "robotics, or culture, or morning calisthenics and company songs, [but by] professional managers who understood their business and paid attention to detail."[5] As a result, Japanese operating costs were as much as 30 percent lower than Harley's.

Beals and his managers tried to implement some of the Japanese management techniques. Each plant was divided into profit centers, with managers assigned total responsibility within their particular area. Just-in-time (JIT) inventory and materials-as-needed (MAN) systems sought to control and minimize all inventories both inside and outside the plants. Quality circles (QCs) were formed to increase employee involvement in quality goals and to improve communication between management and workers. See the following Information Box for further discussion of quality circles. Another new program called statistical operator control (SOC) gave employees the responsibility for checking the quality of their own work and making proper correcting adjustments. Efforts were made to improve labor relations by more sensitivity to employees and their problems as well as better employee assistance and benefits. Certain product improvements were also introduced, notably a new engine and mountings on rubber to reduce vibration. A well-accepted equipment innovation was to build stereo systems and intercoms into the motorcycle helmets.

The production changes between 1981 and 1988 resulted in:[6]

- Inventory reduced by 67 percent
- Productivity up by 50 percent
- Scrap and rework down two-thirds
- Defects per unit down 70 percent

In the 1970s, the joke among industry experts was, "If you're buying a Harley, you'd better buy two—one for spare parts."[7] Now this had obviously changed, but the change still had to be communicated to consumers, and believed.

Marketing Moves

Despite its bad times and its poor quality, Harley had a cadre of loyal customers almost unparalleled. Company research maintained that 92 percent of its customers remained with Harley.[8] Despite such hard-core loyalists, the company had always had a serious public image problem. It was linked to an image of the pot-smoking, beer-drinking, woman-chasing, tattoo-covered, leather-clad biker: "When your company's logo is the

[5] Dexter Hutchins, "Having a Hard Time with Just-in-Time," *Fortune* (June 19, 1986), p. 65.

[6] Hutchins, *op. cit.* p. 66.

[7] *Ibid.*

[8] Mark Marvel, "The Gentrified HOG," *Esquire* (July 1989), p. 25.

INFORMATION BOX

QUALITY CIRCLES

Quality circles were adopted by Japan in an effort to rid its industries of poor quality and junkiness after World War II. Quality circles are worker-management committees that meet usually weekly, to talk about production problems, plan ways to improve productivity and quality, and resolve job-related gripes on both sides.

At the height of their popularity they were described as "the single most significant reason for the truly outstanding quality of goods and services produced in Japan." [9] At one time Mazda had 2,147 circles with more than 16,000 employees involved. They usually consisted of seven or eight volunteers who met on their own time to discuss and solve the issues they were concerned with. In addition to making major contributions to increased productivity and quality, quality circles gave employees an opportunity to participate and gain a sense of accomplishment. [10]

The idea did not originate with the Japanese: it came from two American personnel consultants. But the Japanese refined the idea and ran with it. In the 1980s, American industry, unable to match the quality of Japanese imports, saw quality circles as the elixir in quality enhancement. Firms also found them a desirable way to promote teamwork, good feelings, and to avoid some of the adversarial relations stemming from collective bargaining and union grievances.

Despite the glowing endorsements for quality circles, in the United States they were more a fad that quickly faded. Workers claimed they smacked of "tokenism," and were a façade and impractical, with no lasting benefits once the novelty had worn off. Others saw them as time wasted and, unlike Japan, few U.S. workers accepted the idea of participating in quality circles on their own time.

How would you feel about devoting an hour or more to quality circle meetings every week or so, on your own time? If your answer is, "No way," do you think this is a fair attitude on your part? Why or why not?

Invitation to Research: Can you find any U.S. firms that are still using quality circles?

number-one requested in tattoo parlors, it's time to get a licensing program that will return your reputation to the ranks of baseball, hot dogs, and apple pie." [11]

Part of Harley's problem had been with bootleggers ruining the name by placing it on unlicensed goods of poor quality. Now the company began to use warrants and federal marshalls to crack down on unauthorized uses of its logo at motorcycle conventions. And it began licensing its name and logo on a wide variety of products, from leather jackets to cologne to jewelry—even to pajamas, sheets, and towels. Suddenly retailers realized that these licensed goods were popular, and were even

[9] "A Partnership to Build the New Workplace," *Business Week*, June 30, 1980, p. 101.

[10] As described in a Mazda ad in *Forbes*, May 24, 1982, p. 5.

[11] "Thunder Road," Forbes (July 18, 1983), p. 32.

being bought by a new customer segment, undreamed of until now: bankers, doctors, lawyers, and entertainers. This new breed of customers soon expanded their horizons to include the Harley Davidson bikes themselves. They joined the HOGs, only now they became known as Rubbies—the rich urban bikers. And high prices for bikes did not bother them in the least.

Beals was quick to capitalize on this new market with an expanded product line with expensive heavyweights. In 1989 the largest motorcycle was introduced, the Fat Boy, with eighty cubic inches of V-twin engine and capable of a top speed of 150 mph. By 1991, Harley had twenty models, ranging in price from $4,500 to $15,000.

The Rubbies brought Harley back to a leading position in the industry by 1989, with almost 60 percent of the super-heavyweight motorcycle market; by the first quarter of 1993, this had become 63 percent. See Figure 16.1. The importance of this customer to Harley could be seen in the demographic statistics supplied by the *Wall Street Journal* in 1990: "One in three of today's Harley Davidson buyers are professionals or managers. About 60 percent have attended college, up from only 45 percent in 1984. Their median age is thirty-five, and their median household income has risen sharply to $45,000 from $36,000 five years earlier."[12]

In 1989, Beals stepped down as CEO, turning the company over to Richard Teerlink, who was chief operating officer of the Motorcycle Division. Beals, however, retained his position as chairman of the board. The legacy of Beals in the renaissance of Harley led management writer John Schermerhorn to call him a visionary leader.[13] The following Information Box discusses visionary leadership.

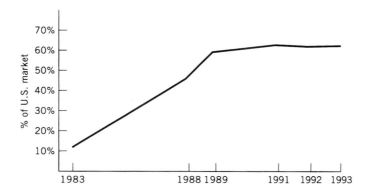

Figure 16.1. Harley Davidson's share of the U.S. heavyweight motorcycle market, selected years, 1983–1993.

Sources: Company reports; R. L. Polk & Company; Gary Slutsker, "Hog Wild," *Forbes* (May 24, 1993), pp. 45–46.

---

[12] Robert L. Rose, "Vrooming Back," *Wall Street Journal* (August 31, 1990), p. 1.

[13] John R. Schermerhorn, Jr., *Management for Productivity*, 4th ed. (New York: Wiley, 1993), pp. 410–411.

INFORMATION BOX

VISIONARY LEADERSHIP

Vision has been identified as an essential ingredient of effective leadership. Having vision characterizes someone who has a clear sense of the future environment and the actions needed to thrive in it.

Undoubtedly, a visionary leader is an asset in a dynamic environment. Such a leader can help a firm grasp opportunities ahead of competitors, revitalize itself, pull itself up from adversity. Schermerhorn states that a visionary begins with a clear vision, communicates that vision to all concerned, and motivates and inspires people in pursuit of that vision. He proposes these five principles of visionary leadership:

1. **Challenge the process.** Be a pioneer—encourage innovation and people with ideas.
2. **Be enthusiastic.** Inspire others through personal example to share in a common vision.
3. **Help others to act.** Be a team player, and support the efforts and talents of others.
4. **Set the example.** Provide a consistent model of how others should act.
5. **Celebrate achievements.** Bring emotion into the workplace and rally "hearts" as well as "minds."[14]

Can you name any visionary leaders? What makes you think they were visionary? Could some of our acclaimed visionary leaders have been merely lucky rather than prophetic?

SUCCESS

By 1993 Harley Davidson had a new problem, one born of success. Now it could not even come close to meeting demand. Customers faced empty showrooms, except perhaps for rusty trade-ins or antiques. Waiting time for a new bike could be six months or longer, unless the customer was willing to pay a 10 percent or higher premium to some gray marketer advertising in biker magazines.

Some of the 600 independent U.S. dealers worried that these empty showrooms and long waiting lists would induce their customers to turn to foreign imports, much as they had several decades before. But other dealers recognized that somehow Beals and company had engendered a brand loyalty unique in this industry, and perhaps in all industries. Assuaging the lack of big bike business, dealers were finding other sources of revenues. Harley's branded line of merchandise, available only at Harley dealers and promoted through glossy catalogs, had really taken off. Harley black leather jackets were bought eagerly at $500; fringed leather bras went for $65; even shot glasses brought $12—all it seemed to take was the Harley name and logo. So substantial was this ancillary business, that in 1992 non-cycle business generated $155.7 million in sales, up from $130.3 million in 1991.

[14] John R. Schermerhorn, Jr., *Management*, 6th ed. (New York: Wiley, 1999) pp. 262–263.

Production

In one sense, Harley's production situation was enviable: it had far more demand than production capability. More than this, it had such a loyal body of customers that delays in product gratification were not likely to turn many away to competitors. The problem, of course, was that full potential was not being realized.

Richard Teerlink, the successor of Beals, expressed the corporate philosophy to expanding quantity to meet the demand: "Quantity isn't the issue, quality is the issue. We learned in the early 1980s you do not solve problems by throwing money at them."[15]

The company increased output slowly. In early 1992 it was making 280 bikes a day; by 1993, this had risen to 345 a day. With increased capital spending, goals were to produce 420 bikes a day, but not until 1996.

Export Potential

Some contrary concerns with the conservative expansion plans of Teerlink surfaced regarding international operations. The European export market beckoned. Harleys had become very popular in Europe. But the company had promised its domestic dealers that exports would not go beyond 30 percent of total production, until the North American market was fully satisfied. Suddenly the European big-bike market grew by an astounding 33 percent between 1990 and 1992. Yet, because of its production constraints, Harley could only maintain a 9 to 10 percent share of this market. In other words, it was giving away business to foreign competitors.

To enhance its presence in Europe, Harley opened a branch office of its HOG club in Frankfurt, Germany, for its European fans.

Specifics of the Resurgence of Harley Davidson

Table 16.1 shows the trend in revenues and net income of Harley since 1982. The growth in sales and profits did not go unnoticed by the investment community. In 1990, Harley Davidson stock sold for $7; in January of 1993, it hit $39. Its market share of heavyweight motorcycles (751 cubic centimeters displacement and larger) had soared from 12.5 percent in 1983, to 63 percent by 1993. Let the Japanese have the lightweight bike market! Harley would dominate the heavyweights.

Harley acquired Holiday Rambler in 1986. As a wholly owned subsidiary, this manufacturer of recreational and commercial vehicles was judged by Harley management to be compatible with the existing motorcycle business as well as moderating some of the seasonality of the motorcycle business. The diversification proved rather mediocre. In 1992, it accounted for 26 percent of total corporate sales, but only 2 percent of profits.[16]

Big motorcycles, made in America by the only U.S. manufacturer, continued the rage. Harley's ninetieth anniversary was celebrated in Milwaukee on June 12, 1993. As many as 100,000 people, including 18,000 HOGS, were there to celebrate. Hotel rooms were sold out for a 60-mile radius. Harley Davidson was up and doing real well.

[15] Gary Slutsker, "Hog Wild," *Forbes* (May 24, 1993), p. 46.
[16] Company annual reports.

TABLE 16.1   Harley Davidson's Growth in Revenue and
Income 1983–1994 (millions)

Year	Revenue	Net Income
1982	$ 210	def $25.1
1983	254	1.0
1984	294	2.9
1985	287	2.6
1986	295	4.3
1987	685	17.7
1988	757	27.2
1989	791	32.6
1990	865	38.3
1991	940	37.0
1992	1,100	54.0
1993	1,210	68.0
1994	1,537	83.0

Source: Company annual reports.

Commentary: The steady climb in sales and profits, except for a pause in 1985, is noteworthy. The total gain in revenues over these years was 631.9%, while income rose more than eightyfold since 1983.

1993–1998

The 1990s continued to be kind to Harley. Demand continued to grow, with the mystique as strong as ever. The company significantly increased its motorcycle production capacity with a new engine plant in Milwaukee completed in 1997 and a new assembly plant in Kansas City in 1998. It expected that demand in the United States would still exceed the supply of Harley bikes.

ANALYSIS

One of Vaughan Beals's first moves after the 1981 leveraged buyout was to improve production efficiency and quality control. This became the foundation for the strategic regeneration moves to come. In this quest, he borrowed heavily from the Japanese, in particular in cultivating employee involvement.

The cultivation of a new customer segment for the big bikes had to be a major factor in the company's resurgence. To some, that more affluent consumers embraced the big, flashy Harley motorcycles was a surprise of no small moment. After all, how could you have two more incompatible groups than the stereotyped black-jacketed cyclists and the Rubbies? Perhaps part of the change was due to high-profile people such as Beals and some of his executives frequently participating at motorcycle rallies and charity rides. Technological and comfort improvements in motorcycles and their equipment added to the new attractiveness. Dealers were also coaxed to make their stores more inviting.

Along with this, expanding the product mix not only made such Harley-branded merchandise a windfall for company and dealers alike, but also piqued the interest of upscale customers in motorcycles themselves. The company was commendably aggressive in running with the growing popularity of the ancillary merchandise, and making this well over a $100 million revenue booster.

Some questions remained. How durable was this popularity, both of the big bikes and the complementary merchandise, with this affluent customer segment? Would it prove to be only a passing fad? If so, then Harley needed to seek diversifications as quickly as possible, even though the Holiday Rambler Corporation had brought no notable success by 1992. Diversifications often bring disappointed earnings compared with a firm's core business.

Another question concerned Harley's slowness in expanding production capability. Faced with a burgeoning demand, was it better to go slowly, to be carefully protective of quality, and to refrain from heavy debt commitments? This had been Harley's most recent strategy, but it raised the risk of permitting competitors to gain market share in the United States and especially in Europe. The following Issue Box discusses aggressive versus conservative planning.

ISSUE BOX

SHOULD WE BE AGGRESSIVE OR CONSERVATIVE IN OUR PLANNING?

The sales forecast—the estimate of sales for the periods ahead—serves a crucial role because it is the starting point for all detailed planning and budgeting. A volatile situation presents some high-risk alternatives: Should we be optimistic or conservative?

On one hand, with conservative planning in a growing market, a firm risks underestimating demand and being unable to expand its resources sufficiently to handle the potential. It may lack the manufacturing capability and sales staff to handle growth potential, and it may have to abdicate a good share of the growing business to competitors who are willing and able to expand their capability to meet the demands of the market.

On the other hand, a firm facing burgeoning demand should consider whether the growth is likely to be a short-term fad or a more permanent situation. A firm can easily become overextended in the buoyancy of booming business, only to see the collapse of such business jeopardizing its viability.

Harley's conservative decision was undoubtedly influenced by concerns about expanding beyond the limits of good quality control. The decision was probably also influenced by management's belief that Harley Davidson had a loyal body of customers who would not switch despite the wait.

Do you think Harley Davidson made the right decision to expand conservatively? Why or why not? Defend your position.

The following numbers show how motorcycle shipments increased from 1993 to 1997, both domestically and export, in thousands of units:

	U.S.	Exports
1997	96.2	36.1
1993	57.2	24.5

Despite continuous increases in production, U.S. consumers still had to wait to purchase a new Harley Davidson bike, but the waits only added to the mystique.

The following shows the growth in revenues and income from 1993 to 1997:

(Millions $)		
	Revenues	Net Income
1997	1,763	174.0
1993	1,217	18.4

Indicative of the popularity of the Harley Davidson logo, Wolverine World Wide, maker originally of Hush Puppies, but now the largest manufacturer of footwear in the United States, entered into a licensing agreement with Harley to use its "sexy" name for a line of boots and fashion shoes.[17]

UPDATE

In its January 7, 2002, issue, *Forbes* declared Harley to be its "Company of the Year," a truly prestigious honor. In supporting its decision, *Forbes* noted that:

In a disastrous year for hundreds of companies, Harley's estimated 2001 sales grew 15 percent to $3.3 billion and earnings grew 26 percent to $435 million. Its shares were up 40 percent in 2001, while the S&P stock average dropped 15 percent. Since Harley went public in 1986, its shares have risen an incredible 15,000 percent. Since 1986, GE generally considered the paragon of American business, had risen only 1,056 percent.

Jeffrey Bleustein, a twenty-six year company veteran now CEO, was diversifying into small, cheaper bikes to attract younger riders as well as women who had shunned the big lumbering machines and who represented only 9 percent of Harley riders. The cult image was stronger than ever. Half of the company's 8,000 employees rode Harleys and many of them appeared at rallies around the country for pleasure and to promote the company. There were now 640,000 owners, the parts-and-accessories catalog numbered 720 pages, and the Harley Davidson name was on everything from blue jeans to pickup trucks. Harley celebrated its 100th birthday in 2003, and some 250,000 riders attended the rally in Milwaukee.[18]

---

[17] Carleen Hawn, "What's in a Name? Whatever You Make It," *Forbes* (July 27, 1998), p. 88.

[18] Jonathan Fahey, "Love Into Money," *Forbes,* January 7, 2002, pp. 60–65.

WHAT CAN BE LEARNED?

Again, a firm can come back from adversity. The resurrection of Harley Davidson almost from the point of extinction proves that adversity can be overcome. It need not be fatal or forever. This should be encouraging to all firms facing difficulties, and to their investors. Noteworthy, however, in comparing Harley with the next case of Continental Air, is the great difference in time these two firms took to turn around. Continental under Bethune achieved spectacular results in only months; it took Harley decades before a Vaughan Beals came on the scene as changemaker.

What does a turnaround require? Above all, it takes a leader who has the vision and confidence that things can be changed for the better. The change may not necessitate anything particularly innovative. It may involve only a rededication to basics, such as better quality control or an improved commitment to customer service brought about by a new positive attitude of employees. But such a return to basics requires that a demoralized or apathetic organization be rejuvenated and remotivated. This calls for leadership of a high order. If the core business has still been maintained, it at least provides a base to work from.

Preserve the core business at all costs. Every viable firm has a basic core or distinctive position—sometimes called an "ecological niche"—in its business environment. This unique position may be due to its particular location, or to a certain product. It may come from somewhat different operating methods or from the customers served. Here, a firm is better than its competitors. This strong point is the basic core of a company's survival. Though it may diversify and expand far beyond this area, the firm should not abandon its main bastion of strength.

Harley almost did this. Its core—and indeed, only—business was its heavyweight bikes sold to a limited and loyal, thought not at the time particularly savory, customer segment. Harley almost lost this core business by abandoning reasonable quality control to the point that its motorcycles became the butt of jokes. To his credit, upon assuming leadership Beals acted quickly to correct the production and employee motivation problems. By preserving the core, Beals could pursue other avenues of expansion.

The power of a mystique. Few products are able to gain a mystique or cult following. Coors beer did in the 1960s and early 1970s, when it became the brew of celebrities and the emblem of the purity and freshness of the West. In the cigarette industry, Marlboro rose to become the top seller from a somewhat similar advertising and image thrust: the Marlboro man. The Ford Mustang had a mystique at one time. Somehow the big bikes of Harley Davidson developed a mystique. Harleys appealed to the HOGS and to the Rubbies: two disparate customer segments, but both loyal to their Harleys. The mystique led to "logo magic": Simply put the Harley Davidson name and logo on all kinds of merchandise, and watch the sales take off.

How does a firm develop (or acquire) a mystique? There is no simple answer, no guarantee. Certainly a product has to be unique, but though most firms strive for this differentiation, few achieve a mystique. Image-building advertising, focusing on the target buyer, may help. Perhaps even better is image-building advertising that highlights the people customers might wish to emulate. But what about the black-leather-jacketed, perhaps bearded, cyclist?

Perhaps in the final analysis, acquiring a mystique is a more accidental and fortuitous success than something that can be deliberately orchestrated. Two lessons, however, can be learned about mystiques. First, they do not last forever. Second, firms should run with them as long as possible and try to expand the reach of the name or logo to other goods, even unrelated ones, through licensing.

CONSIDER

What additional learning insights can you see coming from this Harley Davidson resurgence?

QUESTIONS

1. Do you think Beals's rejuvenation strategy for Harley Davidson was the best policy? Discuss and evaluate other strategies that he might have pursued.

2. How durable do you think the Rubbies' infatuation with the heavyweight Harleys will be? What leads you to this conclusion?

3. A Harley Davidson stockholder criticizes present management: "It is a mistake of the greatest magnitude that we abdicate a decent share of the European motorcycle market to foreign competitors, simply because we do not gear up our production to meet the demand." Discuss.

4. Given the resurgence of Harley Davidson in the 1990s, would you invest money in the company? Discuss, considering as many factors bearing on this decision as you can.

5. "Harley Davidson's resurgence is only the purest luck. Who could have predicted, or influenced, the new popularity of big bikes with the affluent?" Discuss.

6. "The tariff increase on Japanese motorcycles in 1983 gave Harley Davidson badly needed breathing room. In the final analysis, politics is more important than management in competing with foreign firms." What are your thoughts?

HANDS-ON EXERCISES

1. As a representative of a mutual fund with a major investment in Harley Davidson, you are particularly critical of Vaughn Beals's visible presence at motorcycle rallies and his hobnobbing with black-jacketed cycle gangs. He maintains this is a fruitful way to maintain a loyal core of customers. Playing the devil's advocate (a person who opposes a position to establish its merits and validity), argue against Beals's practices.

2. As a vice president at Harley Davidson, you believe the recovery efforts should have gone well beyond the heavyweight bikes into lightweights. What arguments would you present for this change in strategy, and what specific recommendations would you make for such a new course of action? What contrary arguments would you expect? How would you counter them?

3. As a staff assistant to Vaughan Beals, you have been charged to design a strategy to bring a mystique to the Harley Davidson name. How would you propose to do this? Be as specific as you can, and defend your reasoning.

TEAM DEBATE EXERCISE

A major schism has arisen in the executive ranks of Harley Davidson. Many executives believe that a monumental mistake is being made not to gear up production to match the burgeoning worldwide demand for Harleys. The other side believes the present go-slow approach to increasing production is more prudent. Persuasively support your position and attack the opposing view.

INVITATION TO RESEARCH

What is the situation with Harley Davidson today? Has the diversification into lower-priced bikes done well and attracted more women bikers? Is the Harley cult as strong as ever? Are any new competitors or threats emerging?

CHAPTER SEVENTEEN

Continental Airlines: Executing a Recovery

$\boldsymbol{I}$n the fourth edition of *Mistakes*, published in 1994, we described massive management blunders at Continental Airlines as a "confrontational destruction of an organization." In only a few years, in a remarkable recovery under new management, Continental became a star of the airline industry. The changemaker, CEO Gordon Bethune, wrote a best-selling book about his efforts to turn around the moribund company, titled *From Worst to First*. In this chapter we will look first at the unfolding scenario leading to the difficulties of Continental, and then examine the ingredients of the great comeback.

THE FRANK LORENZO ERA

Lorenzo was a consummate manipulator, parlaying borrowed funds and little of his own money to build an airline empire. By the end of 1986, he controlled the largest airline network in the non Communist world: only Aeroflot, the Soviet airline, was larger. Lorenzo's network was a leveraged amalgam of Continental, People Express, Frontier, and Eastern, with $8.6 billion in sales—all this from a small investment in Texas International Airlines in 1971. In the process of building his network, Lorenzo defeated unions and shrewdly used the bankruptcy courts to further his ends. When he eventually departed, his empire was swimming in red ink, had a terrible reputation, and was burdened with colossal debt and aging planes.

The Start

After getting an MBA from Harvard, Lorenzo's first job was as a financial analyst at Trans World Airlines. In 1966, he and Robert Carney, a buddy from Harvard, formed an airline consulting firm, and in 1969, the two put up $35,000 between them to form an investment firm, Jet Capital. Through a public stock offering they were able to raise an additional $1.15 million. In 1971, Jet Capital was called in to fix ailing Texas International and wound up buying it for $1.5 million, and Lorenzo became CEO.

He restructured the debt as well as the airline's routes, found funds to upgrade the almost obsolete planes, and brought Texas International to profitability.

In 1978, acquisition-minded Lorenzo lost out to Pan Am in a bidding war for National Airlines, but he made $40 million on the National stock he had acquired. In 1980, he created nonunion New York Air and formed Texas Air as a holding company. In 1982, Texas Air bought Continental for $154 million.

Lorenzo's Treatment of Continental

In 1983, Lorenzo took Continental into bankruptcy court, filing for Chapter 11. This permitted the corporation to continue to operate but spared its obligation to meet heavy interest payments and certain other contracts while it reorganized as a more viable enterprise. The process nullified the previous union contracts, and this prompted a walkout by many union workers.

Lorenzo earned the lasting enmity of organized labor and the reputation of union-buster as he replaced strikers with nonunion workers at much lower wages. (A few years later, he reinforced this reputation when he used the same tactics with Eastern Airlines.)

In a 1986 acquisition achievement that was to backfire a few years later, Lorenzo struck deals for a weak Eastern Airlines and a failing People Express/Frontier Airlines. That same year Continental emerged out of bankruptcy. Now Continental, with its nonunion workforce making it a low-cost operator, was Lorenzo's shining jewel. The low bid accepted for Eastern reinforced Lorenzo's reputation as a visionary builder.

What kind of executive was Lorenzo? Although he was variously described as a master financier and visionary, his handling of day-to-day problems bordered on the inept.[1] One former executive was quoted as saying, "If he agreed with one thing at 12:15, it would be different by the afternoon."[2] Inconsistent planning and poor execution characterized his lack of good operational strength. Furthermore, his domineering and erratic style alienated talented executives. From 1983 to 1993, nine presidents left Continental.

But Lorenzo's treatment of his unions brought the most controversy. He became the central figure of confrontational labor-management relations, to a degree perhaps unmatched by any other person in recent years. Although he won the battle with Continental's unions and later with Eastern's, he was burdened with costly strikes and the residue of ill feeling that impeded any profitable recovery during his time at the helm.

The Demise of Eastern Airlines

In an environment of heavy losses and its own militant unions, Eastern in 1986, accepted the low offer of Lorenzo. With tough contract demands and the stockpiling of $1 billion in cash as strike insurance, Lorenzo seemed eager to precipitate a strike that he might crush. He instituted a program of severe downsizing and in 1989, after fifteen months

---

[1] See, for example, Todd Vogel, Gail DeGeorge, Pete Engardio, and Aaron Bernstein, "Texas Air Empire in Jeopardy," *Business Week* (March 27, 1989), p. 30.

[2] Mark Ivey and Gail DeGeorge, "Lorenzo May Land a Little Short of the Runway," *Business Week* (February 5, 1990), p. 48.

of fruitless talks, some 8,500 machinists and 3,800 pilots went on strike. Lorenzo countered the strike at Eastern by filing for Chapter 11 bankruptcy, and replaced many of the striking pilots and machinists within months.

At first Eastern appeared to be successfully weathering the strike, while Continental benefited with increased business. But soon revenue dropped drastically with Eastern planes flying less than half full amid rising fuel costs. Fares were slashed in order to regain business, and a liquidity crisis loomed. Then, on January 16, 1990, an Eastern jet sheared the top off a private plane in Atlanta. Even though the accident was attributed to air controller error, Eastern's name received the publicity.

Eastern creditors now despaired of Lorenzo's ability to pay them back in full and they pushed for a merger with Continental, which would expose it to the bankruptcy process. On December 3, 1990, Continental again tumbled into bankruptcy, burdened with overwhelming debt. In January 1991, Eastern finally went out of business.

CONTINENTAL'S EMERGENCE FROM BANKRUPTCY, AGAIN

Lorenzo was gone. The legacy of Eastern remained however. Creditors claimed more than $400 million in asset transfers between Eastern and Continental, and Eastern still had $680 million in unfunded pension liabilities. The board brought in Robert Ferguson, veteran of Braniff and Eastern bankruptcies, to make changes. On April 16, 1993, the court approved a reorganization plan for Continental to emerge from bankruptcy, the first airline to have survived two bankruptcies. However, creditors got only pennies on the dollar.[3]

Still, despite its long history of travail and a terrible profit picture, Continental in 1992 was the nation's fifth largest airline, behind American, United, Delta, and Northwest, and it served 193 airports. Table 17.1 shows the revenues and net profits (or losses) of Continental and its major competitors from 1987 through 1991.

The Legacy of Lorenzo

Continental was savaged in its long tenure as a pawn in Lorenzo's dynasty-building efforts. He had saddled it with huge debts, brought it into bankruptcy twice, left it with aging equipment. Perhaps a greater detriment was a ravished corporate culture. The Information Box on the following page discusses corporate culture.

A devastated reputation proved to be a major impediment. The reputation of a surly labor force had repercussions far beyond the organization itself. For years Continental had had a problem wooing the better-paying business travelers. Being on expense accounts, they wanted quality service rather than cut-rate prices. A reputation for good service is not easily or quickly achieved, especially when the opposite reputation is well entrenched.

---

[3] Bridget O'Brian, "Judge Backs Continental Airlines Plan to Regroup, Emerge from Chapter 11," *Wall Street Journal* (April 19, 1993), p. A4.

TABLE 17.1 **Performance Statistics, Major Airlines, 1987–1991**

	1987	1988	1989	1990	1991	Percent 5-Year Gain
Revenues: (millions $)						
American	6,368	7,548	8,670	9,203	9,309	46.0%
Delta	5,638	6,684	7,780	7,697	8,268	46.6
United	6,500	7,006	7,463	7,946	7,850	20.8
Northwest	3,328	3,395	3,944	4,298	4,330	30.1
Continental	3,404	3,682	3,896	4,036	4,031	18.4
Income (millions $)						
American	225	450	412	(40)	(253)	
Delta	201	286	467	(119)	(216)	
United	22	426	246	73	(175)	
Continental	(304)	(310)	(56)	(1,218)	(1,550)	

Source: Company annual reports.

Commentary: Note the operating performance of Continental relative to its major competitors during this period. It ranks last in sales gain. It far and away has the worst profit performance, having massive losses during each of the years in contrast to its competitors, who, while incurring some losses, had neither the constancy nor the magnitude of losses of Continental. And the relative losses of Continental are even worse than they at first appear: Continental is the smallest of these major airlines.

INFORMATION BOX

IMPORTANCE OF A POSITIVE CORPORATE CULTURE

A corporate or organizational culture can be defined as the system of shared beliefs and values that develops within an organization and guides the behavior of its members.[4] Such a culture can be a powerful influence on performance results:

> If employees know what their company stands for, if they know what standards they are to uphold, then they are much more likely to make decisions that will support those standards. They are also more likely to feel as if they are an important part of the organization. They are motivated because life in the company has meaning for them.[5]

Lorenzo had destroyed the former organizational climate as he beat down the unions. The replacement employees had little reason to develop a positive culture or esprit de corps given the many top management changes, the low pay relative to other airline employees, and the continuous possibility of corporate bankruptcy. Employees had little to be proud of. But this was to change abruptly under new management.

Can a corporate climate be too upbeat? Discuss.

---

[4] Edgar H. Schein, "Organizational Culture," *American Psychologist,* vol. 45 (1990), pp. 109–119.

[5] Terrence E. Deal and Alan A. Kennedy, *Corporate Cultures: The Rites and Rituals of Corporate Life* (Reading, MA: Addison-Wesley, 1982), p. 22

On another dimension, Continental's reputation also hindered competitive parity. Surviving two bankruptcies does not engender confidence among investors, creditors, or even travel agents.

A Sick Airline Industry

Domestic airlines lost a staggering $8 billion in the years 1990 through 1992. Tense fare wars and excess planes proved to be albatrosses. Even when planes were filled, discount prices often did not cover overhead.

A lengthy recession was mostly to blame, inducing both firms and individuals to fly more sparingly. Business firms were finding teleconferencing to be a viable substitute for business travel, and consumers, facing diminished discretionary income and the threat of eventual layoffs or forced retirements, were hardly in an optimistic mood. The airlines suffered.

Part of the blame for the red ink lay directly with the airlines—they were reckless in their expansion efforts—yet they did not deserve total blame. In the late 1980s, passenger traffic climbed 10 percent per year, and in response the airlines ordered hundreds of jetliners.[6] The recession arrived just as the new planes were being delivered. The airlines greatly increased their debt structure in their expansion efforts; the big three, for example—American, United, and Delta—doubled their leverage in the four years after 1989, with debt by 1993 at 80 percent of capitalization.[7]

In such a climate, cost-cutting efforts prevailed. But how much can be cut without jeopardizing service and even safety? Some airlines found that hubs, heralded as the great strategy of the 1980s, were not as cost effective as expected. With hub cities, passengers were gathered from outlying "spokes" and then flown to final destinations. Maintaining too many hubs, however, brought costly overheads. While the concept was good, some retrenchment seemed necessary to be cost effective.

Airlines such as Continental with heavy debt and limited liquidity had two major concerns: first, how fast the country could emerge from recession; second, the risk of fuel price escalation in the coming years. Despite Continental's low operating costs, external conditions impossible to predict or control could affect viability.

THE GREAT COMEBACK UNDER GORDON BETHUNE

In February 1994, Gordon Bethune left Boeing and took the job of president and chief operating officer of Continental. He faced a daunting challenge. While it was the fifth largest airline, Continental was by far the worst among the nation's ten biggest according to these quality indicators of the Department of Transportation:

- In on-time percentage (the percentage of flights that land within fifteen minutes of their scheduled arrival)
- In number of mishandled-baggage reports filed per 1,000 passengers

---

[6] Andrea Rothman, "Airlines: Still No Wind at Their Backs," *Business Week* (January 11, 1993), p. 96.
[7] *Ibid.*

- In number of complaints per 100,000 passengers
- In involuntarily denied boarding (i.e., passengers with tickets who are not allowed to board because of overbooking or other problems)[8]

In late October he became chief executive officer. Now he sat in the pilot's seat.

He made dramatic changes. In 1995, through a "renewed focus on flight schedules and incentive pay" he greatly improved on-time performance, along with lost-baggage claims, and customer complaints. Now instead of being dead last in these quality indicators of the Department of Transportation, Continental by 1996 was third best or better in all four categories.

Customers began returning, especially the higher-fare business travelers, climbing from 32.2 percent in 1994 to 42.8 percent of all customers by 1996. In May 1996, based on customer surveys Continental was awarded the J. D. Power Award as the best airline for customer satisfaction on flights of 500 miles or more. It also received the award in 1997, the first airline to win two years in a row. Other honors followed. In January 1997, it was named "Airline of the Year" by *Air Transport World*, the leading industry monthly. In January 1997, *Business Week* named Bethune one of its top managers of 1996.

Bethune had transformed the workforce into a happy one, as measured by these statistics:

- Wages up an average of 25 percent
- Sick leave down more than 29 percent
- Personnel turnover down 45 percent
- Workers compensation claims down 51 percent
- On-the-job injuries down 54 percent[9]

Perhaps nothing illustrates the improvement in employee morale as much as this: In 1995, not long after he became top executive, employees were so happy with their new boss's performance that they chipped in to buy him a $22,000 Harley-Davidson.[10]

Naturally such improvement in employee relations and customer service had major impact on revenues and profitability. See Table 17.2 for the trend since 1992.

Gordon Bethune

Bethune's father was a crop duster, and as a teenager Gordon helped him one summer and learned firsthand the challenges of responsibility: in this case, preparing a crude landing strip for nighttime landings, with any negligence disastrous. He joined the Navy at seventeen, before finishing high school. He graduated second in his class at the Naval Technical School to become an aviation electronics technician, and over nineteen years worked his way up to lieutenant. After leaving the Navy he joined Braniff, then Western, and later Piedmont Airlines as senior vice president of Operations. He finally

[8] Gordon Bethune, *From Worst to First* (New York: Wiley, 1998), p. 4.
[9] *Ibid.*, pp. 7–8.
[10] *Ibid.*, frontispiece.

TABLE 17.2   Continental Sales and Profits, Before and After Bethune, 1992–1997

	Before Bethune			After Bethune		
	1992	1993	1994	1995	1996	1997
Revenues (millions $)	5,494	3,907	5,670	5,825	6,360	7,213
Net Income (millions $)	−110	−39	−612	224	325	389
Earnings per Share ($)		−1.17	−11.88	3.60	4.25	5.03

Sources: Company annual reports.

Commentary: While the revenue statistics do not show a striking improvement, the net income certainly does. Most important to investors, the earnings per share show a major improvement.

These statistics suggest the fallacy of a low-price strategy at the expense of profitability in the 1992–1994 era. At the same time, we have to realize that the early 1990s were recession years, particularly for the airline industry.

left Piedmont for Boeing as VP/general manager of Customer Service. There he became licensed as a 757 and 767 pilot: "An amazing thing happened. All the Boeing pilots suddenly thought I was a great guy," he writes. "I hope I hadn't given them any reason to think otherwise of me before that, but this really got their attention."[11]

HOW DID HE DO IT?

Bethune stressed the human element in guiding the comeback of a lethargic, even bitter, organization, even by doing the simple things: "On October 24, 1994, I did a very significant thing in the executive suite of Continental Airlines. ... I opened the doors. ... [Before] the doors to the executive suite were locked, and you needed an ID to get through. Security cameras added to the feeling of relaxed charm. ... So the day I began running the company, I opened the doors. I wasn't afraid of my employees, and I wanted everybody to know it."[12] Still, he had to entice employees to the twentieth floor of headquarters, and he did this with open houses, supplying food and drink, and personal tours and chat sessions. "I'd take a group of employees into my office, open up the closet, and say, 'You see? Frank's not here.' Frank Lorenzo had left Continental years before; the legacy of cost cutting and infighting of that era was finally gone, and I wanted them to know it."[13]

Of course, the improved employee relations needed tangible elements to cement and sustain it, and to improve the morale. Bethune worked hard to instill a spirit of teamwork. He did this by giving on-time bonuses to all employees, not just pilots. He burned the employee procedure manual that bound them to rigid policies instead of being able to use their best judgment. He even gave the planes a new paint job to

[11] *Ibid.*, p. 268.
[12] *Ibid.*, p. 14.
[13] *Ibid.*, p. 32.

provide tangible evidence of a disavowal of the old and an embracing of new policies and practices. This new image impressed both employees and customers.

Better communications was also a key element in improving employee relationships and the spirit of teamwork. Information was shared with employees through newsletters, updates on bulletin boards, e-mail, voice-mail, and electronic signs over worldwide workplaces. To Bethune it was a cardinal sin for any organization if employees first heard of something affecting them through the newspaper or other media. The following Information Box contrasts the classic Theory X and Theory Y managers. Bethune was certainly a Theory Y manager, and Lorenzo Theory X.

INFORMATION BOX

THE THEORY X AND THEORY Y MANAGER

Douglas McGregor, in his famous book, *The Human Side of Enterprise*, advanced the thesis of two different types of managers, the traditional Theory X manager with rather low opinion of subordinates, and his new Theory Y manager, whom we might call a human-relations type of manager.

Schermerhorn contrasts the two styles as follows:[14]

Theory X views subordinates as:

- Disliking work
- Lacking in ambition
- Irresponsible
- Resistant to change
- Preferring to be led than to lead

Theory Y sees subordinates this way:

- Willing to work
- Willing to accept responsibility
- Capable of self-direction
- Capable of self-control
- Capable of imagination, ingenuity, creativity

Which is better? With the success of Bethune in motivating his employees for strong positive change in the organization, one would think Theory Y is the only way to go. McGregor certainly thought so and predicted that giving workers more participation, freedom, and responsibility would result in high productivity.[15]

So, is there any room for a Theory X manager today? If so, under what circumstances?

[14] John R. Schermerhorn, Jr., *Management*, 6th ed. (New York: J. Wiley 1999), p. 79.
[15] Douglas McGregor, *The Human Side of Enterprise* (New York: McGraw-Hill), 1960.

Now Continental had to win back customers. Instead of the company's old focus on cost savings, efforts were directed to putting out a better product. This meant emphasis on on-time flights, better baggage handling, and the like. By giving employees bonuses for meeting these standards, the incentive was created.

Bethune sought to do a better job of designing routes with good demand, to "fly places people wanted to go." This meant, for example, cutting back on six flights a day between Greensboro, North Carolina, and Greenville, South Carolina. It meant not trying to compete with Southwest's Friends Fly Free Fares, which "essentially allowed passengers to fly anywhere within the state of Florida for $24.50.[16] The frequent flyer program was reinstated. Going a step further, the company apologized to travel agents, business partners, and customers and showed them how it planned to do better and earn their business back.

Continental queried travel agents about their biggest clients, the major firms that did the most traveling, asking how could it better serve their customers. As a result, more first-class seats were added, particular destinations were given more attention, discounts for certain volumes were instituted. Travel agents themselves were made members of the team and given special incentives beyond normal airline commissions.

This still left financial considerations. Bethune was aggressive in renegotiating loans and poor airplane lease agreements, and in getting supplier financial cooperation. Controls were set up to monitor cash flow and stop waste. Tables 17.3 and 17.4 show

TABLE 17.3 Competitive Position of Continental Before and After Bethune, 1992–1997

	Before Bethune			After Bethune		
	1992	1993	1994	1995	1996	1997
Revenues (millions $):						
AMR (American)	14,396	15,701	16,137	16,910	17,753	18,570
UAR (United)	12,890	14,511	13,950	14,943	16,362	17,378
Delta	10,837	11,997	12,359	12,194	12,455	13,590
Northwest	NA	8,649	9,143	9,085	9,881	10,226
Continental	5,494	3,907	5,670	5,825	6,360	7,213
Continental's Market Share (percent of total sales of Big Five Airlines):		7.1%	9.9%	9.9%	10.1%	10.8%

Sources: Company annual reports.

NA = Information not available.

Commentary: Most significant is the gradual increase in market share of Continental over its four major rivals. This is an improving competitive position.

[16] *Ibid.*, pp. 51–52.

TABLE 17.4   **Profitability Comparison of Big Five Airlines, 1992–1997**

	Before Bethune			After Bethune		
	1992	1993	1994	1995	1996	1997
Net Income (millions $):						
AMR	–474	–96	228	196	1,105	985
UAL	–416	–31	77	378	600	958
Delta	–505	–414	–408	294	156	854
Northwest	NA	–114	296	342	536	606
Continental	–110	–39	–696	224	325	389

Source: Company annual reports.

NA = information not available.

Commentary: Of interest is how the good and bad times for the airlines seem to move in lockstep. Still, the smallest of the Big Five, Continental, incurred the biggest loss of any airline in 1994. Under Bethune, it has seen a steady increase in profitability, but so have the other airlines, although AMR and Delta have been more erratic

the results of Bethune's efforts from the dark days of 1992–1994, and how the competitive position of Continental changed. Remember, Bethune joined the firm in February 1994 and did not become the top executive until late October of that year.

WHAT CAN BE LEARNED?

It is possible to quickly turn around an organization. This idea flies in the face of conventional wisdom. How can a firm's bad reputation with employees, customers, creditors, stockholders, and suppliers be overcome without years of trying to prove that it has changed for the better? This conventional wisdom is usually correct: a great comeback does not often occur easily or quickly. But it sometimes does, with a streetwise leader, and a bit of luck perhaps. Gordon Bethune is proof that negative attitudes can be turned around quickly.

This possibility of a quick turnaround should be inspiring to other organizations mired in adversity.

Still, reputation should be carefully guarded. In most cases, a poor image is difficult to overcome, with trust built up only over time. The prudent firm is careful to safeguard its reputation.

Give employees a sense of pride and a caring management. Bethune proved a master at changing employees' attitudes and their sense of pride. Few top executives ever faced such a negative workforce, reflecting the Lorenzo years. But Bethune changed all this, and in such a short time. His open-door policy and open houses to encourage employees to interact with him and other top executives was such a simple gesture, but so effective, as was his opening wide the channels of communication about company plans. The incentive plans for improving performance, and the freeing up of employee initiatives by abolishing the rigidity of formal policies, were further positives. He engendered an atmosphere of teamwork and a personal image of an appreciative CEO. What is truly remarkable is how quickly such simple actions could turn around the attitudes of a workforce from adversarial with morale in the pits to pride and an eagerness to build an airline.

Try to avoid an adversarial approach to employee relations. Lorenzo used a confrontational and adversarial approach to his organization and the unions. He was seemingly successful in destroying the unions and hiring nonunion replacements at lower pay scales. This resulted in Continental becoming the lowest-cost operator of the major carriers, but there were negatives: service problems, questionable morale, diminished reputation, and devastated profitability.

Bethune used the opposite tack. It is hard to argue against nurturing and supporting an existing organization, avoiding the adversarial mindset of "them or us" if at all possible. Admittedly this may sometimes be difficult—sometimes impossible, at least in the short-run—but it is worth trying. It should result in better morale, motivation, and commitment to the company's best interest.

Contradictory and inconsistent strategies are vulnerable. Lorenzo was often described as mercurial and subject to knee-jerk planning, and poor execution.[17] Clearly focused objectives and strategies mark effective firms. They bring stability to an organization and give customers, employees, and investors confidence in undeviating commitments. Admittedly, some objectives and strategies may have to be modified occasionally to meet changing environmental and competitive conditions, but the spirit of the organization should be resolute, provided it is a positive influence and not a negative one.

The dangers of competing mostly on low price. Bethune inherited one of the lowest-cost air carriers, and it was doing badly. He says "you can make an airline so cheap nobody wants to fly it," [just as] "you can make a pizza so cheap nobody wants to eat it." "Trust me on this—we did it. … In fact, it was making us lousy, and people didn't want to buy what we offered."[18]

We might add here that competing strictly on a price basis usually leaves any firm vulnerable. Low prices can easily be matched or countered by competitors if such low prices are attracting enough customers. On the other hand, competition based on such nonprice factors as better service, quality of product, a good public image or reputation are not so easily matched, and can be more attractive to many customers.

In Chapters 14 and 18, we also find firms competing ever so successfully with a low-price strategy. But Vanguard and Dell have operational efficiencies unmatched in their industries.

CONSIDER

Can you add any other learning insights?

QUESTIONS

1. Could Lorenzo's confrontation with the unions of Continental have been more constructively handled? How?

---

[17] For example, Ivey and DeGeorge, *op. cit.*, p. 48..
[18] Bethune, *op. cit.*, p. 50.

2. Do you see any limitations to Bethune's employee relations, especially in the areas of discipline and acceptance of authority?

3. Compare Bethune's management style with that of Lorenzo. What conclusions can you draw?

4. Bethune gave great credit to his open-door policy when he became CEO. Do you think this was a major factor in the turnaround? How about changing the paint of the planes?

5. How do you motivate employees to give a high priority to customer service?

6. Evaluate the causes and the consequences of frequent top executive changes such as Continental experienced in the days of Lorenzo?

7. How can replacement workers—in this case pilots and skilled maintenance people hired at substantially lower salaries than their unionized peers at other airlines—be sufficiently motivated to provide top-notch service and a constructive esprit de corps?

HANDS-ON EXERCISES

1. It is 1994 and Bethune has just taken over. As his staff adviser he has asked you to prepare a report on improving customer service as quickly as possible. He has also asked you to design a program to inform both business and non-business potential passengers of this new commitment. Be as specific as possible in your recommendations.

2. You are the leader of the machinists' union at Eastern. It is 1986 and Lorenzo has just acquired your airline. You know full well how he broke the union at Continental, and rumors are flying that he has similar plans for Eastern. Describe your tactics under two scenarios:

   a. You decide to take a conciliatory stance.

   b. You plan to fight him every step of the way.

   How successful do you think you will be in saving your union?

TEAM DEBATE EXERCISE

In this case we have a great contrast in management styles. While the participative approach of Bethune seems the winner in this particular case, such is not always so. There are good arguments for the autocratic style, and, indeed, Lorenzo made himself a wealthy man by so doing. Debate the general issue of autocratic versus participative management from as many aspects as you can.

INVITATION TO RESEARCH

What is the situation with Continental today? Is Bethune still CEO? Whatever happened to Lorenzo?

CHAPTER EIGHTEEN

Dell Computer: Rising to Dominate the PC Market

*T*he mettle of a person, or a firm, is best tested and judged not in the euphoria of prosperity and boom conditions but in the bleakness of adversity. The several years before and after the millennium provided the testing ground for personal computer (PC) makers.

By 2002, the lower-price PC market had narrowed to two main adversaries, both the founders of their firms: Michael Dell of Dell Computer and Ted Waitt of Gateway. Both had started their ventures in the mid-1980s on a shoestring, one at age nineteen, the other twenty-two. Both became billionaires before they were thirty-five. But by 2002, the PC boom was over, spending for technology was stagnant, and the high-tech industry was in the vanguard of the stock market collapse. Once-mighty organizations with highly valued names—Lucent, Cisco Systems, Compaq—were only grim reminders of lost chances to cash out in the heady days of 50 percent annual growth.

Some analysts saw the PC market as saturated; everyone who needed and could afford a desktop or laptop already had one. Technological advances had slowed, with the current generation of machines already fast enough for most uses, thus lessening incentive to replace or trade up. The economic downturn further tightened spending. As the product life cycle for PCs lengthened, long-term growth prospects dimmed for computer makers. The high stock multiples of only a few years before were hardly sustainable in a low-growth era. Furthermore, as the market became saturated, not all firms were likely to survive.

DELL COMPUTER

The Start

Michael Dell, a tall, curly-haired youth of nineteen, started Dell Computer in a dorm room at the University of Texas in 1984 with $1,000. He had an idea that computer systems could be sold directly to customers rather than going through middlemen. He thought the manufacturer could better understand the needs of customers and provide them the most effective computing systems at lower prices. This direct marketing would also do away with retailers and their high margins.

Three years later in 1987, Dell began his international expansion by opening a subsidiary in the United Kingdom. The next year, Dell took his enterprise public, with an initial offering of 3.5 million shares at $8.50 each, and became an instant multimillionaire. By 1992, Dell Computer was included in the *Fortune* 500 roster of largest companies. In 1997, the presplit price per share of the common stock reached $1,000, and Michael Dell was a multibillionaire.

With the bruising industry downturn, Dell's stock price fell along with all the rest, its shares by mid-2002 down 55 percent from the early 2001 peak of $59. Michael Dell bought 8.5 million shares of his company to add to the 300 million he already owned.

Competition in 2002

In this troubled environment, Dell's revenue in 2001 grew 2.6 percent while that of the PC industry fell 14 percent. For the quarter ended May 3, 2002, Dell reported $457 million in earnings on sales of $8 billion. These figures were flat from the year-earlier figures, but far better than Dell's competitors.

Compaq, once the master of the PC business, found its stock collapsing from $50 to below $10, and was forced into a merger with Hewlett-Packard (HP) since it could not compete profitably with Dell. Gateway was on the ropes, and even high-end manufacturers like Silicon Graphics and Sun Microsystems were losing sales to Dell. Only IBM seemed insulated from Dell's competitive strength, due to its huge main-frame and services businesses that were not directly competitive.

Dell's Market Share Inroads

The economic downturn provided Dell a golden opportunity to grab market share.It almost doubled its share of the worldwide PC market, from 8 percent to 15 percent in just four years.[1] Much of this came when Dell cut prices as the downturn began, thus pressuring rivals with higher cost structures. Wall Street initially criticized this move as bound to destroy Dell's profits. But the consequent boost in market share instead led to increased profits.

When Hewlett-Packard acquired Compaq Computer for $19 billion in May 2002, it leapfrogged Dell to become the biggest PC maker in the world. But the dominance was short-lived. Next quarter, Dell's share of the PC market grew to 14.9 percent from 13.1 percent a year earlier, while HP's combined share with Compaq fell to 15.5 percent from 18.3 percent before the merger.[2] By fall 2002, Dell regained its No. 1 worldwide ranking, shipping 5.2 million PCs to HP's 5.0 million.[3]

Dell was also engaged in a major battle with HP in the printer arena. HP had long dominated this market of printers and related gear, and with it the very lucrative

[1] "Muscling Into New Markets," *Money,* November 2002, p. 49.

[2] Pui-Wing Tam, Gary McWilliams, and Scott Thurm, "As Alliances Fade, Computer Firms Toss Out Playbook," *Wall Street Journal,* October 15, 2002, pp. A1, A8.

[3] Gary McWilliams, "Gateway's Loss Shrinks, but It Sees Gloomy Year," *Wall Street Journal,* October 18, 2002, p. A7.

ink refills market. These ink and toner refills brought HP some $10 billion annually, 15 percent of its combined annual revenues.[4] See the Information Box: Vulnerability of Cash Cows. Dell's entry into this market through an alliance with No. 2 printer maker Lexmark struck at the vital organs of HP. If Dell could pressure HP's highly profitable printer business, HP would be less able to subsidize its money-losing PC sector, thus adding to Dell's mastery of its core PC operation.

Dell also pursued a potential vulnerability of the HP/Compaq merger. Longtime HP and Compaq customers were justifiably apprehensive about the proposed acquisition and how it would turn out. Dell aggressively wooed these corporate customers, especially those buying PCs and the larger computer systems called servers. Dell believed it could offer them lower prices and better customer service.

Gateway was Dell's most direct competitor. Both firms sold PCs directly to customers by phone or on the Internet, thereby bypassing dealers and allowing customers to design the specifications to their individual needs.

A point of difference was the several hundred "Gateway Country" stores, in which customers could "test drive" PCs in the store. Both companies geared their offerings to the low end of the price range, but Gateway was having serious problems competing with Dell on price. Gateway had lost $1 billion on $6 billion in revenues in 2001, and the company was on the ropes. See Table 18.1 for the trend in operating results from 1994 through 2001 for Dell, Gateway, and Hewlett-Packard, and the relative shifts in market shares for these three major PC competitors. Table 18.2 shows net income comparisons and the trends for these same three competitors.

INFORMATION BOX

VULNERABILITY OF CASH COWS

A cash cow is a product or division that is well entrenched with good profits in a low-growth market. Potential competitors seldom are attracted to such a market or willing to make the investment needed to go against a dominant firm. With no competitive threat, this firm has little incentive to invest more, and is content to "milk" the profits of the cash cow, especially if the cow is as essential as ink is to a printer.

However, danger can lurk in this complacent mind-set. If the product is profitable enough, and if entry into the industry is not prohibitive, then interlopers may still be attracted. In Dell's case, with HP's cash cow subsidizing the money-losing PC sector in direct competition with Dell, it seemed worth attacking.

Therein lies the danger of being greedy with cash cow profitability. Any successful entry will bring prices and profits tumbling down. A more defensible strategy for the dominant firm is to be content with more modest profits and minimize competitive threats.

Do you think Dell will be successful in its "invasion" of the printer and ink refill market? What circumstances might affect its successful entry?

[4] *Ibid.*, p. A8.

Table 18.1: Market Shares of Top Three Competitors, 1994–2001* (in millions)

	2001	2000	1999	1998	1996	1994
Dell						
Revenue	31,168	31,888	25,265	18,243	7,759	3,475
Relative Market Share†	37.8%	35.3	33.1	25.1	15.2	11.2
Gateway						
Revenue	6,080	9,601	8,646	7,468	5,035	2,701
Relative Market Share	7.4%	10.6	11.3	10.3	9.8	8.7
Hewlett-Packard						
Revenue	45,226	48,782	42,370	47,061	38,420	24,991
Relative Market Share	54.8%	54.1	55.6	64.6	75.0	80.1

* The three competitors had slightly different fiscal years. They have been adjusted to the same calendar years.

† The market shares are computed as the revenue relative to the total of these three leading competitors. For example, in 2001 the total revenues of Dell, Gateway, and HP were $82,474 million. Dell's market share then was its own revenues divided by the total revenues for the year: 31,168 ÷ 82,474 = 37.8%

Sources: Company annual reports.

Commentary: The trend information of these statistics is of major significance. It shows that over these seven years, Dell has increased its market share relative to its major competitors from 11.2 percent to 37.8 percent, a major feat in a competitive market. In the same years, HP has had a steady decline in market share from 80.1 percent to 54.8 percent (this is before the merger with Compaq). Gateway, after gaining market share steadily up to 1999, had a precipitous decline in its competitive position.

TED WAITT OF GATEWAY

In the fall of 2002, Ted Waitt, chairman and CEO of Gateway, had to be concerned. It would be bad enough if the computer collapse was affecting all firms equally, with market shares staying about the same. But this was not happening. While Gateway and most others were suffering, one firm—Dell—seemed somehow to be profiting and picking up great chunks of market share, much of it at Gateway's expense.

Waitt's thoughts went back to the beginning, to the farmhouse where in 1985, he and friend Mike Hammond had put their dreams to the test with a used computer, a three-page business plan, and a loan of $10,000 guaranteed by his grandmother. Waitt had dropped out of the University of Iowa to devote full time to this fledging endeavor, to this dream. The business plan was simple and had not changed much even by 2002: Offer products directly to customers and build them to their specifications, with the goal of providing the best value for the money. The enterprise grossed $100,000 in its first year, and was on the way to becoming a multibillion-dollar company.

Now Waitt's thoughts turned to the heady years of growth and unbelievable promise. In 1989, he began selling computers online, taking pride in being the first in the industry to do so. Even mighty Dell did not use the Internet for sales until 1996. In 1991, Waitt got the idea of introducing the cow-print boxes, which brought

Table 18.2: Net Income Comparisons of Dell and Its Major Competitors, 1994–2001* (in millions)

	2001	2000	1999	1998	1996	1994
Dell						
Net income	$1,246	2,236	1,666	1,460	531	149
Percentage of total†	66.6%	37.0	32.1	30.9	15.8	8.1
Gateway						
Net income	(1,014)	253	426	346	251	96
Percentage of total	NM	4.2	8.2	7.3	7.5	5.2
Hewlett-Packard						
Net income	624	3,561	3,104	2,946	2,586	1,589
Percentage of total	33.4	58.8	59.7	61.8	76.7	86.7

* The three competitors had slightly different fiscal years. They have been adjusted to the same calendar years.

†Percentage of the combined net incomes of Dell, Gateway, and Hewlett-Packard. NM means Not Meaningful, in this case because of the net loss.

Sources: Company annual reports.

Commentary: Here again, trend information is very revealing of the shifting competitive strengths in this market. Dell's profitability compared to its two main rivals shows steady gains, with a huge jump in 2001. HP's relative profitability has been steadily declining since 1994, and took a real hit in 2001. Gateway's profitability, which had a nice trend in the boom days of the industry, suffered badly in the industry downturn. With the huge loss in 2001 (a loss that continued in 2002 and into 2003) the company's viability as a separate entity was not looking good.

wide acclaim for Gateway and made its products distinctive. He was then on a roll, and in 1992 began offering customers a choice of software at no additional cost. It was with a great sense of achievement that he learned in 1993 that Gateway had become one of the *Fortune* 500 biggest firms, one year after Dell had joined these prestigious ranks. Not bad for an Iowa farm boy. But that same year, something even more momentous happened. Waitt took the firm public, and investor enthusiasm was so great that he became an instant multimillionaire, and not long after, a multi-billionaire. A person can get used to these accomplishments. In 1996, Waitt introduced a nationwide network of what he called Gateway Country stores—after all, he was a country boy—where customers could try out his products, get advice from technical experts, and learn more about technology in high-tech classrooms. With things going so well, he felt he could ease up a bit, and confidently chose a successor.

He shrugged his shoulders in disgust. In 1999, his one-third share of the business was worth $9 billion. Now in 2002 it was worth $400 million and still falling, an unbelievable personal loss of over $8.5 billion. He felt flummoxed.

At first Waitt blamed his handpicked successor, who was ousted when he returned as CEO. But his magic touch now seemed to elude him. He faced a battle for market share in a down market and a price war to boot with his nemesis Michael Dell. Dell had somehow gotten his costs so low that he could undersell all competitors and still make money. In desperation, Waitt slashed Gateway's workforce by 10 percent. But it was not enough. Then he scaled back the company's international ambitions by exiting Europe and Asia, and reduced the workforce by another 25 percent. But Gateway's U.S. market share dropped from 7.4 percent in 2001 to 5.6 percent in 2002.

Waitt turned his attention to Apple Computer. If he couldn't match Dell on price, maybe he could attack Apple. On August 26, 2002, he launched a nationwide TV brand battle against Apple, with a new computer—the Profile 4, which resembled Apple's iMacs but was $400 cheaper (albeit with fewer features). For years Waitt had struggled to establish Gateway as a cult brand (hoping his rural Holstein theme with the black-and-white cow spots would convey an image of heartland honesty and dependability), one that would appeal to Apple's cultlike followers as well as others. But that had not happened, and he was thinking of putting the cow to rest. Apple had nourished its cult with magazines, chat groups, and a storied twenty-year battle against the standard PC. But could Gateway gain some of this following? Critics were not very complimentary, citing Profile 4's lack of a rewriteable DVD drive and upgraded graphics, its boxiness compared with Apple's sleek design, and a screen that did not swivel as smoothly. Well, critics be d——d; his model was still $400 cheaper.

But the price war with Dell could not be ignored. Trying to reduce costs was cutting into muscle, hurting market share, and still not yielding profits. The loss in the quarter ending June 30, 2002, tripled to $61 million on revenues of $1 billion. By contrast, Dell was prospering with a $501 million profit on sales of $9.5 billion, up 11 percent from the previous year. To add salt to the wounds, a Dell executive gloated in a prominent business journal: "It hasn't been a tough market for us."[5]

Now analysts were picking at Gateway's bones, like jackals on the prowl. They were speculating that many of Gateway's 274 stores would have to be closed, and more production outsourced to foreign manufacturers, if there was any hope of returning to profitability.[6]

Doggedly, Waitt predicted as 2002 drew to a close that Gateway would show a quarterly profit at some point during 2003. But he was disconcerted to learn that both the Council of Institutional Investors and the huge California Public Employees Retirement System had added Gateway to their lists of underperformers.[7]

COMPETITIVE STRENGTH OF DELL

Low Cost Structure

Dell depended heavily on technology developed by others. Essentially, Dell had turned low-end computers into a commodity, so that they could supplant high-priced brands. In the process, once high-flying firms such as Digital Equipment, Apollo Computer, and Data General were now in the graveyard. No one seemed able to match Dell's low prices and still be profitable.

---

[5] Arlene Weintraub, "Gateway: Picking Fights It Just Might Lose," *Business Week*, Sept 9, 2002, p. 52.
[6] *Ibid.*
[7] McWilliams, "Gateway's Loss Shrinks, But It Sees Gloomy Year," p. A7.

Dell's operating costs, and this included research and development (R&D), were around 10 percent of sales in 2001, compared with 20 percent at Compaq, 21 percent at Gateway, 22 percent at HP, and 45 percent at Cisco. Trying to match the costs of Dell was no simple matter. Compaq and HP in their merger hoped to cut $2.5 billion out of their combined costs. Dell, half the size of the two companies after their merger, actually cut $1 billion in operating and manufacturing costs in 2001, and planned to do so again in 2002.[8] See the Information Box: Dell Production Efficiencies.

Dell typically entered a market only after the technology had become standardized and cheap. In the process, it saved on R&D. Cisco, for example, spent 18 percent of its revenue on R&D, while Dell spent a puny 1.5 percent. This allowed Dell to capitalize on its leaner operations to undercut rivals. Seemingly, the march toward standardization had been unstoppable. For example, IBM's Lotus Notes had been largely supplanted by Internet-based hosts that allow users to access their e-mail through any standard browser. But standardization might not make such inroads against the proprietary bastions of storage, mainframe computers, switches, and networking equipment.

Marketing Efforts

In 2000, Dell introduced "Steven" into its PC commercials. Steven, played by actor Ben Curtis, a twenty-one-year-old college student, soon blanketed the pop culture landscape as he shilled for Dell. In the commercials, Steven practically grew up before our eyes, moving from high school to an undisclosed college campus. The original spots showed Steven trying to harangue parents into buying their high school offspring a Dell. Three months later, Steven's famous tag line was added: "Dude,

---

INFORMATION BOX

DELL'S PRODUCTION EFFICIENCIES

In 2001, Dell wrung $1 billion out of it costs, half of this coming from manufacturing. Other areas of cost savings included product design, logistics, and warranty costs. The company vowed to cut another $1 billion in 2002.

Dell reduced manufacturing costs with a more efficient factory layout, computer-directed conveyor systems, robots, and constant attention to simplifying assembly and reducing the number of people needed to complete a product. Purchasing managers worked with suppliers to watch parts inventories hourly, ensuring that just enough parts were on hand to meet expected demand without excess inventory. Its constant attention given to improving efficiency enabled Dell to increase production by a third in two years while cutting manufacturing space in half.[9]

Do you see a downside to constantly trying to improve efficiency and cost-cutting?

---

[8] Daniel Fisher, "Pulled in a New Direction," *Forbes*, June 10, 2002, p. 104.

[9] Fisher, "Pulled in a New Direction," p. 110.

you're getting a Dell." (In his portrayal of Steven, Curtis earned $100,000 a year.) How much this ad campaign contributed to Dell's increasing popularity, especially among younger PC users, is impossible to determine—a deficiency of most advertising—but the company spent one-third of its $226.8 million budget on Steven ads. Most of the remainder was aimed at business customers interested in servers and corporate personal computers.

In late 2002, however, Dell's commercials began downplaying Steven, replacing him with young "Dell interns." Although the emphasis was still directed at the youth market, it looked like Steven's $100,000 contract was in jeopardy.[10]

In late 2002, Dell began opening kiosks in major malls across the country. These booths in heavily trafficked areas gave consumers the chance to touch and play with Dell computers instead of just seeing them in pictures. The rent was far less than for a store in the mall, while visibility was greatly increased.

New Horizons for Dell

In 1997, Dell made a strategic decision to expand beyond PCs into the market for servers, those high-end computers with multiple microprocessors to run complex software. By 2002, servers and other so-called enterprise systems accounted for 20 percent of revenues.

Michael Dell's expanded target list began encompassing the entire $1 trillion information technology (IT) market, going beyond desktop PCs and servers to storage devices, switches, even mainframe-like systems—"enterprise computing," which is technobabble for assembling and running computer networks. Estimates were that Dell could double revenues to $60 billion in four or five years, if it could gain a strong foothold in these expanded markets.[11]

The problems with this ambitious goal were that Dell would be forced to change from assembling boxes depending on technology developed by others to spending billions developing its own engineering service and support talent. At the least, in such expansion of horizons Dell's puny R&D expenditures would have to be significantly increased. There was always the possibility of acquisitions. After all, Dell had a hefty $4 billion in cash at the end of 2002, and its stock was commanding a multiple of twenty-five times 2003 estimated earnings, while its peers traded for fifteen times earnings.[12]

The PC market, though growing only slowly, still offered Dell great potential as it gained ever more dominance in this market. In an interview with *Money* magazine in November 2002, Michael Dell noted that 30 million computers were sold in the previous quarter, most of them being upgrades and replacements. He noted that 180 million computers out there were probably over three years old, and 50 million of those were in large corporations: "A personal computer is like a rubber band: You can

---

[10] Suzanne Vranica, "Dell, Starting New Campaign, Plans for Life Without Steven," *Wall Street Journal,* October 16, 2002, p. B3; and Brian Steinberg of Dow Jones, "Dell Dude's Getting Benched for Interns," reported in *Cleveland Plain Dealer,* October 15, 2002, p. C2.

[11] Fisher, "Pulled in a New Direction," pp. 104ff.

[12] "Muscling Into New Markets."

stretch it and it works. But eventually you can stretch it too hard and it breaks. … The 'maybe we don't need to upgrade' idea won't last long."[13] With just 15 percent of the worldwide PC market, there was plenty of market share to grab.

INDUSTRY FRENETIC PRICE COMPETITION

In fall 2002, with the Christmas season looming, PC makers dropped prices to new lows. Big names like IBM and HP, which usually catered to the higher-end market, went squarely after low-price leader Dell. Other makers dropped their already-low prices even more. For example:

- HP and eMachines had models starting at $399
- Gateway announced its own $399 desktop
- Microtel Computer Systems brought out a bare-bones machine for $199
- HP cut prices for its new HP Compaq Evo to $899, from $1,100 a few months before
- Even laptop prices plummeted: For example, IBM's ThinkPad notebooks were reduced to $950

The severe industry price cutting soon extended beyond PCs. HP reduced operating costs by $800 million by consolidating suppliers and shutting factories. It sought to increase selling efforts direct to customers, thus bypassing middlemen, and expected such direct methods to reach one-third of all sales by November 2003. To be competitive, HP cut prices on computers aimed at business buyers by 10 percent to 15 percent. Dell entered the switch market (the technology linking computer networks) with prices one-half to two-thirds those of comparable models from 3Com and Cisco. 3Com promised "aggressive discounts to meet Dell pricing."[14]

To counter the severe price-cutting of rivals, Dell started selling unbranded PCs through computer dealers that it had traditionally shunned. This program was aimed at small- and medium-size businesses.

ANALYSIS

In the PC industry, Dell reigned supreme with its lowest-cost business model. Competitors with higher operating costs usually could not match Dell's prices without losing money. The PC price war in late 2002 taxed industry profits, but hardly hurt Dell. Still, this market was becoming saturated. In order to justify its high-stock valuations, Dell sought to expand beyond PCs and even beyond servers and storage devices—the larger computers—to designing whole computer systems. Compaq had tried this approach a few years before, buying Digital Equipment in a futile effort to double revenues from entrenched competitors like Cisco Systems and IBM. Dell's

---

[13] *Ibid.*
[14] "As Alliances Fade…," p. A8.

success in these expansion efforts remains to be seen, but the Gateways and Compaqs seem vulnerable.

Can Gateway survive? In late 2002, this was in doubt. A severe price war could be the final blow, although Gateway might be able to prune its costs enough to be reasonably competitive and still make some profit as a niche player. A judicious merger was always possible, or an innovative breakthrough a remote possibility. It seemed unlikely that Gateway could develop the cult following that Apple had, and given nothing particularly distinctive about its products, it was vulnerable to price competition.

A major marketing strategy involves product differentiation, that is, making your product or service unique in some way. The more a firm can attain such distinction, the more latitude it has in pricing. One would think with a product as complex as a computer that differentiation should be easily achieved in the various product features, in the servicing, in customer relations. But increasingly most computers—particularly PCs—have become more standardized, with similar features and peripherals, similar warranties, and similar customer service (or lack thereof).

Another phenomenon that should be affecting the PC market is the price/quality perception: the common notion that the higher the price the higher the quality and, conversely, the lower the price the lower the quality. While this perception held sway in the early years of computer technology, it is far less the case today with many customers. Dell, the lowest-cost producer, still has one of the best reputations for service.

UPDATE

By the end of the Christmas season 2002, Ted Waitt's hopes that this might be a turnaround year were dashed. He had stocked his 274 retail stores with cash-and-carry PCs, and broadened the merchandise assortment to include hot sellers such as digital cameras, $3,000 plasma-screen TVs, and MP3 players, and he spent dearly for advertising. Waitt tried to build PC sales by price-matching, everyday low prices, and even daily specials, but all these only added to Gateway's losses. Now he had to contemplate restructuring again, with the retail chain foolishly created in the heady days of 1996 coming under close scrutiny for new cost cuts. The *Wall Street Journal* noted, however, that Waitt was in no danger of losing his job since he was the largest stockholder.[15]

As 2003 drew to a close, Gateway's situation grew worse. On October 24, its stock price plunged 24 percent after Gateway reported a third-quarter loss of $136.1 million and issued a dour forecast for the fourth quarter. Waitt's push into consumer electronics had failed to offset PC woes. Still, a few analysts saw hope for the company in its having no debt and $1 billion in cash and securities (most of the current assets came from big income tax refunds, but these ended in the first quarter of 2003). But even a good-sized cash horde would not long endure with over $100 million quarterly losses.

Dell, meantime, in August 2003 again slashed PC prices, this time aiming more specifically at HP, which had just reported that its PC unit had slipped into the red in its fiscal third quarter ended July 31 because of overly aggressive price cutting. Dell

[15] Gary McWilliams, "Under Gateway's Tree, Another Shake-up," *Wall Street Journal,* January 6, 2003, pp. A13, A15; and "Slaughterhouse," *Forbes,* January 20, 2003, p. 34.

had a monstrous advantage in its low-cost structure: Dell's overhead in the second quarter of 2003 was 9.6 cents, while HP's was 21.3 cents per dollar of sales.[16]

Dell was also bearding HP by entering the market for printers, the cash cow of HP. Dell's price cuts included 13 percent on printers. Recognizing that most customers want hands-on exposure to printers before buying, Dell expanded its kiosks not only nationwide but also to Canada, Japan, and England. In addition, it courted major retail chains such as Sears for floor space so that customers could try out computers, printers, and other equipment. They could then either place orders online or phone in their orders from home.[17]

INFORMATION BOX

TRYING TO UPGRADE AN IMAGE, MAYBE TO A MYSTIQUE

For years, the Gateway brand has been symbolized by a Holstein cow—the white boxes speckled with black cow spots—and the company carried over this theme in its Gateway Country stores. CEO Ted Waitt even appeared in television commercials with a bovine co-star. He had hoped such a homespun flavor might appeal to many buyers, perhaps conveying an image of integrity and frugality. But as the computer war intensified, with Gateway steadily losing market share, Waitt thought an upgrade was needed, and he killed his beloved cow. "I'm been calling it the de-prairiefication" of the company, he said. The change to sleek black-and-silver PCs and laptops went beyond the product to the stores and advertisements.

Analysts were divided in their endorsement of the shifting strategy. "I don't think consumers will hold it against them that they don't have the cow. Any campaign gets old after a while," said one.

Others disagreed: "The cow motif was one of those odd, quirky, counterintuitive trademarks that succeeded in spite of themselves."

"Odd and quirky" sounds like getting close to a mystique. Do you think Ted Waitt made a good decision in de-prairiefication? Why or why not?

Source: Adapted from Frank Ahrens, *Washington Post*, as reported in *Cleveland Plain Dealer*, "Gateway Changing Its Spots to Create an Upscale Image," November 10, 2002, p. G3.

---

[16] Gary McWilliams and Pui-Wing Tam, "Dell Price Cuts Put a Squeeze on Rival H-P," *Wall Street Journal*, August 21, 2003, pp. B1, B7.

[17] Gary McWilliams and Ann Zimmerman, "Dell Plans to Peddle PCs Inside Sears, Other Large Chains." *Wall Street Journal*, January 30, 2003, pp. B1, B3.

WHAT CAN BE LEARNED?

A price war can be disastrous. A price war developed toward the end of 2002. An economic downturn and disinterested customers were background factors, but Dell initiated it. Generally a price war is detrimental to all participants, because of its effect on profitability, and is shunned by mature industries (though gasoline price wars do flare up from time to time). Most firms in a mature industry have similar costs and innovations are scarce; so all firms suffer from such price wars, even though revenue may increase somewhat because of the lower prices.

For new industries, price wars are more common as technology advances and production economies develop and as inefficient firms are weeded out. But the computer industry has matured, and most marginal firms are long gone. Dell, alone among its competitors, stood to gain from a price war, and Michael Dell had no qualms about starting one.

Survival of the fittest depends on the power of lower costs. If a firm has managed to reduce its operating costs and overhead significantly below its competitors, and if the competitors are not able to quickly match these cost reductions, then a price war can be a shrewd business strategy. While it may reduce profits somewhat, market-share gains could be significant, and such gains may be lasting. In the Vanguard case, we found a similar instance of an organization having significantly lower costs than the rest of the industry; its advantage has not been matched as few firms were willing to cut their costs and profits sufficiently to meet Vanguard's prices. The power of lower costs can make for a survival-of-the-fittest environment and result in greater efficiency and price benefits to customers.

It is difficult to deliberately attract a cult following. A cult following usually depends on a company or brand developing (or acquiring) a sort of mystique. Few brands have been able to do this. Coors beer did back in the 1960s when it became the brew of celebrities and the emblem of the purity and freshness of the West. Marlboro rose to become the top seller on a somewhat similar image, the Marlboro man. The Ford Mustang had a mystique at one time, and Apple also had its devoted followers. But no one has beat Harley Davidson in capitalizing on the mystique of its big motorcycles, as we described in an earlier case.

How does a firm develop a mystique? There is no simple answer, no guarantee. Certainly a company's product has to be distinctive, even if only psychologically. But it takes more than a distinctive product—many firms strive for this and few achieve a mystique. Image-building advertising, focusing on the type of person the firm is targeting, may help. Even better is image-building advertising of the people customers might wish to emulate—such as Nike did so well with athletes.

Perhaps in the final analysis, acquiring a mystique is more fortuitous than deliberate. Two lessons, however, can be learned about mystiques. First, they seldom last forever. Second, once they are gained, the company may be able to exploit them by extending the name or logo to other goods, even unrelated ones, through licensing (more about this in the Harley Davidson case). See the Information Box "Trying to Upgrade an Image, Maybe to a Mystique" for a report on Gateway's efforts to change its image, hopefully to one that might have more potential for a cult following than its black cow spots.

The prescription for great wealth. Great wealth can come from going public with a successful format. We saw in this case how Michael Dell and Ted Waitt both became not only millionaires but billionaires, when they took their enterprises public. They had prior examples and inspirers: Bill Gates of Microsoft and Steve Jobs of Apple.

While these are extraordinary success stories, on smaller scales many small businesses can find themselves attractive to investors seeking growth companies that may offer better potential than existing firms. If the founder of the business keeps a substantial block of the company's stock, the payoff in investors' appraisal of the enterprise can be mind boggling.

CONSIDER

Can you identify additional learning insights that could be applicable to other firms in other situations?

QUESTIONS

1. "Tradition has no place in corporate thinking today." Discuss this statement.

2. Discuss the pros and cons for Dell's decision to start a price war as the downturn worsened in 2000.

3. Do you think Dell should have phased out "Steven" in its commercials? Why or why not?

4. "The computer industry—and most high tech as well—is saturated. This is no longer a growth area, and investors should look elsewhere for growth." Evaluate this statement.

5. "Gateway, with its Holstein cow image, was on the verge of developing a cult following. Now they're doing away with it. I'm selling my Gateway stock." Evaluate this attitude.

6. "I see no one in this foreseeable market who can compete with Dell." Evaluate.

7. How do you judge the quality of a product, computer or otherwise? Is it mostly on price? Discuss your perception of price and quality, as well as any ramifications.

HANDS-ON EXERCISES

1. Be a devil's advocate (one who argues against a proposed decision to test its merits). Argue against Ted Waitt's decision to abandon the cow. Be as persuasive as you can.

2. Be a devil's advocate. You are a staff business planner. Argue against Michael Dell's strategy of cutting prices to the bone in order to gain market share.

Before

1. You are Ted Waitt of Gateway just before the slide of the high-tech industry. What might you have done to prevent the profit collapse and market-share erosion that occurred? Defend your position.

After

2. You are Ted Waitt of Gateway near the end of 2002, with your firm on the ropes. What restorative program do you propose? Defend your ideas.

TEAM DEBATE EXERCISES

1. Debate Dell's ambitious plan to move ahead into other areas, such as servers, storage devices, switches, even mainframelike systems—enterprise computing. Is it likely to overextend itself in search for the ultimate growth? The class may want to divide into two groups, with one arguing as persuasively as possible for the greatest growth. The other group will strongly contest this strategy, proposing a more conservative approach to growth. Each group should be prepared to attack the opponents' arguments as well as defend its own position.

2. "There is no need to be unduly concerned with Dell's price war. Our products are higher quality than Dell's and consumers and business customers alike will quickly recognize that they get what they pay for." Debate this statement by a Hewlett-Packard executive, having one group support it and the other contest it.

INVITATION TO RESEARCH

What is the situation in the PC industry today? Is the price war still on? Has Gateway survived? IIas Dell's market share continued to increase? Has Dell been able to invade HP's printer and ink-refill domain?

PART
FIVE

CONTROLLING

CHAPTER NINETEEN

United Way: Where Were the Controls?

The United Way, the preeminent charitable organization in the United States, celebrated its 100-year anniversary in 1987. It had evolved from local community chests, and its strategy for fund-raising had proven highly effective: funding local charities through payroll deductions. The good it did seemed unassailable.

Abruptly in 1992, the persona of honesty and integrity that United Way had built was jeopardized by investigative reporters' revelations of free-spending practices and other questionable deeds of its greatest builder and president, William Aramony. A major point of public concern was Aramony's salary and uncontrolled perks in a lifestyle that seemed inappropriate for the head of a charitable organization that depended mostly on contributions from working people.

In 1993, another paragon of not-for-profit social enhancement organizations came under fire: the venerable Girl Scouts. Contentions were that multimillion-dollar profits of Girl Scout cookies were found to be used mostly to support bureaucracy instead of the Girl Scout troops that provided the labor in the first place. (This is discussed in an Information Box later in the chapter.)

We are left to question the operations and lack of controls of our major charitable and not-for-profit entities. Business firms have to report to shareholders and creditors, but not-for-profit organizations have been permitted to operate largely without the checks and balances that characterize most other organizations.

THE STATURE AND ACCOMPLISHMENTS
OF THE UNITED WAY

For its 100th anniversary, then-President Ronald Reagan summed up what the United Way stood for:

December 10, 1986

United Way Centennial, 1887–1987
By The President Of The United States Of America
A Proclamation

Since earliest times, we Americans have joined together to help each other and to strengthen our communities. Our deep-roots spirit of caring, of neighbor helping neighbor, has become an American trademark—and an American way of life. Over the years, our generous and inventive people have created an ingenious network of voluntary organizations to help give help where help is needed.

United Way gives that help very well indeed, and truly exemplifies our spirit of voluntarism. United Way has been a helping force in America right from the first community-wide fund raising campaign in Denver, Colorado, in 1887. Today, more than 2,200 local United Ways across the land raise funds for more than 37,000 voluntary groups that assist millions of people.

The United Way of caring allows volunteers from all walks of life to effectively meet critical needs and solve community problems. At the centennial of the founding of this indispensable voluntary group, it is most fitting that we Americans recognize and commend all the good United Way has done and continues to do.

The Congress, by Public Law 99–612, has expressed gratitude to United Way, congratulated it, and applauded and encouraged its fine work and its goals.

NOW, THEREFORE, I RONALD REAGAN, President of the United States of America, by virtue of the authority vested in me by the Constitution and laws of the United States, do hereby proclaim heartfelt thanks to a century of Americans who have shaped and supported United Way, and encourage the continuation of its efforts.

IN WITNESS WHEREOF, I have hereunto set my hand this tenth day of December, in the year of our Lord nineteen hundred and eighty-six, and of the Independence of the United States of America the two hundred and eleventh.

Ronald Reagan

Organizing the United Way as the umbrella charity to fund other local charities through payroll deduction established an effective means of fund-raising. It became the recipient of 90 percent of all charitable donations. Employers sometimes used extreme pressure to achieve 100 percent participation of employees, which led to organizational bonuses. The United Way achieved further cooperation of business organizations by involving their executives as leaders of annual campaigns, amid widespread publicity. It would consequently cause such an executive acute loss of face if his or her own organization did not go "over the top" in meeting campaign goals. A local United Way executive admitted that "if participation is 100 percent, it means someone has been coerced."[1]

For many years, outside of some tight-lipped gripes of corporate employees, the organization moved smoothly along, with local contributions generally increasing every year and with the needs for charitable contributions invariably increasing even faster.

The national organization, United Way of America (UWA), is a separate corporation and has no direct control over the approximately 2,200 local United Way offices. Most of the locals voluntarily contributed one cent on the dollar of all funds they collected, however, and in return, the national organization provided training and promoted local United Way agencies through advertising and other marketing efforts.

Much of the success of the United Way movement in becoming the largest and most respected charity in the United States was due to the twenty-two years of William Aramony's leadership of the national organization. When he first took over, the United Ways were not operating under a common name. He built a nationwide network of agencies, all operating under the same name and using the same logo of outstretched hands, which became nationally recognized as the symbol of charitable giving. Unfortunately in 1992, an exposé of Aramony's lavish lifestyle and questionable dealings led to his downfall and burdened local United Ways with serious difficulties in fund-raising.

WILLIAM ARAMONY

During Aramony's tenure United Way contributions increased from $787 million in 1970 to $3 billion in 1990. Aramony built up the headquarters staff to 275 employees and increased his headquarters budget from less than $3 million to $29 million in 1991. Of this amount, $24 million came from the local United Ways, with the rest coming from corporate grants, investment income, and consulting.[2] Figure 19.1 shows the organizational chart as of 1987.

Aramony moved comfortably among the most influential people in our society. He attracted a prestigious board of governors, including many top executives from America's largest corporations, but only three of the thirty-seven came from not-for-profit organizations. The board was chaired by John Akers, chairman and CEO of IBM. Other board members included Edward A. Brennan, CEO of Sears; James D. Robinson III, CEO of American Express; and Paul J. Tagliabue, commissioner of the National Football League. The presence of such top executives on the board brought United Way prestige and spurred contributions from some of the largest and most visible organizations in the United States.

---

[1] Susan Garland, "Keeping a Sharper Eye on Those Who Pass the Hat," *Business Week* (March 16, 1992), p. 39.

[2] Charles E. Shepard, "Perks, Privileges and Power in a Nonprofit World," *Washington Post* (February 16, 1992), p. A38.

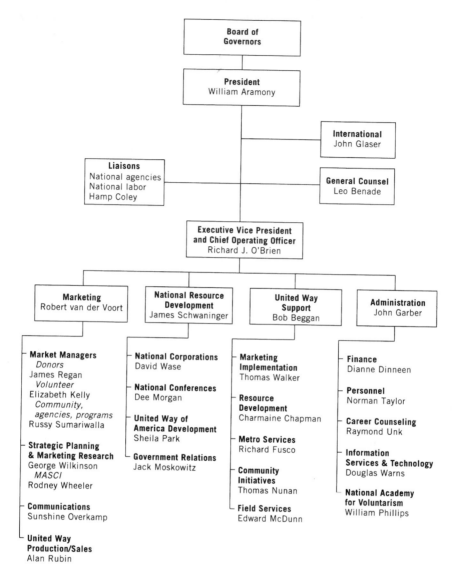

Figure 19.1 United Way: Organizational Chart of 1987.

Aramony was the highest paid executive in the charity field. In 1992, his compensation package was $463,000, nearly double that of the next highest paid executive in the industry, Dudley H. Hafner of the American Heart Association.[3] The board fully supported Aramony, regularly giving him 6 percent annual raises.[4]

---

[3] Shepard, "Perks, Privileges, and Power," A38; and Charles E. Shepard, "United Way of America President Is Urged to Resign," *Washington Post* (February 27, 1992), p. A1.

[4] Joseph Finder, "Charity Case," *New Republic* (May 4, 1992), p. 11.

Investigative Disclosures

The *Washington Post* began investigating Aramony's tenure as president of United Way of America in 1991, raising questions about his high salary, travel habits, possible cronyism, and dubious relations with five spin-off companies. In February 1992, it released the following information on Aramony's expense charges.[5]

- Aramony had charged $92,265 in limousine expenses to the charity during the previous five years.
- He had charged $40,762 on airfare for the supersonic Concorde.
- He had charged more than $72,000 on international airfare that included first-class seats for himself, his wife, and others.
- He had charged thousands more for personal trips, gifts, and luxuries.
- He had made twenty-nine trips to Las Vegas, Nevada, between 1988 and 1991.
- He had expensed forty-nine journeys to Gainesville, Florida, the home of his daughter and a woman with whom he had had a relationship.
- He had allegedly approved a $2 million loan to a firm run by his chief financial officer.
- He had approved the diversion of donors' money to questionable spin-off organizations run by long time aides and provided benefits to family members as well.
- He had passed tens of thousands of dollars in consulting contracts from the UWA to friends and associates.

United Way of America's corporate policy prohibited the hiring of family members within the actual organization, but Aramony skirted the direct violation by hiring friends and relatives as consultants and within the spin-off companies. He paid hundreds of thousands of dollars in consulting fees, for example, to two aides in vaguely documented and even undocumented business transactions.

The use of spin-off companies provided flexible maneuvering. One of the spin-off companies Aramony created to provide travel and bulk purchasing for United Way chapters purchased a $430,000 condominium in Manhattan and a $125,000 apartment in Coral Gables, Florida, for Aramony's use. Another of the spin-off companies hired Aramony's son, Robert Aramony, as its president. Loans and money transfers between the spin-off companies and the national organization raised questions. No records showed that the board of directors had been given the opportunity to approve such loans and transfers.[6]

---

[5] Shepard, "Perks, Privileges, and Power"; Shepard, "President Is Urged to Resign"; Kathleen Telstch, "United Way Awaits Inquiry on its President's Practices," *New York Times* (February 24, 1992), p. A12 (L); Charles E. Shepard, "United Way Report Criticizes Ex-Leader's Lifestyle," *Washington Post* (April 4, 1992), p. A1.

[6] Shepard, "Perks, Privileges, and Power," p. A38.

CONSEQUENCES

When the information about Aramony's salary and expenses became public, reaction was severe. Stanley C. Gault, chairman of Goodyear Tire & Rubber Co., asked, "Where was the board? The outside auditors?"[7] Robert O. Bothwell, executive director of the National Committee for Responsive Philanthropy, said, "I think it is obscene that he is making that kind of salary and asking people who are making $10,000 a year to give 5 percent of their income."[8] At this point let us examine the issue of executive compensation. Are many executives overpaid? The following Issue Box addresses this controversial topic.

ISSUE BOX

EXECUTIVE COMPENSATION: IS IT TOO MUCH?

A controversy is mounting over multimillion-dollar annual compensations of corporate executives. In 1992, for example, the average annual pay of CEOs was $3,842,247; the twenty highest salaries ranged from over $11 million to a mind-boggling $127 million (for Thomas F. Frist, Jr., of Hospital Corporation of America).[9]

Activist shareholders, including some large mutual and pension funds, began protesting pay practices, especially for top executives of firms that were not doing well financially. New disclosure rules imposed in 1993 by the Securities and Exchange Commission (SEC) spotlighted questionable executive pay practices. In the past, complacent board members, themselves well paid and often closely aligned with the top executives of the organization, condoned liberal compensations, but this may be changing. The major argument supporting high executive compensations is that compared with salaries of some entertainers and athletes, they are modest. And are not their responsibilities far greater than those of any entertainer or athlete?

In light of the for-profit executive compensations, Aramony's salary was modest. And results were on his side: He made $369,000 in basic salary while raising $3 billion; Lee Iacocca, on the other hand, made $3 million while Chrysler lost $795 million. Where is the justice?

Undoubtedly Aramony, as head of a large for-profit corporation could have earned several zeros more in compensation and perks, with no raised eyebrows. But is the situation different for a not-for-profit organization, when revenues are derived from donations of millions of people of modest means? This is a real controversy. On one side, shouldn't a charity be willing to pay for the professional competence to run the organization as effectively as possible? But on the other side, how do revelations of high compensation affect the public image and fund-raising ability of such not-for-profit organizations?

What is your position regarding Aramony's compensation and perks, relative to the many times greater compensation of for-profit executives?

---

[7] Susan Garland, p. 39.

[8] Felicity Barringer, "United Way Head Is Forced Out in a Furor Over His Lavish Style," *New York Times* (February 28, 1992), p. A1.

[9] John A. Byrne, "Executive Pay: The Party Ain't Over Yet," *Business Week* (April 26, 1993), pp. 56–64.

As a major consequence of the scandal, some United Way locals withheld their funds, at least pending a thorough investigation of the allegations. John Akers, chairman of the board, noted that by March 7, 1992, dues payments were running 20 percent behind the previous year, saying "I don't think this process that the United Way of America is going through, or Mr. Aramony is going through, is a process that's bestowing a lot of honor."[10]

In addition to the decrease in dues payments, UWA was in danger of having its not-for-profit status revoked by the Internal Revenue Service due to the relationship of loans made to the spin-off companies. For example, it loaned $2 million to a spin-off corporation of which the chief financial officer of UWA was also a director, which is a violation of not-for-profit corporate law. UWA also guaranteed a bank loan taken out by one of the spin-offs, another violation of not-for-profit corporate law.[11]

The adverse publicity benefited competing charities, such as Earth Share, an environmental group. United Way, at one time the only major organization to receive contributions through payroll deductions, now found itself losing donations to other charities able to garner contributions in the same manner. All the building that William Aramony had done for the United Way as the primary player in the American charitable industry was now in danger of disintegration because of his uncontrolled excesses.

On February 28, amid mounting pressure from local chapters threatening to withhold their annual dues, Aramony resigned. In August 1992, the United Way board of directors hired Elaine Chao, the Peace Corps director, to replace Aramony.

Elaine Chao

Chao's story was one of great achievement for one aged only thirty-nine. She was the oldest of six daughters in a family that came to California from Taiwan when Elaine was eight years old. She did not know a word of English. The family prospered through hard work. "Despite the difficulties ... we had tremendous optimism in the basic goodness of this country, that people are decent here, that we would be given a fair opportunity to demonstrate our abilities," she told an interviewer.[12] Chao's parents instilled in their six daughters the conviction that they could do anything they set their minds to, and all the daughters went to prestigious universities.

Elaine Chao earned an economics degree from Mount Holyoke College in 1975, then went on for a Harvard MBA. She was a White House fellow, an international banker, chair of the Federal Maritime Commission, deputy secretary of the U.S. Transportation Department, and director of the Peace Corps before accepting the presidency of the United Way of America.

Her salary was $195,000, less than one-half of Aramony's. She cut budgets and staffs: no transatlantic flights on the Concorde, no limousine service, no plush condominiums. The board of governors was expanded to include more local representatives

---

[10] Felicity Barringer, "United Way Head Tries to Restore Trust," *New York Times* (March 7, 1992), p. 8L.

[11] Shepard, "Perks, Privileges, and Power"; Charles E. Shepard, "United Way Chief Says He Will Retire," *Washington Post* (February 28, 1992), p. A1.

[12] "United Way Chief Dedicated," *Cleveland Plain Dealer* (March 28, 1993), p. 24-A.

and she established committees on ethics and finance. Still, Chao had no illusions about her job: "Trust and confidence once damaged will take a great deal of effort and time to heal."[13]

Local United Way's Concerns

In April 1993, for the second time in a year, United Way of Greater Lorain County (Ohio) withdrew from the United Way of America. The board of the local chapter was still concerned about the financial stability and accountability of the national agency. In particular, it was concerned about Aramony's retirement settlement. The national board and Aramony were negotiating a significant "golden parachute" retirement package in the neighborhood of $4 million.

News of this triggered the Lorain County board's decision to again withdraw from UWA. There were other reasons as well for this decision. The national agency was falling far short of its projected budget because only 890 of the 1,400 affiliates that had paid membership dues two years before were still paying. Roy Church, president of the Lorain agency, explained the board's decision: "Since February ... it has become clear that United Way of America's financial stability and ability to assist locals has been put in question. The benefit of being a United Way of America member isn't there at this time for Lorain's United Way."[14]

Elaine Chao's task of resurrecting United Way of America would not be easy.

See the Information Box on the following page for a discussion of a related example of non-profit callousness to its parties.

ANALYSIS

Executives' lack of accountability of expenditures was a major contributor to the UWA's problems. This lack of controls encouraged questionable practices, since there was no one to approve or disapprove, and it made executives, especially Aramony, vulnerable to great shock and criticism when their practices became known. The fact that voluntary donations were the principal source of revenues made the lack of accountability all the more scandalous.

Where controls and financial reporting are deficient, and where a system of checks and balances is lacking, two consequences tend to prevail, neither one desirable or totally acceptable. The worst-case scenario is outright "white-collar theft," when unscrupulous people find it an opportunity for personal gain. The absence of sufficient controls and accountability can make even normally honest persons succumb to some temptation. Second, insufficient controls tend to promote a mindset of arrogance and allow people to play fast-and-loose with the system. Aramony seemed to fall into this category with his spending extravagances, cronyism, and other conflict-of-interest activities. (Some of the Girl Scout Councils, too, perceived

---

[13] *Ibid.*

[14] Karen Henderson, "Lorain Agency Cuts Ties with National United Way," *Cleveland Plain Dealer* (April 16, 1993), p. 7C.

INFORMATION BOX

ANOTHER CONTROVERSY: GIRL SCOUTS
AND THEIR COOKIES

The main funding source for the nation's 2.6 million Girl Scouts is the annual cookie sale, estimated to generate $400 million in revenue.[15] The practice goes back some seventy years, although in the 1920s, the girls sold homemade cookies. Now each regional council negotiates with one of two bakeries that produce the cookies, sets the price per box, which ranges from $2 to $3, and divides the proceeds as it sees fit. Typically, the Girl Scout troops get 10 to 15 percent, the council takes more than 50 percent, and the rest goes to the manufacturer.

Criticisms have emerged and received public attention regarding the dictatorial handling of these funds by the councils. There are 332 regional councils in the United States, each having an office and a paid staff overseen by a volunteer board. Some councils have dozens of employees, with most serving mainly as policy enforcers and supervisors. At the troop level, volunteer leaders, often women with daughters in the troop, guide their units in the true tradition of scouting, giving their time tirelessly. For the cookie drives, the girls are an unpaid sales force—child labor, as critics assail—that supports a huge bureaucratic structure. Little of the cookie revenue comes back to the local troops.

The bureaucracy does not tolerate dissent well. The *Wall Street Journal* cites the case of a West Haven, Connecticut, troop leader, Beth Denton, who protested both the way the Connecticut Trails council apportioned revenue and the $1.6 million in salaries and benefits paid to forty-two council employees. After she complained to the state attorney general, the council dismissed her as leader.[16]

Admittedly, the individual salaries in the bureaucracy were not high by corporate standards or even by not-for-profit standards. Council administrators' salaries ranged up to about $90,000. Perhaps more disturbing was that volunteer leaders saw no annual financial statements of their council's expenditures and activities.[17]

Evaluate the council's position that annual financial records of their council's activities should be entirely confidential to full-time staff.

themselves as aloof from the dedicated volunteer troop leaders, tolerating no criticism or questioning, dictating and enforcing all policies without consultation or participation, and preventing scrutiny of their own operation.)

The UWA theoretically had an overseer: the boards, similar to the board of directors of business corporations. But when such boards act as rubber stamps, where they are closely in the camp of the chief executives, they are not really exercising control.

---

[15] Ellen Graham, "Sprawling Bureaucracy Eats Up Most Profits of Girl Scout Cookies," *Wall Street Journal* (May 13, 1992), p. A1.

[16] *Ibid.*, p. A4.

[17] *Ibid.*

This appeared to be the case with United Way of America during the "reign" of Aramony; similarly, as discussed in the preceding box, with the regional councils of the Girl Scouts, many of the volunteer boards appear to have exercised little or no control.

Certainly a board's failure to fulfill its responsibility is not unique to not-for-profits. Corporate boards have often been notorious for promoting the interests of the incumbent executives. Although this is changing today, it still prevails. See the following Issue Box for a discussion of the role of boards of directors.

ISSUE BOX

WHAT SHOULD BE THE ROLE OF THE BOARD OF DIRECTORS?

In the past, most boards of directors have tended to be closely allied with top executives and even composed mostly of corporate officials. In some organizations today this is changing, mostly in response to critics concerned about board tendencies to support the status quo and perpetuate the "establishment."

More and more, opinion is shifting to the idea that boards must assume an active role:

> The board can no longer play a passive role in corporate governance. Today, more than ever, the board must assume an activist role—a role that is protective of shareholder rights, sensitive to communities in which the company operates, responsive to the needs of company vendors and customers, and fair to its employees.[18]

Incentives for more active boards have been the increasing risks of liability for board decisions as well as liability insurance costs. Although the board of directors has long been seen as responsible for establishing corporate objectives, developing broad policies, and selecting top executives, these duties are no longer viewed as sufficient. Boards must also review management's performance—acting as a control mechanism—to ensure that the company is well run and that stockholders' interests are furthered. And, today, they must ensure that society's best interests are not disregarded.

But the issue remains: To whom should the board owe its greatest allegiance—the entrenched bureaucracy or the external publics? Without having board members representative of the many special interests affected by the organization, the inclination is to support the interests of the establishment.

Do you think a more representative and activist board will prevent a similar scenario from damaging United Way in the future? Why or why not?

[18] Lester B. Korn and Richard M. Ferry, *Board of Directors Thirteenth Annual Study* (New York: Korn/Ferry International, February 1986), pp. 1–2.

UPDATE

William Aramony was convicted of defrauding the United Way out of $1 million. He was sentenced to seven years in prison for using the charity's money to finance a lavish lifestyle.

Despite this, a federal judge ruled in late 1998 that the charity must pay its former president more than $2 million in retirement benefits. "A felon, no matter how despised, does not lose his right to enforce a contract," U.S. District Judge Shira Scheindlin in New York ruled.[19]

WHAT CAN BE LEARNED?

Beware the arrogant mindset. A leader's attitude that he or she is superior to subordinates and even to concerned outsiders is a formula for disaster, both for an organization and even for a society. Such an attitude promotes dictatorship, intolerance of contrary opinions, and an attitude that "we need answer to no one." We have seen the consequences with William Aramony: moving over the edge of what is deemed by most as acceptable and ethical conduct, assuming the role of the final authority who brooks no questions or criticisms. The absence of real or imagined controls or reviews seems to bring out the worst in people. We seem to need periodic scrutiny to avoid falling into the trap of arrogant decision making devoid of responsiveness to other concerns. The Girl Scout bureaucracy's dealings with its volunteers suggest the inclination toward arrogance and dictatorship in the absence of sufficient real controls.

Checks and balances—controls—are even more important in not-for-profit and governmental bodies than in corporate entities. For profit organizations have "bottom-line" performance (i.e., profit and loss performance) as the ultimate control and standard. Not-for-profit and governmental organizations do not have this control, so they have no ultimate measure of their effectiveness.

Consequently, not-for-profit organizations should be subject to the utmost scrutiny of objective outsiders. Otherwise, abuses seem to be encouraged and perpetuated. Often these not-for-profit organizations are sheltered from competition, which usually also demands greater efficiency. Thus without objective and energetic controls, not-for-profit organizations have a tendency to be out of hand, to be run as little dynasties unencumbered by the constraints that face most businesses. Fortunately, investigative reporting and increasing litigation by allegedly abused parties today act as the needed controls for such organizations. In view of the revelations of investigative reporters, we are left to wonder how many other abusive and reprehensible activities have not as yet been detected.

Nonprofits are particularly vulnerable to bad press. Nonprofits depend on donations for the bulk of their revenues. Unlike most businesses, they depend on people to give without receiving anything tangible in return. Consequently, any

---

[19] Reported in *Cleveland Plain Dealer* (October 25, 1998), p. 24-A.

hint or semblance of waste or misdealings with donated money can quickly dry up contributions or cause them to be shunted to other charities.

With governmental bodies, of course, their perpetuation is hardly at stake with bad publicity, but the administrators can be recalled, impeached, or not reelected with enough adverse publicity.

CONSIDER

Can you add to these learning insights?

QUESTIONS

1. How do you feel, as a potential or actual giver to United Way campaigns, about the "high living" of Aramony? Would these allegations affect your gift giving? Why or why not?

2. What prescriptions do you have for thwarting arrogance in nonprofit and/or governmental organizations? Be as specific as you can, and support your recommendations.

3. How do you personally feel about the coercion that some organizations exert for their employees to contribute substantially to the United Way? What implications, if any, do you see as emerging from your attitudes about this?

4. Given the information supplied about the dictatorial relationships between Girl Scout councils and the local volunteers—and recognizing that such anecdotal information may not be truly representative—what do you see as the pros and cons of Girl Scout cookie drives? On balance, is this marketing fund-raising effort still desirable, or might other alternatives be better?

5. "Since there is no bottom-line evaluation for performance, nonprofits have no incentives to control costs and prudently evaluate expenditures." Discuss.

6. How would you feel, as a large contributor to a charity, about its spending $10 million for advertising? Discuss your rationale for this attitude.

7. Do you think the action taken by UWA after Aramony was the best way to salvage the public image? Why or why not? What else might have been done?

HANDS-ON EXERCISES

1. You are an advisor to Elaine Chao, who has taken over the scandal-ridden United Way. What advice would you give her for as quickly as possible restoring the confidence of the American public in the integrity and worthiness of this preeminent national charity organization?

2. You are a member of the board of governors of United Way. Allegations have surfaced about the lavish life style of the highly regarded Aramony. Most of the board, being corporate executives, see nothing at all wrong with his perks and privileges. You, however, feel otherwise. How would you convince

the other members of the board of the error of condoning Aramony's activities? Be as persuasive as you can in supporting your position.

3. You are the parent of a Girl Scout, who has assiduously worked to sell hundreds of boxes of cookies. You now realize that the efforts of your daughter and thousands of other girls are primarily supporting a bloated central and regional bureaucracy, and not the local troops. You feel strongly that this situation is an unacceptable use of child labor. Describe your proposed efforts to institute change.

TEAM DEBATE EXERCISE

Debate this issue: Should top executives of large charitable organizations be compensated comparable to corporate executives responsible for similar-size organizations?

INVITATION TO RESEARCH

What is the situation with United Way today? Are local agencies contributing to the national? Have donations matched or exceeded previous levels? Was Elaine Chao able to restore confidence? Is she still with United Way, or has she gone on to other challenges?

CHAPTER TWENTY

Maytag: Misplaced Trust With A Foreign Subsidiary

The atmosphere at the annual meeting in the little Iowa town of Newton had turned contentious. As Leonard Hadley faced increasingly angry questions from disgruntled shareholders, the thought crossed his mind: "I don't deserve this!" After all, he had only been CEO of Maytag Corporation for a few months, and this was his first chairing of an annual meeting. But the earnings of the company had been declining every year since 1988, and in 1992, Maytag had had a $315.4 million loss. No wonder the stockholders in the packed Newton High School auditorium were bitter and critical of their management. But there was more. Just the month before, the company had the public embarrassment and costly atonement resulting from a monumental blunder in the promotional planning of its United Kingdom subsidiary.

Hadley doggedly saw the meeting to its close, and limply concluded: "Hopefully, both sales and earnings will improve this year."[1]

THE FIASCO

In August 1992, Hoover Limited, Maytag's British subsidiary, launched this travel promotion: Anyone in the United Kingdom buying more than 100 UK pounds' worth of Hoover products (about $150 in American dollars) before the end of January 1993 would get two free round-trip tickets to selected European destinations. For 250 UK pounds' worth of Hoover products, they would get two free round-trip tickets to New York or Orlando.

A buying frenzy resulted. Consumers had quickly figured out that the value of the tickets easily exceeded the cost of the appliances necessary to be eligible for them. By the tens of thousands, Britishers rushed out to buy just enough Hoover products to qualify. Appliance stores were emptied of vacuum cleaners. The Hoover factory in Cambuslang, Scotland that had been making vacuum cleaners only three days a week was suddenly placed on a twenty-four-hour, seven-days-a-week production

---

[1] Richard Gibson, "Maytag's CEO Goes Through Wringer at Annual Meeting," *Wall Street Journal* (April 28, 1993), p. A5.

schedule—an overtime bonanza for the workers. What a resounding success for a promotion! Hoover managers, however, were unhappy.

Hoover had never expected more than 50,000 people to respond. And of those responding, it expected far less would go through all the steps necessary to qualify for the free trip and really take it. But more than 200,000 not only responded but qualified for the free tickets. The company was overwhelmed. The volume of paperwork created such a bottleneck that by the middle of April only 6,000 people had flown. Thousands of others either never got their tickets, were not able to get the dates requested, or waited for months without hearing the results of their applications. Hoover established a special hotline to process customer complaints, and these were coming in at 2,000 calls a day. But the complaints quickly spread, and the ensuing publicity brought charges of fraud and demands for restitution. This raises the issue of loss leaders—How much should we use loss leaders as a promotional device?—discussed in the following Issue Box.

Maytag dispatched a task force to try to resolve the situation without jeopardizing customer relations any further. But it acknowledged that it's "not 100 percent clear" that all eligible buyers will receive their free flights.[2] The ill-fated promotion was a

ISSUE BOX

SHOULD WE USE LOSS LEADERS?

Leader pricing is a type of promotion with certain items advertised at a very low price— sometimes even below cost, in which case they are known as loss leaders—in order to attract more customers. The rationale for this is that such customers are likely to purchase other regular-price items as well with the result that total sales and profits will be increased. If customers do not purchase enough other goods at regular prices to more than cover the losses incurred from the attractively priced bargains, then the loss-leader promotion is ill advised. Some critics maintain that the whole idea of using loss leaders is absurd: The firm is just "buying sales" with no regard for profits.

While UK Hoover did not think of their promotion as a loss leader, in reality it was: They stood to lose money on every sale if the promotional offer was taken advantage of. Unfortunately for its effectiveness as a loss leader, the likelihood of customers purchasing other Hoover products at regular prices was remote, and the level of acceptance was not capped, so that losses were permitted to multiply. The conclusion has to be that this was an ill-conceived idea from the beginning. It violated these two conditions of loss leaders: They should stimulate sales of other products, and their losses should be limited.

Do you think loss leaders really are desirable under certain circumstances? Why or why not?

[2] James P. Miller, "Maytag U.K. Unit Find a Promotion Is Too Successful," *Wall Street Journal* (March 31, 1993), p. A9.

staggering blow to Maytag financially. It took a $30 million charge in the first quarter of 1993 to cover unexpected additional costs linked to the promotion. Final costs were expected to exceed $50 million, which would be 10 percent of UK Hoover's total revenues—this for a subsidiary acquired only four years before that had yet to produce a profit.

Adding to the costs were problems with the two travel agencies involved. The agencies were to obtain low-cost space available tickets, and would earn commissions selling "packages," including hotels, rental cars, and insurance. If consumers bought a package, Hoover would get a cut. However, despite the overwhelming demand for tickets, most consumers declined to purchase the package, thus greatly reducing support money for the promotional venture. So, Hoover greatly underestimated the likely response, and overestimated the amount it would earn from commission payments.

If these cost-overruns added greatly to Maytag and Hoover's customer relations and public image, the expenditures would have seemed more palatable. But with all the problems, the best that could be expected would be to lessen the worst of the agitation and charges of deception. And this was proving to be impossible. The media, of course, salivated at the problems and were quick to sensationalize them:

> One disgruntled customer, who took aggressive action on his own, received the widest press coverage, and even became a folk hero. Dave Dixon, claiming he was cheated out of a free vacation by Hoover, seized one of the company's repair vans in retaliation. Police were sympathetic: they took him home, and did not charge him, claiming it was a civil matter.[3]

Heads rolled also. Initially, Maytag fired three UK Hoover executives involved, including the president of Hoover Europe. Mr. Hadley, at the annual meeting, also indicated that others might lose their jobs before the cleanup was complete. He likened the promotion to "a bad accident ... and you can't determine what was in the driver's mind."[4]

The issue receiving somewhat less publicity was why corporate headquarters allowed executives of a subsidiary such wide latitude that they could saddle parent Maytag with tens of millions in unexpected costs. Did not top corporate executives have to approve ambitious plans? A company spokesman said that operating divisions were "primarily responsible" for planning promotional expenses. While the parent may review such outlays, "if they're within parameters, it goes through."[5] This raises the issue, discussed in the following Issue Box, of how loose a rein foreign subsidiaries should be allowed.

---

[3] "Unhappy Brit Holds Hoover Van Hostage," *Cleveland Plain Dealer* (June 1, 1993), p. D1; and Simon Reeve and John Harlow, "Hoover Is Sued Over Flights Deal," *London Sunday Times* (June 6, 1993).

[4] Gibson, "CEO Goes Through Wringer," p. A5.

[5] Miller, "Maytag UK Unit," p. A9.

ISSUE BOX

HOW LOOSE A REIN FOR A FOREIGN SUBSIDIARY?

In a decentralized organization, top management delegates considerable decision-making authority to subordinates. Such decentralization—often called a "loose rein"—tends to be more marked with foreign subsidiaries, such as UK Hoover. Corporate management in the United States understandably feels less familiar with the foreign environment and more willing to let the native executives operate with less constraints than it might with a domestic subsidiary. In the Maytag/Hoover situation, decision-making authority by British executives was evidently extensive, and corporate Maytag exercised little operational control, being content to judge performance by ultimate results achieved. Major deviations from expected performance goals, or widespread traumatic happenings—all of which happened to UK Hoover—finally gained corporate management attention.

Major advantages of extensive decentralization or a loose rein are: First, top management effectiveness can be improved since time and attention is freed for presumably more important matters; second, subordinates are permitted more self-management, which should improve their competence and motivation; and third, in foreign environments, native managers presumably better understand their unique problems and opportunities than corporate management, located thousands of miles away, possibly can. But the drawbacks are as we have seen: Parameters within which subordinate managers operate can be so wide that serious miscalculations may not be stopped in time. Since top management is ultimately responsible for all performance, including actions of subordinates, it faces greater risks with extensive decentralization and giving a free rein.

"Since the manager is ultimately accountable for whatever is delegated to subordinates, then a free rein reflects great confidence in subordinates." Discuss.

BACKGROUND ON MAYTAG

Maytag is a century-old company. The original business, formed in 1893, manufactured feeder attachments for threshing machines. In 1907, the company moved to Newton, Iowa, a small town thirty miles east of Des Moines, the capital. Manufacturing emphasis turned to home-laundry equipment, and wringer-type washers.

A natural expansion of this emphasis occurred with the commercial laundromat business in the 1930s, when coin meters were attached to Maytag washers. Rapid growth of these coin-operated laundries took place in the United States during the late 1950s and early 1960s. The 1970s hurt laundromats with increased competition and soaring energy costs. In 1975, Maytag introduced new energy-efficient machines, and "Home Style" stores that rejuvenated the business.

The Lonely Maytag Repairman

For years Maytag reveled in a coup, with its washers and dryers enjoying a top-quality image, thanks to decades-long ads in which a repairman laments his loneliness because of Maytag's trouble-free products.[6] The result of this dependability and quality image was that Maytag could command a price premium: "Their machines cost the same to make, break down as much as ours—but they get $100 more because of the reputation," grumbled a competitor.[7]

During the 1970s and into the 1980s, Maytag continued to capture 15 percent of the washing machine market, and enjoyed profit margins about twice that of competitors. Table 20.1 shows operating results for the period 1974–1981. Whirlpool was the largest factor in the laundry equipment market, with a 45 percent share, but this was largely because of sales to Sears under the Sears brand.

Acquisitions

For many years, until his retirement December 31, 1992, Daniel J. Krumm had influenced Maytag's destinies. He had been CEO for eighteen years and chairman since 1986, and his tenure with the company encompassed forty years. In that time, the home-appliance business encountered some drastic changes. The most ominous occurred in the late 1980s with the merger mania, in which the threat of takeovers by hostile raiders often motivated heretofore conservative executives to greatly increase corporate indebtedness, thereby decreasing the attractiveness of their firms. Daniel Krumm was one of these running-scared executives, as rumors persisted that the company was a takeover candidate.

TABLE 20.1 Maytag Operating Results, 1974–1981 (in millions)

	Net Sales	Net Income	Percent of Sales
1974	$229	$21.1	9.2%
1975	238	25.9	10.9
1976	275	33.1	12.0
1977	299	34.5	11.5
1978	325	36.7	11.3
1979	369	45.3	12.3
1980	346	35.6	10.2
1981	409	37.4	9.1
Average net income percent of sales: 10.8%			

Source: Company operating statistics.

Commentary: These years show a steady, though not spectacular growth in revenues, and a generally rising net income, except for 1980. Of particular interest is the high net income percentage of sales, with this averaging 10.8 percent over the eight-year period, with a high of 12.3 percent.

---

[6] Jesse White, the actor who first portrayed this repairman, died in early 1997.

[7] Brian Bremmer, "Can Maytag Clean Up Around the World?" *Business Week* (January 30, 1989), p. 89.

Largely as a defensive move, Krumm pushed through a deal for a $1 billion buy-out of Chicago Pacific Corporation (CPC), a maker of vacuum cleaners and other appliances with $1.4 billion in sales. As a result, Maytag was burdened with $500 million in new debt. Krumm defended the acquisition as giving Maytag a strong foothold in a growing overseas market. CPC was best known for the Hoover vacuums it sold in the United States and Europe. Indeed, so dominant was the Hoover brand in England that many people did not vacuum their carpets, but "hoovered the carpet." CPC also made washers, dryers, and other appliances under the Hoover brand, selling them exclusively in Europe and Australia. In addition, it had six furniture companies, but Maytag sold these shortly after the acquisition.

Krumm had been instrumental in transforming Maytag, the number-four U.S. appliance manufacturer—behind General Electric, Whirlpool, and Electrolux—from a niche laundry-equipment maker into a full-line manufacturer. He had led an earlier acquisition spree in which Maytag had expanded into microwave ovens, electric ranges, refrigerators, and freezers. Its brands now included Magic Chef, Jenn-Air, Norge, and Admiral. The last years of Krumm's reign, however, were not marked by great operating results. As shown in Table 20.2, revenues showed no gain in the 1989–1992 period, while income steadily declined.

Trouble

Although the rationale for internationalizing seemed inescapable, especially in view of a recent wave of joint ventures between U.S. and European appliance makers, still the Hoover acquisition was troublesome. While it was a major brand in England and in Australia, Hoover had only a small presence in Europe. Yet, this was where the bulk of the market was, with some 320 million potential appliance buyers.

The probabilities of the Hoover subsidiary being able to capture much of the European market were hardly promising. Whirlpool was strong, having ten plants there in contrast to Hoover's two plants. Furthermore, Maytag faced entrenched European competitors such as Sweden's Electrolux, the world's largest appliance

TABLE 20.2 Maytag Operating Results, 1989–1992

	Revenue	Net Income	% of Revenue
	(in millions)		
1989	$3,089	131.0	4.3%
1990	3,057	98.9	3.2
1991	2,971	79.0	2.7
1992	3,041	(315.4)	(10.4)

Source: Company annual reports.

Commentary: Note the steady erosion of profitability, while sales remained virtually static. For a comparison with profit performance of earlier years, see Table 20.1 and the net income to sales percentages of this more "golden" period.

maker; Germany's Bosch-Siemens; and Italy's Merloni Group. General Electric had also entered the market with joint ventures. The fierce loyalty of European to domestic brands raised further questions as to the ability of Maytag's Hoover to penetrate the European market without massive promotional efforts, and maybe not even then.

Australia was something else. Hoover had a good competitive position there, and its refrigerator plant in Melbourne could easily be expanded to include Maytag's washers and dryers. Unfortunately, the small population of Australia limited the market to only about $250 million for major appliances.

Britain accounted for half of Hoover's European sales. But at the time of the acquisition its major appliance business was only marginally profitable. This was to change: After the acquisition it became downright unprofitable, as shown in Table 20.3 for the years 1990 through 1992, as it struggled to expand in a recession-plagued Europe. The results for 1993, of course, reflected the huge loss from the promotional debacle—hardly an acquisition made in heaven.

Maytag's earlier acquisitions also were becoming soured. Its acquisitions of Magic Chef and Admiral were diversifications into lower-priced appliances, and these did not meet expectations. But they left Maytag's balance sheet and its cash flow weakened (see Table 20.4). Perhaps more serious, Maytag's reputation as the nation's premier appliance maker became tarnished. Meanwhile, General Electric and Whirlpool were attacking the top end of its product line. As a result, Maytag found itself in the number-three or -four position in most of its brand lines.

TABLE 20.3 Operating Results of Maytag's Principal Business Components, 1990–1992

	Revenue (in millions)	Income[a] (in thousands)
1990		
North American Appliances	$2,212	$221,165
Vending	191	25,018
European Sales	497	(22,863)
1991		
North American Appliances	2,183	186,322
Vending	150	4,498
European Sales	486	(865)
1992		
North American Appliances	2,242	129,680
Vending	165	16,311
European Sales	502	(67,061)

Source: Company annual reports.

[a] This is operating income, that is, income before depreciation and other adjustments.

Commentary: While these years had not been particularly good for Maytag in growth of revenues and income, the continuing, and even intensifying, losses in the Hoover European operation had to be troublesome. And this is before the ill-fated early 1993 promotional results.

TABLE 20.4   **Long-Term Debt as a Percent of Capital from Maytag's Balance Sheets, 1986–1991**

Year	Long-Term Debt/Capital
1986	7.2%
1987	23.3
1988	48.3
1989	46.8
1990	44.1
1991	42.7

Source: Company annual reports.

Commentary: The effect of acquisitions, in particular that of the Chicago Pacific Corporation, can be clearly seen in the buildup of long-term debt: In 1986, Maytag was virtually free of such commitments; two years later its long-term debt ratio had increased almost sevenfold.

ANALYSIS

Flawed Acquisition Decisions

The long decline in profits after 1989 should have triggered strong concern and corrective action. Perhaps it did, but the action was not effectual as the decline continued, culminating in a large deficit in 1992 and serious problems in 1993. As shown in Table 20.2, the acquisitions brought neither revenue gains nor profitability. One suspects that in the rush to fend off potential raiders in the late 1980s, the company bought businesses it might never have under more sober times, and that it also paid too much for these businesses. Further, they cheapened the proud image of quality for Maytag.

Who Can We Blame in the UK Promotional Debacle?

Corporate Maytag management was guilty of a common fault in their acquisitions: It gave newly acquired divisions a loose rein, letting them continue to operate independently with few constraints: "After all, these executives should be more knowledgeable about their operations than corporate headquarters would be." Such confidence is sometimes misguided. In the UK promotion, Maytag management would seem as derelict as management in England. Planning guidelines or parameters were far too loose and undercontrolled. The idea of subsidiary management being able to burden the parent with $50 million of unexpected charges, and to have such erupt with no warning, borders on the absurd.

Finally, the planning of the UK executives for this ill-conceived travel promotion defies all logic. They vastly underestimated the demand for the promotional offer and they greatly overestimated paybacks from travel agencies on the package deals. Yet, it took no brilliant insight to realize that the value of the travel offer exceeded the price of the appliance—indeed, 200,000 customers rapidly arrived at this conclusion—and that such a sweetheart of a deal would be irresistible to many, and that it could prove to be costly in the extreme to the company. A miscalculation, or complete naivete on the part of executives and their staffs who should have known better?

How Could the Promotion Have Avoided the Problems?

The great problem resulting from an offer too good could have been avoided, and this without scrapping the whole idea. A cost-benefit analysis would have provided at least a perspective as to how much the company should spend to achieve certain benefits, such as increased sales, greater consumer interest, and favorable publicity. See the Information Box for a more detailed discussion of the important planning tool of a cost–benefit analysis.

INFORMATION BOX

COST–BENEFIT ANALYSIS

A cost–benefit analysis is a systematic comparison of the costs and benefits of a proposed action. Only if the benefits exceed the costs would we normally have a "go" decision. The normal way to make such an analysis is to assign dollar values to all costs and benefits, thus providing a common basis for comparison.

Cost–benefit analyses have been widely used by the Defense Department in evaluating alternative weapons systems. In recent years, such analyses have been sporadically applied to environmental regulation and even to workplace safety standards. As an example of the former, a cost–benefit analysis can be used to determine if it is socially worth spending X million dollars to meet a certain standard of clean air or water.

Many business decisions lend themselves to a cost–benefit analysis. It provides a systematic way of analyzing the inputs and the probable outputs of particular major alternatives. While in the business setting some of the costs and benefits can be very quantitative, they often should be tempered by nonquantitative inputs to reach the broadest perspective. Schermerhorn suggests considering the following criteria in evaluating alternatives:[8]

Benefits: What are the "benefits" of using the alternatives to solve a performance deficiency or take advantage of an opportunity?

Costs: What are the "costs" to implement the alternatives, including direct resource investments as well as any potential negative side effects?

Timeliness: How fast will the benefits occur and a positive impact be achieved?

Acceptability: To what extent will the alternatives be accepted and supported by those who must work with them?

Ethical soundness: How well do the alternatives meet acceptable ethical criteria in the eyes of multiple stakeholders?

What numbers would you assign to a cost–benefit analysis for Maytag Hoover's plan to offer the free airline tickets, under an assumption of 5,000 takers? 20,000 takers? 100,000 takers? 500,000 takers? (Make any assumptions needed as to costs.) What would be your conclusions for these various acceptance rates?

---

[8] John R. Schermerhorn, Jr., *Management,* 6th ed. (New York: Wiley, 1999), p. 61.

A cost-benefit analysis should certainly have alerted management to the possible consequences of various acceptance levels, and of the significant risks of high acceptance. However, the company could have set limits on the number of eligibles: perhaps the first 1,000, or the first 5,000. Doing this would have held or capped the costs to reasonably defined levels, and avoided the greater risks. Or the company could have made the offer less generous, perhaps by upping the requirements, or by lessening the premiums. Such more moderate alternatives would still have made an attractive promotion, but not the major uncontrolled catastrophe that happened.

FINALE

Maytag's invasion of Europe proved a costly failure. In the summer of 1995, Maytag gave up. It sold its European operations to an Italian appliance maker, recording a $135 million loss.

Even by the end of 1996, the Hoover mess was still not cleaned up. Hoover had spent $72 million flying some 220,000 people and had hoped to end the matter. But the fight continued four years later, with disgruntled customers who never flew taking Hoover to court. Even though Maytag had sold this troubled division, it still could not escape emerging lawsuits.

Leonard Hadley

In the summer of 1998, Leonard Hadley could look forward and backward with some satisfaction. He would retire the next summer when he turned sixty-five, and he had already picked his successor. Since assuming the top position in Maytag in January 1993 and confronting the mess with the UK subsidiary his first few months on the job, he had turned Maytag completely around.

He knew no one expected much change from him, an accountant who had joined Maytag right out of college. He was known as a loyal but unimaginative lieutenant of his boss, Daniel Krumm, who died of cancer shortly after naming Hadley his successor. After all, he reflected, no one thought that major change could come to an organization from someone who had spent his whole life there, who was a clone so to speak, and an accountant to boot. Everyone thought that changemakers had to come from outside, like Al Dunlap of Scott Paper and Sunbeam (described in Chapter 5). Well, he had shown them, and given hope to all number-two executives who resented Wall Street's love affair with outsiders.

Within a few weeks of taking over, he'd fired a bunch of managers, especially those rascals in the UK who'd masterminded the great Hoover debacle. He determined to get rid of foreign operations, most of them newly acquired and unprofitable. He just did not see that appliances could be profitably made for every corner of the world, because of the variety of regional customs. Still, he knew that many disagreed with him about this, including some of the board members who thought globalization was the only way to go. Still, over the next eighteen months he had prevailed.

He chuckled to himself as he reminisced. He had also overturned the decades-long corporate mindset not to be first to market with new technology because they would "rather be right than be first." His "Galaxy Initiative" of nine top-secret new products was a repudiation of this old mindset. One of them, the Neptune, a front-loading washer retailing at $1,100, certainly proved him right. Maytag had increased its production three times and raised its suggested retail price twice, and still it was selling like gangbusters. Perhaps the thing he was proudest of was getting Maytag products in Sears stores, the seller of one-third of all appliances in the United States. Sears's desire to have the Neptune was what swung the deal.

As an accountant, he probably should be focusing first on the numbers. Well, 1997 was certainly a banner year with sales up 10.9 percent over the previous year, while profitability as measured by return on capital was 16.7 percent, both sales and profit gains leading the industry. And 1998 so far was proving to be even better, with sales jumping 31 percent and earnings 88 percent.

He remembered the remarks of Lester Crown, a Maytag director: "Len Hadley has—quietly, softly—done a spectacular job. Obviously, we just lacked the ability to evaluate him [in the beginning]."[9]

Leonard Hadley retired on August 12, 1999. He knew he had surprised everyone in the organization by going outside Maytag for his successor. He was Lloyd Ward, age fifty, Maytag's first black executive, a marketing expert from PepsiCo, and before that Procter & Gamble, who had joined Maytag in 1996, and was currently president and chief operating officer.

Hadley's choice of successor proved to be flawed, or maybe Ward was just a victim of circumstances mostly beyond his control. After fifteen months, Ward left citing differences with Maytag's directors amid sorry operating results. Hadley came out of retirement to be interim president and CEO. Some 3,400 Maytag workers, a quarter of Newton's population, roared when they heard the news. They had feared the company would be moved to either Chicago or Dallas, or that it would be sold to Sweden's Electrolux. Hadley assured them that such would never happen as long as he's at the helm.[10]

UPDATE

Hadley retired again in June 2001, and Ralph F. Hake succeeded him. Hake came to Maytag from Fluor Corporation, an engineering and construction firm, where he had been executive vice president. Before that he had been with Maytag's chief rival, appliance manufacturer Whirlpool.

Hake kept headquarters in Newton, Iowa, but moved three plants to Reynosa, Mexico, intensifying fears that Maytag might export even more jobs to countries with

[9] Carl Quintanilla, "Maytag's Top Officer, Expected to Do Little, Surprises His Board," *Wall Street Journal* (June 23, 1998), pp. A1, A8.

[10] "Maytag Chief Quits as Profits Plummet," *Cleveland Plain Dealer* (November 10, 2000), p. 3C; and Emily Gersema, "Maytag Re-hires Former CEO After Time of Internal Turmoil, *Wall Street Journal* (January 15, 2001), p. 3H.

cheap labor. However, Hake tried to allay such concerns: "I do not anticipate multiple plant shutdowns or restructuring here." However, some analysts cautioned that consumers were becoming increasingly cost conscious—and less concerned with whether a product is made in the United States or abroad.

Hake also sought to move the company's product line beyond the traditional to more unusual products. He created a Strategic Initiatives Group with ten to twelve members to introduce a premium-priced line of mixers, blenders, toasters, and coffee makers under the brand name Jenn-Air Attrezzi. The hope was that such a focus on creative thinking would move the company out of its slump.[11]

WHAT CAN BE LEARNED?

Again—beware overpaying for an acquisition. Hoping to diversify its product line and gain overseas business, Maytag paid $1 billion for Chicago Pacific in 1989. As it turned out, this was far too much, and the debt burden was an albatross. Hadley conceded as much: "In the long view, it was correct to invest in these businesses. But the timing of the deal, and the price of the deal, made the debt a heavy burden to carry."[12]

Zeal to expand, and/or the desire to reduce the attractiveness of a firm's balance sheet with heavy debt and thus fend off potential raiders, do not excuse foolhardy management. The consequences of such bad decisions remain to haunt a company, and the ill-advised purchases often have to be eventually sold off at substantial losses (as we saw in the Snapple case). The analysis of potential acquisition candidates must be soberly and thoroughly done, and rosy projections questioned, even if this means the deal may be soured.

In decision planning, consider a worst-case scenario. There are those who preach the desirability of positive thinking, confidence, and optimism—whether it be in personal lives, athletics, or business practices. But expecting and preparing for the worst has much to commend it, since a person or a firm is then better able to cope with adversity and to avoid being overwhelmed, and more likely to make prudent rather than rash decisions.

Apparently the avid acceptance of the promotional offer was a complete surprise; no one dreamed of such demand. Yet, was it so unreasonable to think that a very attractive offer would meet wild acceptance?

In using loss leaders, put a cap on potential losses. Loss leaders, as we noted earlier, are items promoted at such attractive prices that the firm loses money on every sale. The expectation, of course, is that the customer traffic generated by such attractive promotions will increase sales of regular profit items so that total profits will be increased.

[11]David Pitt, Associated Press, as reported in "Maytag's Moves to Mexico Under Fire," *Cleveland Plain Dealer,* August 6, 2003, p. C2; and Fara Warner, *New York Times,* as reported in "Maytag Cookin' With New Twist on Tools for the Kitchen," *Cleveland Plain Dealer,* September 14, 2003, pp. G1 and G6.)

[12] Kenneth Labich, "Why Companies Fail," *Fortune* (November 14, 1994), p. 60.

The risks of uncontrolled or uncapped loss leader promotions are vividly shown in this case. For a retailer who uses loss leaders, the loss is ultimately capped as the inventory is sold off. With UK Hoover there was no cap. The solution is clear: Attractive loss leader promotions should be capped, such as the first 100 or the first 1,000 or for one week only. Otherwise, the promotion should be made less attractive.

Beware giving too loose a rein, thus sacrificing controls, especially of unproven foreign subsidiaries. Although decentralizing authority down to lower ranks is often desirable and results in better motivation and management development than centralization, it can be overdone. At the extreme, where divisional and subsidiary executives have almost unlimited decision-making authority and can run their operations as virtual dynasties, then corporate management essentially abdicates its authority. Such looseness in an organization endangers cohesiveness; it tends to obscure common standards and objectives; and it can even dilute unified ethical practices.

Such extreme looseness of controls is not uncommon with acquisitions, especially foreign ones. It is easy to make the assumption that these executives were operating successfully before the acquisition and have more firsthand knowledge of the environment than the corporate executives.

Still, there should be limits on how much freedom these executives should be permitted—especially when their operations have not been notably successful. In Maytag's case, the UK subsidiary had lost money every year since it was acquired. Accordingly, one would expect prudent corporate management to have condoned less decentralization and insisted on tighter controls that it might otherwise.

The power of a cost–benefit analysis. For major decisions, executives have much to gain from a cost–benefit analysis. It forces them to systematically tabulate and analyze the costs and benefits of particular courses of action. They may find that likely benefits are so uncertain as to not be worth the risk. If so, now is the time to realize this, rather than after substantial commitments have already been made.

Without doubt, regular use of cost–benefit analyses for major decisions improves executives' batting averages for good decisions. Even though some numbers may have to be judgmental, especially as to probable benefits, the process of making this analysis forces a careful look at alternatives and most likely consequences. For more important decisions, input from diverse staff people and executives will bring greater power to the analysis.

CONSIDER

What other learning insights can you add?

QUESTIONS

1. How could the promotion of UK Hoover have been better designed? Be as specific as you can.

2. Given the fiasco that did occur, how do you think Maytag should have responded?

3. "Firing the three top executives of UK Hoover is unconscionable. It smacks of a vendetta against European managers by an American parent. After all, their only 'crime' was a promotion that was too successful." Comment on this statement.

4. Do you think Leonard Hadley, the Maytag CEO for only two months, should be soundly criticized for the UK situation? Why or why not?

5. Please speculate: Why do you think this UK Hoover fiasco happened in the first place? What went wrong?

6. Evaluate the decision to acquire Chicago Pacific Corporation (CPC). Do this both for the time of the decision, and for now—after the fact—as a post mortem. Defend your overall conclusions.

7. Use your creativity: Can you devise a strategy for UK Hoover to become more of a major force in Europe?

8. Evaluate the reflections of Hadley in the summer of 1998. Do you agree with all of his convictions and actions? Why or why not?

HANDS-ON EXERCISES

1. You have been placed in charge of a task force sent by headquarters to England to coordinate the fire-fighting efforts in the aftermath of the ill-fated promotion. There are neither enough productive capacity nor enough airline seats available to handle the demand. How would you propose to handle this situation? Be as specific as you can and defend your recommendations.

2. As a staff vice president at corporate headquarters, you have been charged to develop companywide policies and procedures that will prevent such a situation from ever occurring again. What would you recommend?

TEAM DEBATE EXERCISE

How tightly should you supervise and control a foreign operation? This Maytag example suggests very tightly. But is this an aberration, unlikely to be encountered again? Debate the issue of very tight controls versus relative freedom for foreign operations.

INVITATION TO RESEARCH

Is Maytag still independent or has it been acquired? Is Maytag's headquarters still in Newton, Iowa? Can you find further information on the effectiveness of the Strategic Initiatives Group in generating innovative new products? How is the company doing since Ralph Hake took over as CEO? Have any more plants been moved abroad?

CHAPTER TWENTY-ONE

MetLife: Deceptive Sales Tactics—Condoned or Poorly Controlled?

*I*n August 1993, the state of Florida blew the whistle on giant Metropolitan Life, a company dating back to 1868, and the country's second largest insurance firm. MetLife agents based in Tampa, Florida, were alleged to have duped customers out of some $11 million. Thousands of these customers were nurses, lured by the sales pitch to learn more about "something new, one of the most widely discussed retirement plans in the investment world today."[1] In reality, this was a life-insurance policy in disguise, and what clients were led to think were savings deposits were actually insurance premiums.

As we will see, the growing scandal rocked MetLife, and brought it millions of dollars in fines and restitutions. What was not clear was the full culpability of the company: Was it guilty only of not monitoring agent performance sufficiently to detect unethical and illegal activities, or was it the great encourager of such practices?

RICK URSO: THE VILLAIN?

The first premonitory rumble that something bad was about to happen came to Rick Urso on Christmas Eve 1993. Home with his family, he received an unexpected call from his boss, the regional sales manager. In disbelief, he heard there was a rumor going around the executive suites that he was about to be fired. Now, Urso had known that the State of Florida had been investigating, and that company auditors had also been looking into sales practices. And on September 17, two corporate vice-presidents had even shown up to conduct the fourth audit that year, but on leaving they had given him the impression that he was complying with company guidelines.

Urso often reveled in his good fortune and attributed it to his sheer dedication to his work and the company. He had grown up in a working-class neighborhood, the son of an electrician. He had started college, but dropped out before graduating.

[1] Suzanne Woolley and Gail DeGeorge, "Policies of Deception?" *Business Week* (January 17, 1994), p. 24.

His sales career started at a John Hancock agency in Tampa, in 1978. Four years later, he was promoted to manager. He was credited with building up the agency to number two in the whole company.

He left John Hancock in 1983 for MetLife's Tampa agency. His first job was as trainer. Only three months later he was promoted to branch manager. Now his long hours and overwhelming commitment were beginning to pay off. In a success story truly inspiring, his dedication and his talent as a motivator of people swept the branch from a one-rep office to one of MetLife's largest and most profitable. In 1990 and 1991, Urso's office won the company's Sales Office of the Year award. By 1993, the agency employed 120 reps, seven sales managers, and thirty administrative employees. And Urso had risen to become MetLife's third-highest-paid employee, earning $1.1 million as manager of the branch. With such a performance history, the stuff of legends, he became the company's star, a person to look up to and to inspire trainees and other employees.

His was the passion of a TV evangelist: "Most people go through life being told why they can't accomplish something. If they would just believe, then they would be halfway there. That's the way I dream and that's what I expect from my people."[2] He soon became known as the "Master Motivator," and increasingly was the guest speaker at MetLife conferences.

On the Monday after that Christmas, the dire prediction came to pass. He was summoned to the office of William Groggans, the head of MetLife's Southeast territory, and was handed a letter by the sober-faced Groggans. With trembling hands he opened it and read that he was fired for engaging in improper conduct.

The Route to Stardom

Unfortunately, the growth of his Tampa office could not be credited to simple motivation of employees. Urso found his vehicle for great growth to be the whole-life insurance policy. This was part life insurance and part savings. As such, it required high premiums, but only part earned interest and compounded on a tax-deferred basis; the rest went to pay for the life insurance policy. What made this so attractive to company sales reps was the commission: A Met whole-life policy paid a 55 percent first-year commission. In contrast, an annuity paid only a 2 percent first-year commission.

Urso found the nurses' market to be particularly attractive. Perhaps because of their constant exposure to death, nurses were easily convinced of the need for economic security. He had his salespeople call themselves "nursing representatives." And his Tampa salespeople carried their fake retirement plan beyond Florida, eventually reaching thirty-seven states. A New York client, for example, thought she had bought a retirement annuity. But it turned out to be life insurance even though she didn't want such coverage because she had no beneficiaries.[3]

As the growth of the Tampa agency became phenomenal, his budget for mailing brochures was upped to nearly $1 million in 1992, ten times that of any other MetLife office. This gave him national reach.

---

[2] Weld F. Royal, "Scapegoat or Scoundrel," *Sales & Marketing Management* (January 1995), p. 64.

[3] Jane Bryant Quinn, "Yes, They're Out to Get You," *Newsweek* (January 24, 1994), p. 51.

Urso's own finances increased proportionately because he earned a commission on each policy his reps sold. In 1989, he was paid $270,000. In 1993, as compensation exceeded $1 million, he moved his family to Bay Shore Boulevard, the most expensive area of Tampa.

End of the Bonanza

A few complaints began surfacing. In 1990, the Texas insurance commissioner warned MetLife to stop its nursing ploy. The company made a token compliance by sending out two rounds of admonitory letters. But nothing apparently changed. See the following Information Box about the great deficiency of token compliance without follow-up.

An internal MetLife audit in 1991 raised some questions about Urso's pre-approach letters. The term *nursing representative* was called a "made-up" title. The auditors also questioned the term *retirement savings policy* as not appropriate for the product. However, the report concluded by congratulating the Tampa office for its contribution to the company. Not surprisingly, such mixed signals did not end the use of misleading language at that time.

In the summer of 1993, Florida state regulators began a more in-depth examination of the sales practices of the Urso agency. As a result of this investigation, Florida Insurance Commissioner Tom Gallagher charged MetLife with several violations. Now MetLife began more serious investigation.

INFORMATION BOX

THE VULNERABILITY OF COMPLIANCE, IF IT IS ONLY TOKEN

A token effort at compliance to a regulatory complaint or charge tends to have two consequences, neither good in the long run for the company involved:

1. Such tokenism gives a clear message to the organization: "Despite what outsiders say, this is acceptable conduct in this firm." Thus is set the climate for less than desirable practices.
2. Vulnerability to future harsher measures. With the malpractice continuing, regulators, convinced that the company is stalling and refusing to cooperate, will eventually take more drastic action. Penalties will move beyond warnings to become punitive.

Actually, the firm may not have intended to stall, but that is the impression conveyed. If the cause of the seemingly token effort is really faulty controls, one wonders how many other aspects of the operation are also ineptly controlled so that company policies are ignored.

Discuss what kinds of controls MetLife could have imposed in 1990 that would have made compliance actual and not token.

The crux of the investigations concerned promotional material Urso's office was sending to nurses nationwide. From 1989 to 1993, millions of direct-mail pieces had been sent out. Charges finally were leveled that this material disguised the product agents were selling. For example, one brochure coming from Urso's office depicted the Peanuts character Lucy in a nurse's uniform. The headline described the product as "retirement savings and security for the future a nurse deserves." Nowhere was insurance even mentioned, and allegations were that nurses across the country unknowingly purchased life insurance when they thought they were buying retirement savings plans.

As the investigation deepened, a former Urso agent, turned whistleblower, claimed he had been instructed to place his hands over the words "life insurance" on applications during presentations.

METLIFE CORRECTIVE ACTIONS

With Florida regulators now investigating, the company's attitudes changed. At first, MetLife denied wrongdoing. But eventually it acknowledged problems. Under mounting public pressure, it agreed to pay $20 million in fines to more than forty states as a result of unethical sales practices of its agents. It further agreed to refund premiums to nearly 92,000 policyholders who bought insurance based on misleading sales information between 1989 and 1993. These refunds were expected to reach $76 million.

MetLife fired or demoted five high-level executives as a result of the scandal. Urso's office was closed, and all seven of his managers and several reps were also discharged. Life insurance sales to individuals were down 25 percent through September 1994 over the same nine-month period in 1993. And Standard & Poor's downgraded Met's bond rating based on these alleged improprieties.

Shortly after the fines were announced, the Florida Department of Insurance filed charges against Urso and eighty-six other MetLife insurance agents, accusing them of fraudulent sales practices. The insurance commissioner said, "This was not a situation where a few agents decided to take advantage of their customers, but a concerted effort by many individuals to dupe customers into buying a life insurance policy disguised as a retirement savings plan."[4]

The corporation, in attempting to improve its public image, instituted a broad overhaul of its compliance procedures. It established a corporate ethics and compliance department to monitor behavior throughout the company and audit personal insurance sales offices. The department was also charged to report any compliance deficiencies to senior management and to follow up to ensure the implementation of corrective actions.

In MetLife's *1994 Annual Report*, Harry Kamen, CEO, and Ted Athanassiades, president, commented on their corrective actions regarding the scandal:

> We created what we think is the most effective compliance system in the industry. Not just for personal insurance, but for all components of the company. We installed systems

---

[4] Sean Armstrong, "The Good, The Bad and the Industry," *Best's Review, P/C* (June 1994), p. 36.

to coordinate and track the quality and integrity of our sales activities, and we created a new system of sales office auditing.

Also, there were organizational changes. And, for the first time in twenty-two years, we assembled all of our agency and district managers—about a thousand people—to discuss what we have done and need to do about the problems and where we were going.[5]

Meantime, Rick Urso started a suit against MetLife for defamation of character and for reneging on a $1 million severance agreement. He alleged that MetLife made him the fall guy in the nationwide sales scandal.

The personal consequences on Urso's life were not inconsequential. More than a year later he was still unemployed. He had looked for another insurance job, but no one would even see him. "There are nights he can't sleep. He lies awake worrying about the impact this will have on his two teenagers." And he laments that his wife cannot go out without people gossiping.[6]

WHERE DOES THE BLAME LIE?

Is Urso really the unscrupulous monster who rose to a million-dollar-a-year man on the foundations of deceit? Or is MetLife mainly to blame for encouraging, and then ignoring for too long, practices aimed at misleading and even deceiving? Probably the final reckoning will not be reached outside the courtroom. And who can say that the judgment then rendered will be completely valid?

The Case Against MetLife

Undeniably Urso did things that smacked of the illegal and unethical. But did the corporation knowingly provide the climate? Was his training such as to promote deceptive practices? Was MetLife completely unaware of his distortions and deceptions in promotional material and sales pitches? There seems to be substantial evidence that the company played a part; it was no innocent and unsuspecting bystander.

At best, MetLife top executives may not have been aware of the full extent of the hard selling efforts emanating at first from Tampa and then spreading further in the organization. Perhaps they chose to ignore any inkling that things were not completely on the up and up, in the quest for exceptional bottom-line performance. "Don't argue with success" might have become the corporate mindset.

At the worst, the company encouraged and even demanded hard selling and tried to pretend that such could still be accomplished with the highest ethical standards of performance. If such ethical standards were not met, then, company top executives could argue, they were not aware of such wrongdoings.

There is evidence of company culpability (more will undoubtedly be introduced during Urso's suit). Take the training program for new agents. Much of it was designed to help new employees overcome the difficulties of selling life insurance. In

[5] *MetLife 1994 Annual Report*, p. 16.

[6] Royal, p. 65.

so doing, they were taught to downplay the life insurance aspects of the product. Rather, the savings and tax-deferred growth benefits were to be stressed.

In training new agents to sell insurance over the phone, they were told that people prefer dealing with specialists. It seemed only a small temptation to use the title *nursing representative* rather than *insurance agent.*

After the scandal, MetLife admitted that the training might be faulty. Training had been decentralized into five regional centers, and the company believed that this may have led to a less standardized and less controlled curricula. MetLife has since reorganized so that many functions, including training and legal matters, are now done at one central location.[7]

The company's control or monitoring was certainly deficient and uncoordinated during the years of misconduct. For example, the marketing department promoted deceptive sales practices while the legal department warned of possible illegality but took no further action to eliminate it.

An Industry Problem?

The MetLife revelations focused public and regulatory attention on the entire insurance industry. The Insurance Commissioner of Florida also turned attention to the sales and marketing practices of New York Life and Prudential. The industry itself seems vulnerable to questionable practices. With millions of transactions, intense competition, and a widespread and rather autonomous sales force, opportunity exists for misrepresentation and other unethical dealings.

For example, just a few months after the Tampa office publicity, MetLife settled an unrelated scandal. Regulators in Pennsylvania fined the company $1.5 million for "churning." This is a practice of agents replacing old policies with new ones, in which additional commissions are charged and policyholders are disadvantaged. Class-action suits alleging churning have also been filed in Pennsylvania against Prudential, New York Life, and John Hancock.

But problems go beyond sales practices. Claims adjusters may attempt to withhold or reduce payments. General agents may place business with bogus or insolvent companies. Even actuaries may create unrealistic policy structures.

With a deteriorating public image, the industry faces further governmental regulation, both by states and by the federal government. But cynics, both within and outside the industry, wonder whether deception and fraud are so much a part of the business that nothing can be done about them.[8]

ANALYSIS

We could have placed this case under an Ethics and Social Responsibility section. The choice to include it under Controlling assumed a lapse in complete feedback to top executives. But maybe they did not want to know. After all, nothing was life-threatening

---

[7] "Trained to Mislead," *Sales & Marketing Management* (January 1995), p. 66.

[8] Armstrong, p. 35.

here, no product safety features were being ignored or disguised, nobody was in physical danger.

This raises a key management issue. Can top executives hide from less than ethical practices—and even illegal ones—under the guise that they did not know? The answer should be *No!* See the Information Box below for a discussion of management accountability.

So, we are left with top management of MetLife grappling with the temptation to tacitly approve the aggressive selling practices of a sales executive so successful as to be the model for the whole organization, even though faint cries from the legal staff suggested that such might be subject to regulatory scrutiny and disapproval.

The harsh appraisal of this situation is that top management cannot be exonerated for the deficiencies of subordinates. If controls and monitoring processes are defective, top management is still accountable. The pious platitudes of MetLife management that they have now corrected the situation hardly excuse them for permitting this to have developed in the first place.

Ah, but embracing the temptation is so easy to rationalize. Management can always maintain that there was no good, solid proof of misdeeds. After all, where do aggressive sales efforts cross the line? Where do they become more than simply puffing, and become outright deceptive? See the Information Box on the following page regarding puffing, and this admittedly gray area of the acceptable. Lacking indisputable evidence

INFORMATION BOX

THE ULTIMATE RESPONSIBILITY

In the Maytag case in Chapter 20 we examine a costly snafu brought about by giving executives of a foreign subsidiary too much rein. With MetLife the problem was gradually eroding ethical practices. In both instances, top management still had ultimate responsibility and cannot escape blame for whatever goes wrong in an organization. Decades ago, President Truman coined the phrase, "The buck stops here," meaning that in this highest position rests the ultimate seat of responsibility.

Any manager who delegates to someone else the authority to do something will undoubtedly hold them responsible to do the job properly. Still, the manager must be aware that his or her own responsibility to higher management or to stockholders cannot be delegated away. If the subordinate does the job improperly, the manager is still responsible.

Going back to MetLife, or to any corporation involved with unethical and illegal practices, top executives can try to escape blame by denying that they knew anything about the misdeeds. This should not exonerate them. Even if they knew nothing directly, they still set the climate.

In Japan, the chief executive of an organization involved in a public scandal usually resigns in disgrace. In the United States, top executives often escape full retribution by blaming their subordinates and maintaining that they themselves knew nothing of the misdeed. Is it truly fair to hold a top executive culpable for the shortcomings of some unknown subordinate?

of misdeeds, why should these executives suspect the worst? Especially since their legal departments, not centralized as they were to be later, were timid in their denunciations?

Turning to controls, a major caveat should be posed for all firms: In the presence of strong management demands for performance—with the often implicit or imagined pressure to produce at all costs, or else—the ground is laid for less than desirable practices by subordinates. After all, their career paths and even job longevity depend on meeting these demands.

In an organizational climate of decentralization and laissez faire, such abuses are more likely to occur. Such a results-oriented structure suggests that it's not how you achieve the desired results, but that you meet them. So, while decentralization is, on balance, usually desirable, it can, in the right environment of top management laxity of high moral standards, lead to undesirable—and worse—practices.

At the least, it leads to opportunistic temptation by lower- and middle-level executives. Perhaps this is the final indictment of MetLife and Rick Urso. The climate was conductive to his ambitious opportunism. For a while it was wonderful. But the clinks and the abuses of accepted practices could not be disguised indefinitely.

And wherever possible, top management will repudiate its accountability responsibilities.

The Handling of the Crisis

MetLife responded slowly to the allegations of misconduct. A classic mode for firms confronted with unethical and/or product liability charges is to deny everything, until evidence becomes overwhelming. Then they are forced to acknowledge problems under mounting public pressure—from regulatory bodies, attorneys, and the media—and have to scramble with damage control to try to undo the threats to public image and finances. In MetLife's case, fines and refunds approached $100 million early on. They would eventually reach almost $2 billion.

Being slow to act, to accept any responsibility, and, for top executives exhibiting aloofness until late in the game, are tantamount to inflaming public opinion and regulatory zeal. We saw something similar in the Coca-Cola product-safety crisis in Europe: First there was denial, then grudging admission, then uncoordinated remedial efforts, and only after the crisis had received alarming attention did top management become involved to finally lead massive restorative efforts.

How much better for all involved, victims as well as the organization itself, if initial complaints are promptly followed up? And, if complaints are serious, they should be given top management attention in a climate of cooperation with any agencies involved as well as the always-interested media.

LATER DEVELOPMENTS

On August 18, 1999, MetLife agreed to pay out at least $1.7 billion to settle final lawsuits over its allegedly improper sales practices. In the agreement (in which MetLife admitted no wrongdoing), about six million life insurance policyholders and a million annuity contract holders were involved. Essentially, these customers were expected to get one to five years of free term-life insurance coverage.

MetLife argued for years that it had done nothing wrong. It had previously dispensed with most of its litigation problems by settling rather than going to trial. The incentive for settling these final class-action suits even at the cost of a massive charge, was to clear the way for MetLife's planned conversion to a stockholder-owned company from its current status as a policyholder-owned mutual company. "Clearly it's something they needed to put behind them before they demutualized," or went public.[9]

Harry Kamen, CEO of MetLife, brought Robert Benmosche, age fifty-seven, an ex-Wall Streeter, on board in 1995 to turn things around. Benmosche solved many of MetLife's problems and became chairman when Kamen retired in 1998. In April 2000, he took the company public and the stock offering raised $5.2 billion.

In his relentless restructuring, Benmosche axed poor performers, some 1,300 including 154 assistant vice presidents and higher in 2001—and demanded better results and ethical standards. He required agents to work full time, instead of part time, as many had previously done: "I knew this was needed after I met someone who complimented one of my agents for his plumbing skills," explained Benmosche. He also compelled all agents to get securities licenses so they could sell investments like variable annuities. Bonuses were now tied into performance reviews and a division's financial results, and officer's bonuses were partly paid in stock that they were discouraged from selling: "If the top people … don't do what they have to do to make sure the company strongly survives, we should lose our shirts." MetLife's revenues in 2001 were $32 billion, up 18 percent since Benmosche became chairman.[10]

[9] Deborah Lohse, "MetLife Agrees to Pay Out $1.7 Billion or More to Settle Policyholder Lawsuits," *Wall Street Journal*, August 19, 1999, p. B14.

[10] Carrie Coolidge, "Snoopy's New Tricks," *Forbes*, April 15, 2002, pp. 100–102.

WHAT CAN BE LEARNED?

Beware the head-in-the-sand approach to looming problems or public complaints. Ignoring or giving only token attention to suspected problems and regulatory complaints sets a firm up for a possible massive crisis. Covering one's eyes to malpractices and danger situations does not make them go away; they tend to fester and become more serious. Prompt attention, investigation, and action is needed to prevent these problem areas from getting out of hand. MetLife could have saved itself several billion dollars if it had acted on the early complaints of misrepresentation and misleading customers.

Unethical and illegal actions do not go undetected forever. It may take months, it may take years, but a firm's dark side will eventually be uncovered. Its reputation may then be besmirched, it may face loss of customers and competitive position, and it may face heavy fines and increased regulation.

The eventual disclosure may come from a disgruntled employee (a whistleblower). It may originate from a regulatory body or an investigative reporter. Or it may come from revelations emanating from a lawsuit. Eventually, the deviation is uncovered, and retribution follows. Such a scenario should be—but is not always—enough to constrain those individuals tempted to commit unethical and illegal actions.

What made the MetLife deceptive practices particularly troubling is that they were so visible, and yet were so long tolerated. Much of the sales organization seemed to lack a clear definition of what was acceptable and what was not. Something was clearly amiss both in the training and in the controlling of agent personnel.

The control function is best centralized in any organization. Where the department or entity that monitors performance is decentralized, tolerance of bad practices is more likely than when centralized. The reason is rather simple. Where legal or accounting controls are decentralized the persons conducting them are more easily influenced and are likely to be neither as objective nor as critical as when they are further from the situation. So, reviewers and evaluators should not be close to the people they are examining. And they should report only to the top management.

A strong sales incentive program invites bad practices. The lucrative commission incentive for the whole-life policies—55 percent first-year commission—was almost bound to stimulate abusive sales practices, especially when the rewards for this type of policy were so much greater than for any other. Firms often use various incentive programs and contests to motivate their employees to seek greater efforts. But if some are tempted to cross the line, the end result in public scrutiny and condemnation may not be worth whatever increases in sales might be gained.

Large corporations are particularly vulnerable to public scrutiny. Large firms, especially ones dealing with consumer products, are very visible. This visibility makes them attractive targets for critical scrutiny by activists, politicians, the media, regulatory bodies, and the legal establishment. Such firms ought to be particularly careful in any dealings that might be questioned, even if short-term profits have to be restrained. In MetLife's case, the fines and refunds eventually approached $2 billion. Although the firm in its *1994 Annual Report* maintained that all the bad publicity was behind it, that there were no ill effects, some analysts wondered how quickly a besmirched reputation could truly be restored, especially with competitors eager to grab the opportunity presented.

Sometimes a tarnished reputation can be rather quickly restored. Contrary to some experts, there is compelling evidence that customers tend to quickly forget misdeeds, as they apparently did with MetLife under the new management of Benmosche. We saw a similar restoration of reputation with the unsafe tires of Firestone in Ford Explorers in Chapter 3. While the poor image of Continental Airlines was not due to product safety or deception, but rather to years of deteriorating service, this image was quickly turned around with enlightened, fresh management. Perhaps these experiences should be comforting to a firm that incurs image damage, perhaps through its own fault, or maybe because of factors not directly under its control. It does help, however, if there is a change in top management. Still, in cases of unethical conduct, fines and perhaps a plethora of lawsuits are more immediate consequences of culpability.

CONSIDER

What additional learning insights do you see?

QUESTIONS

1. Do you think Rick Urso should have been fired? Why or why not?
2. Do you think the MetLife CEO and president should have been fired? Why or why not?
3. Why was the term, "life insurance," seemingly so desirable to avoid? What is wrong with life insurance?
4. Given the widespread publicity about the MetLife scandal, do you think the firm could regain consumer trust in a short time?
5. "This whole critical publicity has been blown way out of proportion. After all, nobody was injured. Not even in their pocketbook. They were sold something they really needed. For their own good." Evaluate.
6. "You have to admire that guy, Urso. He was a real genius. No one else could motivate a sales organization as he did. They should have made him president of the company. Or else he should become an evangelist." Evaluate.
7. Do you think the arguments are compelling that the control function should be centralized rather than decentralized? Why or why not?

HANDS-ON EXERCISES

Before

1. It is early 1990. You are the assistant to the CEO of MetLife. Rumors have been surfacing that life insurance sales efforts are becoming not only too

high pressure but also misleading. The CEO has ordered you to investigate. You find that the legal department in the Southeast Territory has some concerns about the efforts coming out of the highly successful Tampa office of Urso. Be as specific as you can about how you would investigate these unproven allegations, and explain how you would report this to your boss, assuming that some questionable practices seem apparent.

2. It is 1992. Internal investigations have confirmed that Urso and his "magnificent" Tampa office are using deceptive selling techniques in disguising the life insurance aspects of the policies they are selling. As the executive in charge in the Southeast, describe your actions and rationale at this point. (You have to assume that the later consequences are completely unknown at this point.)

After

3. The _____ has hit the fan. The scandal has become well publicized, especially with such TV programs as *Dateline* and *20/20*. What would you do as top executive of MetLife at this point? How would you attempt to save the public image of the company?

TEAM DEBATE EXERCISE

The publicity is widespread about the "misdeeds" of MetLife. Debate how you would react. One position is to defend your company and rationalize what happened and downplay any ill effects. The other position is to meekly bow to the allegations and admit wrongdoing and be as contrite as possible.

INVITATION TO RESEARCH

Is MetLife still prospering under Benmosche? Can you find any information that contradicts that the situation has virtually been forgotten by the general public? Can you find out whether Rick Urso has found another job? Could you develop the pros and cons of a mutual (policyholder owned) firm and a public firm owned by stockholders?

ENTREPRENEURIAL
ADVENTURES

CHAPTER TWENTY-TWO

Boston Beer—Revisited

Jim Koch was obsessed with becoming an entrepreneur. He wasn't quite sure where he should do his entrepreneuring. Maybe the brewing industry? Years before, his great-great-grandfather, Louis Koch, had concocted a recipe at his St. Louis brewery that was heavier, more full-bodied than such as Budweiser or Miller. However, it was much more expensive to produce than mass-market beers. It involved a lengthy brewing and fermentation process, as well as such premium ingredients as Bavarian hops that cost many times more than those regularly used by other brewers.

Jim had a well-paying job with the prestigious Boston Consulting Group. He had been with them for six and a half years already, but still he was haunted by that dream of becoming his own man. Of late, the thought pursued him that maybe the brewing industry might be ripe for a new type of product and a new approach, a good tasting brew something like his ancestor's. He wondered if he might have a strategic window of opportunity in a particular consumer segment: men in their mid-twenties and older who were beer aficionados and would be willing to pay a premium for a good-tasting beer. What he couldn't be certain of was how large this segment was, and he knew from his consulting experience that too small a segment doomed a strategy. So, were there enough such sophisticated drinkers to support the new company that he envisioned?

In 1984, he thought he detected a clue that this might indeed be the case: Sales were surging for import beers such as Heineken and Beck's with their different tastes. Didn't this portend that enough Americans would be willing to pay substantially more for a full-bodied flavor?

As he studied this more, Koch also came to believe that these imports were very vulnerable to well-made domestic brews. They faced a major problem in maintaining freshness with a product that goes sour rather quickly. He knew that the foreign brewers, in trying to minimize the destructive influence of the time lag between production and consumption, were adding preservatives and even using cheaper ingredients for the American market.

Some small local brewers offered stronger tastes. But they were having great difficulty producing a lager with consistent quality. And he sensed they were squandering their opportunity. Although they could produce small batches of well-crafted beer, albeit of erratic quality, what they mainly lacked was ability and resources to aggressively market their products.

He thought now that he had indeed found the right niche, a strategic window of opportunity, for becoming an entrepreneurial success. See the following Information Box for further discussion of a strategic window of opportunity and its desirable accompaniment, a SWOT analysis.

He decided to take the plunge, and gave up his job.

Amassing sufficient capital to start a new venture is the common problem with almost all entrepreneurs, and so it was with Koch. Still, he was better off than most. He had saved $100,000 from his years with Boston Consulting, and he persuaded

INFORMATION BOX

STRATEGIC WINDOW OF OPPORTUNITY AND SWOT ANALYSIS

A strategic window is an opportunity in the marketplace, one that is currently neglected by competitors and one that fits well with the firm's or prospective firm's competencies. Strategic windows often last for only a short time before they are filled by alert competitors, but sometimes they may be more lasting if competitors deem it difficult to enter the particular niche. Potential competitors may pass because of price or image advantages they see the first firm as having, or perhaps because they judge—correctly or incorrectly—that the niche does not have sufficient potential.

SWOT Analysis

Strategic windows are usually found by systematically analyzing the environment, examining the threats and opportunities it holds. The competencies of the firm, its physical and financial resources, and, not the least, its people resources—management and employees and their strengths and weaknesses—should be assessed. The objective is to determine what courses of action might be appropriate for that particular firm and its orientation.

These are the elements of SWOT analysis:

Strengths and

Weaknesses of the firm, and

Opportunities and

Threats in the environment

Although SWOT analysis may be a formal part of the planning, it may also be informal and even intuitive. We suspect that Jim Koch, having worked six and a half years with a prestigious consulting firm, would have formalized this analysis. (In the next case, OfficeMax, Michael Feuer may have been more informal and intuitive in his assessment of entrepreneurial opportunity.)

Why do you think all the big brewers overlooked the possibilities of the highest-priced end of the market?

family and friends to chip in another $140,000. But while this might be enough to start a new retail or service venture, it was far less than the estimated $10 million or more needed to build a state-of-the-art brewery.

Koch got around this major obstacle. Instead of building or buying he contracted an existing firm, Pittsburgh Brewing Company, to brew his beer. It had good facilities, but more than this, its people had the brewing skills coming from more than twenty years of operation. He would call his new beer Samuel Adams, after a Revolutionary War patriot who was also a brewer.

PROBLEMS

A mighty problem still existed, and the success of the venture hinged on this. Koch would have to sell his great-tasting beer at $20 a case to break even and make a reasonable profit. But this was 15 percent more than even the premium imports like Heineken. Would anyone buy such an expensive beer, and one that didn't even have the cachet of an import? See the Information Box "Competing on Price, Revisited."

It fell to Koch as the fledgling firm's only salesperson to try to acquaint retailers and consumers with his new beer, this unknown brand with the very high price. "I went from bar to bar," he said. "Sometimes I had to call fifteen times before someone would agree to carry it."[1]

He somehow conjured up enough funds for a $100,000 ad campaign in the local market. Shunning the advertising theme of the big brewers that almost without exception stressed the sociability of the people drinking their brand, Koch's ads attacked the imports: "Declare your independence from foreign beer," he urged. And the name Samuel Adams was compatible with this cry for independence. Foreign brews were singled out as not having the premium ingredients and quality brewing of Samuel Adams. Koch appeared on most of his commercials, saying such things as: "Hi, I'm Jim Koch. ... It takes me all year to brew what the largest import makes in just three hours because I take the time to brew Samuel Adams right. I use my great-great-grandfather's century-old recipe, all malt brewing and rare hops that cost ten times what they use in the mass-produced imports."[2]

Gradually his persistence in calling on retailers and his anti-import ads, some of which garnered national attention in such periodicals as *Newsweek* and *USA Today*, induced more and more bartenders and beer drinkers to at least try Samuel Adams. Many liked it, despite the high price. (Or, perhaps, because of it?)

Now his problem became finding distributors, and this proved particularly troubling for a new firm in this industry where major brands often had a lock on existing wholesalers. The situation was so bad in Boston—no wholesaler would carry Samuel Adams, even though it was a local brand—that Boston Beer bought a truck and delivered the cases itself.

Koch slowly expanded his distribution one geographical area at a time, from Boston into Washington, D.C., then to New York, Chicago, and California, taking care that production could match the steady expansion without sacrificing quality. He

[1] Jenny McCune, "Brewing Up Profits," *Management Review*, April 1994, p. 18.

[2] *Ibid.*, p. 19.

INFORMATION BOX

COMPETING ON PRICE, REVISITED: THE PRICE/QUALITY PERCEPTION

In the Vanguard and Dell Computer cases, we examined the potent strategy of offering the lowest prices in the industry—if this could be done profitably due to a lower expense and overhead structure than competitors.

Here, Boston Beer was attempting to compete while having some of the highest prices in the industry. Was this the height of foolishness? Why would anyone pay prices higher even than the expensive imported beers, just for a different taste?

The highest price can convey an image of the very highest quality. We as consumers have long been conditioned to think this. With cars, we may not be able to afford this highest quality, such as an Infiniti, Lexus, or Mercedes convertible. But with beer, almost anyone can afford to buy the highest-priced brew sometimes, maybe to impress guests or to simply enjoy a different taste that we are led to think is better.

Sometimes such a price/quality perception sets us up. It might be valid, or might not be. Especially is this true where quality is difficult to ascertain, such as with beer and liquor, with bottled water, with perfume, as well as other products with hidden ingredients and complex characteristics.

Have you have ever fallen victim to the price/quality misperception? How does one determine quality for an alcoholic beverage such as vodka, gin, and scotch, as well as beer? By the taste? The advertising claims? Anything else?

---

brought in his secretary at Boston Consulting, Rhonda Kaliman, to assist him in building a sales organization. This grew from less than a dozen sales reps in 1989 to seventy nationwide by 1994, more than any other microbrewer and about the same number as Anheuser-Busch, the giant of the industry. Now Samuel Adams salespeople could give more personalized and expert attention to customers than competitors whose sales reps often sold many beverage lines.

Sales soared 63 percent in 1992 when the company went national and achieved distribution in bars and restaurants in forty-eight states. In a continual search for new beer ideas, Boston Beer added a stout, a wheat beer, and even a cranberry lambic, a type of beer flavored with fruit. Helping to fuel the growing popularity were the numerous industry awards and citations Samuel Adams had received since 1984. Not only was it voted the Best Beer in America four times at the annual Great American Beer Festival, but it received six gold medals in blind tastings.

In April 1994, Jim Koch and two of his brewmasters were testing their entry into the Great American Beer Festival—"Triple Bock." They had not yet tried to market this creation, although their expectations were high. But this was so different. It boasted a 17 percent alcoholic content with no carbonation, and they planned to package it in a cobalt bottle with a cork. It was meant to be sipped as a fine brandy. "It's a taste that nobody has ever put into a beer," Koch said.[3] Too innovative? Jim and his colleagues pondered this as they sipped on this beautiful spring day.

[3] McCune, "Brewing Up Profits," p. 20.

THE BREWING INDUSTRY IN THE 1990s

In ten years, Boston Beer had forged ahead to become a major contender in its industry and the largest U.S. specialty brewer. But a significant change in consumer preferences was confronting the industry in the 1990s. The big brands that had been so dominant, to the extent that smaller brewers could not compete against their production efficiencies, now were seeing their market shares decline. The brand images they had spent millions trying to establish were in trouble. Many were cutting prices in desperate attempts to keep and lure consumers. For example, special price promotions in some markets were offering twelve-packs of Budweiser, Coors, and Miller for just $1.99.

The shifting consumer preferences, and the severe price competition with their regular brands, were compelling the big brewers to seek the types of beers that would command higher prices. Imports were still strengthening, growing at an 11 percent rate between 1993 and 1994. But microbrews seemed the wave of the future, with prices and profit margins that were mouth-watering to the big barons of the industry.

Consequently, the major breweries came up with their own craft brands. For example, Icehouse, a name that conveys a microbrewery image, was actually produced in megabreweries by Miller Brewing. So, too, the pseudo-import Killian's Irish Red was made by Coors in Golden, Colorado. Killian's, stocked in retailer's import cases and commanding a high price, muscled its way abreast of Samuel Adams as the largest specialty beer in the United States.

The brewing industry was desperately trying to innovate. But no one saw anything revolutionary on the horizon, not like the 1970s when light beer made a significant breakthrough in the staid industry. Now, "ice" beers became the gimmick. First developed in Canada, these are beers produced at temperatures a little colder than ordinary beer. This gives them a slightly higher alcohol content. Whether because of this or the magic of the name "ice," these products captured almost 6 percent of total industry sales in 1994, more than all the imports combined. But, still, the potential was limited.

Anheuser-Busch, with a still-dominant 44 percent of U.S. beer sales despite its 9 percent sales volume slide in the early 1990s, asserted its reluctance to change: "The breweries that we have are designed to produce big brands. Our competition can't compete with big brands. That's why they've had to introduce lots of little brands."[4] But even Anheuser, despite its words, was sneaking into microbrewing by buying into Redhook Ale Brewery, a Seattle microbrewery that sold 76,000 barrels of beer in 1993, versus Anheuser's 90 million. Anheuser's distributors applauded this move as a badly needed step in giving them higher-profit, prestige brands. When Anheuser tiptoed into this market, other giants began to look for microbreweries to invest in.

This troubled Jim Koch: "I'm afraid of the big guys. They have the power to dominate any segment they want." Then he expressed his confidence: "Still, my faith is that better beer will win out."[5]

---

[4] Patricia Sellers, "A Whole New Ballgame in Beer," *Fortune*, September 19, 1994, p. 86.

[5] *Ibid.*

THE CONTINUING SAGA OF BOSTON BEER

In August 1995, Boston Beer announced an initial public stock offering (IPO) of 5.3 million shares, of which 990,000 shares would be made available directly to the public through a coupon offer. This selling of shares to the general public was unlike any other IPO, and as such caught the fancy of the national press.

The company put clip-and-mail coupons on Samuel Adams six-packs and other beer packages. These offered customers a chance to buy thirty-three shares of stock at a maximum price of $15, or $495 total. Only one subscription was allowed per customer, and these were honored on a first-come, first-served basis. The success was overwhelming. First distributed in October, by the first of November the offering was oversubscribed. The company expected that the total funds generated from the IPO would be $75 million.[6] But when the new stock offering finally came out on November 20, 1995, heavy demand led to it being priced at $20 a share. Two days later it was selling on the New York Stock Exchange for $30. Interestingly, its stock symbol is SAM.

Boston Beer was riding a high. It reported an impressive 50 percent growth in 1994 over 1993, brewing 700,000 barrels and becoming the largest microbrewery in the country. The entire microbrewing industry was producing more than double the volume that it was in 1990. By now Boston Beer had twelve different beers including six seasonals, and was distributing in all fifty states through 300 wholesalers. Its newest beer, the 17 percent alcohol content Triple Bock, had been introduced to the market.[7]

Most of Boston Beer's production continued to be contract brewed. In early 1995, it encountered difficulties with Pittsburgh Brewing, the first of the three contract breweries it was now using. Because of an alleged overdraft of $31 million by its owner, Michael Carlow, who was accused of fraud, the brewery was to be auctioned off. Jim Koch stoutly professed having no interest in buying the brewery and that any problems of Pittsburgh Brewery would have no affect on Boston Beer.[8]

See the following Information Box for a discussion of contracting out rather than building production facilities.

TOWARD THE MILLENNIUM

By 1998, Samuel Adams had become the seventh-largest brewer overall, and was the largest independent craft brewer, in the sector that had grown 39 percent in a five-year period while U.S. beer total shipments remained virtually flat. Samuel Adams Boston Lager, the company's flagship product, grew faster than the overall craft beer sector, and accounted for the majority of Boston Beer's sales in 1997.

For 1997, revenues were $184 million, down 3.8 percent from the year before, but a major increase from the $77 million in 1994, the year before Boston went public. Net income at $7.6 million was a decline of 9.9 percent from the year before, but this still compared favorably with $5.3 million in 1994.

[6] "Boston Beer's Plan for Offering Stock," *New York Times*, National Edition, August 26, 1995, p. 20.

[7] "Little Giants," *Beverage World*, December 1994, p. 26.

[8] "Sam Adams Brewer May Be On Block," *Boston Business Journal*, February 24, 1995, p. 3.

INFORMATION BOX

THE MERITS OF EXPANDING SLOWLY AND KEEPING FIXED COSTS TO A MINIMUM

There is much to be said for any enterprise, new or older, to keep its fixed overhead to a minimum. If it can escape having to commit large sums to physical plant and production facilities, its breakeven point is far less, which means that fewer sales are needed to cover expenses and interest payments, leaving more to go into profits. In the event of adversity, such a firm can retrench much more nimbly than if burdened with heavy overhead. In every such decision of renting or buying, the economics of the particular situation need to be carefully analyzed.

Arguments against such contracting out usually maintain that efficiency will be sacrificed since direct control is lacking. So, this argument would maintain that Pittsburgh Brewing could not do as good a job as Boston Beer could have done itself. Yet, the empirical evidence is that Boston's contract brewers were giving it the high standards it wanted. Boston Beer set the standards and insisted on their being met, or it would find another contract brewery.

Still, the "edifice complex" tantalizes most top executives, as it does hospital and school administrators, who see the stone and mortar of their buildings and factories as tangible evidence of their own importance and accomplishments. They will claim that such is important to the public image of their organization.

Given the approximately $100 million that Boston Beer received from its IPO, would you predict some of this would go for "stones and mortar"?

Boston Beer produced more than two dozen styles of beer, and was selling in all fifty states and several foreign countries. Its sales force was still the largest of any craft brewer, and one of the largest in the domestic beer industry.

The acute disappointment had to be the stock market valuation of its shares. An exuberant public reaction to the initial stock offering had bid the price up to $30 a share. Almost immediately, the share price began a slow decline. By late 1998, shares were trading around $8.

The situation had not improved significantly by the millennium. Indeed, the growth that had so bedazzled Koch and early investors seemed only an illusion. Samuel Adams had been the forefather of microbrews, but this specialty market had now spawned 3,000 microbrews, all competing within the $3 billion beer market—a market that represented just 3 percent of the U. S. beer market—with a mind-boggling array of ciders, ales, stouts, and so-called better beers. "After people got inundated with so many choices ... they kind of stepped back," said one industry analyst.[9]

[9] Hillary Chura, "Boston Beer Crafts Strategy: Slumping Brewer Abandons Some of Its Specialty Beers," *Advertising Age*, November 8, 1999, p. 20.

Koch drastically cut back his assortment of different brews, concentrating only on bestsellers: the flagship lager and four seasonal brews. He went through four advertising agencies in six years trying to find the right pitch, but without much success. Experts were wondering if Koch would eventually sell out to a big brewer such as Miller. By mid-2001, the stock price ranged from $8 to $10 a share, still a disaster for its IPO investors.

UPDATE

Table 22.1 shows the trend in revenues and net income for 1998 through 2002. Sales and profits show little growth trend during this five-year period. The stock price has ranged between $10 and $18 a share for 2003.

In August—National Beer Month—of 2002, Koch led a ten-city "Liquid Lunch" taste-test tour, pitting three Samuel Adams beers and local craft beers from each of the cities against leading international brews such as Heineken, Corona, and Guinness. The beers were scored according to appearance, aroma, flavor, mouthfeel, and overall impression. The taste testers included beer enthusiasts, consumers, journalists, and winners from local radio station promotions.

In one-on-one taste tests, Samuel Adams was preferred over the imports in all thirty blind taste-offs. Many of the local brews also bested their foreign competition. Koch's crusade against imports received a good promotional push. He declared: "These imports have been considered the world standards. ... But I believe when you take away the fancy bottles and marketing mystique of imported beer, you discover that Samuel Adams and other American brewers simply make better tasting beers."[10]

Table 22.1: Boston Beer Revenue and Net Income, 1998–2002 (in millions)

	1998	1999	2000	2001	2002
Revenue	$183.5	$176.8	$190.6	$186.8	$215.4
Net Income	7.9	11.1	11.2	7.8	8.6

Source: Company annual reports

Commentary: Here we see a company with practically no growth, even though revenue for 2002 was the highest ever. But it was not accompanied by the highest net income; that was back in 1999 and 2000. Yet these statistics do show a stable company, one comfortably established in its own niche. Unfortunately, this is little consolation for those investors who bought at the initial public stock offering (IPO) at $20 a share, or bought a few days later at $30 a share, expecting big growth.

[10] Boston Beer Company News, August 25, 2000, www.samadams.com.

ANALYSIS

Entrepreneurial Character

Although many entrepreneurial opportunities come in the retail and service industries, mostly because these typically require less start-up investment, Jim Koch saw the possibility in beer, even without a huge wallet. He started with $100,000 of his own money and $140,000 from friends and relatives. He had the beer recipe and the determination. By contracting out the production to an existing brewery with unused capacity, the bulk of the start-up money could be spent on nonproduction concerns, such as advertising.

His determination to gain acceptance of his beer, despite its high price and lack of foreign cachet, is characteristic of most successful entrepreneurs. They press on, despite obstacles in gaining acceptance. They have confidence that their product or concept is viable. They are not easily discouraged.

At the same time, Koch believed he had something unique, a flavor and quality that neither domestic nor imported brews could deliver. He had the audacity to further make his product unique by charging even higher prices than the imports, thus conveying an image of highest quality.

His search for uniqueness did not end with the product. He developed an advertising theme far different from that of other beers by stressing quality and aggressively attacking the imports: "Declare your independence from foreign beer."

And he was the spokesman on TV and radio commercials, giving a personal and charismatic touch.

As Boston Beer moved out of regional into national distribution, Koch developed a sales force as large as Anheuser-Busch, the giant of the industry. His grasping of uniqueness even went to Boston Beer's initial public stock offering, in which customers were invited to buy into the company through coupons on six-packs. And it was oversubscribed in only a few weeks.

Controlled Growth (Aggressive Moderation)

When demand seems to be growing insatiably, the temptation for any firm, but especially for newer, smaller firms, is to expand aggressively: "We must not miss this opportunity." Such optimism can sow the seeds of disaster, when demand suddenly lessens because of a saturated market and/or new competition. And our firm is left with too much plant and other fixed assets, and a burdensome overhead.

Controlled growth—we might also call this "aggressive moderation"—is usually far better. Now our firm is not shunning growth, even vigorous growth, but is controlling it within its present resources, not overextending itself. Boston Beer showed this restraint by expanding within its production capability, adding several more contract brewers as needed. It expanded market by market at the beginning, moving to a new geographical area only when it could supply it. First was Boston, then Washington, D.C., then New York, Chicago, California, and finally all fifty states.

Besides husbanding resources, both material and personnel, aggressive moderation is compatible with the tightness of controls needed to ensure high-quality product and service standards. Even more than this, moderation allows a firm to build the accounting and financial standards and controls needed to prevent the dangerous buildup of inventories and expenses.

Limits on Potential

It is difficult to perceive, in the heady days of growth for a new firm, that the growth potential is sorely limited without drastic and risky changes. Limits on potential usually are due to two factors:

> Ease of entry into the industry, which encourages a host of competitors. This turned out to be especially true with the influx of microbrewers, to 3,000 in just a few years.

> Finite potential in demand. (This also affected the high-tech industry and the collapse of the NASDAQ at the turn of the millennium.) Demand for specialty beer, while at first robust and rising, was certainly not going to take over the mainstream beer market.

Given the rush to microbreweries in an environment of limited demand, the aspirations of Jim Koch to be a dominant force in the brewing industry had to be curbed. He could still be a profitable firm and do well in his niche, but he would never be a challenge beyond that. Perhaps that is enough for most entrepreneurs. They can hardly expect to grasp the golden ring of complete market dominance.

WHAT CAN BE LEARNED?

The price-quality perception, again. We have a curious phenomenon today regarding price. More consumers than ever are shopping at discount stores because they supposedly offer better prices than other retailers. Airlines competing with lowest prices, such as Southwest and JetBlue, are clobbering higher-cost carriers. As is Dell with PCs. Yet for many products, especially those that are complex and have hidden ingredients, a higher price than competitors is the major indicator of higher quality. Boston Beer certainly confirms that higher price can successfully differentiate a firm. This is especially so if the taste is robustly different, and if the theme of highest quality is constantly stressed in advertising.

Perhaps the moral is that both low prices and high prices can be successful. A strategy of lowest prices, however, tends to be more vulnerable since competitors can so easily and quickly match these low prices (not always profitably, of course), while a high-price strategy stressing quality tends to attract less competitors. But it will also attract fewer customers, as with higher-priced goods such as office furniture. The high-price strategy should generally be more successful with products that are relatively inexpensive to begin with, such as beer, and ones where the image of prestige and good taste is attractive.

The challenge of the right approach to growth. In the analysis section we discussed the desirability of controlled growth or aggressive moderation and noted that Boston Beer practiced this well. There are some who would challenge such a slowness in grabbing opportunities. Exuberant expansion instead is advocated, when and if the golden opportunity is presented (some would call this "running with the ball"). Operations should be expanded as fast as possible in such a situation, some would say. But there are times when caution is advised.

Risks lie on all sides as we reach for these opportunities. When a market begins to boom and a firm is unable to keep up with demand without greatly increasing capacity and resources, it faces a dilemma: Stay conservative in the expectation that the burgeoning potential will be short-lived, and thereby abdicate some of the growing market to competitors, or expand vigorously and take full advantage of the opportunity. If the euphoria is short-lived, and demand slows drastically, the firm is then left with expanded capacity, more resource commitment than needed, high interest and carrying costs, and perhaps even jeopardized viability because of overextension. Above all, however, a firm should not expand beyond its ability to maintain organizational and accounting control over the operation. To do so is tantamount to letting a sailing ship brave the uncertainties of a storm under full canvas.

Keep the breakeven point as low as possible, especially for new ventures. Fixed investments in plant and equipment raise the breakeven point of sales needed to cover overhead costs and make a profit. Boston Beer kept its breakeven point low by using contract breweries. Now this would have been a mistake if the quality of production at these breweries was erratic or not up to Boston Beer expectations. These were indeed vital requirements if it were to succeed in selling its high-priced beer. But by working closely with experienced brewers, quality control apparently was no problem.

Certainly the lower breakeven point makes for less risk. And the future is always uncertain, despite research and careful planning. Mistakes will be made. The environment is constantly changing as to customer attitudes and preferences, and particularly in actions of competitors.

When a decision involves high stakes and an uncertain future—which translates into high risks—is it not wiser to approach the venture somewhat conservatively, not spurning the opportunity, but also not committing major resources and efforts until success appears more certain?

The importance of maintaining quality. For a high-priced product, a brief letdown in quality control can be disastrous to the image. The story is told of Jim Koch ordering a draft of his own Samuel Adams at a restaurant across from Lincoln Center in New York City. He was horrified at the taste. He called the manager and they went to the basement and looked at the keg. "It was two and a half months past its pull date." The manager quickly changed the past-its-prime keg, which the distributor, intentionally or not, had sold the restaurant.[11] Sometimes a lapse in quality is not the fault of the manufacturer, but of a distributor or dealer. Whoever

---

[11] Example related in McCune, "Brewing Up Profits," p. 16.

is at fault, the brand image is tarnished. And it is difficult to resurrect a reputation of poor or uncertain quality.

For investors, consider the risk of initial public offerings (IPOs). IPOs are often bid up to unreasonable prices in public enthusiasm with new offerings. While Boston Beer did well as a niche brewer, and dominated its niche, it has to be a major disappointment to its investors who bought in at the beginning. Perhaps the better investor strategy is to wait for public enthusiasm to calm down before taking a stake in a new enterprise.

CONSIDER

Can you think of other learning insights?

QUESTIONS

1. Have you ever tried one of the Boston Beer brews? If so, how did you like the taste? Did you think it was worth the higher price?

2. The investment community evidently thought Boston Beer had great growth probabilities to have bid up the initial price so quickly. Why do you suppose so many fell into this trap? Or was Jim Koch a poor executive in not bringing Boston Beer up to their expectations?

3. "The myriad specialty beers are but a fad. People will quickly tire of an expensive, strong-flavored beer. Much of it is just a gimmick." Discuss.

4. What problems do you see retailers facing with the burgeoning number of different beers today? What might be the implications of this?

5. Playing the devil's advocate (one who takes an opposing view for the sake of argument and deeper analysis), critique the strategy of charging some of the highest prices in the world for your beer.

6. We saw the detection of a problem with the freshness of a beer at a restaurant by Jim Koch himself. How can Boston Beer prevent such incidents from happening again? Can such distributor negligence or short-sighted actions be totally prevented by Boston Beer?

7. Do you think Boston Beer can continue to compete effectively against the giant brewers who are now moving with their infinitely greater resources into the specialty beer market with their own microbrews? Why or why not?

8. In 1998, Boston Beer produced more than two dozen styles of beer. Now it is down to just a few. Do you see any problems with this?

HANDS-ON EXERCISES

1. You are Jim Koch. You have just learned that Michael Feuer, founder of OfficeMax, described in Chapter 23, has grown his entrepreneurial endeavor to a $1.8 billion enterprise in just seven years. It has taken you ten

years to grow Boston Beer to a $50 million firm. You are depressed at this but determined to greatly increase your company's growth. How would you go about setting Boston Beer on this great growth path? Be as specific as you can. What dangers do you see ahead?

2. It is 1986 and Boston Beer is beginning its growth after hiring Pittsburgh Brewery to produce its beer. Jim Koch has charged you with coordinating the efforts at Pittsburgh Brewery, paying particular attention to assuring that your quality standards are rigidly maintained. How would you go about doing this?

TEAM DEBATE EXERCISE

Debate how Boston Beer should commit the $100 million it received in late 1995 from the public stock offering. In particular, debate whether the bulk of the proceeds should go to building its own state-of-the-art brewery, or something else. (For the group arguing for the brewery, do not be dissuaded by my comments about aggressive moderation. You should be able to muster a strong case for a state-of-the-art brewery.)

INVITATION TO RESEARCH

How is Boston Beer faring today? Has its expansion accelerated or stalled? Is it facing any particular problems? Has the stock price risen to the $30 initial issuance price? Are any merger rumors circulating?

CHAPTER TWENTY-THREE

OfficeMax: To the End

Michael Feuer had a passion to be an entrepreneur. He realized this passion was rather late in coming, but by age forty-two he was bored with the corporate life. Still, perhaps it had been there all along, this passion.

He had started with Fabri-Centers of America, a 600-store chain, seventeen years before, and had quickly rose through the ranks. He liked to describe himself in those days as suffering from the Frank Sinatra syndrome—"I wanted to do it my way." And he got tired of what he called CYB, "covering your backside," which he saw most executives spending too much of their time trying to do, at the expense of total effectiveness. If he only had his own business he could escape these drains on career satisfaction and constraints on his potential. However, he couldn't accept the common notion of the true entrepreneur as one who has enormous self-confidence, enough to give up the security of the paycheck and go off on his or her own. "I'm not a true entrepreneur because I suffer acutely from what I call 'F of F,' the fear of failure."[1]

In his pursuit of entrepreneurship, Feuer turned down a number of big-money corporate jobs and the perks that go with them. Increasingly he felt an overwhelming urge to be his own man, to succeed or fail on his own terms. He soon realized, however, the reality of starting a small business from scratch and the contrast with what might have been if he had chosen the corporate option.

THE START

Feuer found a partner, Robert Hurwitz, and the two recognized a flaw in the way office products were distributed and sold. The traditional channel of distribution for this merchandise was from manufacturers to wholesalers or distributors and finally to stationers, who were usually small retailers. This rather lengthy process imposed

---

[1] Until late 1993, little had been written about the success of OfficeMax. Much of the early material and quotes have come from speeches that Feuer made to various business and graduate business school classes.

markups at each stage of the distribution and resulted in relatively high prices for the end user. Feuer saw this as archaic, akin to the "old-time mom-and-pop groceries on every corner," which were eventually replaced by more efficient and much lower-priced supermarkets. These for the most part bypassed wholesalers and distributors and went directly to manufacturers.

Feuer and Hurwitz (who became no longer active in the firm on a full-time basis) were able to mass $3 million from fifty investors, some friends and family members as well as a number of doctors and lawyers. The two partners did not use any debt financing, nor did they seek venture capitalists. They shunned these most common sources of capital for new firms, not wanting to give up some control of their enterprise; neither did they want to answer to skeptics and defend every major decision. However, for many promising small businesses, venture capital can provide needed startup funds difficult to obtain otherwise. See the following Information Box for more discussion of venture capitalists and their role in fostering small enterprises.

While Feuer and Hurwitz recognized what seemed an attractive opportunity, they were not the only ones to do so. In May 1988, an industry trade paper listed all the embryonic firms in the emerging office products superstore industry. OfficeMax rated number fourteen on a list of fifteen. "We would have been dead last, but another company had started a week later than we did, although neither one of us had any stores."[2]

Feuer and Hurwitz established headquarters offices in a tiny 500-square-foot brick warehouse. It had little heat or air conditioning. The company owned only a few pieces of office furniture, a coffee-maker, and a copy machine, but no fax. The restroom had to be unisex since there was only space for one toilet. They had recruited seven people who were only half-jokingly told that they needed to have small appetites because there was little money to pay them. But Feuer promised that they would share in the financial success of the company, and for these seven their faith and hope for the future was enough. Feuer likes to tell the story of how he reinterviewed a candidate for a vice president's position who had turned him down in 1988. Had he accepted the job then he would have been a multimillionaire by 1993.

THE FIRST YEAR

Even with $3 million of seed money from the fifty investors, OfficeMax had limited resources for what it proposed to do. A major problem now was to convince manufacturers to do business with this upstart firm in Cleveland. Most manufacturers were satisfied with the existing distribution channels and were reluctant to grant credit to a revolutionary newcomer with hardly a store to its name.

The key to winning the support of these manufacturers lay in convincing them that OfficeMax had such a promising future that it could offer them far more business potential than they would ever have with their present distributors—that OfficeMax would soon be a 30-, 50-, even 300-store chain in a few years. "We explained to them that it was in *their* best interest to help us today—to guarantee a place with us tomorrow."

---

[2] John R. Brandt, "Taking It to the Max," *Corporate Cleveland* (September 1988), p. 17.

INFORMATION BOX

VENTURE CAPITALISTS: AID TO ENTREPRENEURS

The biggest roadblock to self-employment is financing. Banks tend to be unreceptive to funding unproven new ventures, especially for someone without a track record. Given that most would-be entrepreneurs have limited resources from which to draw, where are they to get the financing needed?

Feuer and Hurwitz bypassed conventional sources of financing by finding fifty willing investors. For many other would-be entrepreneurs venture capitalists may be the answer.

Venture capitalists are wealthy individuals (or firms) looking for extraordinary returns for their investments. At the same time, they are willing to accept substantial risks. Backing nascent entrepreneurs in speculative undertakings can be the route to a far greater return on investment than possible otherwise—provided that the venture capitalist chooses wisely who to stake. This decision is much easier after a fledgling enterprise has a promising start. Then venture capitalists may stand in line for a piece of the action. But until then, the entrepreneur may struggle to get seed money.

How do these sources of funding choose among the many business ideas brought to them? "They look at the people, not the ideas," says Arthur Rock, one of the foremost venture capitalists. "Nearly every mistake I've made has been because I picked the wrong people, not the wrong idea."[3]

For a would-be entrepreneur seeking venture capital, then, the most important step may be in selling yourself, in addition to your idea. Intellectual honesty is sometimes mentioned by venture capitalists as a necessary ingredient. This may be defined as a willingness to face facts rigorously and not be deluded by rosy dreams and unrealistic expectations.

Those who win the early support of venture capitalists will likely have to give away a good piece of the action. Should the enterprise prove successful, the venture capitalists will expect to share in the success. Indeed, the funds provided by a venture capitalist may be crucial to even starting, or they may mean the difference in being adequately funded or so poorly funded that failure is almost inevitable.

Selling a definitive business plan to a prospective venture capitalist is usually a requirement for such financing. In the process, of course, you are selling yourself. You may want to do this exercise. Choose a new business idea, develop an initial business plan, and attempt to persuasively present it to a would-be investor.

To make its message credible, OfficeMax needed to create an image of stability and of a firm poised to jump. To help convey this image, Feuer convinced a major Cleveland bank to grant the company an unsecured line of credit. There was only one condition: OfficeMax had to promise that it would never use it. But this impressive-looking line of credit, bespeaking the faith that a major bank seemingly had in the embryonic firm, brought respect from manufacturers. Then OfficeMax even went so far as to ask them for unheard-of terms of sale—such as 60, 90, even 120 days with a discount.

---

[3] John Merwin, "Have You Got What It Takes?" *Forbes* (August 3, 1981), p. 61.

Xerox was somehow persuaded to grant a year's payment delay for purchases. Many other manufacturers also accepted the outlandish requests. The bold promise of growth was realized, and many manufacturers five years later found OfficeMax to be their best customer. OfficeMax became so important at Xerox that the account became handled by a divisional president and chief financial officer.

The first store was opened July 5, 1988, three months after the enterprise itself was started. This was an amazingly short time to fine-tune the concept, find a site, remodel as needed, and merchandise and staff the store. Feuer explains that the firm urgently needed some cash to survive, hence the desperate efforts to bring the first unit on line. In addition to providing needed cash flow, the first store had to confirm the viability and promise of the superstore concept to investors and suppliers alike.

This the first store quickly did. Customers eagerly embraced the great variety yet lowest prices of the superstore, more commonly known today as a category killer store for office products. The only publicity had been a newspaper story two days before. Yet, the store racked up $6,400 in sales that first day.

In the next ninety days, stores two and three were opened, also in metropolitan Cleveland. The fourth store opened in Detroit, not far from the executive offices of Kmart, destined a few years later to become a majority shareholder. Within six months the company was breaking even before corporate expenses.

As Feuer describes his work schedule in those early days, he typically was in the corporate office from 7:00 A.M. to 7:00 P.M., stopping at his home just long enough to change into nondescript clothing before going to the first store, where he could inconspicuously observe the shopping activity and talk to customers, asking them what they liked and didn't like about the store. He likes to recount how he would even follow customers who left without buying anything out to the parking lot to ask them why OfficeMax did not meet their needs.

Following the example of Feuer, from its inception the company has had a strong commitment to its customers. For example, OfficeMax accepted collect calls from customers. Any complaints had to be resolved in less than twenty-four hours, complete with an apology from OfficeMax. The company's objective was to build loyalty. "We're not embarrassed to say that we were wrong—and the customer was right."

As the company began making a small profit, Feuer's worst nightmare was that the accounting had been "screwed up," and that OfficeMax was on the verge of bankruptcy without realizing it. With this tormenting thought, he went back to the existing shareholders after six months to raise additional capital. The early success of the enterprise enabled them to raise the per share price 75 percent over the original placement.

By the end of the first full year, OfficeMax had six stores operational in Ohio and Michigan, with total sales of $13 million. The stores were profitable due to undeviating cost-consciousness.

GROWTH CONTINUES

By early 1990, two years into the operation, OfficeMax had seventeen stores in operation. Unexpectedly, Montgomery Ward proposed a merger between OfficeMax and Office World, a similar operation that Ward had funded along with a number of venture capitalists. Office World had been started with what seemed to OfficeMax executives as almost a king's ransom. But it proceeded to lose $10 million in a very short time. In the negotiations, OfficeMax was in the power position, and it acquired Office World and its seven Chicago locations on rather attractive terms: Its major concession was to relinquish two of its ten board seats to Montgomery Ward and the venture capitalists, but it acquired along with the stores several million dollars in badly needed cash.

By the summer of 1990, OfficeMax had about $25 million in cash, with thirty stores in operation. It raised another $8 million in a third private placement, at a share price 600 percent higher than the original investors had paid just two years before. Corporate offices were now moved into a building with space for both men's and women's restrooms.

Feuer began an aggressive new expansion program, calling for opening twenty additional stores. Competition was heating up in this new superstore industry, and several competitors had gone public to raise funds for more rapid expansion. Several others had gone bankrupt.

The Kmart Connection

The biggest threat facing OfficeMax now came from news that Kmart was poised to roll out its new Office Square superstore chain, which would be a direct threat to OfficeMax. With all the resources of Kmart—financial, managerial, and real estate expertise and influence—Feuer and company saw themselves being crushed and driven into Lake Erie. Feuer consoled himself that being left penniless would at least be character building.

Mostly as a defensive strategy, Feuer sought to open talks with Kmart. Kmart top executives proved to be receptive, and in November 1990, an agreement was negotiated in which Kmart made an investment of about $40 million in return for a 22 percent equity stake in OfficeMax. As a part of the agreement, the feared Office Square became a possession of OfficeMax, and Kmart received one seat on the OfficeMax board.

Now the expansion program could begin accelerating, with Kmart's full cooperation and support. So good was the rapport that within ten months of the initial transaction, discussions were started concerning a broader business relationship with Kmart.

As the original goals of the business were being realized, it was perhaps time to cash in some of the chips, Michael Feuer thought. Two options seemed appropriate for the original investors: (1) go public, or (2) structure a new deal with Kmart. The company decided to go with Kmart. Kmart agreed to buy out all of the shareholders, with the exception of 50 percent of the shares of Feuer and partner Hurwitz, for a total market capitalization of about $215 million. This was up from zero just forty-two months earlier. What made the deal particularly attractive was the fact that while 92 percent of OfficeMax was sold to a well-heeled parent, it could still retain total autonomy.

Onward and Upward, Without Kmart

By the end of July 1995, OfficeMax had 405 superstores in more than 150 markets in 41 states and Puerto Rico. The typical store was 23,500 square feet and had 6,000 items. Faster growth had been achieved through two major acquisitions: the 46-store Office Warehouse chain and the 105-store BizMart chain.

Sales were primarily to small and medium-sized businesses employing between 1 and 100 employees, home office customers, and individual consumers. But institutions such as school boards and universities were also targets, and the low prices of OfficeMax were a powerful inducement. A new program was established for next-day delivery of office supplies, based on calls to telephone centers with toll-free lines.

The company was planning to open up to twenty new FurnitureMax stores, which were to be 8,000 to 10,000 square feet additions to existing OfficeMax stores devoted to office furniture. It also was testing five to ten new CopyMax stores. Along with a multimedia advertising strategy, the company now had a 220-page merchandise catalog featuring about 5,000 items with toll-free telephone ordering.

Meanwhile, Kmart was seeking additional money to provide badly needed facelifts for its stores in the desperate attempt to hold off the mighty Wal-Mart. This led Kmart to sell its 25 percent share of OfficeMax, as well as some of its other subsidiaries, in order to raise a needed $3 billion in cash. This was finalized in July 1995. OfficeMax sold through underwriters 24,555,375 common shares, including all of the 18,803,526 shares held by Kmart, at $19.875 a share. OfficeMax itself netted $110 million to be used to fund its store expansion. Its future as a public company rather than a subsidiary of Kmart now presented a heady dream to Feuer and his investors. The following Information Box discusses the prescription for great wealth in going public.

By fiscal 1995 (year ending January 31), revenues were over $1.8 billion. Net income was $30.4 million, up 181 percent from the year before. Figures 23.1 and 23.2 show the growth in sales and in number of stores.

INFORMATION BOX

THE PRESCRIPTION FOR GREAT WEALTH FOR ENTREPRENEURS

An entrepreneur often has much to gain by going public with an enterprise after a few years if it shows early success and a promising future. The entrepreneur keeps a portion of the stock and offers the rest to the public. With an attractive new venture, the offering price may be high enough to make the entrepreneur an instant multimillionaire.

Take Office Depot, for example. This was the largest office supply superstore chain in North America, although it is not that much bigger than OfficeMax. It was listed on the New York Stock Exchange and its 94,143,455 shares of common stock sold for about $39 a share, giving a total market value of about $3.7 billion. If OfficeMax went public and had a similar relative market value and if Feuer and Hurwitz held 8 percent of the total capitalization, they would be worth about $296 million or almost $150 million apiece.

What rationale do you see for Feuer's decision to structure a new deal with Kmart rather than go public? Do you agree with his rationale?

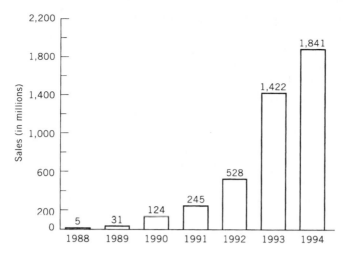

Figure 23.1 Sales growth (fiscal years ending Jan. 31 of the next year). In 1988, OfficeMax projected 1993 sales of less than $100 million; actual 1993 sales were fourteen times larger.

STORM CLOUDS

In 1996, OfficeMax became only the fourth company up to that time to exceed $3 billion in revenues in less than nine years. As of September 1998, it had 769 stores in 48 states and Puerto Rico. Through joint ventures, it also had nine stores in Mexico and a first store in Japan. In addition, there were 129 CopyMax outlets

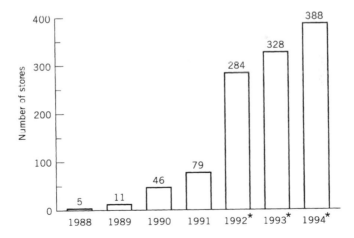

Figure 23.2 Growth in number of stores (fiscal years ending Jan. 31 of the next year). OfficeMax's 1988 business plan called for fifty stores by 1993; the company ended the year with nearly seven times that number.

*Includes BizMart stores.

targeting the estimated $9 billion "print-for-pay" industry, as well as 129 FurnitureMax stores tapping the estimated $12 billion office furniture industry.[4]

In 1999, it planned to open 120 new superstores in the United States on top of the 150 opened in 1998. Revenues had steadily climbed to $3.765 billion in 1997, while net income had grown to $89.6 million, an increase of 30 percent from 1996.[5] Over the three-year period from January 31, 1994 to January 31, 1997, OfficeMax's market share compared to its largest competitor, Office Depot, rose from 30.1 percent to 35.9 percent, as shown below:

	Fiscal Year 1997	1994
Office Depot revenues	$6.716 billion	$4.266 billion
OfficeMax revenues	3.765	1.841
Market share of OfficeMax relative to Office Depot	35.9%	30.1%

Yet, OfficeMax's stock price had fallen precipitously to under $10 a share by September 1998. By late 1998, analysts began attacking OfficeMax: It was showing up more poorly than competitors Office Depot and Staples. In particular, sales were lagging at its older stores, and OfficeMax warned that third- and fourth-quarter earnings would not hit expectations, mostly because of heavy price-cutting on computers. Critics were quick to point out that Office Depot and Staples were not so adversely affected.[6] Was this just a temporary aberration?

The situation was to worsen, as businesses began cutting back in a slowing economy in 2000, and the office-supply industry faced an oversaturated market: too many stores from years of vigorous expansion in the 1990s.

The fourth quarter of 2000, which should have been the strongest quarter of the year, was particularly nasty. OfficeMax posted an $85 million loss, while Office Depot and Staples posted $168 million and $112 million losses respectively. All announced sharp cuts in expansion and closings of underperforming stores. OfficeMax, now grown to 995 stores, planned fifty store closings.[7] Company stock was trading around $2 a share.

ANALYSIS

Here we see what initially was an outstanding entrepreneurial success. The growth rate in only a few years rivaled the best at that time. In the same year that OfficeMax was started, 685,095 other new businesses were also formed in the United States, but

---

[4] *1998 OfficeMax Annual Report.*

[5] *Ibid.*

[6] For example, Teresa Dixon Murray, "Office Max Predicts Shortfall in Earnings," *Cleveland Plain Dealer* (October 7, 1998), pp. 1C, 2C; and "OfficeMax Opens New Stores While Sales Lag at Old Ones," *Cleveland Plain Dealer* (October 29, 1998), p. 2C.

[7] Mya Frazier, "Bad Day at the Office [Supplier]," *Cleveland Plain Dealer* (March 7, 2001), p. C1.

more than half of these eventually failed. Of the survivors, only a small percentage would ever achieve a net worth over $50 million. Only a handful would ever reach $200 million. What made OfficeMax so uniquely successful?

It was not that it had identified a great idea and nurtured it exclusively. While OfficeMax launched on to a business opportunity arising from the archaic distribution structure of the office-supplies industry, it was far from unique in this identification. Indeed, the concept of category-killer stores was in the ascendancy for all kinds of retail goods.[8] The competition could become intense when category-killer stores competed with each other. Eventually, only three chains of superstores remained in the office-products industry, and OfficeMax was one of these, although the smallest. Why did OfficeMax succeed so well, while most of its competitors failed or were acquired?

Much of the success was due to the efforts of the principal founder, Michael Feuer. His vision was to retain control of the nascent enterprise by shunning venture capitalists and debt financing. While the money initially raised, $3 million, would seem adequate for most ventures, for a category-killer chain it was barely sufficient. But severe austerity combined with the promise of great future rewards motivated both employees and suppliers. This required optimism and an enthusiastic selling job by Feuer. And it also required a trusting relationship with investors, employees, and suppliers.

Great attention to customer service, to cost containment to the point of austerity, to the myriad details needed for opening stores with adequate employees and merchandise in severe deadline situations—all of these were part of the success package.

Building on the growth without losing sight of the austerity heritage was perhaps even more important as the enterprise grew from a few stores to twenty, fifty, and more.

Of particular interest for any growing enterprise is the opportunity to make attractive acquisitions of former competitors who have fallen into desperate straits. The successful firm is in a position to quickly build on the bones of former competitors who could not make it.

Alas, some of the early virtues of austerity and moderate borrowing (and consequent modest interest expenses) were disregarded in the heady rush to expansion in the late 1990s. A saturated market and an economic slowdown forced retrenchment, not only for OfficeMax but for its bigger competitors as well.

THE END

On July 14, 2003, OfficeMax announced that it had agreed to be acquired by Boise Cascade Corp., a big lumber and paper company. In a $1.15 billion buyout, OfficeMax shareholders would get $9 a share, about a 25 percent premium over the current share price. Feuer himself would stand to make $22.3 million from the shares he held, in addition to at least five years of his $983,000 salary for having a consulting role in the new operation.

Feuer had actively sought a buyer since Fall 2002, having concluded that he had taken the company about as far as he could with his resources, and with being the

---

[8] A *category-killer* store gets its name from the strategy of carrying such a huge assortment of merchandise at good prices in a particular category of goods that they practically destroy traditional merchants of such goods.

smallest firm in office-products retailing. In spite of all his efforts, OfficeMax had had eight losing quarters before regaining profitability in late 2002. He felt worst about those investors who had enthusiastically joined him when he took his enterprise public in 1994. Their faith in him was largely unrewarded, and many of these investors were his friends, and they had paid $19 a share then. In the bad days of 2000 and 2001, their shares had sunk 92 percent to $1.56 at the lowest point. Perhaps he had been too ambitious, had opened too many stores, more than OfficeMax was able to assimilate. These brought a hefty debt load that became an unhealthy burden. Now he had finally turned the company to profitability, but the stock price remained only a fraction of what it had been a few years earlier, and was well below the $19 a share many of these people paid.

Feuer reflected on the drawbacks of being a distant third in a strongly competitive industry. He had never been able to gain a foothold with the large customers his rivals had. No, his main customer base was consumers and small businesses; the profitable volume was just not there.

Boise had been endeavoring to move away from the severe price competition of being a commodity supplier to distributors, and get into the more profitable business of selling paper products to end users. It had already made more than forty acquisitions in recent years to expand its office products business, and it offered the potential of tapping into the larger customer base.

Would this turn out to be one of the few mergers "made in heaven" or another of the ill-fated ones? At least Feuer came out of his fifteen years of entrepreneurship a very wealthy man.[9]

WHAT CAN BE LEARNED?

Successful entrepreneurship is not easy. Not many who opt to go into business for themselves expect this to be an easy road, a comfortable and lazy lifestyle. Yet the work ethic of successful entrepreneurs can be awesome, even for those prepared for long hours and worries in the night. Michael Feuer customarily put in twelve to eighteen-hour days between corporate headquarters and keeping in close touch with stores and customers and suppliers. He would wake up at 3 A.M. to stare at the ceiling while wondering if he made the right decision. He felt a responsibility to his employees, even after they had grown from the seven original ones whose jobs depended on his decisions. By the end of 1993, he had more than 19,000 reasons to worry in the night.

Would he have been less successful with a more moderate work ethic? Maybe. But the personal stake in a growing business drives many entrepreneurs to become workaholics even to the point of sacrificing other aspects of their lives, including family.

[9] Jim Carlton, "Boise Cascade Expects OfficeMax to Shore Up Profit, *Wall Street Journal,* July 15, 2003, p. B5; Teresa Dixon Murray and Janet H. Cho, "Michael Feuer Drove OfficeMax and Himself," *Cleveland Plain Dealer,* July 20, 2003, pp. A1 and A10.

There is power in a growth image, even if it is only an illusion. In perhaps one of the most crucial moves taken in the early and most vulnerable months of the embryonic enterprise, Feuer and his people were able to sell both bankers and manufacturers on the great growth prospects for the company, that "we would rapidly become a 20-, 50-, or even 300-store chain. We explained that it was in *their* best interest to help us today—to guarantee a place with us tomorrow."

What makes a strong growth company so attractive to investors, creditors, suppliers, and employees? Part of the attractiveness certainly is that everyone likes to be associated with a winner. The greatest appeal of growth companies is their economic promise. This embraces investors, of course, because their investment grows with the business. Creditors and suppliers see more and more business coming their way as the company grows ever larger. And employees see great career opportunities continually opening up in a rapidly growing organization.

Perhaps in creating the image of OfficeMax as a company on the threshhold of great growth, Feuer was simply very persuasive. But perhaps many of the people he talked with were so eager to be convinced and to be offered the opportunity to get in on the ground floor of what might be the stuff of dreams that they would accept even grandiose conjecture.

Go the extra miles in customer relations. It is easy for an organization to proclaim its dedication to customer service and good customer relations. Too often, however, such is only lip service, pious pronouncements without real substance. OfficeMax went far beyond lip service. Feuer and his executives, at least in the early years, sought close contact with customers in stores, even to the point of following them to the parking lot to see what might have been lacking in the merchandise or service that discouraged a purchase. The company accepted collect calls from customers who might have problems or complaints or special needs. A promise of satisfaction of all complaints within twenty-four hours, the guiding "How can we make you happy?" question in all customer dealings, and readiness to apologize, attest to a customer commitment beyond the ordinary. With few exceptions, all businesses depend on customer loyalty and repeat business for their success. Perhaps in office products, where many customers are businesses, customer loyalty is all the more important. But it is easy to delude yourself and an organization that the loss of any single customer is not all that important, and that the firm must guard against being taken advantage of by unreasonable customers. Where should a firm, particularly a retailer, draw the line? Can any retailer be too liberal in the handling of customer complaints?

Again, the power of "lean and mean." In several earlier cases we noted problems of bloated bureaucracies and/or uncontrolled spending, and the dire effect on profitability. We examined several highly successful firms, notably Dell Computer and Vanguard, that followed a policy of continued frugality despite increasing size. The temptation with great growth is to let down the barriers and open the spending spigots. OfficeMax resisted this urge in the early years, but then got caught up in the frenzy of opening stores as fast as it could.

Again, dedicated employees can give a powerful advantage. OfficeMax in its early years was able to stimulate employees to move beyond individual concerns to a higher level of performance, a true team approach. This dedication, and the vague promise of future great expectations, brought employees to OfficeMax for very low wages, some turning down much higher paying jobs for the dream that might or might not come to pass. The dedication of these employees made possible opening the first store from scratch barely three months after the company was founded, with other stores quickly following.

The hope for great growth, a trusted leader, and an organization geared to a team effort seem to be most compatible in producing dedicated employees. One suspects there is also a close relationship in lean-and-mean organizations, where limited bureaucracy and management levels bring ease of communication. Unfortunately for a maturing OfficeMax, such motivational factors began to wane. The hope for great growth had to be more soberly appraised in a competitive environment where OfficeMax was number three behind two other aggressive competitors and in an almost-saturated market.

Beware market saturation. How many office-supply superstores can one metro area handle and still enable all outlets to prosper? Especially when there is little to choose from among the major competitors? OfficeMax, Staples, and Office Depot all have large box stores, widest possible assortment of goods, and reasonably low prices, and all push employees to be friendly, knowledgeable, and to provide the best possible service. In such an environment with little distinctiveness possible, market saturation or overstoring becomes a real problem. It hurts profitability, until weaker competitors leave the market, and certainly curbs the growth potential.

CONSIDER

Can you identify other learning insights coming from this case?

QUESTIONS

1. In the hiring process, how would you identify candidates who are most likely to become dedicated employees?
2. Can a firm be too liberal in handling customer complaints?
3. "OfficeMax is number three in its industry. This is a severe disadvantage, as it can never match the resources of its two larger competitors." Evaluate this assertion.
4. Do you think Feuer was being entirely ethical when he sold manufacturers on the desirability of doing business with OfficeMax in the very early days of the company? Why or why not?
5. Do you see any limitations to the future of category-killer stores?
6. Can you think of some types of merchandise where category-killer stores are unlikely to be successful?
7. Feuer regularly put in twelve to eighteen-hour days in the early years. Do you think he would have been as successful with less of a work ethic? Why or why not?

8. Do a SWOT analysis—analyzing strengths and weaknesses, opportunities and threats (see Chapter 22) for OfficeMax. What do you conclude as far as future prospects?

9. Would you like to work for OfficeMax today? (You may want to do a little investigation of job opportunities there to support your position.)

HANDS-ON EXERCISES

1. You own a small office-supply store. Business has been steady and sufficient for a good living for you and your family up to now. Now an OfficeMax has opened less than a mile away. Discuss how you possibly can compete against such a superstore when you cannot come close to matching their variety of goods or their prices.

2. You are the assistant to Feuer. He wants you to draw up plans for targeting large institutions and businesses. Be as specific as you can, making assumptions where needed, and persuasively support your recommendations.

TEAM DEBATE EXERCISE

On October 25, 1995, the largest office-products retailer, Office Depot, announced it was planning to open a dozen stores on OfficeMax's home turf, metropolitan Cleveland, where OfficeMax has its headquarters and seventeen stores. "When we enter a major market, our usual policy is to go in rather quickly and saturate the market with six to a dozen to twenty stores within the first couple of years," Office Depot said. Michael Feuer was unfazed. "We think the advantage we have is such a fierce sense and focus of local pride. I don't think there will be much of a test," he said. Debate the challenge OfficeMax now faces: It should be badly worried, because the market already is close to saturation; it should not be worried since the market potential is still increasing and it can outperform Office Depot.[10]

INVITATION TO RESEARCH

1. How has Boise's acquisition of OfficeMax gone in the opinions of the press and other experts? Has Boise instituted any major changes with OfficeMax? Has the headquarters been moved from Cleveland?

2. Feuer was fifty-eight at the time of the agreement to merge. Has he taken money and gone into self-satisfied retirement?

[10] Bill Lubinger, "Office Depot Is Taking on OfficeMax," *Cleveland Plain Dealer* (October 25, 1995), p. C1.

CHAPTER TWENTY-FOUR

What Can Be Learned?

*I*n considering mistakes, three things are worth noting: (1) Even the most successful organizations make mistakes but survive as long as they maintain a good "batting average" of satisfactory decisions; (2) mistakes should be effective teaching tools for avoiding similar errors in the future, and (3) firms can bounce back from adversity, and turnaround.

We can make a number of generalizations from these mistakes and successes. Of course we recognize that management is a discipline that does not lend itself to laws or axioms; exceptions to every principle or generalization can be found. Still, the decision maker does well to heed the following insights. For the most part they are based on specific corporate experiences and are transferable to other situations and other times.

INSIGHTS REGARDING OVERALL ENTERPRISE PERSPECTIVES

Importance of Public Image

The impact, for good or bad, of an organization's public image was a common thread through a number of cases—for example, Continental, Harley Davidson, United Way, Boston Beer, Perrier, Johnson & Johnson, and the Ford Explorer and Firestone tires.

Continental Airlines is a case for hope. It shows that a reputation in the pits, not only with employees but with the general public, can be resurrected and revitalized, even over a short period of time, but it takes inspired leadership to do so. And this its new CEO, Gordon Bethune, supplied.

Harley Davidson, the cycle maker, showed an image turnaround also, only it took decades to accomplish. The image of the black-jacketed motorcyclist was originally a disaster, but in the 1980s this turned around to become even a status symbol. Harley executives helped develop the new mystique, and then exploited it.

The nonprofit United Way was brought to its knees by revelations about the excesses of its longtime chief executive, William Aramony. Donations dwindled and local chapters withheld funds from the national organization as the reputation of the largest charitable organization was sullied.

Johnson & Johnson gained a great image of undeviating concern for its customers, regardless of cost. At the other extreme, both Ford and Firestone showed their callousness and refusal to take responsibility for product deficiencies that resulted in hundreds of deaths.

Other examples of capitalizing on a positive image were Vanguard and Boston Beer. On the other hand, Perrier and MetLife let their images slip.

The importance of a firm's public image is undeniable, yet some firms continue to disregard this and either act in ways detrimental to image or else ignore the constraints and opportunities that a reputation affords.

Power of the Media

We have seen or suspected the power of the media in a number of cases. Coca-Cola, United Way, Perrier, and Ford and Firestone are obvious examples. This power is often used critically—to hurt a firm's public image. The media can fan a problem or exacerbate an embarrassing or imprudent action. In particular, media focus can trigger the herd instinct, in which increasing numbers of people join in protests and public criticism. And the media in their zeal can sometimes cross the line, as did the media in England in denigrating Maytag for the ill-advised promotion of its Hoover Europe subsidiary.

We can make these generalizations regarding image and its relationship with the media:

1. It is desirable to maintain a stable, clear-cut image and undeviating objectives.

2. It is difficult and time consuming to upgrade an image.

3. In order to satisfy negative media mindset, in dire circumstances new top management may be needed if image is to be more quickly upgraded.

4. A good image can be quickly lost if a firm relaxes in an environment of aggressive competition, or else has an episode of product-safety concerns.

5. Well-known firms, and not-for-profit firms dependent on voluntary contributions, are especially vulnerable to critical public scrutiny and must use great care in safeguarding their reputations.

No Guarantee of Success

That success does not guarantee continued success or freedom from adversity is a sobering realization that must come from examining these cases. Many of the mistakes occurred in notably successful organizations, such as Harley Davidson, Euro Disney, Boeing, Maytag, MetLife, United Way, even Coca-Cola and Pepsi. How could things go so badly for such firms conditioned to success? The three C's mind-set offers an explanation for this perversity.

The Three Cs Mind-set

We can also call this the "king of the hill" syndrome. With such an organizational climate, success actually brings vulnerability. The three C's—complacency, conservatism, and conceit—can blanket leading organizations. To avoid this, a constructive attitude of never underestimating competitors can be fostered by

- Bringing fresh blood into the organization for new ideas and different perspectives

- Establishing a strong and continuing commitment to customer service and satisfaction—this should be more than just lip service

- Conducting periodic corporate self-analyses designed to detect weaknesses as well as opportunities in their early stages

- Continually monitoring the environment and being alert to any changes (more about this later)

The environment is dynamic, sometimes with subtle and hardly recognizable changes, at other times with violent and unmistakable changes. To operate in this environment, an established firm must be on guard to defend its position.

Adversity Need Not Be Forever

Just as a dominant firm can lose its momentum and competitive position, so can a faltering organization be turned around. If a faltering firm can at least maintain some semblance of viability, then it has hope. Continental Airlines and Harley Davidson are examples of such comebacks.

PLANNING INSIGHTS

What Should Our Business Be?

An organization's business, its mission and purpose, should be thought through, spelled out clearly, and well communicated by those involved in policy making. Otherwise, the organization lacks unified and coordinated objectives, which is akin to trying to navigate without a map.

Good judgment suggests choosing safe rather than courageous goals. But in the heady optimism for high-techs in the 1990s, few such firms could resist the temptation to go for the moon, and spend and plan accordingly with no semblance of frugality. Rather, we suggested controlled growth (aggressive moderation) for firms as they plan their growth, and Boston Beer exemplified this.

Determining what a firm's business is or should be gives a starting point for specifying goals. Several elements help with this determination.

The firm's resources and distinctive abilities and strengths should play a major role in determining its goals. It is not enough to wish for a certain status or position if resources and competence do not warrant this. To take an extreme example, a railroad company can hardly expect to transform itself into an airline, even though both may be in the transportation business. A Wal-Mart is hardly likely to successfully imitate a Neiman Marcus.

Environmental and competitive opportunities ought to be considered. The initial inroads of foreign carmakers in the United States stemmed from environmental opportunities for energy-efficient vehicles at a time when U.S. carmakers had ignored this area. Vanguard found opportunity in lower expense ratios for its mutual funds than the rest of the fund industry was willing or able to match. Dell Computer, with its lower overhead, came to dominate the PC market by offering its PCs at lower prices than anyone else could match and still make a profit. McDonald's for almost half a century dominated the fast food industry by its highest standards for quality, service, and cleanliness that its competitors could not seem to match.

The Right Growth Orientation

The opposite of a growth commitment is a status quo philosophy, one uninterested in expansion or the problems and work involved. Harley Davidson was content, despite being pushed around by foreign competitors, until eventually a new management reawakened it decades later.

In general, how tenable is a low-growth or no-growth philosophy? Although at first glance it seems workable, such a philosophy sows the seeds of its own destruction. More than four decades ago the following insight was pointed out:

> Vitality is required even for survival; but vitality is difficult to maintain without growth, at least in the American business climate. The vitality of a firm depends on the vigor and ambition of its members. The prospect of growth is one of the principal means by which a firm can attract able and vigorous recruits.[1]

Consequently, a firm not obviously growth-minded finds it difficult to attract able people. Customers see a growing firm as reliable, eager to please, and constantly improving. As we saw with OfficeMax, suppliers and creditors tend to give preferential treatment to a growth-oriented firm because they hope to retain it as a customer and client when it reaches large size.

But emphasizing growth can be carried too far. The growth must be kept within the abilities of the firm to handle. Cases such as McDonald's and Vanguard showed how firms can grow rapidly without losing control. But we also have the bungled growth efforts of Maytag's Hoover Division in the United Kingdom, where controls were loosened far too much for a foreign subsidiary. Not to be outdone, we saw the unethical growth climate at MetLife. Good financial judgment and decent ethical behavior must not be sacrificed to the siren call of growth. With relatively new firms, growth can easily outpace management competence and the ability to effectively utilize mass infusions of investment capital. OfficeMax, in its desire to become a bigger factor in its industry, destroyed its profitability.

---

[1] Wroe Alderson, *Marketing Behavior and Executive Action* (Homewood, IL.: Irwin, 1957), p. 59.

In our championing of aggressive moderation, we can make these generalizations about the most desirable growth perspectives:

1. Growth targets should not exceed the abilities and resources of the organization. Growth at any cost—especially at the expense of profits and financial stability —should be shunned. In particular, tight controls over inventories and expenses should be established, and performance should be monitored closely.

2. The most prudent approach to growth is to keep the organization and operation as simple and uniform as possible, to be flexible in case sales do not meet expectations, and to seek a low breakeven point, especially for new and untried ventures.

3. Rapidly expanding markets pose dangers from both too conservative and overly optimistic sales forecasts. The latter may overextend resources and jeopardize viability should demand contract; the former opens the door to more aggressive competitors. There is no right answer to this dilemma, but management should be aware of the risks and the rewards of both extremes.

4. A strategy emphasizing rapid growth should not neglect other aspects of the operation. For example, older stores should not be ignored in the quest to open new outlets, as OfficeMax was in danger of in its rapid opening of new stores. The giant aircraft producer Boeing found itself unable to cope with burgeoning demand partly because of too much attention given to assimilating McDonnell Douglas.

5. Decentralized management is more compatible with rapid growth than centralized, because it puts less strain on home office executives. However, delegation must have well-defined standards and controls as well as competent subordinates. Otherwise, the Maytag Hoover fiasco may be repeated.

6. The integrity of the product and the firm's reputation must not be sacrificed in pursuit of rapid growth. This is especially important when customers' health and safety may be jeopardized.

Search for Uniqueness

Most firms seek some differential advantage or uniqueness over existing competitors. Some never find it, or they rely on gimmicks, such as a new package or some product feature of little consequence to customers. All the successes we examined had uniqueness: Boston Beer, McDonald's, Vanguard, Dell, even Harley Davidson at last, with its fortuitous mystique.

Uniqueness, though, may not be long lasting. Snapple, the ill-fated acquisition of Quaker Oats, soon found the uniqueness that had permitted a higher price waning. Perrier, the premium bottled water, found publicity about contamination at a plant destroying its advantage. Boston Beer faced the constant danger of losing its premium product advantage. Even McDonald's, for decades unique in its control of product quality and service, became no longer unique among its competitors.

So, uniqueness is widely sought, but not always achieved nor lasting. It is a mistake to believe that uniqueness has to come from a distinctive product. It can come from simply doing some things better, such as service, quality control, dependability, or efforts toward pleasing customers.

We can make these generalizations regarding finding opportunities and strategic niches:

1. Opportunities often exist when a traditional way of doing business has prevailed in the industry for a long time—maybe the climate is ripe for a change.

2. Opportunities often exist when present firms are not completely satisfying customers' needs.

3. Innovations are not limited to products but can involve customer services as well as such things as methods of distribution.

4. For industries with rapidly changing technologies—usually new industries— heavy research and development expenditures are usually required if a firm is to avoid falling behind its competitors. But heavy R&D expenditures do not guarantee being in the forefront, as shown by Dell Computer's competitors.

Power of Judicious Imitation

Some firms are reluctant to copy successful practices of their competitors; they want to be leaders, not followers. But successful practices or innovations may need to be copied if a firm is not to be left behind. Sometimes the imitator outdoes the innovator. Success can lie in doing the ordinary better than competitors.

Michael Feuer with OfficeMax took a similar format of other category-killer stores, but did things better, at least in the beginning. On the other hand, many competitors of McDonald's long ignored its successful format, even though the high standards and rigid controls were obvious to all. The same has been true of the great values of Vanguard and Dell. These two firms defy competitors to match their prices and efficiency. Admittedly, it is not easy to develop high standards and to insist that they be followed, or to become so efficient that prices can be lowered to the point where competitors cannot match them without losing money. We can make this generalization: It makes sense for a company to identify the characteristics of successful competitors (and even similar but noncompeting firms), and then to adopt these characteristics if they are compatible with its resources. Let someone else do the experimenting and risk taking. The imitator faces some risk in waiting too long, but this usually is far less than the risk that the innovator faces.

EXECUTION INSIGHTS

The Austerity Mind-set

Four of the firms we studied exemplified this philosophy. Two were rather new firms, Boston Beer and OfficeMax, but with greater size they eased the austerity reins.

Another firm, Vanguard, steadfastly adhered to the frugality of its founder, John Bogle. And Dell seems unassailable with its low overhead, although the temptation for growth beyond PCs may at least partly mute its present advantage.

We have seen the opposite in the organizational bloat of a Boeing. Besieged Scott Paper and Sunbeam, reeling from the drastic cuts of Al Dunlap, deserved some of this because their organizations had grown cumbersome. Chrysler, at the time of its merger with Daimler, also brought with it a recently bloated organization.

Lean and mean is the order of the day with many firms. The problem with the lemming-like pursuit of the lean-and-mean goal is knowing how far to downsize without counterproductively cutting into bone and muscle. As thousands of managers and staff specialists can attest, the loss of jobs and destruction of career paths has been traumatic for individuals as well as society. So it is much better not to become bloated in the first place.

Resistance to Change

People, as well as organizations, are naturally reluctant to embrace change. Change is disruptive; it destroys routines and muddies interpersonal relationships with subordinates, coworkers, and superiors. Previously important positions may be downgraded or even eliminated, and persons who view themselves as highly competent may be forced to assume unfamiliar duties, with the fear that they cannot master the new assignments. When the change involves wholesale terminations in a major downsizing, such as the ones Dunlap engineered and the restructuring that the new German top brass forced on Chrysler and that Newell forced on Rubbermaid, resistance and fear of change can become so great that overall efficiency is seriously jeopardized.

Normal resistance to change can be combated by good communication with participants about forthcoming changes. Without such communication, rumors and fears may be blown far out of proportion. Acceptance of change is facilitated if employees are involved as fully as possible in planning the changes, if their participation is solicited and welcomed, and if assurance can be given that positions will not be impaired, only changed. Gradual rather than abrupt changes also make a transition smoother.

In the final analysis, however, possible negative repercussions should not deter making needed changes and embracing different opportunities, as Disney found confronting it in Europe. If change is desirable, as it usually is with long-established bureaucratic organizations, it should be initiated. Individuals and organizations can adapt to change—it just takes some time.

Beware the Rush to Merge

Mergers create the most disruption. Even mergers that seem to combine similarities often miss serious relationship subtleties, as Quaker Oats with its costly acquisition of Snapple found out too late.

The confidence of Newell management that it could quickly bring Rubbermaid up to its standards in meeting the demands of Wal-Mart were misguided, and Newell Rubbermaid became a troubled firm. On the other hand, Hewlett-Packard's acquisition of Compaq still seems a model of quick and effective assimilation.

When a merger involves an acquisition of an old and cherished U.S. firm by a foreign firm, a one-time enemy in World War II, the resistance to change is all the greater. When subterfuge is added to such a merger, with U.S. management mistakenly expecting this to be a "merger of equals," personnel and assimilation problems become all the greater. As this is written, DaimlerChrysler has still not smoothed out this merger of unequals.

Studies increasingly show that most mergers and acquisitions do not meet expectations. For example, a study of seventy-eight deals over a two-year period done by the consulting firm Booz Allen Hamilton found that in mergers of similarly sized companies the failure rate was 67 percent. If the acquirer was more than twice the size of the target company, the failure rate was still 38 percent. Reasons given for the failures were loss of key staff members, culture clashes, poor or clumsy integration, and the loss of key customers.[2]

Prudent Crisis Management

Crises are unexpected happenings that pose threats to the organization's well-being, ranging from modest to catastrophic. A number of cases involved crises: for example, United Way, Maytag, Euro Disney, Coca-Cola, MetLife, Perrier, Boeing, Ford and Firestone, and Johnson & Johnson (J&J). Some handled their crisis reasonably well, such as United Way, Euro Disney, and the paragon of crisis management, J&J, although we can question in the first two cases how such crises were allowed to happen in the first place. However, Maytag, Perrier, Boeing, Ford/Firestone, and MetLife either overreacted or else failed badly in salvaging the situation.

Most crises can be minimized if a company practices risk avoidance, has contingency plans, and is alert to changes in the environment. For example, it is prudent to prohibit key executives from traveling on the same plane; it is prudent to insure key executives so their incapacity will not endanger the organization; it is prudent to set up contingency plans for a strike, an equipment failure or plant shutdown, the loss of a major customer, unexpected economic conditions, or a serious lawsuit; and it is prudent to back up records and, for financial firms in particular, to have such backups in distant locations. With contingency plans, it is best to work backward from a worst-case scenario. Some crises can be anticipated, such as a looming oil embargo, a shortage of certain raw materials, a growing union militancy in the industry. When the business environment looks particularly troubling, as was the case after the destruction of the World Trade Center on September 11, 2001, a firm in a vulnerable industry might consider organizing a crisis management team.

Insurance usually covers certain risks, but the mettle of any organization can be severely tested by an unexpected crisis not covered adequately by insurance, for example, a major product recall because of serious safety or health concerns. Such may have major impact on profits, as Johnson & Johnson found with its Tylenol recall, and Perrier lost market share never to be regained. Crises may necessitate some

---

[2] Janet Whitman, Dow Jones News, as reported in "Mergers Often Look Better on Paper, Consultant's Study of 78 Deals Finds," *Cleveland Plain Dealer,* August 5, 2001, p. H3.

changes in the organization and the way of doing business, but they need not cause the demise of the company if alternatives are weighed and actions taken only after due deliberation. Firms should avoid making hasty disruptive changes or, the other extreme, making too few changes too late.

Don't Rock the Boat

This philosophy advocates not making changes unless problems warrant it. If things are going well, even if not as well as desired, don't tamper, since the consequences might be worse. This is also commonly known as the "if it's not broke, don't fix it" philosophy. The Coca-Cola case is the strongest confirmation of this idea: Changing the flavor of Coke slightly did not improve demand but simply aroused condemnation.

As with most things, however, this admonition of not changing that which seems to be satisfactory should not be graven in stone. An operation may be improved through fine-tuning; an alternative may be better. Boeing and United Way were slow in making changes, and severe problems caught up with them. Scott Paper and Sunbeam likewise needed to make changes long before Dunlap brought his drastic ones. Continuance of the status quo is usually just a wistful fancy, one that deludes any organization not geared to the possibility of change.

Environmental Monitoring

A firm should be alert to changes in the business environment: changes in customer preferences and needs, in competition, in the economy, in government regulation, and even in international events such as nationalism in Canada, NAFTA, OPEC machinations, changes in Eastern Europe and South Africa, economic developments in the Far East, and the threats and consequences of terrorist activities here and abroad. Harley Davidson and Boeing failed to detect and act upon significant changes in their industries. Disney encountered different customer attitudes in Europe than it had experienced before. McDonald's had difficulty coming to grips with the realization that its industry was maturing and a different business strategy might be needed. Philip Morris and the tobacco industry failed to detect or accept the burgeoning public and political opinion swinging against it, until confronted with lawsuits and judgments in the hundreds of billions of dollars.

How can a firm remain alert to subtle and insidious or more obvious changes? It must have sensors constantly monitoring the environment. The sensor may be a marketing or economic research department, but in many instances such a formal organizational entity is not really necessary to provide primary monitoring. Executive alertness is essential. Most changes do not occur suddenly and without warning—but we well know this still can happen; the danger exists, and should not be disregarded. Feedback from customers, sales representatives, and suppliers; news of the latest relevant projections in business journals; and even simple observations of what is happening in stores, advertising, prices, and new technologies can provide information about a changing environment. Unfortunately, in the urgency of handling day-to-day operating problems, managers may miss clues of imminent changes in the competitive environment.

Following are generalizations regarding vulnerability to competition:

1. Initial market advantage tends to be rather quickly countered by competitors.

2. Countering by competitors is more likely when an innovation is involved than when the advantage comes from more commonplace effective management, such as superb cost controls or customer service.

3. An easy-entry industry is particularly vulnerable to new and aggressive competition, especially if the market is expanding. In new industries, severe price competition usually weeds out the marginal firms.

4. Long-dominant firms tend to be vulnerable to upstart competitors because of their complacency, conservatism, and conceit (the three C's). They frequently are resistant to change and myopic about the environment.

5. Careful monitoring of performance at strategic control points can detect weakening positions needing corrective action before situations become serious. (This will be further discussed shortly.)

6. In expanding markets it is unwise to judge performance by increases in sales rather than by market share; an increase in sales may hide a deteriorating situation as competitors increase sales more.

7. A no-growth policy invites competitive inroads.

The Power of Giving Employees a Sense of Pride and a Caring Management

The great turnaround of Continental from the confrontational days of Frank Lorenzo has to be mainly attributed to the people-oriented environment fostered by Gordon Bethune. The marvel is how quickly it was done, started with such a simple thing as an open-door policy to the executive suite, and encouragement of full communication with employees.

Still, Continental was not unique is this enlisting of employees to the team. Other successful firms have done so, although perhaps none so strikingly or so suddenly. Ray Kroc of McDonald's fostered this as McDonald's began its great charge, although in recent years relations with franchisees grew more fragile under new top management. Michael Feuer gained dedicated employees in the early growth years of OfficeMax and John Bogle imbued Vanguard with his concept of frugality and customer service.

Then we have the other extreme, the mechanistic handling of employees by Al Dunlap. Any temporary improvement of profits, through cutting expenses to the bone with vast layoffs, finally came to roost as he himself was fired at Sunbeam.

Boeing's problems with its peaks and valleys of layoffs and hiring destroyed pride and esprit de corps of employees, except perhaps for a nucleus. This sense of pride was certainly latent with such a prestigious product, but without workplace stability a great opportunity was lost to cement employee morale.

In addition to a people-oriented management, another key factor in cultivating employee morale and teamwork lies in the perceived growth prospects of the firm. Where growth prospects look good, even coming back from the adversity of Continental, then employees can grasp that extra measure of enthusiasm and motivation.

CONTROL INSIGHTS

Delegation Overdone

Good managers delegate as much as possible to subordinates. By giving them some freedom and as much responsibility as they can handle, future leaders are developed. More than this, delegation allows higher executives to concentrate on the most important matters. Other areas of the operation need come to their attention only where performances deviate significantly from what is expected at strategic control points. This is known as management by exception.

Management by exception failed, however, with Maytag and its overseas Hoover division. The flaw lay in failing to monitor faulty promotional plans. By the time results were coming in, it was too late. Admittedly, with diverse and far-flung operations it becomes more difficult to closely monitor all aspects, but still there should be strategic control points to warn of impending dangers. At the least, home office approval of expenditures above a certain amount must be enforced.

We found delegation problems in other cases. The ridiculous acquisition of Snapple—a product at the end of its faddish life cycle and incompatible with the existing distribution structure of Gatorade—smacks of dependence on incompetent researchers to whom too much delegation had been placed.

The Euro Disney difficulties may have resulted from not enough autonomy: The European operation did not adjust well to a somewhat different playing field, in which customers were far more price-conscious than had been experienced before.

At the top executive level, United Way found the excesses of its chief, William Aramony, to be unacceptable. Here, the board of directors could be faulted for being far too tolerant of a chief executive's questionable behavior. This raises another issue: How closely should the board exercise control?

Board of Directors Patsies

A board of directors can monitor top management performance closely and objectively. Or it can be completely supportive and uncritical. In the latter situation, the board exercises no controls on top management; in the former, it becomes an important control factor at the highest level.

Given the potential control power of the board, top executives find their own interests best served by packing the board with supporters. Aramony of United Way had such a sympathetic and supportive board that permitted his excesses to go unmonitored, until investigative reporters blew the whistle.

Instead of assuming the status of watchdogs for investors' best interests, such patsy boards disserve them.

Systematic Evaluations and Controls

Organizations need feedback to determine how well something is being done, whether improvement is possible, where it should occur, how much is needed, and how quickly it must be accomplished. Without feedback or performance evaluation, a worsening situation can go unrecognized until too late for corrective action.

As firms become larger, the need for better controls or feedback increases, because top management can no longer personally monitor all aspects of the operation. Mergers and diversifications, which often result in loosely controlled decentralized operations—for example, again, Maytag and its overseas Hoover division—all the more need systematic feedback on performance.

Financial and expense controls are vital. After all, if costs and inventories get severely out of line—and worse, if this is not recognized until late—then the very viability of the firm can be jeopardized. Many of the exuberant high-tech enterprises found their heedless extravagances hastened their demise, leaving the field to such stalwarts as Hewlett-Packard and Dell.

Performance standards are another critical means of control for widespread operations. Unless operating standards are imposed and enforced, uniformity of performance is sacrificed, resulting in unevenness of quality and service and a lack of coordination and continuity among the different units. Even unethical and illegal practices may ensue, as we saw with MetLife. Instead of running a tight ship, managers face a loose and undisciplined one. McDonald's had long been the model of a tight ship, with its enduring insistence on the tightest standards in the industry; its problems began when it allowed these to slip.

INSIGHTS REGARDING SPECIFIC STRATEGY ELEMENTS

Appeal of Price

In several cases we have seen an anomaly regarding the effective use of price. Dell Computer owed its great strategic advantage to offering the lowest prices in its industry and doing so profitably with a cost structure lower than competitors. Similarly, mutual fund giant Vanguard brought frugality and lowest prices to investors while still giving them the best service in the industry.

Still, the low-price strategy of Frank Lorenzo almost destroyed Continental Air in the absence of good service and morale. Discount stores base their customer appeal in offering lower prices than conventional retailers. Undoubtedly customers are strongly attracted by low prices, but low prices must not be at the expense of reasonable customer service and product quality.

We saw several cases where high prices attracted. The entrepreneur Jim Koch targeted Boston Beer as having a robust flavor with the highest prices in the industry. Harley Davidson customers were willing to wait months to obtain its high-priced bikes. Perrier led the bottled-water industry with its high prices for the simple commodity of water, and this was successful until the contamination exposé.

Yet, high prices did not work to Disney's advantage in Euro Disney. The French and most other Europeans were more frugal than Disney executives expected; only when prices were cut significantly was viability more certain. Quaker Oats also found high prices of Snapple left it vulnerable to lower-priced competitors. Hewlett-Packard has so far been able to milk its printer ink business with exorbitantly high prices. But such a cash cow invites competitors eager to participate, and this advantage may not be enduring.

With price it seems we face the twin appeals to bargains and to highest quality. Although customers are attracted to bargains and low prices, some will pay a lot more for something they believe is the highest quality. And the great majority of customers believe that high price equates to high quality—which it does sometimes, but not always.

Can Advertising Do the Job?

We are left with contradictions regarding the power and effectiveness of advertising. Boston Beer, despite its larger competitors and its own rather modest expenditures for advertising, carved a significant niche in the beer market with an unusual theme. At the time of Coca-Cola's blunder with its New Coke it was spending $100 million more for advertising than Pepsi, and all the while was losing market share. Does advertising have much relationship with success?

The right theme can bring success, although with the sheer volume of advertising, finding an appealing and unique theme is a mighty challenge. Of course, you can give the store away, as Maytag Hoover's promotional campaign almost did: It certainly created great attention and interest.

Thus we see the great challenge of advertising. One never knows for sure how much should be spent to get the job done, to reach the planned objectives of perhaps increasing sales or market share by a certain percentage. However, despite the inability to measure directly the effectiveness of advertising, it is the brave—or foolhardy—executive who stands pat in the face of aggressive increased promotions by competitors. We draw these conclusions:

1. There is no assured correlation between expenditures for advertising and sales success. But the right theme or message can be powerful.

2. In most cases, advertising can generate initial trial. But if the other elements of the strategy are relatively unattractive, customers will neither be won nor retained.

Analytical Management Tools

We identified several of the most useful analytical tools for decision making. In Euro Disney we discussed breakeven analysis, a highly useful means for making go/no-go decisions about new ventures and alternative business strategies. In the Maytag case, we described the cost-benefit analysis that might have prevented the bungled promotion in England. And we encountered the SWOT analysis in the Boston Beer case. While these analyses do not guarantee best decisions, they do bring order and systematic thinking into the art of management decision making.

ETHICAL CONSIDERATIONS

A firm tempted to walk the low road in search of greater short-run profits may eventually find that the risks far outweigh the rewards. We have examined more than a few cases dealing with ethical controversies—for example, MetLife's indictment for deceptive sales practices and the exposés of undesirable practices by United Way. Nor can we forget the callousness toward life and injury by Ford and Firestone regarding Explorers fitted with Firestone tires. While it is beyond the scope of this book to delve very deeply into social and ethical issues,[3] two insights are worth noting:

1. A firm can no longer distance itself from the possibility of critical scrutiny. Activist groups and/or investigative reporters often publicize alleged misdeeds long before governmental regulators will. Legal actions may follow.

2. Public protests may take a colorful path, with marches, picketing, billboard whitewashing, and the like, and may enlist public and media support for their cause.

Should a firm attempt to resist and defend itself? The overwhelming evidence is to the contrary. The bad press, the adversarial relations, and the effect on public image are hardly worth such a confrontation. The better course of action may be to back down as quietly as possible, repugnant though such may be to a management convinced of the reasonableness of its position.

Most ethical problems we saw came with a hostile media. Sensationalism, exaggeration, and taking sides against the big corporation usually sell more copies or gain more audience. Many executives are uncomfortable and even hostile toward an inquisitive press. So, they create a bad impression, frequently one of trying to hide something. Even worse is to be confrontational, as Philip Morris and the tobacco industry have long practiced.

Johnson & Johnson's secret for gaining rapport with the media was corporate openness and cooperation. After the Tylenol catastrophe, it sought good two-way communication with media furnishing information from the field while J&J gave full and honest disclosure of its own investigation and actions. To promote good rapport, top-level company officials were readily available to the press.

GENERAL INSIGHTS

Impact of One Person

In many cases one person had a powerful impact on the organization. Ray Kroc of McDonald's converted a small hamburger stand into the world's largest restaurant chain. John Bogle of Vanguard started a crusade against the high-priced mutual funds of competitors, and led his firm to become one of the biggest of all. Less well known are the entrepreneurs Jim Koch of Boston Beer and Michael Feuer of OfficeMax.

---

[3] For more depth of coverage, see R. F. Hartley, *Business Ethical Mistakes* (New York: Wiley, forthcoming).

For turnaround accomplishments, Gordon Bethune, who turned around a demoralized Continental Airline, stands tall, with Vaughn Beals of Harley Davidson no slouch. The young Michael Dell is on track to be one of the notables in the computer world, and join Bill Gates.

One person can also have a negative impact on an organization. Al Dunlap, the decimator of sick companies, who finally got his comeuppance with Sunbeam, is perhaps best known. Then there was William Aramony, who almost destroyed United Way by his high living and arrogance. Geoffrey Bible, longtime chairman of Philip Morris, led an aggressively confrontational stand against those who sought to curb smoking, and delayed action against the industry for years. The impact of one person, for good or ill, is one of the recurring marvels of history, whether business history or world history.

Prevalence of Opportunities for Entrepreneurship Today

Despite the maturing of our economy and the growing size and power of many firms in many industries, opportunities for entrepreneurship still abound. This last decade witnessed the greatest proliferation ever of entrepreneurship. Much of this came in the high-tech arena, with technological advances proliferating and thousands of entrepreneurs, many in their twenties, jumping into the arena only to crash. Still, opportunities exist not only for the changemaker or innovator, but also for the person who seeks only to do things a little better than existing, and complacent, competition.

Most entrepreneurial successes are unheralded, although dozens are widely publicized. While we dealt specifically with new business ventures in Part VI with such rising stars as Boston Beer and OfficeMax, two other cases are not so many years away from their births: for example, Vanguard and Dell. Bill Gates of Microsoft is the premier entrepreneur.[4] Opportunities are there for the dedicated. Venture capital to support promising new businesses helped many fledgling enterprises, and became a flood during the wild boom of the 1990s. As a new business shows early promise, initial public offerings (IPOs)—i.e., new stock issues—become important sources of capital, as we saw with Boston Beer and OfficeMax.

But entrepreneurship is not for everyone. In prudent times, the great venture capitalists look at the person, not the idea. Typically they distribute their seed money to resourceful people who are courageous enough to give up security for the unknown consequences of their embryonic ventures, who have great self confidence, and who demonstrate a tremendous will to win.

CONCLUSION

We learn from mistakes and from successes, although every management problem and opportunity seems cast in a somewhat different setting. But there are still common elements. One author has likened business strategy to military strategy:

> Strategies which are flexible rather than static embrace optimum use and offer the greatest number of alternative objectives. A good commander knows that he cannot

[4] This case is described in R. F. Hartley, *Marketing Mistakes*, 7th ed. (New York: Wiley, 1998), pp. 217–233.

control his environment to suit a prescribed strategy. Natural phenomena pose their own restraints to strategic planning, whether physical, geographic, regional, or psychological and sociological.[5]

He later adds:

> Planning leadership recognizes the unpleasant fact that, despite every effort, the war may be lost. Therefore, the aim is to retain the maximum number of facilities and the basic organization. Indicators of a deteriorating and unsalvageable total situation are, therefore, mandatory. … No possible combination of strategies and tactics, no mobilization of resources … can supply a magic formula which guarantees victory; it is possible only to increase the probability of victory.[6]

Thus, we can pull two concepts from military strategy to help guide business strategy: the desirability of flexibility in an unknown or changing environment and the idea that a basic core should be maintained in crises. The first suggests that the firm should be prepared for adjustments in strategy as conditions warrant. The second suggests that there is a basic core of a firm's business that should be unchanging; it should be the final bastion to fall back on for regrouping if necessary. Harley Davidson stolidly maintained its core position, even though it let expansion opportunities slither away.

In regard to the basic core of a firm, every viable firm has some distinctive function or "ecological niche" in the business environment:

> Every business firm occupies a position which is in some respects unique. Its location, the product it sells, its operating methods, or the customers it serves tend to set it off in some degree from every other firm. Each firm competes by making the most of its individuality and its special character.[7]

Woe to the firm that loses its ecological niche.

QUESTIONS

1. Design a program aimed at mistake avoidance. Be as specific, as creative, and as complete as possible.

2. Would you advise a firm to be an imitator or an innovator? Why?

3. "There is no such thing as a sustainable competitive advantage." Discuss.

4. How would you build controls into an organization to ensure that similar mistakes do not happen in the future?

5. Array as many pros and cons of entrepreneurship as you can. Which do you see as most compelling?

---

[5] Myron S. Heidingsfield, *Changing Patterns in Marketing* (Boston: Allyn & Bacon, 1968), p. 11.

[6] *Ibid.*

[7] Alderson, *Marketing Behavior and Executive Action*, p. 101.

6. Do you agree with the thought expressed in this chapter that a firm confronted with strong ethical criticism should abandon the product or the way of doing business? Why or why not?

7. We have suggested that the learning insights discussed in this chapter and elsewhere in the book are transferable to other firms and other times. Do you completely agree with this? Why or why not?

HANDS-ON EXERCISE

Your firm has had a history of reacting rather than anticipating changes in the industry. As the staff assistant to the CEO, you have been assigned the responsibility of developing adequate sensors of the environment. How will you go about developing such sensors?

TEAM DEBATE EXERCISE

Debate the extremes of forecasting for an innovative new product: conservative versus aggressive.

INDEX

A page number with a *t* indicates a table.